AFRICAN POLITICS

AFRICAN POLITICS

Crises and Challenges

J. GUS LIEBENOW

Indiana University Press
Bloomington and Indianapolis

Maps by Cathryn L. Lombardi

First Midland Book Edition 1986

Manufactured in the United States of America

Library of Congress Cataloging-in-Publication Data

Liebenow, J. Gus, 1925–
African politics.

Includes index.
1. Africa, Sub-Saharan—Politics and government—1960–
2. Africa, Sub-Saharan—Economic conditions—1960–   .   I. Title.
DT352.8.L53   1986   320.967   85-45469
ISBN 0-253-30275-7
ISBN 0-253-20388-0 (pbk.)

1   2   3   4   5   90   89   88   87   86

For Beverly

CONTENTS

MAPS

TABLES

PREFACE

This volume is the culmination of over three and a half decades of research in East, West, Central, and Southern Africa; of teaching courses and seminars on African politics and development at both the undergraduate and graduate levels in the United States and Africa; and of thinking through many of the political problems which have faced the more than forty-five countries of sub-Saharan Africa under colonial rule and since independence. Through those long years, I have come not only to share the hopes and aspirations of Africans for a better way of life but also to agonize with them over the disappointments in coming to grips with the problems of nation-building, surmounting poverty, and achieving popular control over governments.

Many institutions and foundations over the years have assisted me in my thinking and research about African politics. The former would include the faculties at universities where I have studied (University of Illinois, Harvard University, and Northwestern University) as well as at universities where I have taught (University of Texas, Indiana University, and the University of Dar es Salaam). Funding for research during those three and a half decades has come from the Social Science Research Council, the American Council on Learned Societies, the Ford Foundation, the Midwest Universities Consortium on International Affairs, the Universities Field Staff International, Carnegie Foundation, and other smaller foundations.

Of the many individuals who should be singled out for acknowledgments, none is more important to me than my wife, Beverly Bellis Liebenow. She has not only given me invaluable assistance over the years in gathering data on field research trips in Africa, but she has also been my most attentive and rigorous editorial critic. Above all, she has suffered with me during the long gestation period as this volume has progressed, with frequent interruptions caused by academic, administrative, and family responsibilities. At the next level of recognition are my children, Diane, Debra, Jay, and John, who in many cases enjoyed (as well as endured) their trips to Africa with Beverly and me.

There are many in the academic world who should be given special recognition for the ideas which came to fruition in this study. Among those to whom I owe much because of their direction and inspiration during my formative years are the late Rupert Emerson, Roland Young, Melville J. Herskovits, and Charles S. Hyneman. Among my contemporaries, there are a number who could be singled out for acknowledgments, but there is one in particular who deserves special mention for reasons both academic and personal—Carl G. Rosberg. My students have also been in the fullest sense my "teachers," since they have challenged me to go more deeply into some of the issues dealt with in this volume. At the risk of neglecting some in an enumeration of the many, I want to limit my mention to one who has read portions of this manuscript and who has nurtured at Indiana University the tradition of African Studies which I helped create, namely Patrick O'Meara. Finally, a special note of thanks to Barbara Hopkins, who displayed efficiency, speed, and the needed good humor in the preparation of this volume.

AFRICAN POLITICS

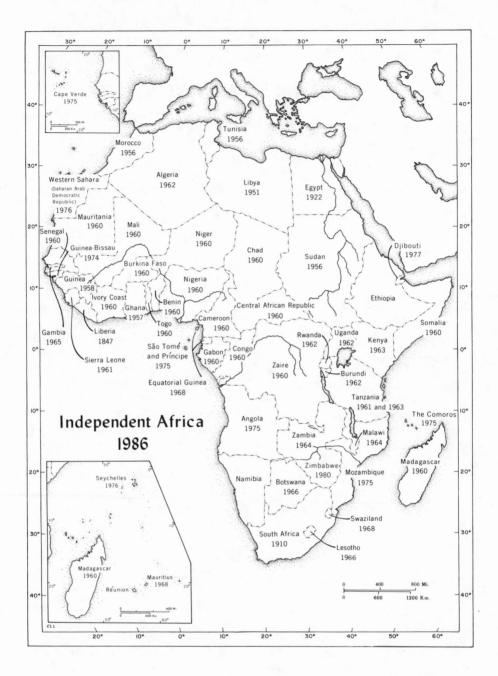

Cape Verde
1975

Morocco
1956

Tunisia
1956

Western Sahara
(Saharan Arab
Democratic
Republic)
1976

Algeria
1962

Libya
1951

Egypt
1922

Mauritania
1960

Mali
1960

Niger
1960

Chad
1960

Sudan
1956

Djibouti
1977

Senegal
1960

Guinea-Bissau
1974

Burkina Faso
1960

Nigeria
1960

Guinea
1958

Ivory Coast
1960

Ghana
1957

Benin
1960

Cameroon
1960

Central African Republic
1960

Ethiopia

Somalia
1960

Gambia
1965

Liberia
1847

Togo
1960

São Tomé
and Príncipe
1975

Gabon
1960

Congo
1960

Rwanda
1962

Uganda
1962

Kenya
1963

Sierra Leone
1961

Equatorial Guinea
1968

Zaire
1960

Burundi
1962

Tanzania
1961 and 1963

The Comoros
1975

**Independent Africa
1986**

Angola
1975

Zambia
1964

Malawi
1964

Madagascar
1960

Seychelles
1976

Namibia

Botswana
1966

Zimbabwe
1980

Mozambique
1975

Madagascar
1960

Mauritius
1968

Réunion

Swaziland
1968

South Africa
1910

Lesotho
1966

0   400   800 Mi.
0   600   1200 Km.

CLL

I

INTRODUCTION

The emergence of more than forty-five Black African states as significant actors in international politics has been one of the more surprising developments of the latter half of the twentieth century. This phenomenon must be reckoned with other major transformations that have reshaped the way in which the world community engages in political behavior. These transformations would certainly include the decline of Britain and France as superpowers and their subsequent integration within Western Europe; the consolidation of power at the national level in China after a century of domestic turmoil; the Islamic resurgence and new assertiveness of oil-producing states, most of them in the Middle East; and above all, of course, the potential for nuclear confrontation.

What makes the entry of independent African states on the world scene so startling is that until the mid-1950s that continent had been relegated to the fringes of international politics. It was an area where the six European colonial powers proposed and disposed of the political, economic, and social fate of the 150 to 200 million inhabitants of the sub-Saharan region. By their own choice or the intention of the colonial powers, the two major superpowers, the United States and the Soviet Union, had few direct contacts with Africa during the colonial era, primarily with the three independent states of South Africa, Ethiopia, and Liberia. The continent had only been minimally involved in the First and Second World Wars, and the agenda of the United Nations in the immediate postwar period had comparatively few situations of crisis magnitude relative to Africa. Only the issue of colonialism in general, the U.N. Trust territories in Africa in particular, and several persistent situations relating to South Africa systematically received attention at the U.N. in the late 1940s and the 1950s.

There was a similar lack of attention and understanding on the part of the rest of the non-African world to developments taking place within the continent. For the most part, only the specialized and relatively small pool of colonial administrators and military officers, Christian missionaries, and European investors, miners, traders, and other economic entrepreneurs provided direct linkages between Africans and the outside world. The shared and often distorted images of these expatriates were in many cases the only available data to dispel the still uniformly accepted external view of Africa as the "dark continent"—the place of "primitives," the unknown, the mysterious, and the romantic. Few scholars had made Africa their major area of concern in the colonial era. Most of the major news services did not regularly post agents to Africa, and if they did, they operated from the relative comfort of Johannesburg, Dakar, Nairobi, and Cairo while reporting "authoritatively" on events thousands of miles distant from those major cities.

Africans themselves were often no better informed regarding developments within their own continent. Pass laws, residential segregation, and other devices kept most Africans rigidly rooted to their parochial villages. If Africans did migrate in search of education, work, or some other goal, they were often limited to the arbitrary colonial territory of which their ethnic group had become a part or to neighboring territories of the same colonial power. Except for mission publications, newspapers were virtually nonexistent, and modern associations that transcended the village or ethnic group were severely restricted both in membership and in the scope of their activities. Mission schools, when they went beyond exposing Africans to the Bible, invariably taught them more about French or English history and geography than they did about Africa.

Events of the past two or three decades have rudely shattered the appearance of calm and stability associated with Africa. The independence struggle, which owed its success to developments both within and external to Africa, swept everything before it, leaving only Namibia and the Republic of South Africa subject to white minority control in the 1980s. Starting with the independence of the Sudan in 1956 and Ghana in 1957, each new African state has taken seriously its membership in the United Nations. The African bloc has become the largest of the regional voting groups in the General Assembly. Most African states have also vigorously pursued the creation of an expanding network of diplomatic, cultural, economic, and other links within the region and the continent as well as with other states at the global level. As the "sleeping giant" has awakened and expanded its interests externally, however, the realization has come that external involvement is a double-edged sword. Africa has reluctantly become the extended arena for conflict (and occasionally accommodation) between the United States and the Soviet Union; Israel and the Arab-Muslim World; China and the Soviet Union; Libya and the West; and other protagonists whose own concerns are not always directly relevant to African interests.

While European colonialism has virtually finished its course, the legacy of colonial rule remains. This is apparent not only in the way in which many African states conduct their foreign affairs, but even more when we examine the many domestic crises that have focused world attention on Africa in the past quarter of a century. In contrast to the virtual neglect of journalistic coverage of African affairs in the 1950s, hardly a day goes by when Africa does not figure prominently in the American and European press, radio, and television news. The riots in South Africa and the Ethiopian famine in 1985 were literally brought directly into the living rooms of people halfway around the globe—courtesy of satellite telecommunications.

It is usually the crises that absorb the attention of headline writers and television commentators. Comparatively little notice is taken of African success stories, and yet they abound. Drought-stricken Tanzania, for example, has made a most dramatic assault on both its legacy of illiteracy and the endemic diseases that have plagued the rural poor. Malawi, one of the poorest of the Fourth World countries, has risen to the challenge of feeding its own people and its neighbors as well. Malawi's leaders have also undertaken to provide clean water from its high mountain streams to millions of rural farmers at lower altitudes. Swaziland has engaged in one of the more imaginative programs of reforesting the mountain slopes which had been denuded during centuries of overgrazing by cattle and unrestrained cutting of timber. There has been a resurgence of interest in African art in its various forms—sculpture, dance, music, and poetry—and it is no longer rejected in the West as "primitive" and "pagan." Beneath the attention-absorbing crises, Africans have been successfully restoring or fashioning de novo political, economic, social, and religious institutions which are often better calculated to meet their needs than the ones that had been imposed upon them during the European occupation of their land. Indeed, the achievement of independence in defiance of all predictions is itself a remarkable feat.

These success stories and other creative challenges to crisis situations will certainly not be ignored in this volume. At the risk, however, of dwelling on the negative, one of my purposes is to probe behind the headlines and to analyze why the series of African crises exist and persist. It is this kind of realistic analysis that many former colonialists refuse to undertake, preferring instead to lament the destruction or erosion of the alleged legacy of democracy and development they claim to have left behind. Realistic analysis, unfortunately, is an exercise that many African nationalist leaders also refuse to assume, preferring instead to lay all of their problems at the doorstep of the former colonialists. Admittedly the origins of many of these crises are indeed traceable to the philosophies, policies, and programs of the European colonial powers that dominated Africa for close to a century. But after almost three decades of independence in the case of the Sudan, Ghana, and Guinea, and more than two decades in the case of the majority of African states, the leaders of these new societies must themselves begin to assume some of the responsibility for the failures that persist. The defeatist acceptance of crises must be displaced by the decision to treat Africa's problems as challenges which can be overcome with greater resourcefulness and sacrifice.

What are these African crises that can creatively be viewed as challenges? The first crisis, which is central to our understanding of the others, is the struggle for national identity. The liberation movement of the past three decades did not restore to independence nation-states that had previously existed. What it did was to free from external control peoples who had been arbitrarily grouped together within larger European colonial territories. Only a few of the forty-five states in sub-Saharan Africa at independence had national leaders who could regularly command the loyalties of the overwhelming majority of the citizenry and who could meet the many material, psychological, and cultural needs of their people. What we had in Africa was literally some forty or more states in search of nationhood. It has been in many cases the conflicts over achieving this goal in Nigeria, the Sudan, Zimbabwe, and Angola that have been central to those leaders' successfully responding to the other crises that dominate the news.

The second and closely related crisis has been that of overcoming poverty. In popular parlance the developing states have been referred to as the Third World, in contrast to the Western industrialized states (the First World) and the leading socialist societies (the Second World). Within the Third World category the World Bank each year identifies thirty to forty lowest income states, popularly called the Fourth World. Two-thirds of the latter are located in Africa. A combination of factors limits the ability of Africans to overcome their poverty. The physical environment is only the most dramatic of these factors; we must also consider the residue of colonial relationships, the paucity of education, official corruption, the reluctance of the developed states to generously share their wealth, and the political instability associated with nation-building itself.

The third crisis is the unresolved issue of white supremacy in Southern Africa. The leaders of most African states—and in particular those who received fraternal support from sources both internal and external to Africa—have assumed a moral debt to continue the struggle against white supremacy to its ultimate conclusion. This means not only the termination of South Africa's colonial control over Namibia but the dismantling of the structures of apartheid in South Africa itself. It has been apartheid which has denied to the Black majority and others the ability to control their own political, economic, religious, and social destinies. For the external world, the policies of non-African governments with respect to the whole of the continent tend to be judged in terms of the sole litmus test of their policies with respect to South Africa.

The fourth crisis addressed in this volume is one which has economic and social consequences but is considered primarily as a political problem since it relates so critically to the issue of nation-building and to governmental policy in a range of areas. This is the dilemma of the political community in the African urban setting. Africa is one of the least urbanized of the world's regions, but the rate of urban growth is twice the global average. This phenomenon of urban expansion relates very closely to another statistic which finds many African states drastically exceeding world averages, namely population growth. Kenya alone—one of the few cases of relative economic success—has attained twice the global average in that respect.

Two chapters deal with the fifth crisis, that of popular control over government. The political parties, which served as vehicles for the successful liberation struggles and were to lead the new countries into the brighter tomorrow, have failed in most cases to live up to expectations. Many of the dominant parties ossified as they asserted their claims to be the sole representatives of the people within single-party states. The majority, however, have succumbed to military coups. Indeed, military intervention rather than openly contested elections has become the more predictable instrument for changing the top personnel and policies of government. The causes for this intervention and an evaluation of military versus civilian performance are analyzed in the chapter on the African military.

Finally, since many of the readers of this volume will be Americans, it is useful to analyze the dramatic transformation in American thinking and action with respect to sub-Saharan Africa. With the exception of Liberia, America's interests in the continent were marginal during most of the nineteenth and twentieth centuries. The achievement of African independence has changed all that. Now, potentially every country in Africa has some form of economic, diplomatic, political, educational, and other relationships with America. The ways in which African states and the United States deal with each other in official terms have not been altogether satisfactory from the standpoint of either. Why this is the case is explored in the final chapter.

The Nature of Political Authority in Africa

Although the author is not an African, after thirty-five years of studying the continent's political development, it is hoped that the analysis presented here does provide a sympathetic understanding of the African perspective on the issues covered. Throughout, however, efforts are made to be comparative—to link African situations with parallel if not similar developments taking place not only in other Third World areas but in the more developed states of the West and the Soviet bloc. The crisis of nation-building in the Sudan, for example, is analogous in many respects to the multiple cleavages caused by religion, language, and history within Northern Ireland. The contemporary emergence of ethnic associations in the growing cities of Africa has had earlier as well as continuing manifestations in urban America and Mexico. The phenomenon of military intervention in African politics can be better understood if one also examines similar deviations from the civilian supremacy model in Pakistan, Chile, and Poland.

In searching for analogous or parallel situations for comparative purposes, however, one runs the risk of assuming too basic a commonality in the way in which people pursue political problems. To only a limited extent is this the case. As Harold Lasswell pointed out decades ago, every society, both ancient and modern and without respect to geographic location, has pursued the same categories of values.[1] Individuals in society seek power (the ability to affect the outcome of important situations); wealth (command over the accumulation and distribution of resources); health; respect (the allocation of deference and prestige); enlightenment; skills (both for the survival of the society and enhancement of the individual); affection (group loyalty, companionship, and sexual gratification); and rectitude (establishing a moral basis for individual and group actions).

The diversity of human choice and preference with respect to each of the values delineated above, however, is staggering—as is the diversity of institutional forms which are created for the pursuit and allocation of these values within particular societies. Hence, if one assumes a basic commonality of human pursuits, one is bound to regard the actions and preferences of people in other societies as amusing, wrong-headed, or even dangerous when their choices differ from one's own. This not only presents a problem for a Westerner viewing African political behavior, it applies as well to the way in which Africans view each other within an arbitrarily constituted single state. As we shall point out in the chapter on nation-building, the majority of the states in sub-Saharan Africa are multi-ethnic. This was a consequence of the haphazard way in which the European diplomats in the nineteenth century drew the lines on the map of Africa. It is a situation, however, with which most African nationalist leaders have elected to live.

It is not merely the number of ethnic groups that were included within a single state such as Tanzania (120) or Nigeria (an estimated 250–300) that presents a problem. Nor is the mere size of the ethnic communities a major factor, even though some groups consisted of a limited number of interrelated families while others, such as the Ganda (Baganda) of Uganda, numbered close to a million at the time of the European arrival. What is pertinent to many of the issues dealt with in this book is the diversity of attitudes toward political authority found within a single African state.

With respect to recognition of this problem, anthropologists were well in advance of their fellow social scientists. Indeed, political scientists in the United States and Western Europe had barely averted their vision from a narrow concern with politics in Western society prior to the Second World War. The Soviet Union, Latin America, India, China, and the Middle East were regarded as being beyond the pale as far as comparative polities were concerned. Thus, the neglect of African politics as a legitimate area of concern for political scientists was not surprising. The seminal work of two British anthropologists, Meyer Fortes and E. E. Evans-Pritchard, in 1950 came as a revelation not only to young scholars like myself but to older generations of American and European political scientists as well regarding the range of political systems manifest in Africa.[2] Even greater refinements of the Fortes and Evans-Pritchard classifications were presented by other British social anthropologists such as John Middleton, Paula Brown and Lucy Mair.[3]

Essentially what the work of Fortes and Evans-Pritchard and others has demonstrated is that a variety of types of political systems were represented in Africa at the time of the European arrival. One of those types was not unlike the political systems that emerged in Europe during the latter part of the Middle Ages. That is, there were societies with governments in which centralized political authority was exercised within a roughly defined geographic area. The leadership group exercising that authority tended to claim a monopoly over the legitimate use of force both internally and with respect to external challenges to that society. Political offices and roles, moreover, were sharply defined even though they were not entirely divorced from the performance of economic, religious, and social roles within that society. Hence the early European adventurers, merchants, and missionaries could with some degree of accuracy recognize a chief, king, or other official with whom they could negotiate to pursue their purposes. These political offices were often organized in a hierarchical fashion, with different rights, duties, and privileges attached to each level.

Buganda, Kanem-Bornu, and the other societies with well-defined government structures, moreover, had specialized military establishments and roles; when an occasion for defense arose, the entire population of young adult males was not required to take responsibility. Specialized bureaucracies within these state societies not only collected taxes or tribute payments but were expected to organize the maintenance of roads and the provision of social services—including relief during time of famine. Those societies possessing the formal trappings of government were further marked by the accumulation of economic surplus which permitted degrees of social stratification, with the more privileged classes or caste groups having a disproportionate role in the politics and religious performances of the society.

By way of extreme contrast, the same European colonial territory in Africa that included several of these large, structured communities could include as well communities that were no more than small hunting bands: a series of families, loosely tied together by birth and marriage and by their mutual need for survival in a hostile environment. Political roles were not precisely defined. Depending upon the occasion and the situation which the band faced, the same adult male might be considered a social leader (the head of his family segment), an economic leader (the organizer of a hunting expedition), a religious leader (one who makes propitiations to a revered ancestor), or a political leader (organizing the security of the community against an external threat or arbitrating an intra-band dispute).

There were political communities in traditional Africa far larger than hunting bands, however, which also lacked formal structures of government. The attitudes toward political authority in these governmentless societies were significantly different than in the societies with formal government. Decisions on security, distribution of goods, and other functions in these politically headless (or "acephalous") societies were made by clan elders either singly or collectively, depending upon the number of clans involved in a specific situation of conflict or cooperation. Like the heads of hunting bands, the clan leaders intermittently exercised, roles that were social, economic, religious, and political. There was no clearly defined group within the society that enjoyed a monopoly with regard to the legitimate use of force. Hence the defense of the community and the maintenance of internal order was the result of the recognition of previously agreed-upon rules of seniority among the relevant lineage heads and the application of rules or procedures with respect to the appropriate type of force which could legitimately be applied in particular circumstances. In a delicately balanced situation such as this, the emphasis in law and justice was not on the punishment of individual wrongdoers but on the maintenance of the corporate strength and integrity of the family units who were parties to a conflict. Although some groups were considered less important, such as slaves captured from external tribes, and some lineages were considered more important, because of their reputed proximity to the ancestral founder of the broader family unit, nevertheless there were relatively few, sharp cleavages based upon rank, status, or wealth. Economic roles, moreover, were only minimally differentiated. Age and sex categories of labor were the primary distinctions in the way in which that society pursued its predominant activity, whether it be agriculture, pastoralism, hunting, or trading. Each male and each female respectively "did the work of all."

Intermediate between those traditional societies which possessed centralized political authority and those in which political functions were diffused among clan segments were societies we can call multiple kingdoms. These were ethnic groupings which were broadly linked by language, historic memories, similarity of economic and social institutions across the territory occupied by the group, and the web of kinship and marital ties. Political authority, however, was decentralized, with chiefs or kings and their respective councils and hierarchies of sub-chiefs having authority with respect to only a portion of the larger group. Geographic boundaries were seldom sharply defined. Political allegiance was easily shifted; a disaffected family could gather its members and all of its properties and relocate outside the jurisdiction of a tyrannical chief in the domain of a more lenient or hospitable ruler. My own research among the Sukuma people of Tanzania, for example, demonstrated that political power was dispersed among fifty to sixty relatively autonomous chiefdoms at the time of the German imposition of colonial rule. The large Yoruba grouping in Nigeria was also divided into many distinct political communities, linked by the myth of their descent from a common founder.

In addition to the broad structural differences in the political systems of traditional societies, which complicated administration for both the colonial officers and the successor nationalist leadership, there are other problems that have limited the establishment of legitimacy in the new African states. Although each group pursues the same categories of values, the content varies considerably. A political program calling for election of leadership on the basis of achievement criteria (education, prior government service, or ability to communicate effectively) is not necessarily well received or under-stood by members of a society who had "sacred" leadership presented to them rather than chosen by election and where the qualifications were ascrip-tive (sex, age, birth into a particular family, ethnicity, or physical traits). Power as a value is pursued in a great variety of ways. An economic program based on increasing the protein intake of the population by raising cattle for slaughter encounters resistance among those pastoralists within the state who view cattle as central to the assignment of prestige. Cattle, to those groups—as will be noted in Chapter 3—are only marginally related to the exchange economy and the satisfaction of nutritional needs. The allocation of the value called affection is also a highly sensitive issue. Thus, a social program emphasizing family planning as a way of coping with Africa's mount-ing population explosion encounters resistance from members of those so-cieties—perhaps the majority—who view large families as a prestige factor or as necessary insurance against the endemic diseases that in the past regu-larly contributed to high infant mortality rates.

Finally, the comprehension of contemporary African attitudes toward po-litical authority is complicated by the varying weights given by traditional societies to the various sanctions, or supports, for political authority. The authority system in every society, whether committed to radical change or the retention of tradition, is sustained by the same categories of sanctions. These include the use of force, resort to ritual, economic distribution and deprivation, education, and symbiotic or group sanctions. Not only does the content of each sanction vary from society to society, but the weight given to the various categories varies considerably as well. Contemporary Euro-pean and American society, for example, places the highest priority on eco-nomic, educative, and symbiotic or group sanctions while giving only casual attention to ritual and regarding force as the sanction of last resort. Nazi Germany—another product of Western Europe—gave the highest priorities to force and ritual, and the content of its educative sanctions was marked by an emphasis on rote learning rather than on giving free rein to intellectual dialogue.

Within many traditional societies in Africa a heavy reliance was placed upon ritualistic behavior in sustaining political authority. As will be covered in the section on the religious factor in nation-building, the notion that ancestors, gods, spirits, and other types of extra-human intervention pro-vided props for political authority was a pervasive one. In societies that possessed formal political roles, moreover, the syndrome of divine kingship manifested itself in various forms in many parts of the continent. The per-sistence of such ritualistic sanctions not only complicates the modern tasks of nation-building but also limits efforts to establish a secular society.

Two other sanctions for authority upon which traditional African societies relied also present problems for contemporary African politics. The first is the difference in the character of educative sanctions in contemporary and traditional society. Most African societies lacked written forms of their language although there were other ways in which some coded information vital to their history or technology. Most communication was verbal, which limited the amount of data that could be transmitted and stored. Education therefore in many instances emphasized rote learning or relied upon some more artistic form of retaining and replaying vital information, such as proverbs, recitation of poetry, tapestries, and music. Traditional educative sanctions, however, are of limited utility when the national leadership is attempting to consolidate authority within a large-scale political community above the level of the family, the neighborhood, or other parochial units. The provision of Western education, moreover, must overcome not only the high rates of illiteracy in Africa but the fact that much of the traditional data being transmitted is at variance with or even contradicts the scientific and technological information provided in contemporary schools.

The other sanction which was significant with respect to traditional authority systems in Africa—symbiotic or group supports—also enjoys a high priority in sustaining authority in the emerging political systems. Here again, there are decided differences. Groups in traditional society were few in number and largely limited to face-to-face situations with membership being determined on the narrowly ascriptive grounds of birth, sex, age, neighborhood, and ethnic grouping. Each group in a sense reinforced the other in what was regarded as a highly homogeneous community. In contrast, the tendency within the Western societies that many African leaders attempt to emulate is for groups to be virtually unlimited in number and to embrace all facets of human interest unless restrictions are imposed by the state itself. Although these new associations in Western societies bring individuals together on one plane of commonality, the members may have radically divergent interests when it comes to other affairs within that society. Since many of the groups seek to influence, if not control, the machinery of state and the policies of the national government, the ability of the members of political parties, trade unions, and churches to enjoy personalized contacts with each other or even with the leadership is severely limited. Indeed, many political party and military leaders in Africa fear the flowering of groups which are beyond their ability to control; hence they attempt to restrict this aspect of the Western democratic model.

One of the basic groups in the African traditional system—namely the family—provides special problems for the construction of post-independence authority systems. One frequently cited problem is the alleged drain upon creativity and economic innovation posed by the demands of the extended family. Here, the tradeoffs in terms of social security are not sufficiently appreciated by the Western observer. A similar misperception is involved in the criticism of the recurrent patterns of political nepotism that prevail in many parts of the continent. Perhaps the greatest problem with respect to family organization is in the framing of national laws regarding marriage, divorce, parental responsibility, and the inheritance of property. The fact that the arbitrarily defined territories include representatives of both matrilineal and patrilineal societies—whose members increasingly interact within the contexts of the emerging society—makes it difficult to arrive at acceptable legal codes in the vital area of family relationships.

The diversity of attitudes within a multi-ethnic African state with respect to political authority becomes a problem of considerable magnitude in the face of increasing efforts not only to achieve a better way of life for Africa's people but to give legitimacy to those who claim to govern in their behalf. In many respects "modernization"—as defined below—has become the secular religion not only of the party elites that assumed command of the state upon the withdrawal of European administrators, but of the military leadership that has in many cases displaced civilians. Modernization most visibly entails the physical transformation of a society—new roads, harbors, and buildings, and the introduction of factories, mechanization, and other technological changes in order to meet the society's material needs. Above all, however, modernization is an attitude of mind that demands a political program. It is an attitude that assumes that mankind is capable of changing the environment and that change is *at least potentially* good. Second, modernization assumes that mankind itself—rather than ancestors, spirits, gods, and other supernatural forces—is ultimately responsible for improvements in the human condition. Third, modernization implicitly assumes that the talents to bring about this transformation are not the monopoly of any one race, ethnic group, sex, or age category, or of any arbitrary social stratum based upon religion, region, or wealth. In keeping with the theory, it is incumbent upon political leadership in a modernizing society to create institutions and to remove barriers so as to permit these widely shared talents to emerge and be put to work in behalf of the entire society. Finally, modernization assumes that a broadening of the scale of social, economic, and political interactions among individuals is essential to the better utilization of human and physical resources of an expanding community. The aspirations of African leaders to modernize, however, have often fallen short in terms of actual delivery. Instead of institution-building we witness institutional decay if not outright destruction. Instead of the flowering of many groups and the liberation of human talents without regard to race, sex, region, or religion, the leadership group acts in behalf of its own narrow corporate interests and erects new ascriptive requirements which limit participation at both the leadership and the mass levels.

Each of the crises and challenges enumerated previously as the concern of this volume relates to the quest for a better way of life, stability, and other goals in the face of varying attitudes toward legitimate political authority. It is apparent that not all Africans share the passion of some nationalist leadership for modernization or at least do not share the same vision of modernization. Islamic fundamentalists in northern Nigeria, for example, approve of some facets of modernization, such as the expansion in the scale of the political community, but reject the secularization of society and the changing role of women in contemporary Nigeria. The Masai pastoralists of Tanzania and Kenya accept the commitment of the leaders of the new society to search for the causes and cures of diseases of humans and animals, but reject urbanization and other changes associated with improved agricultural and educational programs. The search for more efficient mechanisms for popular participation in politics, furthermore, encounters the resistance of those who still adhere to traditional notions of succession to office based upon birth and other ascriptive qualifications. Hence, even where modernization is perceived as a positive, integrative force by the African elites, the pursuit of modernization has actually been a significant factor in the instability that plagues contemporary Africa.

II

THE IMPACT OF
COLONIAL RULE

From the midpoint of the nineteenth century to the midpoint of the twentieth, sub-Saharan Africa stood at the frontier of international politics. It was an area of the globe where outsiders proposed and outsiders disposed of the major interests of the inhabitants of that world region. Basic issues of war and peace, the nature of the emerging national community, the establishment of priorities in economic development, and other matters were decided essentially by Europeans. Africans either reaped the benefits or suffered the consequences—depending upon the nature of the activity and the perspective of the observer. This is not to suggest that Europeans monopolized all aspects of the pursuit of power, wealth, health, and the other values which people universally hope to satisfy through political action. Indeed, given the paucity of the European population even in the "settler" territories they could not have exercised total control even if they had attempted to do so. Many of the day-to-day decisions affecting marriage, procreation, the cultivation of crops, the feeding and clothing of one's family, and the worship of deities and other supernatural forces continued to be made by Africans without reference to European political control. The extended family, neighborhood groups, age grade societies, and the remnants of traditional political authority systems continued to function as did more modern structures, such as churches, trade unions, and political parties where Africans had assumed control. The broad parameters of African participation within the broader colonial state, however, continued to be established by Europeans until they were effectively challenged by African nationalism in the 1950s.

The European domination of other peoples in the Americas, the Middle East, much of Asia, and sub-Saharan Africa has been one of the most significant phenomena of that period of history called the modern age. It rivals for the political, social, and economic realms the technological explosion of that same period which has dramatically transformed the way men and women everywhere not only meet their basic needs for survival but also come to view their own cultural heritage. With respect to Africa these two phenomena of the modern era have been closely interrelated. In many instances it was this alleged technological superiority of the West Europeans that led them to believe that they were destined as a matter of right to govern people elsewhere on the globe.

At base, the Western European version of imperialism was a unique historical phenomenon. Previous empires, such as those of the ancient Assyrians, the Macedonians, the Romans, and the Mongols, had been established and maintained substantially by resort to superior weaponry. Imperial rule in those instances was not established until there had been an actual defeat of the defending armies on the field of battle. In contrast, European colonialism was far more insidious and complex. It was in many instances established and maintained without the continued application of naked force. It survived because both the representatives of the imperial power and many of the subordinated peoples themselves came to assume a generalized superiority of Europeans to non-Europeans on a wide range of matters beyond brute force and technology. In their actions, their words, and in other respects the subordinated people went far beyond the pro forma appearance of having accepted this generalized notion of European superiority. From the arrogant European perspective other peoples and places did not actually exist or have a history until they had come within the purview of Europeans and had reality breathed into their existence. This view was neatly summarized as recently as 1954 in a keynote address delivered by a former governor of Kenya, Sir Philip Mitchell, at Johns Hopkins School of Advanced International Studies in Washington: "The forty-two years I have spent in Africa," the governor said, "forty of them in public service, cover a large part of the history of sub-Saharan Africa, for it can hardly be said to extend much further back than about 1870."[1]

This ethnocentric view of history is still with us today in our continued reference to the European "Age of Discovery." Africans and Indians in the New World, it is assumed, only began to exist at the point that they were "discovered" by Portuguese, Spanish, or other European voyagers. Worse yet was the corollary notion that the act of "discovery" established a political claim to dominion over the land and inhabitants by the nation-state associated with the "discoverer." This applied whether the initial European contact took place for the purposes of trade, extending the influence of the Christian faith, or the satisfaction of purely scientific curiosity. Treaties of friendship negotiated by the Europeans with local political personages—or even evidence of conversations alone—became converted in the nineteenth century diplomatic scramble into European deeds of ownership to the land, the people, and all their resources. The rules of the game were neatly established in 1884–1885 at the Berlin Conference on African Affairs.

Today we would have no difficulty in dealing with a hypothetical situation in which a Soviet cosmonaut strayed off course, landed in some remote area of the Canadian Yukon or the Brazilian Amazon, and—following the old European practice—presumed to lay claim to the area and its residents in the name of the Soviet state and world socialism. Our altered mores would lead to this claim being laughed out of court. And yet still today European, American, and even some African textbooks continue to make reference, for example, to David Livingstone having "discovered" Victoria Falls instead of being referred to—as the altered guidebooks in Zimbabwe now do—as the "first overseas visitor" to Victoria Falls.

The absorption of three-quarters of the globe into the European imperial system began with the steady probing of the Western African littoral in the early fifteenth century by Portuguese mariners in search of a sea route to India. The Portuguese mariners became more emboldened as they rounded Cape Verde and defied predictions by not falling off the face of the earth. Curiously, however, it was not until almost four hundred years later—long after North and South America, southern Asia, and Australia had succumbed to European domination—that the bulk of Africa was subjected to the European colonial yoke. At the time of the scramble in the nineteenth century, only the British and Boer areas in South Africa and the isolated coastal enclaves of St. Louis, El Mina, Luanda, Lourenço Marques, and other ports were under European control.

There are various explanations for the roughly 400-year delayed reaction to the earlier European acquisitions in Africa. One rationale is that the gold of the western hemisphere and the spices and other exotic commodities of the Asian sub-continent and Indonesia quickly proved to be much more attractive commodities to the Portuguese and Spanish who had launched the European colonial era. Indeed, the naming by the Portuguese of the two harbors at Port Elizabeth and Maputo as Algoa and Delagoa Bays indicated the subordinated importance of Africa in terms of the more lucrative trade with Goa and India. Similarly, when the Dutch entered the East Indian trade in 1652, they established the colony at Cape Town not as an area of intrinsic value but rather as a victualing station for ships bound to and from the "spice islands" of the East Indies. Specific instructions were given to the Dutch settlers not to venture into the interior and create conflicts with the local population that would jeopardize the primary victualing mission of Cape Town.

A similar attitude regarding Africa as of only marginal importance compared to some other region is detectable in the scramble for territory in the nineteenth century and in the maintenance of the African empire. East Africa, for example, tended to be important to Great Britain because it related to the strategic defense of India. The British and French concentration on the Horn of Africa was of less intrinsic importance than the concern of those two powers regarding the intrusion of the Russians into that region. Russia, in turn, had designs on that area as a countermove to Turkish influence.

This is not to assume that Africa had no direct significance to Europe. There were, of course, commodities from West Africa such as gold and ivory which were of direct interest to Europeans. Even more significant were the slaves, which were instrumental to the European exploitation of the agricultural and mineral resources of the Americas from Virginia to Uruguay.

The magnitude of the slave trade in particular is only now being fully appreciated; Philip Curtin, Paul Lovejoy, and others have estimated the numbers involved at roughly 11.5 million.[2] For a combination of reasons, however, slaves and other commodities were extracted from Africa without the Europeans effectively penetrating the interior. First of all, it was not necessary to do so. The depiction in Alex Haley's first chapter of *Roots* notwithstanding, it was basically Africans who captured and enslaved other Africans and brought them to the European vessels at the coast for sale prior to their passage to the new world.

Secondly, the African middlemen who profited from the traffic in human beings were reluctant to permit Europeans to compete with them in the interior trade, and they had the military means to prevent such a situation from materializing. As my historian colleague George Brooks notes, Africans along the coast asserted in those days that "the sea may belong to the white man, but the land belongs to the Africans." This is not intended to absolve Europeans of their culpability in the slave trade, for certainly the appearance of ever-increasing numbers of European slaving vessels at the coast both accelerated the traffic in human cargo from the interior of Africa and redirected West African lines of trade away from the more legitimate exchange of salt, leather, gold, and other goods across the Sahara.

In any event, a third factor limited European incursion prior to the middle of the nineteenth century: the harsh physical environment, coupled with limits on technology, would have made it a very costly proposition for the Europeans to attempt to penetrate the West African interior. Africa as a whole suffers from the relative absence of natural harbors. The continent's smooth coastline stands in sharp contrast to the rough and highly indented coastlines of the other continents. For every mile of coast in Europe there are 107 square miles of land; in North America the ratio is one to 97. For Africa the ratio is one to 510. Since water transport is still the least expensive means of transport, Africa thus starts out with a significant barrier to easy low-cost penetration of the hinterland. Africa, moreover, lacks the great rivers of commerce such as the Rhine and Danube in Europe or the Mississippi-Missouri network in North America. The Zaire and most other river systems in Africa have unpredictable year-long flow, are marked by a series of falls or cataracts, and invariably have sand bars, high surf, and other obstacles to easy navigation at the mouths of the rivers.

The physical barriers to European penetration were matched by the disease factor. The persistence of malaria, yellow fever, and other tropical diseases contributed to the West African coast being informally labeled "the white man's grave." The cemetery on Bunce Island in Freetown harbor in Sierra Leone which I visited in 1961 has many grave markers with such indications as: "Lt. J. Bradshaw / landed 15 February 1790 / died 24 February 1790 / of the fever." It was not altogether in jest that one West African nationalist leader, Kwame Nkrumah, just before Ghana's independence, was alleged to have said that the flag of his country should carry the likeness of a mosquito, since that insect had done so much to limit European settlement in West Africa.

With the suppression of the slave trade during the middle decades of the nineteenth century, Africa became even less attractive to European and New World merchants in general than it had been previously. In both economic and strategic terms Africa became so much real estate in the path of the more lucrative and highly prized political contacts with India and southeast Asia. Hence, the objective in constructing the Suez Canal in the 1860s was to make the longer and more expensive journey around the Cape of Good Hope unnecessary. The political incorporation of Africa into the Western European colonial nexus at the end of the nineteenth century, moreover, did not substantially alter economic linkages. The main lines of world trade continued to be between Europe and the New World, between Europe and Asia through the Suez Canal, or between America and the Far East. Africa still remained on the sidelines.

Theories of Imperialism

Why then, after nearly four hundred years of "waiting for the other shoe to drop," did the Europeans at the end of the nineteenth century engage in a frantic scramble to bring virtually the entire continent into the colonial system? This question has several facets. First we must deal with the question of why it suddenly became possible to penetrate Africa, after so many years in which the physical and human environment presented serious obstacles. Most obviously, the changes in technology during the nineteenth century on a broad front prepared Europeans to cope with problems that had previously been insurmountable. The development of the steamship and the railroad provided at least some solutions to both internal and external transport problems. Feeding large numbers of soldiers in a series of wars from the Napoleonic era to the American Civil War and the Franco-Prussian War had taught Europeans a great deal about preservation of foods. There were also medical advancements—particularly knowledge of the relationship between proper sanitation and good health, even though the causes of malaria, schistosomiasis, and sleeping sickness were still not known. Equally important was the improved military technology: the Gatling gun dramatically increased the advantage in weaponry that Europeans enjoyed over the firepower of more traditional rifles available to Africans. It was now possible for Europeans to challenge the trade monopoly of African middlemen in the West and Arabs in the East. European missionaries and scientifically inclined explorers (who provided advanced claims for European politicians) no longer had to pay tribute after tribute as they made their way in search of souls or the sources of the Nile, the Niger, and other potential avenues of commerce.

The reasons why imperialism was not possible earlier do not explain why it actually happened when it did. Why was the colonial relationship the consistent byproduct of European-African interaction in the nineteenth and early twentieth centuries? Both supporters and critics of European imperialism had their theories. Stewart Chamberlain and other apostles of the Social Darwinism school, for example, misapplied both Darwin and the canons of the scientific method to explain the forcible subordination of non-whites to whites around the globe as the "survival of the fittest." In the process, the Social Darwinists seemed to forget that Darwin had intentionally not applied his thesis on natural selection to the human species. Nor did his thesis enthrone the status quo; rather it looked to evolution as a continuing process. Darwin, moreover, certainly identified cooperation, isolation, and other non-violent mechanisms as equally valid explanations for survival of a particular species. Violent conquest was only one among several alternatives.

Other supporters of nineteenth-century European colonial expansion justified imperialism on humanitarian grounds.[3] European domination was presented as a self-assumed obligation on the part of the technologically advanced Europeans to "take up the white man's burden"—to quote Rudyard Kipling. In most instances, of course, the humanitarian explanation was an effort—usually after the fact—to put a charitable interpretation on what were rather base, avaricious motives in bringing an unwilling people into the political orbit of those who possessed superior military or technological skills. No one bothered to explain why humanitarianism was a trait peculiar to the imperialism of the nineteenth century but not characteristic of imperialism in the past, or why humanitarianism, while bringing education, better health, and Christianity to Africans, required their political subordination, or why Africans had to be bludgeoned into accepting what was supposed to be in their best interests. There was nothing resembling a consensus on the part of Africans about setting aside their traditional views on religion, organization of the family, and other values and institutions.

Opponents of European colonial expansion also had their explanations regarding the nineteenth-century acquisition of empires in Africa and elsewhere. The most vigorous critics were the Marxists, although it fell to Lenin in 1917 rather than Marx himself to provide the most systematic socialist indictment of imperialism.[4] Recognizing that imperialism had existed almost from the beginning of human experience, Lenin argued that the imperialism of the late nineteenth and early twentieth centuries differed significantly from earlier examples of political domination. Whereas the earlier examples were *casually* related to the mode of production of a given society or epoch, the imperialism which found most of Africa coming under European colonial control was *causally* related to that mode of production called capitalism. Indeed, the concentration of financial institutions and activities among the leading capitalist countries at the global level had not only produced the demand for territorial expansion to further control markets both for raw materials and consumer goods, but it had also given capitalism one last gasp of breath before its ultimate collapse. Hence, to Lenin, the appearance of western imperialism—the "highest stage of capitalist development"—provided an intervening stage not foreseen by Marx in terms of the dialectic and helped account for the delay in the transition to the next stage of history, socialist revolution.

Leninist criticism of imperialism has had a certain attraction because it is frequently easier to identify and measure economic activities that either precede or follow political conquest than it is to measure spiritual, social, or other alleged "causes." It has also been attractive to African nationalists because in attacking capitalism one also appeared to be attacking the dominant economic mode of production and the system of racial and class privilege associated with the colonial rule of Britain and other Western powers. But there are a number of limitations to the Leninist thesis. First, there are often significant gaps between the economic results of specific cases of imperial expansion and the alleged economic "causes" which brought about the political relationship in the first place. Despite the political incorporation of Africa into the European political system, moreover, the main lines of world trade and investment continued to link Western Europe with the British Commonwealth, the United States, Latin America, Japan, and other independent states. Insofar as Africa is concerned, the Germans, who had been united under the Prussian dynasty in the 1860s and 1870s, and Britain were the only colonial powers among those involved in the carve-up of that continent that manifested the characteristics of industrial capitalism, the later stage of economic development that according to Marx was a necessary prior stage to the socialist revolution. Portugal, Spain, and Italy were still in the feudal stage, and France and Belgium in the nineteenth century were examples of commercial, rather than industrial, capitalism. Indeed, one of Marx's prime examples of industrial capitalism, the United States, had steadfastly refused to take up Kipling's colonial challenge. The opportunities for the United States had been there with respect to Liberia, the Congo Basin Treaty, the Moroccan affair, and the formation of the League of Nations Mandates System after World War I, but in each instance the colonial responsibility was rejected.

A more plausible rationale than the Social Darwinian, humanitarian, or Leninist explanations of the European scramble for Africa is contained in the writings of the Austrian political economist Joseph Schumpeter.[5] Rather than attributing imperialism to rational motivations, Schumpeter suggests that over time imperial domination has been a consequence of unspent energies left over from consolidation of nationalism. Hence the year 1492 was important not only for the beginning of Spanish conquest of the New World, but also for the culmination of the struggle to expel the Moors and bring together the autonomous kingdoms of Aragon and Castile with other Hispanic principalities. A further example would be the expansion of the United

States beyond its Atlantic frontiers (including the proposed incorporation of Canada in the government under the Articles of Confederation), a movement which was already contemplated long before the issue of national independence and unity had actually been resolved. Finally, the nineteenth-century scramble for territory in Africa was preceded by the nationalist separation of Belgium from the Netherlands, the success of Garibaldi's plan for the unification of Italy, and the consolidation of Bismarck's efforts to unite the Germans under Prussian leadership. It was the reaction of France, Britain, and Portugal to (a) the imperial designs of Germany in various regions of the continent, (b) the ill-fated activities of the Italians in the Horn, and (c) the personal ambitions of Leopold in the Congo that precipitated the frenetic carve-up of Africa. Given the principles of Adam Smith's laissez faire capitalism, imperialism was, according to Schumpeter, a totally irrational response rather than—as Lenin had insisted—an inevitable consequence of the internal inconsistencies within capitalism itself. Imperialism was an aspect of the mercantilist system that Adam Smith's capitalism was to counteract. The moves of latecomers Belgium, Italy, and Germany created a "stampede" situation among the other Europeans who felt that they had deeper roots and more significant stakes in Africa.

The General Character of European Imperialism

Whatever the motivations that launched the European carve-up of Africa, the task of incorporating Africa within the several imperial orbits was not only all-encompassing, but accomplished virtually within a quarter of a century. The external imperial intervention, moreover, stimulated to action locally based groups that extended their imperial control over their neighbors. This included those entities that managed to secure international recognition as independent states. The case of South Africa is explored in a later chapter. It is sufficient at this point to note that the majority of the population, suffering under the policies of apartheid, consider themselves victims of imperial rule. A similar situation, however, had long prevailed in the other two states, Ethiopia and Liberia, which were recognized as independent states. Ethiopia maintained its independence in the nineteenth century by matching the French, British, and especially the Italian imperialists at their own game. Under Menelik II, the Amhara people of the Abyssinian highlands extended their jurisdiction over the domain of the Oromo, the Tigre, the Somali, and other ethnic groups that the Europeans were similarly coveting. Liberia, which had been founded in the 1820s as a refuge for freed persons of color from the New World, took on all the mannerisms of an imperial power as the Americo-Liberians at the coast expanded inland. Until the military coup in Ethiopia in 1974 and a similar development in Liberia in 1980, the majority of the inhabitants of both states considered themselves to be colonial subjects of a culturally distinct minority at the political center. The African-based imperialists also included ethnic groups who were themselves ultimately subordinated to European domination, such as the Moroccans and the Ganda (Baganda).

As Table 1 and Map 2 indicate, the task which had been tentatively launched with the Berlin Conference in 1884–1885 was all but completed on the eve of the First World War. The reshuffling of colonial territories in the First and Second World Wars as well as the occupation of Ethiopia by the Italians in 1936 constituted for the most part a change in the character of the imperial power rather than a de novo subordination of African people to imperial rule.

Ironically, the windup of colonial rule in the period following the Second World War was accomplished with almost the same breakneck speed that had characterized its initial imposition. The early and relatively unexpected achievement of independence by the Sudan in 1956, Ghana in 1957, and Guinea in 1958 came amid insistent predictions of some colonialists that the imperial relationship between Africa and Europe would endure anywhere from twenty-five more years to a full century. This author in 1951 heard the Belgian Minister of State for the colonies boast in a speech at Harvard University that the Congolese were so satisfied by their material gains under Belgian rule that he did not envision any demands for independence for several generations to come. Yet by the year 1960 the entire colonial house of cards began to come tumbling down. By 1986 only Namibia—a dependency of South Africa—and South Africa itself remain colonial situations for the majority of their African citizens. The rationale for the independence of each state is as complex and idiosyncratic as the rationale for the initial inclusion of that territory under colonial rule. A common thread, however, is the fact that the pressures for decolonization were in many cases as much external as they were internal. Without detracting from the courage of national liberation forces, there were only a few instances (Kenya, Zimbabwe, Mozambique, Angola, and Guinea-Bissau) in which prolonged armed struggle preceded the achievement of independence. Some analysts argue that it was the abandonment of India by the British and of Viet Nam and Algeria by the French that logically extended the principle of independence to other dependent areas. In some cases, it was a change of government in Britain, France, Belgium, or Portugal at a critical stage in the independence movement that hurried this situation along to a peaceable surrender of European authority to African leadership. Laborite and socialist parties tended to be more anti-imperialist than the conservative parties they displaced. Anti-colonial pressure by Latin American, Asian, and Middle East states in the United Nations was very often as significant in the liberation effort as the direct pressure applied by African nationalists against their respective colonial administrators.

Considering the magnitude of the colonial network and the lasting impact

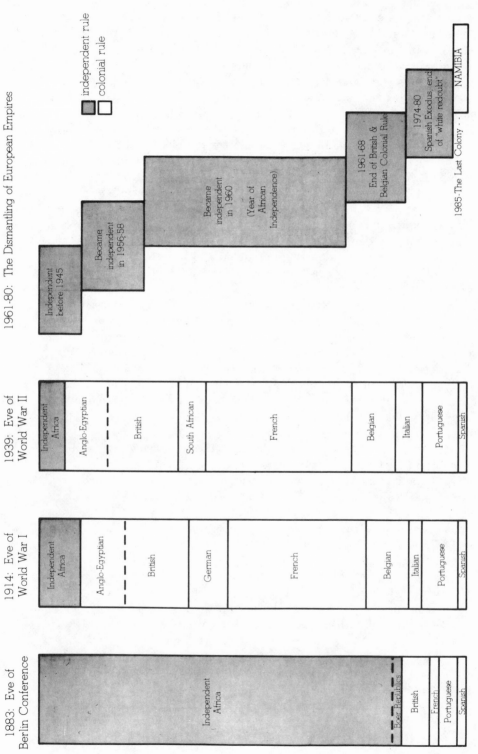

TABLE 1

The Rise and Fall of European Colonialism in Sub-Saharan Africa

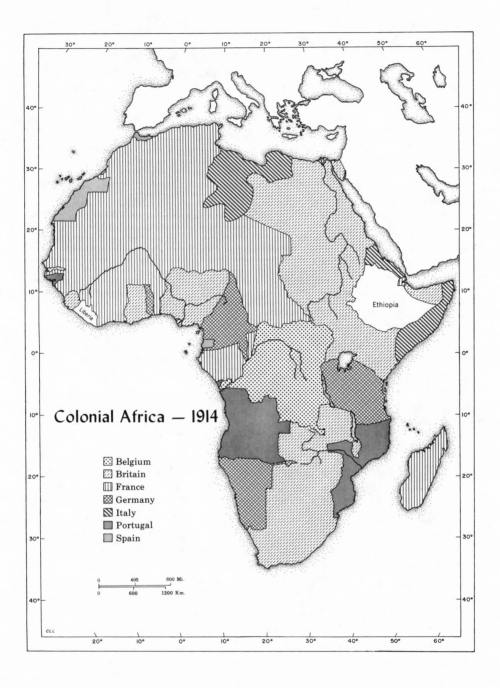

Colonial Africa — 1914

Ethiopia

Liberia

Belgium
Britain
France
Germany
Italy
Portugal
Spain

| 0 | 400 | 800 Mi. |
| 0 | 600 | 1200 Km. |

CLL

that European colonial rule has had upon African values and institutions, it must be recalled that it was one of the shorter-lived colonial experiences in history. Although the distant ancestors of some of the coastal people at Dakar, Cape Town, and Luanda had experienced the yoke of imperialism centuries ago, for most Africans the colonial presence was measured in decades rather than centuries. As Ali Mazrui has pointed out for Kenya, the period of colonial subjugation of the people of that modern state was briefer than the lifespan of its first president, Jomo Kenyatta. For particular people, it was in fact, even if not in legal terms, far briefer than that, since colonial rule made an uneven impact upon the peoples of the sub-continent. Compared to Africans residing in the interior, those on the coast tended to experience a more in-depth exposure to wage employment, Christianity, modern medicine, and Western education. Those Africans who had resisted the imposition of European rule tended to witness a great erosion—if not destruction—of traditional political and other institutions than did those who acquiesced in the assertion of European rule. The impact of colonial rule was also felt more strongly by those Africans who lived in areas where European settlers had coveted and confiscated land, where the mineral wealth and agriculture potential was considered suitable for exploitation, and where Christian missionaries had been proselytizing. In the absence of the above conditions, the writ of the colonial authority was only dimly perceived even at the eve of independence. This author in the mid-1950s visited an island in Lake Victoria where most of the younger generation had never previously seen a European and where colonial taxes were collected in only a perfunctory way.

In both de jure and de facto terms there was a wide range of variations in the way in which colonial rule was applied to the Africans of more than fifty territories in sub-Saharan Africa. Taking the British imperial system alone, there were wide discrepancies between a settler colony at the one extreme and a United Nations Trust Territory at the other. In the former, the rights and privileges of the small European minority were given far higher priority than the African majority. Intermediate between a colony and a trust territory, a given dependency might be designated as a protectorate, a condominium, a high commission territory, or a treaty state. Most dependencies were administered by the Colonial Office, but several (Botswana, Lesotho, and Swaziland) were under the British Foreign Office. Dependencies in this intermediate category were governed from the 1920s onward in accordance with the principle of the "paramountcy of African interests," on the theory that the rights of the Africans ought to take precedence over the interests of settlers, miners, planters, and other European and Asian entrepreneurs. It was a principle, however, which was usually invoked when an exception was being made to its observance. Most protective of the interests of Africans was the category of U.N. Trust Territory. The U.N. system was a successor to the League of Nations Mandates System, established at the end of World War I. The U.N. system not only committed the trust power to either self-government or independence as the ultimate goal of the dependency relationship, but it also provided mechanisms for international supervision of and accountability for the way in which the Trust Authority administered a territory. These protective mechanisms included annual reports, triennial and special visitations by members of the U.N. Trusteeship Council, and the right of residents to petition the Council directly.

Despite the diversity in legal status and the variation in policies among the several colonial powers, the dependency situation throughout the continent tended to be a similar experience for most Africans. The latter tended to be subordinated in all respects to the interest of Europeans and others who augmented the European presence. This applied whether the colonial relationship was established by conquest or as a result of an innocuous and deceptive "treaty of friendship and commerce," and whether the dependency was ultimately destined for a resumption of independent status or was considered an overseas extension of the French or Portuguese state. Treaties of friendship were literally converted into deeds of ownership when the European powers convened at Brussels, Berlin, Paris, and other places to divide the spoils during the scramble for African territory.

Although slavery and the slave trade had been terminated, the European colonial overlords tended, nevertheless, to assert total control over the person and the personality of the African residents of a dependency. Adult African males could be conscripted into the army to maintain the peace elsewhere in the territory or the broader empire and even to fight in Europe, Asia, or the Middle East, as they did in both World Wars. African males were also liable to provide up to thirty days free service in road construction and other communal labor projects. Although the practice was invariably denied, in fact African males were forcibly recruited to work in European-owned mines or on plantations at wages which in some cases barely provided for their maintenance with a little left over to pay taxes and buy a few pieces of cloth or other consumer goods. Other compulsory means were utilized to control the way Africans employed their talents and energies. In some areas Africans were required to plant trees and crops which would provide them with cash for the payment of taxes and give the territory a better trade balance. Even with respect to subsistence agriculture the colonists used fines, imprisonment, and other coercive means to force Africans to make use of agricultural techniques which the Europeans felt were technologically superior to traditional methods (often they were not!). With respect to social, political, and economic modernization, Africans were seldom permitted under colonial authority to opt for the activity or lifestyle which would have been their choice. Africans in Zimbabwe were discouraged from living in towns; Africans in Kenya could not cultivate coffee in competition with Europeans; Africans in Nyasaland and Zaire were harassed for joining the Watchtower Movement; Africans in Zambia were not permitted to join white mineworker unions; and Africans in most territories were not permitted to join political parties. Formally and informally Africans tended to be restricted to the areas that were regarded as their traditional homelands, and passes as well as other obstacles limited their mobility, a practice that is still the rule in South Africa under its Homelands policy.

In other ways than those cited above, Africans were restricted in their utilizing of natural resources. This was particularly the case with respect to the most significant element in production, namely land. Even in West Africa, where disease, climate, and other factors had limited European settlement, the colonial authorities had ultimate control over land use. Traditional systems of land tenure and ownership would be superseded when the mineral or agricultural potential of a given area became attractive to Europeans. The exploitation of iron ore and diamonds in Sierra Leone, for example, and the planting of cocoa and palm oil trees in the Ivory Coast tended to become the monopoly of European entrepreneurs on land that was "leased" to Europeans.

In areas that were attractive to white settlement, the designation of land as "alienated" for European settlement was far out of proportion to settlers' numbers or even their ability to exploit it efficiently. Thus, in the areas designated for Europeans, those Africans who remained on the land of their ancestors were regarded as illegal squatters or permitted to remain only because they provided a pool of cheap labor to the new white owners. In the case of South Africa, the residue of this historic alienation of land to Europeans underscores the ultimate failure of the Homelands policy, since only 13 percent of the land has been reserved for the 77 percent of the population that is Black. Needless to say, the reserved land is among the most eroded and overworked land in the Republic and with the exception of Bophuthatswana, contains none of the mineral resources which have underwritten South Africa's economic development. A travesty of similar proportions was characteristic of land distribution in pre-independence Zimbabwe. Ian Smith, the leader of the white Rhodesians, once boasted during the liberation struggle that he believed in racial equality with respect to land ownership: the Africans under land "reform" got 50 percent of the land and the Europeans got the same. It was a kind of Orwellian equality, however, since the Africans outnumbered the Europeans by a ratio of twenty to one. In Kenya, although the European minority controlled smaller percentages of the land than was true of whites further south, there were qualitative differences between the land held by Africans and that held by Europeans. The latter, for example, had purchased land or "leased" it for 999 years— despite the absence of a traditional African concept of land sale. European land also differed from African reserved land in that the former generally was at higher altitudes, more predictably received adequate rainfall, was relatively free of the tsetse fly, which carries human or animal sleeping sickness, and had a low population density.[6]

The all-encompassing control by Europeans over the labor and land of

Africans was a sufficient indictment of colonialism. What made it even more intolerable was the assertion of racial and cultural superiority of European values and institutions over those which were African. Every aspect of indigenous culture and behavior was subject to manipulation if not destruction. Except in those rare cases like Northern Nigeria under Lord Lugard where Islam was given preference, Christian missionaries were literally given carte blanche to substitute Christianity for traditional forms of religious worship and to desecrate or dispose of "pagan" art. European languages or lingua franca such as KiSwahili and KiKongo displaced African traditional languages as vehicles for commerce, administration, and educational enlightenment. Certain traditional dance forms and songs were expressly outlawed in Kenya and Tanzania. African styles of dress, body decoration, and other aspects of personal hygiene were severely regulated. Most humiliating of all, however, was the assumption that Africans were like children and had to be treated accordingly in terms of restraints on the use of alcohol, gambling, and other activities. This attitude was epitomized by the use of the term "boy" to describe an African male servant no matter what his age.

Finally, in terms of a wide range of human transactions, Africans became second- or even third-class citizens in their own countries. No matter how minuscule the European minority in a given territory, the whites stood at the top of a political, economic, and social hierarchy based on a fairly rigid racial caste system. The Europeans, including administrators, missionaries, merchants, and miners, were exempt from the application of African law. Since they operated without the normal moral and other restraints of their democratic home societies, expatriates tended frequently to give vent to their most base instincts in their dealings with Africans. Many developed what East Africans termed a *bwana mkubwa* (big master) complex. Those whites who considered themselves permanent settlers, moreover, were permitted to engage in politics long before the African majority, and had access to economic privileges denied to Africans. Ironically, even the Indians, Pakistanis, Lebanese, and other third parties who were invited or permitted in to assist the Europeans in administrative, commercial, and other tasks could claim a middle rung on the ladder of privilege superior to that of Africans.

Contrasts in Colonial Policies and Practices

In starting our analysis of the commonality of the colonial experience, it was stressed that colonial rule affected some Africans more deeply than others, depending upon their location, the presence of exploitable resources, and other factors. The colonial experience also differed from territory to territory and even within a single territory, depending upon the broad policies of the European power in charge. Over the long haul, this has shaped the way in which Africans sought independence, the nature of the future relationship with the colonial metropole, and the manner in which the nationalist leadership has faced its problems of nation-building and economic development.[7]

FRENCH COLONIAL POLICY. The attitudes of the French with respect to their African dependencies were undoubtedly the most radical and far-reaching in their implications. It was assumed until well into the 1950s that the objective of French colonial policy was both to convert Africans into Black Frenchmen and to incorporate African dependencies into a broader Francophone political community led by the French Republic. Depending upon one's perspective, French policy could be viewed as either ethnocentric or altruistic. It was ethnocentric in its implicit assumptions that French culture was superior to that of all other societies, and that—having been exposed to the French language, manners, and other facets of culture—dependent people would inevitably prefer the imported French values and institutions to their own. It therefore became an obligation of Frenchmen to assume a civilizing mission (mission civilisatrice) with respect to those people under French political control. As Boissy d'Anglas said during the French Revolution: "There can only be one kind of good government. If we have found it for Europe, why should the colonies be deprived of it?"

It was, on the other hand, altruistic in its assumption that people without regard to race or ethnicity were indeed capable of becoming like Frenchmen. Having accepted the French language, Christianity, monogamy, and the virtue of French ideas and institutions, they should be treated as the political, social, and economic equals of Frenchmen of European origin. Indeed, the inclusion of Léopold Senghor of Senegal and Félix Houphouet-Boigny of the Ivory Coast in the governments of the French Republic following the Second World War is often cited as proof of the sincerity of the French position on the issue of equality and substantiation of the rejection of racism in French colonial rule.[8]

In practice the French policy of incorporation of African territories into the French Republic fell far short of the theory. The constitutions of the Third (1870–1940) as well as the Fourth (1940–1958) and the Fifth (1958–) Republics left open the possibility of incorporation of African territories into an expanding French Republic in the same way that the United States expanded from thirteen to fifty states. Despite the theory of the Fourth Republic's French Union or the Fifth Republic's French Community, incorporation was never considered to be a viable option for sub-Saharan Africa except for the four communes in the Dakar region of Senegal. The latter area had long sent deputies to the National Assembly in Paris. The theoretical option nevertheless had negative consequences in terms of African political development. It meant that the French and many Francophone Africans rejected the concept of independence until nationalist movements elsewhere in Africa finally compelled them to accept the inevitability of separation.[9] Léopold Senghor told the National Assembly in 1957: "We do not wish to leave the French compound. We have grown up in it and it has been pleasant to live in it. We simply want to build our own house which will enlarge and strengthen the family compound, or rather the French hexagon."[10] It meant, furthermore, that there was a long delay before territorial political institutions were developed in the Francophone dependencies. Political parties, trade unions, and other associations were organized with respect to participation in the politics of France or French West Africa rather than being relevant to the development of the individual territories of Senegal or the Ivory Coast, for example. It was not until the *loi cadre* of 1956 that the French seriously addressed the question of territorial political assemblies; even then they excluded Africans from sharing in executive power. Similarly, the French did not attempt to develop relatively self-sufficient and integrated economies for any of the territories. Even in the areas where the post–World War II infusion of development capital contrasted sharply with the neglect of the preceding period, the efforts actually linked the dependency ever closer to the economy of France. The military as well was organized less in terms of the security needs of a given dependency than of the strategic interests of France, the French Empire, or an administrative region such as West or Equatorial Africa. Administration, finally, in theory at least, was highly centralized with local and territorial officials allowed less initiative and having to take far more orders from Paris or the regional headquarters at Dakar or Brazzaville than was true of their British counterparts. In fact, however, the *commandant de cercle*, the man on the spot, tended to govern without administrative restraints and in an arbitrary manner.[11]

As a consequence, states in Francophone Africa have continued to maintain far closer linkages both with each other and with the former metropole than has been the case with other independent African states. This is true in the economic, diplomatic, military, educational, and cultural fields, and it has led to the term "neo-colonialism" having special application to the former French dependencies.

The second facet of French colonial policy, the cultural transformation of Africans, achieved some measure of success. Surprisingly, this was accomplished despite political independence and despite the fact that the overwhelming majority of Africans in the French Empire did not achieve French citizenship until after World War II. That status was reserved under previous constitutions for the few *évolués* (evolved persons), that is, persons who had been taught in French, accepted the values and institutions of Frenchmen, and had in other respects—such as service in the French army or outstanding support of colonial administrative efforts—demonstrated their commitment to French rule. The évolué was, as a consequence of his status, exempt from military conscription; compulsory labor; the application of both customary law and the arbitrary and capricious system of justice administered by colonial officials (the *indigénat*); and the restrictions on residential mobility and rights of association which limited the freedom of the majority, who were considered merely French subjects. Although these formal distinctions ultimately disappeared, it was still this minority of French-speaking Africans who were permitted to join political parties and trade unions and to become journalists, administrators, and fill other roles normally reserved for Europeans. Évolués largely escaped the kind of racism inflicted on their more traditional fellow Africans. This was a universal characteristic of colonial rule—the French theory of equality and fraternity notwithstanding.

The cultural transformation sought by the French succeeded despite the paucity of évolués during the colonial era. It did so because it was this elite which inherited the reins of power when the French reluctantly acceded to the necessity of African independence. French administrators, moreover, as well as businessmen, priests, educators, technicians, and even military leaders, remained on hand and in some cases dramatically increased their numbers after independence. This made it possible for this Francophone elite to expand instruction in French, give assistance to Roman Catholic and Protestant missionary efforts, and in other respects to continue the links with France. Finally, the policy succeeded because the primary domestic rivals to the political authority of the Francophone elite, the traditional chiefs, had either been eliminated under the policy of direct rule or had had their power considerably curtailed where they were permitted to govern on sufferance. The latter situation occurred in areas where the local chiefs had proved to be worthy allies of the French or where the French lacked the administrative manpower or the economic interest to institute direct rule.

BRITISH COLONIAL POLICY. In analyzing British colonial policies in Africa it is necessary to differentiate between the territories that had some modicum of European settlement (South Africa, the two Rhodesias, and Kenya) and those territories not considered climatically and otherwise hospitable to European settlers. In the former, the British government over the long haul was prepared to accede to the demands of the white minority for something approximating the status of Canada, New Zealand, and Australia as independent or autonomous dominions within the Commonwealth of Nations.[12] Long before the legal, political, economic, and other rights of the African majority were recognized and protected, the British established "national" parliaments and cabinets-in-embryo (legislative and executive councils) in which the interests of the elected white minority were represented either exclusively or far out of proportion to their numbers. Gradually the representatives of the British Crown surrendered one portfolio after another to the local whites, leaving them free to manage not only their own affairs but those of the African majority and the Asian and other minorities as well. In the case of South Africa this surrender was all but total. In the case of the two Rhodesias (now Zimbabwe and Zambia) the federation introduced after the Second World War left all but foreign affairs, security, and some aspects of "native policy" in local white hands. In Kenya this process of devolution was only interrupted by the so-called Mau Mau uprising of the 1950s.

In the rest of British Africa the tendency was to give paramount concern to the interests of the African residents.[13] As national institutions were established, Africans gradually attained a majority of the seats in the legislative councils and assumed the major portfolios in the executive councils. This is not to suggest that the British were more benign or radically different than the French in terms of granting African self-government. True, the British did create meaningful territorial institutions and permit "national" parties at a far earlier point than was generally true of the French. Concessions only came, however, in response to organized demand and when the higher costs of resisting reform outweighed any advantages that might accrue by maintaining the status quo. The devolution of authority was hardly a case of enthusiastic capitulation, as the example of Sierra Leone in Table 2 indicates. Inclusion of Africans, for example, in legislative and executive councils came initially by appointment of the governor and only much later by popular election. The British preferred to give greater representation to traditional chiefs than to the modernized elite, thereby slowing the pace of reform. Legal and other barriers, moreover, were frequently placed in the path of Africans organizing effective political parties or other associations, such as trade unions, which might accelerate the demands for independence. Africans were often encouraged to focus their energies on local government before turning their attention to territorial or "national" politics. Despite the foot-dragging and incrementalism of the British approach, Africans in Sierra Leone ultimately came into control of their own destinies—albeit almost a century after the 1863 introduction of the Legislative Council (Leg-Co).

Despite the differences between settler and non-settler territories, there are several common threads which run through British colonial policy and practice which differentiate the British from the French. First, from the American Revolution until the present day the British government has never accepted the notion of the integration of overseas areas beyond the British Isles themselves into the British state. Outright independence, self-government, or continued dependency status with linkages through the Crown and the Commonwealth have been the only acceptable outcomes in the relationship between Britain and its colonies. Second, as a corollary to the preceding, Britain saw no advantage in converting Africans into Black Englishmen, since they were not expected to enjoy legal, political, and other rights in the United Kingdom. Third, since Africans were expected to develop politically, economically, and in other respects as Africans (or Yoruba or Nigerians), preference was given to the retention of African traditional values and institutions to the extent that they were not "repugnant to British standards of justice and morality." This preference had been informally recognized in the past, but under Lord Lugard's administration in northern Nigeria it developed into the formal policy of Indirect Rule and was extended to other parts of British Africa and pursued as almost a religious philosophy.[14] Although it

TABLE 2

Evolution of Self-Government in Sierra Leone

Year	Event	Legislative Power	Executive Power
1787	Founding of Sierra Leone Colony (COL) as refuge for freed slaves	COL administered by private company, the Sierra Leone Company, through its local agent, who exercised both legislative and executive powers	
1808	S.L. designated as Crown Colony	COL under authority of United Kingdom Colonial Office, and administered locally by appointed Governor (GOV)	
1811	Creation of quasi-legislative Advisory Council	Advisory Council: GOV & Senior Officers (SR OFS)	
1863	Creation of governmental structures	Legislative Council (LEG-CO): 5 Officials: GOV & 4 SR OFS ‖ 4 Unofficials: 3 White (WH), 1 African (AFR) Nominated (NOM) by GOV	Executive Council (EX-CO): GOV & SR OFS
1872	Increases in African representation	5 Officials: GOV & SR OFS ‖ 4 Unofficials: 3 AFR, 1 WH NOM by GOV	
1896	Establishment of Protectorate (PROT) over hinterland behind coastal COL	LEG-CO denied authority to legislate for PROT; limited to COL	
1913	Beginning of "national" system of government	LEG-CO given authority to legislate for PROT and COL as separate units	
1924	LEG-CO reorganized and given limited power to deal with COL and PROT as a national unit	12 Officials: GOV & 11 SR OFS ‖ 10 Unofficials: 3 from PROT (NOM by GOV) ‖ 7 from COL (4 NOM by GOV ‖ 3 Directly Elected (DIR EL))	

1943/48 — Local representation in EX-CO

6 Officials	3 Unofficials
GOV & SR OFS	2 COL; 1 PROT Paramount Chief (PC)

1951 — Post World War II reforms in both LEG-CO & EX-CO

4 Officials	6 Unofficials
GOV & SR OFS	NOM by GOV

8 Officials	23 Unofficials		
	7 fr COL	14 fr PROT	2 At-Large
GOV & 7 SR OFS	DIR EL	12 INDIR EL by District / 2 PC, Nom by PROT Assembly	NOM by GOV

1953/54 — Introduction of Ministerial System

4 Officials	6 Unofficials
GOV & SR OFS	Chief Minister (CM) & 5 Unofficials Elected by LEG-CO

1956/57 — Delegation of responsibility to locals

4 Officials	9 Unofficials
GOV & SR OFS	Chief Minister & 8 Unofficials EL by LEG-CO

4 Officials	53 Unofficials		
	14 fr COL	37 fr PROT	2 AT-LARGE
4 SR OFS; Speaker replaces GOV	DIR EL	25 DIR EL / 12 PC IN-DIR EL	NOM, no vote

1958 — Creation of Parliamentary System

Conversion of LEG-CO into House of Representatives (HR); Removal of Official members

1960/61 — Transition to Cabinet government; withdrawal of GOV from executive power

GOV retains reserved powers	CM becomes Prime Minister; PM & 10 MINS assume all portfolios except defense, foreign affairs, police & public services

1961 — Independence; admission to the Commonwealth

GOV becomes GOV-GENL	PM & 14 Cabinet MINS assume all portfolios

Assumption of full power by House of Representatives

was presented as a more humane way of exposing Africans to the modern world through institutions that were familiar to them, it was also presented as being "cost effective" in that it constituted less of a drain on the financial and personnel resources of the British administration. The task was largely that of "finding the chief" and governing through him. On the other hand, it could also be viewed as racism, since it implicitly rejected the idea of equality between Englishmen and Africans even if the latter adopted Christianity, were educated at Eton and Oxford, accepted a monetized economy, and in other respects became "modernized." Unlike the French évolué, the evolved African in a British territory had no privileged political, legal, or economic status that differentiated him from his fellow traditional Africans.

The consequence was that the British not only accepted self-government or independence for the colonies as inevitable, but left behind stronger territorial political institutions than was true of the French. On the theory that a dependency should pay for its own administration, security, and social services, the British tended to establish more viable national economies and educational systems than did the French. Administrative decision-making was decentralized at the territorial level. Since the British declined to make a place for the evolved Africans in the politics of Great Britain itself, Jomo Kenyatta, Kwame Nkrumah, and others tended to regard their own national territories as the proper arena for the development of their talents and interests. The continued preference for traditional authorities, moreover, meant that the independence struggle was often a triangular affair pitting the British, the chiefs, and the modernized elite against one another. In many cases, such as Lesotho, Swaziland, western and northern Nigeria, and Sierra Leone, the traditional authorities have continued to exercise influence if not real power. This makes national politics considerably different in English-speaking as opposed to Francophone Africa.

BELGIAN COLONIAL POLICY. In many respects the Belgians got the lion's share of tropical Africa's wealth. Only South Africa rivals the former Belgian Congo in terms of its stores of copper, tin, uranium, diamonds, gold, and cobalt—mostly located in the Shaba (Katanga) region. But it was its agricultural potential that led Leopold II to put in his bid to have the Congo Free State recognized in 1885 as the personal property of the Belgian monarch. It was this acquisition, coupled with the German annexations in other parts of Africa, that precipitated the "scramble for Africa." Having perpetrated one of the more sordid examples of colonial exploitation of human and other resources under Leopold's personal rule, the Belgian state in 1908 assumed responsibility for the Congo and set it on a course of "scientific colonialism" that differed radically from the policies and practices of its European colleagues. Accepting neither the British goal of eventual self-government and/or independence nor the French ideal of incorporation, the

Belgians were prepared to leave the Congo in a relationship of political dependency to Belgium that could last for a hundred years.

Internally, the Belgian Congo was to become an economically advanced but politically neutral zone in the heart of Africa. Like France, Belgium created a legal class of évolués who would be better educated, better trained in skills, better housed and fed, and more modernized in terms of acceptance of monogamy, the nuclear family, Christianity, and other attributes of Western civilization than their countrymen. Unlike their French counterparts, however, the Congolese évolués were in effect to be political eunuchs. The entire emphasis of the Belgian colonial program was upon "stomach rather than status." That is, the material needs of the évolués were to be satisfied in a paternalistic way in the new urban communities established around the mining enterprises in the Katanga, but the évolués were to be prevented from developing political aspirations. Parties and other associations that might become political were banned until virtually the eve of independence. School education abruptly halted at the end of the secondary level for everyone except priests. Indeed, there were only an estimated dozen college graduates in a society of 16 million in 1960.[15] And although Congolese had been trained to run much of the complicated mining machinery, there was not a single Congolese in a supervisory position in any of the mining operations. This experiment in controlled colonial development was in the hands of a triad: the Belgian administration; the Union Minière du Haut Katanga and other companies, which ran the most significant aspects of the economy; and the Roman Catholic Church, which provided much of the schooling and carried out the "civilizing mission" among the évolués and their families. The end product of this enterprise was to be a Congolese who was not Belgian, no longer tribal, and only partially modern. In effect, the évolué was expected to remain in psychological and political limbo.

To avoid the political turmoil of other African dependencies, moreover, the linguistic and language conflicts within Belgian society itself were not to be "exported" to the Congo. The French language and the Catholic version of Christianity were the preferred instruments of colonial rule. The Europeans, whose skills were needed not only in mining but in agriculture and administration, were carefully screened in terms of economic status, political leanings, and other factors that might be disruptive. Their numbers were consciously limited, and they were denied the political privileges accorded European settlers elsewhere.

Despite their "best laid plans" the Belgian experiment could not be insulated from the forces that were alive in other quarters of the continent, leading Africans to demand political independence. Belgium's delay in creating territorial institutions with relevance to Africans, its reluctance to permit Africans to identify with the developing national community, and its ban on political parties until the middle 1950s account in great measure not only

for the explosive nature of Zaire's birth as an independent state but also for its many problems since.

for the explosive nature of Zaire's birth as an independent state but also for the many problems which have plagued that society in the past quarter of a century.

PORTUGUESE COLONIAL POLICY. Portugal had the longest history of colonial rule in Africa; yet it was the power that least prepared its colonial territories and their residents for independence.[16] Only Portugal was dislodged from each of its dependencies as a result of armed resistance on the part of African liberation forces. Just as in the former Belgian territory, many of the problems in the post-independence era of Mozambique, Angola, and Guinea-Bissau are the direct reflection of flawed colonial policies. Unlike those of the Belgians, however, the policies of the Portuguese were marked by neglect, oppression, and calculated efforts to deny Africans even a modicum of development.

Being one of the poorest of the colonial powers, Portugal lacked the resources to develop the mineral and agricultural potential of its colonies; and it was fearful of being displaced by any outsiders that it may have called in to do the job in its behalf. Not until the period following World War II, when the prospects of losing its colonies by default were increasing, did the Portuguese began to seek the American, British, German, and South African capital needed to launch mineral, agricultural, and industrial development in Angola. In Mozambique primary government revenues (other than port and railway transit fees paid by South Africans and Rhodesians) came from the fees paid to the government for the recruitment of Africans to work in the South African mines. The civil administration of vast areas was left to the private companies that had concessions for the agricultural exploitation of the country instead of becoming a direct responsibility of the Portuguese government.

In outward form the political aspects of Portuguese colonial rule resembled those of the French, but there were profound differences in application. Going even further than the French, for example, the Portuguese claimed that they had no colonies—only overseas provinces of the Portuguese state. In fact, the legal fiction meant nothing in terms of African participation in Lisbon politics or any other significant arena of Portuguese affairs. Like France and Belgium, Portugal created a legal status for evolved Africans, called *assimilados*, which gave them equality with Portuguese of European origin. It meant little, however, in terms of political participation since openly contested elections were not held in Portugal itself under the Salazar fascist dictatorship. Indeed, the educational, financial, and other requirements qualifying one for assimilado status were constantly being raised. Consequently, not more than one percent of the African population attained this rank. Many of the jobs in government, business, industry, and the church that were being handled by Africans elsewhere on the continent were monopolized by poor whites in the Portuguese colonies. Despite the claims of being non-racial, the whites and *mestiços* (persons of mixed European and African ancestry) discriminated against Blacks in all phases of life.[17]

Balance Sheet on Colonial Rule

The world is still too close to the actual experience of colonial rule in Africa to present an objective assessment of its impact. Ghana, after all, has only been independent since 1957, and Zimbabwe since 1980. Neither Africans nor Europeans are of one mind about the consequences of colonialism. Any assessment is bound to be distorted by the ideology, national origin, and other perspectives of the particular analyst. European critics, like the members of the Fabian Society in Britain, were often far harsher in their condemnation of imperialism than many Ghanaian, Nigerian, or Senegalese nationalists. On the other hand, many Frenchmen today view with a measure of pride the sharing of their language, culture, and institutions with the people of Senegal and the Ivory Coast. Still other Europeans exaggerate the heritage of democracy and capitalism which the colonialists allegedly bequeathed to Africa and hence are critical of the military interventions and single-party systems which appear to erode that heritage.

Africans are also ambivalent about the full significance of their subordination to Europe during the nineteenth and twentieth centuries. Some, like Félix Houphouet-Boigny of the Ivory Coast and Léopold Senghor of Senegal, have always seen some positive financial, cultural, and political merit in the Euro-African connection. Indeed, there are four times as many Frenchmen in the Ivory Coast today as there were at independence, indicating a continuity of the Francophone linkage. Over 4,000 men of the French Foreign Legion remain in Djibouti, years after its 1977 independence. Other African leaders, such as Dos Santos in Angola and Samora Machel in Mozambique, who were vigorous armed opponents of Portuguese rule, and who welcomed the mass departure of Portuguese nationals in 1974–75, have recently reassessed their Lusophone connection. During 1983, Angola and Mozambique actually intensified their diplomatic, economic, linguistic, and other linkages with the former metropole. Similarly, Robert Mugabe and his colleagues in Zimbabwe—after having fought the European settler minority over the issue of land ownership—have nevertheless asked the European farmers to remain in order to maintain Zimbabwe's advanced status in food production. For the most part, however, it is difficult for Africans to avoid holding the former colonial powers responsible for many of their crises of nation-building, poverty, and lapses from democracy. The Europeans, after all, were not intentionally invited in to serve as political overlords. Even where treaties had been honestly negotiated, there was little awareness by African leaders that the economic, social, and educational development of the continent would be Eurocentric in perspective rather than constructed to give primary attention to the needs of Africans. Even with respect to those aspects of the colonial experience which have endured and are now working to the good of Africans, the intended initial beneficiaries were usually European or Asian rather than African. Hence, many of the positive assertions regarding colonial rule have to be countered by negative evaluation.

Political Impact of Colonial Rule

This balancing of consequences is readily apparent in the realm of political behavior and relationships. Apologists for colonial rule note that the imposition of European peace terminated what for many ethnic groups had been a perpetual Hobbesian "state of nature, a continuous war of every man, against every man," in which life was "solitary, poor, nasty, brutish, and short." The European-imposed *pax* contributed to breaking down traditional African parochialism based upon clan, ethnic, and other local affiliations. Over a larger extent of territory than in the past, Africans were permitted to engage in a whole range of positive interactions with other Africans. These activities included long distance trade, cooperation in the grazing of cattle, and pursuit of religious objectives such as pilgrimages to Mecca or the Holy Land.

This is not to suggest that Africans in the pre-European era lived in isolated hamlets or that they did not have contacts over considerable distances. However negative its impact, the intertribal warfare which was terminated under colonial rule did nevertheless bring some Africans into a wide-ranging imperial system. The Zulu-Ngoni military diaspora, which emanated from South Africa, reached as far north as the shores of Lake Victoria and incorporated many groups into the Zulu-Ngoni militocracy. Similar developments at an earlier period in West Africa had led to the establishment of the Islamic empires of Gao, Mali, and Ghana. Interethnic contacts also had long histories with respect to the network of trade routes established across the Sahara and from east to west in the Sahara/Sahelian region. The 1324 overland pilgrimage to Mecca by Mansa Musa, the ruler of ancient Mali, required many less celebrated but similar demonstrations of courage in facing human and physical obstacles in order to gain the revered title of El Hadj—evidence of having made the required pilgrimage to Mecca. Territorial boundaries, moreover, among ethnic groups were seldom precisely defined, and social passage from one group to another was often possible. Strangers from a neighboring society who wished to take up cultivation were often welcomed on a probationary basis as long as they accepted the political and other rules established by the original occupants.

On balance, however, both environmental barriers to unimpeded travel and political, social, and economic resistance to migration did make interethnic contact the exception rather than the rule in pre-European Africa.

Early Manding, Hausa, and other traders in West Africa—like the European missionaries and merchants in the nineteenth century—literally had to buy from the local political authorities the privilege of passage through, and residence in, the areas in which they operated. Traders, smiths, and others considered alien to the host community were frequently required to live in separate quarters called *zongoes*, which persist today, to limit their contact with the local community. At a minimum, then, the European-imposed peace and the establishment of a network of roads and railroads did for nineteenth-century Africa what the establishment of the King's Highways by the Normans did for eleventh-century England. Hence, it potentially widened African contacts not only on the continent but beyond as well, as Africans were permitted to take advantage of educational opportunities in Europe, America, and elsewhere.

A second general political claim made by the colonialists in their own behalf is that they brought an end to many tyrannical authority situations in which whole ethnic groups were subordinated to oppressive conquering marauders. The imperialists pointed out, moreover, that colonial adminis-trators had terminated the institution of domestic slavery, and that under colonial rule there was a curtailment of the kind of personalized rule which exacted tribute payments, military service, and other forms of expropriation of property, labor, and women from relatively defenseless subjects. In place of inhumane political systems, the colonialists argued, they had introduced the values and institutions associated with parliamentary democracy.

Finally, there is a political consequence of European rule which contem-porary African leaders explicitly if not implicitly recognize: the expansion of the scale of political community from the isolated clan, neighborhood, or "tribal" segment to the level of the nation-state. From as many as nine hundred to a thousand relatively autonomous polities, sub-Saharan Africa under colonial rule was reduced to roughly fifty colonial dependencies. A few of these territories were consolidated at the time of independence. This included the union of Ghana and British Togoland, the fusion of Italian and British Somaliland, and the division of British Cameroon between Nigeria and the former French Cameroon. Another series of territories which had been fused were reestablished as separate political entities immediately be-fore or after independence. Examples of this are the dissolution of the Mali Federation (Senegal and Mali) and the fragmentation of the Federation of Rhodesia and Nyasaland (Malawi, Zambia, and Zimbabwe). Essentially, how-ever, the arbitrary lines drawn on the map of Africa by European diplomats in the nineteenth and early twentieth century remain the political boundaries of post-independence Africa, and these are the geographic boundaries within which most Africans are prepared to live. The commitment of African states to "the frontiers existing on their achievement of national independence" has been enshrined in the July 1964 Cairo Resolution of the Organization of African Unity regarding border disputes as well as the Charter of the

United Nations. Thus, this "heritage" of European rule remains a constant in contemporary African politics, setting the parameters both for interstate political relationships and for the formation of national political communities.

This somewhat sanguine assessment of the political heritage of colonial rule must be offset by some rather candid counterevidence. In the first place, Europeans were seldom invited in to establish themselves as political overlords, and certainly not with the understanding that their control over the people, the land, and the resources would be unrestrained. If the contemporary African leaders did inherit an augmented political community, with parlimentrary institutions in place, they were—as Jawaharlal Nehru said of India—"the *unintended* beneficiaries of European colonial exploitation." Take the case of the European-imposed peace under colonial rule. The prime beneficiaries were the English settlers, Belgian mining entrepreneurs, French merchants, German missionaries, and Portuguese planters who desired to pursue their objectives over a wider domain unimpeded by interethnic warfare and the demands for tribute payment by local African autocrats. For some people, such as the Nandi in Kenya or the Hehe in German Tanganyika, "peace" was imposed through an annihilation of large segments of their populations. And while the *pax* permitted Europeans to move relatively freely about a colonial territory, this was not always the case with Africans. The establishment of "tribal reserves" and the imposition of identity cards or pass laws in East, Central, and Southern Africa and of "stranger" or zongo quarters within West African cities limited interethnic contact. Those Africans who did move over great distances (other than Muslim pilgrims, Hausa traders, and traditional migrants) were those who were compelled to do so in order to pay taxes to the colonial administration or provide labor to European planters and mine owners. The new territorial boundaries, with their customs officials and currency restrictions, set limits on how far one was free to roam without official harassment, resembling the traditional barriers to long distance passage.

With respect to political behavior, it is true that some of the worst manifestations of traditional autocracy were eliminated under colonial rule, but this was only late in the scheme of things. Domestic slavery, for example, was not eliminated in the protectorate area of Sierra Leone or in Tanganyika until the 1920s nor in Mauritania until twenty years after independence. Some traditional political relationships, moreover, were not as abusive as they appeared. Tribute payments to chiefs, for example, did appear to transfer the limited resources of impoverished people to their political leaders. But times of famine, pestilence, or a military threat to that society revealed the true nature of tribute as a tribal bank: the grain and other foodstuffs were returned to those who had paid tribute during times of relative prosperity.[18] As pointed out elsewhere in this chapter and in the chapter on political parties, the introduction of parliamentary democracy, moreover, did not always come willingly nor early. Much of the instability of post-independence Africa can be attributed to the fact that the fledgling parliamentary institutions had only been in African hands for a few years (only a few months, in the case of Zaire). In any event the arbitrary system of government by administrative command and petitioning over ad hoc grievances was hardly a suitable hothouse for the nurturing of a democratic system marked by compromise and negotiation over diverse interests in a continuing and systematic fashion.

Finally, increasing the scale of political community to the territorial level was hardly a European "gift" to Africans. Territorial administration was introduced to serve European rather than African purposes. Indeed, most Africans were by one means or another prevented from identifying politically or legally with an entire colonial territory until the eve of independence. Ethnic membership, such as Hausa-Fulani, or regional residence (e.g., "northern Nigerian") were more frequent designations than "Nigerian." In all but a few instances, moreover, the growing interethnic contacts in various fields as well as the erosion of traditional ethnic polities would have made it difficult for nationalist movements to have been organized around units smaller than the territorial state.

Social, Religious, and Economic Impact of Colonial Rule

In addition to the termination of domestic slavery, former colonial administrators reckon other achievements in terms of the social, religious, and economic impact of European rule upon Africans. Exposing Africans to two of the major world religions was certainly one of the consequences. Christianity was, of course, directly encouraged since in many respects it served as an adjunct to the political and economic objectives of colonial administrators. In the case of the French and Belgians, the Roman Catholic Church in particular was one of the pillars of the colonial structure. Islam, however, as Trimingham has pointed out, also flourished under the European-imposed peace, even though in some areas—such as the Southern Sudan—it did so in the face of calculated efforts of the British administration to discourage its spread.[19] On the other hand, in Nigeria Lord Lugard and his successors gave Islam a preferred position over Christianity and permitted the Muslim emirs to consolidate their religious as well as their political holds over the people of the north. In areas where the colonial powers were even-handed in dealing with religious conversion, moreover, Islam was an effective challenger to Christianity since it required less of a drastic break with traditional institutions and values, such as polygamy and the status of women.

The exposure of Africans to these two world religions, especially Christianity, had ramifications beyond religious conversion. Koranic teachers, for example, did provide many Africans with literacy in Arabic, but, on balance, the exposure to Christianity had wider consequences. Christian missionaries, in an effort to bring the Bible closer to the people, transcribed many of Africa's roughly 900 languages, the overwhelming majority of which lacked any written form.[20] Of greater long-term significance, since the Christian missionaries were European, Africans were introduced to languages which later became the effective vehicles of nation-building and of communication in government, commerce, the courts, the universities, and other areas. Knowledge of a European language linked Africans to the scientific and technological resources of the West and provided them with the indispensable tools of contemporary global diplomacy.

Beyond language, missionaries until a decade or two prior to independence provided most of the formal primary and secondary schooling in sub-Saharan Africa, with government lagging far behind. Often as the price for being given carte blanche to carry out their proseletyzing efforts, missionaries were required to set up clinics and other medical facilities; other times they engaged in this activity without government pressure. They thus helped to convince Africans that they need not be condemned by "fate" to the risk of endemic and epidemic disease, high infant mortality rates, and a short life span.

Under the imperial umbrella, missionaries of course were not the only agents of social change. The colonial administrators as well as European miners and planters, Asian traders, and others contributed to an erosion of the old social and economic order and the introduction of new values and institutions. Collectively these forces for change transformed the relatively static economies based upon subsistence agriculture to more dynamic economies based upon cash transactions and marked by a diversification of agriculture, commerce, and a modicum of manufacturing. Instead of an individual being narrowly tied to the traditional economic roles peculiar to that society, such as herder, cultivator, fisherman, or smith, a diversity of economic roles were now available to both males and females, including those of teacher, priest, mason, bank clerk, merchant, agricultural agent, miner, or mechanic. This permitted the rival nationalist elites to challenge those surviving traditional authorities whose claims to power were based on traditional ownership of cattle, allocation of land, collection of tribute payments, and other more narrow and static forms of wealth. Inclusion of Africa in the global capitalist economy, moreover, resulted in the availability of consumer goods far greater in variety and at far cheaper prices than could be provided by the long-distance African traders of the past. Finally, the advantages of urban residence in a continent that was overwhelmingly rural at the time of the imposition of colonial rule made it possible for the talents and personalities of Africans to be developed in ways which the grandparents of the present generation would have thought to be inconceivable.

It may be, however, that the most abiding influence of West European colonial rule—particularly in the case of the British, French, and Belgian experiences—is that it hastened for Africa as a whole the spread of the essential ideas associated with modernization. That is, modernization assumes implicitly that things can get better if mankind applies rationality to the solution of human problems. Instead of being bound by fate, magic, and other external forces, mankind can be in control of its destinies. Modernization, moreover, assumes that individual actions and commitment can make a difference in the quality of life, and that the talents for improvement in man's condition are not the monopoly of any one race, ethnic or religious group, sex, age category, or other ascriptively defined group.

As was true of the political impact of colonial rule, however, the accomplishments of which the colonialists boast in the social, religious, and economic spheres only tell part of the story. Although, for example, missionaries were frequently invited in to provide schooling and medical services to a chiefdom, it was not always appreciated that Africans would as a consequence have to surrender their traditional religions. The term "pagan" or "primitive" religion is, after all, one employed from the outside without serious consideration of how an indigenous religion satisfies a whole range of needs of the actual practitioners. Religion is not compartmentalized in traditional society. It underwrites the moral code; it sustains the social relationships among generations in a community and between members of an extended family; it sanctifies economic activities; and it guides artistic endeavors. Hence, the transition from belief in a traditional religion to acceptance of Christianity, or even Islam, was a disruptive one for most Africans since few realized how much of their culture and social relationships was being lost in accepting a global religion.

The literacy and vocational skills that missionaries imparted to Africans, moreover, initially served the primary interest of those who were more directly exploitative of African labor. In this way the missionaries either intentionally or unwittingly contributed to making colonial rule more pervasive and oppressive. Furthermore, the introduction of schools and hospitals was often concentrated in those areas where the economic interests of European miners or planters were significant and where the medium-range skills of cheap African labor was in greater demand. Research on schistosomiasis, onchocerciasis, and other diseases of tropical Africa did not proceed where the economic payoff was not apparent.

Both at the macro and the micro level the general configuration of economic development during the colonial era found Africans to be largely the indirect beneficiaries of change. The transport network was not designed to develop a well-integrated domestic economy or to get more consumer goods to Africans; it was designed, rather, to get raw materials transported out and capital and expatriate personnel into Africa in the most expeditious manner. Innovation in agriculture was often introduced capriciously and by coercive means, rather than being demonstrably in the best interest of Africans. Indeed, the neglect of food production at the expense of cash export crops is part of the bitter harvest that food-short Africa is now reaping.

It is apparent from the foregoing that the final assessment of the impact of colonial rule will have to await the next generation. One already perceives in observation of African politics over the last twenty-five years a diminishing tendency to blame all of Africa's ills upon colonial rule and an increased realization that Africa's future can still be controlled by Africans. It is at that point that some of the consequences of colonial rule—whether intended or incidental to European selfish interests—will be viewed positively, as a legacy rather than a curse.

Curiously, one of the most significant contributions of colonial rule to contemporary African politics was one that was not intended by the European overlords. I refer to the fact that hostility toward the capricious and arbitrary administration of African people and the often ruthless and callous behavior of those associated with colonial rule may have provided the significant "glue" to enable the nationalist elite to succeed in its liberation efforts. The intensity of that lingering hostility toward the more degrading aspects of white supremacy may have bought the African leadership time to respond to the challenges of nation-building, overcome poverty, and achieve a workable African form of democracy. In this respect the former colonialists have usefully served the role of "enemy at the gates" which has been so indispensable to nationalist movements elsewhere.

III

THE CHALLENGE OF NATION–BUILDING

Africa today is a continent of roughly forty-five states in search of nationhood. The last quarter of a century has witnessed the surprising victory of the African peoples in their struggle to govern their own lives free from external dictation. In all but the southern tip of the continent, African politicians, military leaders, and others have inherited the machinery of government once monopolized by Europeans as well as the responsibility for the welfare of those included within the territorial jurisdictions of the post-colonial states. Independence, however, has not immediately brought into existence that sense of national political community which would permit Africans to enjoy all the fruits of their victory over colonial rule. The achievement of peace— both internally and between neighboring state communities—remains elusive in various quarters of the continent. Without internal peace and stability, the realization of the good life—better food, housing, and living conditions— seems to be beyond the grasp of many of Africa's people. Hence, much of the energies and talents of Africa's leaders in the years since the Sudan and Ghana led the way to independence in 1956–57 have been directed at matching the concept of state sovereignty with the concept of national community.

The concept of the nation-state remains an imprecise tool in the literature of the social sciences. In most cases there is an imperfect fit between the nation and the state in practice. But despite its analytical flaws, this concept continues to be the basis upon which both scholarly analysis and pragmatic politics proceed in Africa and elsewhere on the globe. No person and no place is free from the all-absorbing embrace of the nation-state system. We are rudely reminded of this fact when remote regions like the Malvinas, or Falkland Islands, become arenas for some major contest of political wills between two substantial powers, or when the United Nations attempts to find an equitable solution to the conflicting claims of ownership of the Antarctic polar wastelands. With all the arbitrariness and fickleness to which the human personality is subjected, individuals are required to be assigned to the jurisdiction of one political state or another. This is so even when the ultimate fate of some of those individuals is continued subordination or, worse yet, ultimate extermination, as was the case with the Jews in Nazi Germany.

The process today of shaping the sense of national community to match the exercise of state power within territorially defined boundaries is a universal phenomenon. It is observable in Africa, Asia, the Middle East, and the other areas of the world recently liberated from West European colonial rule. Ironically, it is a process that continues even in Western Europe itself, where the modern system of nation-states was purportedly founded. For, in a convenient but highly ethnocentric fashion, Western scholars date the launching of the nation-state system from the 1648 signing of the Treaty of Westphalia. This treaty formally recognized the collapse of the Holy Roman Empire. More importantly, it established the principle (for Europe at least) that any large group of people who, by virtue of history, culture, and similarity of institutions, considered themselves to be a "nation" had earned the right to constitute themselves as a political state. The latter concept involved not only the right to create the machinery of government necessary to preserve and advance its peculiar interest, but also the right to sovereignty— that is, to manage or mismanage its affairs without external dictation or interference. Thus, independence—not merely autonomy—was the rightful goal of each nation. Finally, this state sovereignty implicitly assumed that each nation-state, no matter how large or small, how well armed or weak, how wealthy or poor, was considered to be the equal of any other in international affairs.

Ironically, Africans have entered the nation-state system just as the operations of that system are being challenged in Western Europe itself. The Scots, the Basques, and the Bretons, for example, confront the internal integrity respectively of the British, Spanish, and French nation-states at the very moment when others have launched an external assault on the shape of European nationhood. I refer in particular to the "new Europeans," the businessmen, educators, churchmen, military leaders, and others who are attempting to reorient the thinking and actions of their fellow West Europeans toward the Common Market, the Parliament at Strasbourg, NATO, and other supranational institutions.

Despite the basic similarity between the nation-building process in Africa and in Western Europe, it is readily apparent that the task confronting Africans is far more complex. One of the leading scholars on West European nationalism, Hans Kohn, could with some degree of accuracy describe nationalities as

> products of the living force of history [most of them possessing] certain objective factors distinguishing them from other nationalities like common descent, language, territory, political entity, customs and traditions, or religion. . . . Although objective factors are of great importance for the formation of nationalities, the most essential element is a living and active corporate will. . . .[1]

The forty-five states in Sub-Saharan Africa today can hardly be described as the products of the "living force of history," inasmuch as their establishment is the product of conscious, arbitrary acts—primarily at the initiative of outsiders—which have occurred within the lifetimes of many of Africa's older citizens. With the qualified exceptions perhaps of Somalia, Swaziland, Lesotho, and Botswana, moreover, the citizens of most African states lack the psychological commitment to their fellow citizens that emanates from the widespread sharing of language, religion, race, history, and traditions.

The complexities of the European versus the African versions of nation-building aside, there are, however, several basic assertions. First, the process of establishing political community at increasingly larger geographic scales is neither a European nor a European-related pnenomenon, nor is it a process that is limited to the modern era. Efforts to establish political community at levels higher than the extended family or the parochial hunting band have characterized human behavior since people first emerged from the primitive conditions for survival in forests and caves. Indeed, evidence of archaeologists suggests that the creation of ever-larger communities is one of the distinguishing features which sets man apart as a social animal. That is so whether that community is established by force of arms or by mutual recognition of the benefits of cooperation within a more substantial community. Africa—which may well be the cradle of mankind—has ample evidence of this human characteristic. Historical research of the past three decades has provided ever-increasing evidence of the pre-colonial existence in Africa of relatively stable political communities that spanned vast amounts of territory, manifested sophisticated machinery of government, successfully integrated peoples of diverse cultural, linguistic, and religious backgrounds, and endured over centuries. The ancient empires of Ghana, Mali, Songhai, and others in West Africa and the Monomatapa empire and other polities in east and central Africa provide some early data on successful state-building.

The second basic assertion relates to the critical role of leadership in the process of nation-building. Because it happened in the past, the creation of nations in Western Europe and elsewhere appears to have been an evolutionary process, with people at the mass level interacting and developing common institutions and bonds of solidarity. In Africa, the process is taking place before our very eyes, so we can easily perceive the extent to which it is revolutionary rather than evolutionary. This is not to say that state-formation has never occurred spontaneously in Africa or elsewhere in the world. But to a far greater extent, it has universally been the product of self-conscious acts on the part of a committed elite that is determined to fashion, maintain, or even realign the bonds of solidarity between itself and some or all of the masses included within its territorial jurisdiction. In establishing the links between itself and the citizenry, a nationalizing elite seeks to neutralize (if not destroy) the influence of competing kinship, ethnic, religious, and economic elites that might pull the citizenry in either centrifugal or centripetal directions away from the authority of the governing state elite. The success of that elite depends on its ability to establish effective means of social communication between itself and the masses as well as an expanding network of significant social interactions which link the relevant segments of the masses with each other. If the construction of social communication and interactions is successful—it is argued by the governing elite—the citizens to whom the efforts are directed will in the long run come to enjoy psychic and material satisfaction from seeking marital, trade, religious, and other goals in association with those who are equally members of that same emerging national community. These satisfactions will outweigh benefits secured from consorting with those who have come to be defined as "aliens," "foreigners," "pariahs," or "outsiders." This process of mutual identification involves the use by the governing elite of both positive and negative sanctions of force, ritual, and education, as well as the application of economic rewards and deprivations. To the extent that satisfaction of goals is significant and relatively continuous, this citizen identification with the arbitrary national community becomes over time a form of moral obligation. The individual citizen no longer engages in protracted internalized debate about the legitimacy of his or her virtually automatic response to the suggestions and commands emanating from the nationalizing elite. At that point, the legitimacy of both the community and its leadership is established. This legitimacy gives the governing elite the ability to claim a more generalized monopoly on loyalties within that select community as well as a monopoly on the use of force, both internally and externally, in pursuit of community goals.

Lest the reader assume that nation-building is a multiple-sum game in which all come out winners, we should hasten to make explicit that it is often a painful process. Not only are many citizens expected to put aside their value preferences in a whole range of matters but there may be whole groups of citizens (even a majority, in the case of South Africa) who are consciously excluded from the politically relevant masses that the governing elite is addressing. Nation-building in Africa and elsewhere has led not only to the physical removal of certain groups from the territory of the state but to their actual physical annihilation.

As described here, the process of nation-building is to a considerable degree a product of social engineering rather than the result of natural or inevitable evolutionary forces. Nations do not exist in the abstract, waiting only to be found and brought into existence. There may be so-called objective criteria such as language or religion that post hoc come to be associated with the life of a particular national community. These are for the most part, however, instruments upon which a committed governing elite may draw in establishing the bonds of solidarity between itself and the relevant masses.

What is the nature of this nationalizing elite? A nationalizing elite is "political" in the sense that it ultimately becomes associated with the operation of the machinery of government, independent of external direction. It is not necessarily, however, a monolithic group. That is, to achieve its objective it may have to confront other elites which are equally "political." The political party leaders in Africa, for example, had to challenge others whose roles were also essentially political, the colonial administrators. The nationalizing role, however, may be assumed by elites who are not normally associated with the whole range of affairs that are the domain of governments. Thus, in both Nigeria and Ghana in 1966 the civilian party leaders were successfully challenged by those usually associated with only one aspect of state authority, namely the military. In the emergence of modern Turkey out of the ashes of the Ottoman Empire it was the military under Ataturk who took on the primary task of shaping national institutions and values.

In many instances, however, the nationalizing elite may emanate from those structures within society which we label religious and which are associated with the code of moral behavior of that society and the relationship between individual citizens and their creator. The clergy of the Roman Catholic Church, for example, provided the crucial nationalizing role during the century and a quarter of dismemberment of the Polish nation, and they continue to exert a nationalizing influence today. Modern Cyprus and post-Shah Iranian society provide two other contemporary examples of religious elites playing nationalizing roles. In the United States in 1787 and in western Europe today, it has been members of the business community—investors, bankers, merchants, and others—who have assumed a crucial role in the launching of national institutions. In Africa, for reasons which will be dealt with in Chapter 7, the initial nation-buliding role was assumed largely by leaders of political parties rather than traditional chiefs, clerics, military leaders, and others. In the post-independence era, however, that role has been shared or alternated with leaders drawn from the military.

Beyond the creation of effective systems of social communication and social interaction, the nationalizing elite in Africa has had to create new unifying symbols for the members of the heterogeneous state society it has inherited. Whether based on "facts" that can be objectively verified or on fabrications that defy social science testing, the leadership must create and sustain social myths of common origin and destiny, as well as engage in the designation of national heroes, events, and places of ritualistic significance in terms of the survival of the national political community. The symbolism must be strong enough in its appeal and believability to be able to compete effectively with the more parochial or localized symbols of those previously independent or autonomous societies which are included in the new state. And finally, the nationalizing elite must be able to establish a unified code for moral behavior that effectively integrates what may be radically diverse attitudes and behavior. This diversity may apply to rather basic considerations, such as the value of life itself, proper sexual relationships, the nature of the family, the definition of property rights, and the assumption of economic roles needed for survival of the community.

Ethnic Fragmentation and Pluralism

The problems of nation-building confronting most African leaders in the past quarter of a century would have staggered the creativity and imagination of Mazzini, Bismarck, Paderewski, and other nineteenth and twentieth century leaders of European nationalist movements. Those leaders had relatively little difficulty in "finding" citizens who had already identified themselves as members of the Italian, the German, or the Polish "nation." A European nationalizing elite could capitalize upon a widely shared commitment to use of a particular language, the existence of social links and moral values based upon a shared religious tradition, the absence of severe cleavages based upon racial differences, and a perceived common history. Its main task was thus to press for the creation of a unified political state which would consolidate and protect much of this pre-existing common pursuit of values. There was, of course, still the task of deciding which Germans—for example—were to be included or excluded from the emerging Bismarckian German state. The African governing elite, by contrast, have inherited the political apparatus of the colonial state but have yet to establish those bonds which effectively orient a diverse people toward each other and toward the leadership cadre itself.

The territorial boundaries within which the current efforts at nation-building are taking place were not initially of African choosing, and with the possible exception of Rwanda and Burundi they do not conform to the pre-existing boundaries of political community. The European diplomats who divided the continent in the last century did so on the basis of highly imperfect knowledge of and concern for the human and environmental realities faced by the Africans who actually lived there. Their actions led to the creation of political, social, and economic absurdities such as The Gambia, a territory two hundred miles long and roughly thirty miles wide. Essentially it consists of both banks of one of the few rivers in West Africa which is navigable the year round. In assigning the banks of the Gambia River to British control while leaving the hinterland as part of the French colony of Senegal, the Europeans not only created considerable barriers to the continuity of social, political, and religious ties among the Manding inhabitants, but they politically and administratively separated the river from its natural economic hinterland. The 1981 Senegalese rescue of the beleaguered government of President David Kairaba Jawara from a threatened police-directed coup provided the first real opportunity for serious discussion which could lead to the creation of a unified Senegambian state. This arbitrary division of formerly unified peoples throughout the continent took place again and again. The Ewe in West Africa, the Masai in the east, and the Swazi, Sotho, and Tswana in the south represent cases where the imposition of colonial boundaries—however poorly manned they were during the European era—have compelled the various segments of a fractured society to

accept different languages for administration and education, separate monetary systems, and diverse codes of family law. Territorial boundaries have
distorted the ways in which members of a formerly unified society can effectively relate to each other in family, religious, and other circumstances.
One of the most serious cases of fractured nationhood, with both regional
and international ramifications, is that of the Somali people on the Horn of
Africa. This case of fractured nationhood will be dealt with in greater detail
in the final section of this chapter, on alternative strategies of nation-building.
Suffice it at this point to note that the Somali people were divided among
five territories (including the Ethiopian Empire) during the nineteenth century carve-up of Africa. Although two of the segments have been rejoined,
the irredentist campaign to regain control over the three "lost provinces"
has not only affected the stability of the several states in the Horn but has
led to external intervention by both the Soviet Union and the United States.

Tragic as the fragmentation of previously unified people may be, the more
frequently encountered problem of nation-building in Africa is that of ethnic
heterogeneity. The elite committed to nation-building must contend not only
with the racial, religious, and other divisions introduced during colonial rule,
but also with the potential for conflict arising from the arbitrary inclusion
of members of several indigenous ethnic groups within a single colonial
territory. Multi-ethnicity is the more common situation which the leaders
of forty of the forty-five states in sub-Saharan Africa have to confront in their
nation-building efforts.

The terms ethnicity and ethnic group are used by most contemporary
political analysts in preference to "tribalism" and "tribe" since the latter have
not only come to have pejorative connotations of "backwardness" or "sav-
agery" but convey a false impression of group political cohesion under a
unified leadership. Ethnicity refers to the particular configuration of cultural
norms, language, institutions, and values which set one group of people
apart from another. What is a significant point of differentiation with respect
to one people may be a relatively insignificant distinction for another. Preferable as ethnicity and ethnic group are as social science terms, they are
still politically offensive to those philosophers and political practitioners who
stress pan-Africanism, négritude, and other concepts which suggest the basic
underlying unity of African peoples. Ethnicity is viewed as a divisive concept.
Many political leaders who have created unity out of the heterogeneous
populations they govern attempt to deal with ethnicity as if it did not exist.
In some cases legal steps have been taken to eliminate ethnic-based traditional chieftainship, to ban political parties and other associations based on
one ethnic group, to redraft administrative and electoral boundaries to cut
across ethnic boundaries, to omit ethnic origin data from the national census,
and to penalize those who make public reference to the separate ethnic
identity of citizens.

These efforts to reduce conflict within a heterogeneous state may be laudable, but ethnic diversity and tension are facts of life in Africa. Refusing to discuss the existence of ethnicity does not facilitate one's understanding of the problems ethnic differences create. It overlooks the fact, too, that people everywhere—not merely in Africa—tend to pursue power, respect, health, wealth, skills, rectitude, enlightenment, and affection in ways that are culturally unique to each group. There is a certain patterning and interrelationship, moreover, between the manner in which a given people pursue clusters of two or more of these values. This value patterning of a given ethnic group tends to persist over time because it becomes sanctified as the morally *right* way of pursuing values, rather than being left to individual choice or preference. Holding to the *correct* value patterning helps to differentiate "us" from "them," and it leads to stylized ways of dealing with members of the internal as well as the external groups. With respect to how an individual pursues a given value, his or her society may be dogmatically rigid. Alternatively that society may appear to be flexible, but this is flexibility within bounds. Even the classic examples of traditional societies could not remain static in the face of exposure to other societies and their unique ways of pursuing value. For any society that endures, the integrity of the patterning and interrelationship of value pursuit remains relatively constant. Thus, political leadership in a multi-ethnic state ignores this value patterning at its peril.

Before examining some of the complications that ethnic heterogeneity presents in terms of nation-building in Africa, several observations must be made. First of all, although the pluralistic nature of the post-independence state is a creature of the colonial past and not necessarily an African choice, the decision to live within those arbitrary boundaries after independence has been an African choice. Indeed, the commitment is embedded in Resolutions of the Organization of African Unity. The only adjustments in those boundaries that are acceptable to African leaders generally are those which have received the assent of the parties directly involved and are accomplished by peaceable means. This includes, for example, the fusion of Italian and British Somaliland creating the Republic of Somalia; the union of British Togoland with Ghana at the time of the latter's independence; the partition of British Cameroon, with the north being joined to Nigeria and the south federated with the former French Cameroon; and the post-independence union of Tanganyika and Zanzibar as the Republic of Tanzania. Even before most of the African states had achieved independence (and three years before the establishment of the OAU), African leaders rejected the implication of a fragmented Congo (Zaire) which the threatened secession of the Katanga (Shaba) province under Moise Tshombe presented in 1960. Liberia, Ghana and several other African countries contributed armed forces to maintain the integrity of the arbitrary colonial boundaries.[2] In the late 1960s the attempted secession on the part of the Igbo and other eastern Nigerians in the Biafran War was similarly rejected although the heads of state of both the Ivory

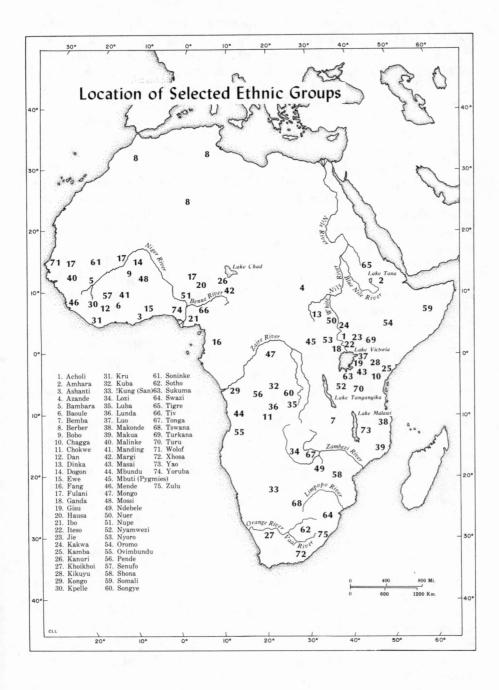

Location of Selected Ethnic Groups

1. Acholi	31. Kru	61. Soninke
2. Amhara	32. Kuba	62. Sotho
3. Ashanti	33. !Kung (San)	63. Sukuma
4. Azande	34. Lozi	64. Swazi
5. Bambara	35. Luba	65. Tigre
6. Baoule	36. Lunda	66. Tiv
7. Bemba	37. Luo	67. Tonga
8. Berber	38. Makonde	68. Tswana
9. Bobo	39. Makua	69. Turkana
10. Chagga	40. Malinke	70. Turu
11. Chokwe	41. Manding	71. Wolof
12. Dan	42. Margi	72. Xhosa
13. Dinka	43. Masai	73. Yao
14. Dogon	44. Mbundu	74. Yoruba
15. Ewe	45. Mbuti (Pygmies)	75. Zulu
16. Fang	46. Mende	
17. Fulani	47. Mongo	
18. Ganda	48. Mossi	
19. Gisu	49. Ndebele	
20. Hausa	50. Nuer	
21. Ibo	51. Nupe	
22. Iteso	52. Nyamwezi	
23. Jie	53. Nyoro	
24. Kakwa	54. Oromo	
25. Kamba	55. Ovimbundu	
26. Kanuri	56. Pende	
27. Khoikhoi	57. Senufo	
28. Kikuyu	58. Shona	
29. Kongo	59. Somali	
30. Kpelle	60. Songye	

0   400   800 Mi.
0   600   1200 Km.

Coast and Tanzania did recognize Biafra when it looked as if the continued fighting would only result in considerable suffering and loss of life. The forcible occupation of the former Spanish Western Sahara by Morocco and by Mauritania (which later abandoned its occupation, permitting Morocco to claim the entire territory) has also been generally rejected, and the 1984 vote to recognize Polisario as the legitimate government of the Western Sahara actually led to Morocco's withdrawal from OAU membership. Similarly, the OAU states generally have rejected the attempts of South Africa's apartheid government to cede territory to Swaziland, despite the historic claim of the latter to the area in question. The effort was opposed by OAU states on the grounds that the relevant Black inhabitants of South Africa had not been properly consulted. Most significant of all, perhaps, was the total absence of support for Somalia's 1977 invasion of the Ogaden province of Ethiopia in an effort to forcibly assert its irredentist claim to one of the "lost segments" of the Somali nation.

The second observation is that ethnic heterogeneity is not necessarily a curse; it can be regarded as a creative challenge. Diversity of culture has certainly broadened the horizons of many Africans by permitting a considerable sharing of art, music, folklore, and philosophy. It has encouraged the widespread borrowing of political and legal norms and institutions from traditional societies in fashioning structures and behavior patterns within the emerging national society. In providing psychological and other forms of support to sub-national groups, several advantages accrue to the leadership of a fledgling African state. Local problems, such as crime and unemployment or the resolution of minor legal disputes involving only members of a particular ethnic group, can be settled at the grass-roots level without requiring a further strain on the limited human and physical resources available to the nationalizing elite. A more positive attitude toward local autonomy, moreover, may actually bring forth more talents and resources in the solution of recurrent national problems. The willingness of Kenyans to lay out private funds for "Harambee" schools is a case in point. Allowing experimentation with social, economic, and other governmental programs at the local level, furthermore, reduces the risk that blame for any failures will always be laid at the feet of the precarious national government. Federalism, as one form of accommodation to ethnic pluralism, actually permits a "squaring of the circle" by permitting otherwise incongruous values and institutions to persist in a politically united society.

The third observation is derived from the second: there are mechanisms for coping with and containing some of the negative manifestations of ethnic pluralism. Federalism is only one of those mechanisms. Provision for the separation of church and state in countries where religious conflict is divisive is another. Switzerland, Belgium, and other multilingual countries have developed strategies for dealing with the complications of communicating in several languages.

Ethnic pluralism, however, does become a serious problem for nation-building in several respects. One of these is the incompatibility of values which are not easily subject to change. Family relationships, for example, are firmly fixed within most societies, and not only parental obligations but also rules on incest, inheritance of property, and other issues and relationships are at stake. As long as most people agree on the proper ordering of family links, there is no problem. In the United States, however, when the Mormons accepted the institution of polygamy it presented a challenge to the basic commitment to monogamy within the American social system. The situation in Africa is far more complicated. The contacts enjoyed by peoples of diverse cultures under the European-imposed peace have intensified as the rural to urban migration, economic development, the expanding educational system, and other opportunities for interethnic contact have broadened in the post-colonial era. In the formulation of a code of national family law, in holding parents accountable for the discipline of youngsters or the payment of school fees, in deciding issues of inheritance where members of two different ethnic groups are involved, and in other areas as well, the diverse nature of traditional African family relationships has become a serious problem. Attitudes toward polygamy versus monogamy are already an issue where Christianity has presented a standard that differs from Islam and most African traditional social systems. More serious is the basic conflict between matrilineal versus partilineal systems of reckoning kinship, which involves widely differing patterns of family obligations and privileges. Unlike the bilaterialism of the Western family model, Africans in traditional society normally count only their relatives and ancestors on the father's side, or only those on the mother's side, but not both. In a matrilineal society one's biological father is far less significant to a youth than the social father, namely the mother's oldest brother. As long as people from the matrilineal and patrilineal societies lived apart, there was no great problem. Increasing urbanization which involves considerable interethnic mixing makes it an issue, however, which must be addressed in a satisfactory way by a nationalizing elite.

The incompatibility of values in a plural society also presents problems with respect to agricultural development, particularly where pastoral people are involved. Among the Masai, the Somali, and other cattle-raising people in east, central, and southern Africa, one does not change occupation as one would change a shirt—according to preference or whim. Rather, one is born into a pastoral society and all males at the appropriate age are expected to begin acquiring cattle. Although the meat of the cattle may be consumed on ceremonial occasions, generally the animals are not regarded as a source of "protein on the hoof" but rather as an element in the prestige economy. Cattle are an economic asset and do fit into the exchange economy in that one may trade a cow for something else of value or sell it in order to buy food, pay school fees, or acquire capital for some other enterprise. The ownership of cattle is associated with the allocation of respect within society, and cattle are exchanged at key points in a person's life (birth, marriage, divorce) as a way of establishing bonds of solidarity or dissolving them. Ownership of many head of cattle marks a man as a person of great importance. Today, however, when African governments are concerned about malnutrition and particularly protein deficiency, a drive to encourage the greater consumption of meat encounters resistance. Even greater resistance is encountered when agricultural development schemes intrude upon the land which the pastoral people regard as essential to the proper grazing of their herds.

A further way in which ethnic pluralism complicates the nation-building task is the sheer numbers involved. Depending upon how one defines an ethnic group, there are anywhere between 250 and 300 groupings in Nigeria alone. In the last census in which ethnic (or tribal) origins of citizens was revealed, Tanzania could count more than 120 such groups in its population of 16 million inhabitants. The Ivory Coast has approximately thirty-five ethnic groups, Liberia sixteen, and Zaire forty—to cite just a few additional cases. Since each group tends to have its distinctive language, the problems of social communication are considerable, as will be noted in more detail shortly. The potential demand for the duplication of institutions in already poor societies is almost as great as the conflict over the incompatibility of values.

There are other problems relating to ethnic pluralism that have both quantitative and qualitative implications. The relative size of the ethnic groups and special characteristics associated with the larger groups may be an issue. In Tanzania, none of the 120 groups constitutes as much as 10 percent of the total, and the largest group—the Sukuma—are not viewed as "threatening" to the other groups. In Uganda, on the other hand, the size of the largest group, the Ganda (Baganda), along with its degree of development and its history of imperialism with respect to its neighbors, created nation-building problems even prior to independence and has continued to do so. The hostility of other Ugandan groups was exacerbated by the manner in which the British used the Baganda in administration. Roughly 75 percent of the colonial bureaucracy was drawn from this one ethnic group. In Kenya, the tension between two of the three largest and most economically advanced of the roughly forty ethnic groups, the Kikuyu and the Luo, has taxed the skills of the nationalizing elite in assuring the continued stability and economic growth of that country.

The problems relating to numbers and diversity of values become intensified when the *clustering* of value positions by two or more major groups in that society reinforces conflict on each plane of analysis. Such situations, of course, are not unique to Africa, as the examples of Northern Ireland, Canada, Cyprus, and Lebanon will demonstrate. One of the classic cases for Africa is the Sudan, which experienced more than a decade of civil war

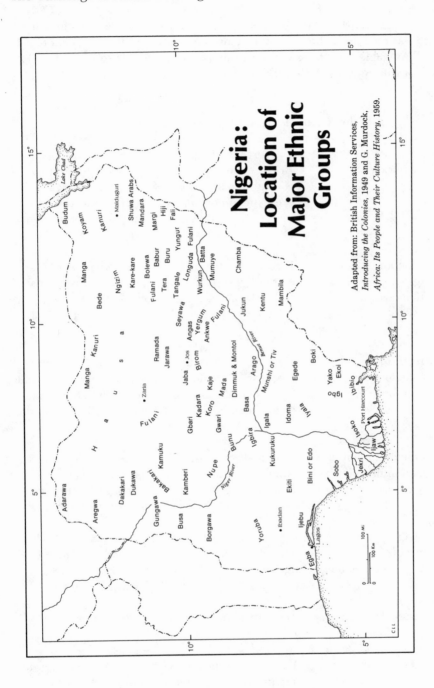

Nigeria:
Location of
Major Ethnic
Groups

Adapted from: British Information Services,
Introducing the Colonies, 1949 and G. Murdock,
Africa: Its People and Their Culture History, 1959.

between the north and the south shortly after independence and which since 1983 has once more been experiencing the renewal of interregional hostilities. As Table 3 indicates, value incompatiblity extends to virtually every area of consequence within that society.

TABLE 3
Value Conflicts within the Republic of the Sudan

Value	Northern Region	Southern Region
1. power	British turned over control of national government to northerners	Autonomy under colonial rule ended; South underrepresented in national government
2. affection (group identification)	Part of broader Arab cultural group; "Semitic" in terms of racial categories	Divided among Nuer, Dinka, and other parochial ethnic groups; "Nilotic" in physical type
3. rectitude (religious structure, morality)	Predominantly Muslim; Koran provides fundamental moral code—Shar'ia law	Traditional religion and Christianity; Bible and oral tradition provide moral code; British discouraged Islam
4. enlightenment (communications)	Arabic used in courts, commerce and education; Koranic schools at primary level	Preference for English officially, traditional language locally; secular or missionary education
5. wealth (type of economic activity)	Trading, commercial agriculture	Pastoralism, subsistence agriculture, barter
6. residential patterns	Town dwellers	Rural hamlets, nomadism
7. external orientation	Emphasis on ties with Egypt, other Muslim Arab countries	Internal orientation to family, clan; bonds with other Nilotics in Uganda, Chad, Zaire

The Racial Factor in Nation-Building

Race is one of the most controversial and the least precise of the many concepts used in the social sciences. There are, nevertheless, two indisputable facts about race. The first of these is that in relatively static populations certain physical traits are biologically transmitted and recur within that human group. These traits include distinct skin pigmentation, average height, predominant color and shape of eyes, typical color and texture of hair, steatopygia in certain females, distinct facial features, and—only recently appreciated—certain clusters of blood types. There are, however, considerable ranges of variation for any of these traits within a given population. Moreover, as human mobility intensifies around the globe and as social, legal, and other barriers to sexual interaction across these racial lines are relaxed or ignored, delineating racial groupings with any degree of precision becomes more complicated.

The second observation is that despite the lack of precision in classification, people today, as in the past, tend to structure their preferred social, political, economic, and religious contacts with others on the basis of assumed continuity of these differences in physical traits. People form judgments as well about the alleged intellectual, moral, and artistic qualities of members of their own racial grouping as opposed to others with whom they must contend. In the absence of specific information to the contrary, members of both small-scale and large, complex societies find that differences and similarities in physical character still tend to serve as latent signals that an approaching stranger is either a potential friend or potential enemy. The subsequent speech or actions of the stranger may either confirm or contradict the initial predisposition. Differences in physical type, of course, are not the only signaling devices in such circumstances. The various coded messages incorporated into style of dress, ornamentation, the manner of cutting or plaiting hair, and even body mutilation (lip and nose plugs, cicatricing) may also serve as relevant signaling mechanisms.

Given the prominent role that racial issues played in European and African relations during the past four hundred years, it is inevitable that they should also play a prominent role in African politics today. Indeed, a good deal of the political energies of many nation-building elites in Africa today are directed to denigrating differences in physical traits to a secondary or tertiary level of importance, stressing instead such unifying concepts as "pan-Africanism," "multi-racialism," or *harambee*, the Kenya expression that signals the desire of Africans, Europeans, and Asians to pull together without respect to racial differences. In South Africa, on the other hand, the effort since 1948 has gone patently in the opposite direction by creating rigid—and frequently absurd—racial categories, which affect the way in which values are allocated within a broad range of categories. The South African whites who use skin color as a badge of privilege, however, are not alone in using race as a factor in politics. Even in Zimbabwe, for example, where Blacks have assumed the reins of political power and the leadership is committed to multiracial cooperation, race remains a factor. It is irritating to many of Robert Mugabe's followers that after a long and violent struggle for Blacks to come into control of their own affairs, the small but diminishing white minority continue to occupy positions of consequence in the economy, in the bureaucracy, in education, and in religious structures. In nearby Angola the racial issue is no longer simply one of white versus Black conflict, but rather a reaction to a residue of the Portuguese presence and racial policies. I refer to the fact that the Ovimbundu leadership of the dissident UNITA group capitalizes upon Black hostility to the *mestiço* or mulàtto minority (persons of mixed European and African ancestry) that are disproportionately represented in leadership positions under the MPLA regime. Under the Portuguese rule, many of the mestiços were considered assimilados and given privileges denied to the Black majority.

The emphasis on race has also been apparent in many states where white domination or its residue is no longer the issue. Idi Amin Dada of Uganda, for example, was not the only political leader in East Africa who tried to forge a common racial link for an otherwise heterogeneous African society by conducting an overt campaign of hostility against long-time Asian residents in that country. Both Kenya and Tanzania have had moments since independence when Asians were presented as the scapegoat for economic failure and other crises in society. The continuing legacy of the colonial experience, in which imported Asian clerks, masons, shopkeepers, and others served as a middle tier in a racially structured caste society, has been difficult to overlook. It was often the Asians in East Africa or the Lebanese and Syrians in West Africa that made colonial rule profitable for Europeans. These bitter memories of Afro-Asian contacts provide the extreme nationalist with the "evidence" needed to stir up xenophobic hostility in an attempt to strengthen his own role as a unifying leader.

Even among those Africans whom the outside world might uniformly classify as "Black," differences in physical type are not only readily apparent but have political, social, and economic consequences. Some of this racial conflict within the African community is a residue in part of the colonial experience. One example is the long-festering conflict in the Sudan, which appears to be heating up again in the early 1980s. The hostility stems from the fact that withdrawing British authorities in 1956 turned over the reins of power to those who were identified with the people of the north. While there are many points of differentiation between the northerners and southerners in Sudan—as was noted in Table 3—one of the main points is variation in physical type. The people of the north are considered to be "Semitic," and have much in common physically with the Arab populations of the Middle East. The people of the south are "Nilotic," are generally more slender and taller than the people of the north, with darker skin pigmentation and facial and hair features that to the astute observer identify them with the Dinka, Nuer, Shilluk, and other southern people. Political, economic, and social power and conflict relate to these differences in racial characteristics. In Ethiopia as well, the way in which the nineteenth-century boundaries were established between the expansionist forces of Emperor Menelik and those of the encroaching Europeans created a number of situations in which domination can be defined in racial terms. Ethiopians are certainly aware of the differences between a Somali or an Oromo and an Amharic-speaker from the Abyssinian highlands.[3]

It is an error, however, to assume that racial conflict or domination of one African group over other physically dissimilar groups is entirely a product of the European colonial experience. Categorization of African peoples on the basis of differing physical traits existed long before Europeans and Asians appeared on the scene. The fallacious assumption that Africans perceive both themselves and all other dark-skinned residents of the continent as "Black" is a view strangely shared by both the prejudiced white external observer and the philosophical African proponent of "pan-Africanism." Ironically, the simple white-versus-Black dichotomy is also shared, for example, by white and Black politicians in South Africa and Zimbabwe, respectively, who attempt to stress the alleged racial commonality of their constituency in opposing other racially defined groups who confront the political, social, or economic status of the political leader's own racial group. The diversity of the ways in which Africans classify themselves was early brought home to this author while doing research in colonial Tanganyika in the 1950s. Just among my immediate staff of research and household assistants, various individuals defined themselves and each other as "Black," "red," or "yellow" in terms of skin pigmentation. Later, in analyzing the early foundations of the Liberian Republic, I found a similar categorization of nominally Black citizens as "bright skinned," "red," or "Black." I soon realized that these designations were significant in my comprehension of how political, social, and economic privilege was allocated within Africa's first Black republic.

Perhaps most interesting of all, however, were the various caste societies that emerged several hundred years ago in eastern Africa. Two of the clearest cut cases were those obtaining in the present states of Rwanda and Burundi.[4] In each, political, economic, military, and social control was monopolized by roughly ten percent of the population, who were considered to be Nilo-Hamitic in origin. This group, generally referred to as Tusi, were of very tall stature, slender in build, lighter in skin color, and differing in other respects from the two other groups within Burundi and Rwanda which could be differentiated in physical type. Those in the larger of these two latter groups—constituting roughly 85 to 90 percent of the population—were darker in skin pigmentation, of medium stature and build, and possessing more rugged facial and other features than the Tusi. These were the Hutu. The second subordinate group, which was limited in numbers and in the types of contact maintained with the Hutu and Tusi, were the Twa, a pygmoid people who lived in the forested areas. The political, economic, and social significance of these variations in physical type was manifested in several ways. Rules about marriage and sexual contact were tightly controlled in order to protect the alleged racial superiority of the Tusi overlords. The Tusi monopolized political power based on divine kingship; they bore the primary responsibility for the military defense of the society; they owned the cattle that were tended by the Hutu on a patron-client basis; they enjoyed a higher standard of living through the exploitation of Hutu labor; and their religion was the transcendant one for the whole of the society. Although the German and Belgian colonial systems did alter the character of the caste relationship, it remained largely in place until the post-independence era. The political upheaval in both Rwanda and Burundi since the 1960s, as we shall see, is essentially attributable to social and other stereotypes based on differences in physical type.

The Legacy of White Supremacy

Although European political domination of those generally regarded as "Blacks" has ceased in all but South Africa and Namibia, the legacy of the ideology of white supremacy has persisted as a factor in African politics. Unfortunately, almost from the outset European relationships with Africans have been tainted by racism. Slavery, of course, was the worst manifestation of this racism even though it is acknowledged that the institution had a history in many African communities that predated any contact with Europeans. The notion that all Black Africans were potential slaves persisted in European thought long after the concept of involuntary servitude in all its forms had ceased to be applied to Caucasians. And although Indians in the New World, as well as Arabs and Asians who were swept into the European political orbit, suffered all the indignities associated with colonial rule, they were largely spared legal designation as slaves with all the deprivations associated with that condition. Few indignities rivaled in character or magnitude the fact of roughly eleven and a half million West Africans being extricated from their home environment and transported several thousand miles across the Atlantic.[5] On a reduced scale, a similar fate awaited the East Africans who fell into the clutches of the Arab slave traders and were transported to the Middle East.[6]

For those Black Africans who survived the inhumane conditions of the passage to the Americas, domestic slavery in the New World turned out to be an even more dehumanizing experience than slavery in Africa itself. Freed Blacks as well as slaves were denied the rights of political participation in the governing of their own affairs, property ownership was forbidden them, and they were not permitted to establish enduring family and other social relationships of their own choosing. Even when emancipated in America, Blacks lacked the right, in many cases, to sue and be sued or to pursue certain professional careers. Prior to the U.S. Civil War, the Dred Scott decision of 1857 designated Blacks as property rather than persons.

Some four hundred years after the Portuguese initiated the practice of taking Africans back to Europe as slaves, the slave trade and then slavery itself were outlawed in Europe, the British Empire, and the United States. Eventually Blacks were freed in the rest of the Americas, including Brazil, which gave total emancipation in 1888. Curiously, in many European colonies in Africa, such as Sierra Leone and Tanganyika, the European administration did not feel able to deal with the total abolition of slavery until the mid-1920s. Mauritania, despite having been a French colony, did not actually terminate the legal status of slaves until the early 1980s, following independence.

The stigma of bondage, however, lasted longer than the actual institution of slavery. Even those Europeans and Americans who were viewed by their contemporaries as humanitarians for their efforts in behalf of Black emancipation and abolition of slavery were never fully committed to the idea of integration of Blacks into the fabric of American, Canadian, or European life. The recurrent solution for the debased Black condition was invariably a proposal involving "repatriation to Africa," even though many freed Blacks were in fact second or third generation residents of America or the West Indies. It was out of this limited form of assumed humanitarianism that the colonies of Freetown, Libreville, and Fernando Po emerged as refuges for freed persons of color from the New World as well as for the "recaptives," those taken from slave ships bound for the Americas and deposited in the repatriation settlements.

Two other developments during the nineteenth century reinforced the notion of white superiority over Blacks. The first was the misapplication of Darwin's theory of evolution to the development of the human species, referred to in Chapter 2. In the hands of Herbert Spencer, William Graham Sumner, and others Darwin's theory was used to justify the domination of Europeans over non-Europeans as evidence of the "survival of the fittest." Hence, Africans and others who were subordinated to Europeans were assumed to be deficient in those traits which guarantee success in the human struggle.

The emergence of the Social Darwinist ideology served in part as a prelude to, and in part as a justification after the fact for, the second development, namely, the imposition of European colonial rule in Africa. As noted in Chapter 2, the absorption of Africa into the colonial network was arbitrary, capricious, and brutal. Although the formal institution of slavery persisted in only a few territories during the dependency period, various practices of the colonials bordered on it. The demands that the colonial administration could make upon the labor of African males as well as upon the land and other resources of value were initially unlimited. Relations between whites and Africans were exacerbated in those territories where the colonial government pursued a conscious and vigorous policy of white settlement. In both settler and non-settler territories, Blacks found themselves relegated to the bottom rung of a rigidly maintained caste system which extended to every phase of social activity and interaction, while Europeans were automatically assigned to the highest rungs, without regard to whether they derived from aristocratic or humble social and economic origins in their home countries. Most European residents underwent a "sea change" en route to Africa and took on most of the airs, opinions, and prerogatives of the colonial privileged caste. This applied not only to the long term settlers but included as well colonial administrators, commercial entrepreneurs, operators of mining and industrial concerns, and sometimes even Christian missionaries.[7] As a corporate group Europeans were exempt from the application of native law and custom; from compulsory military or public service; from the requirements of the pass laws; and from the other restrictions imposed upon Africans with respect to mobility, use of one's talents, and the privilege of forming associations. The European minority enjoyed special preference with respect to salaries, housing, education for their children, and other prerequisites denied to Africans until the eve of independence. They monopolized access to the supervisory and better salaried positions in government, the commercial sector, and even in the churches. And, with the exception of the Portuguese territories under the paternalistic Salazar regime, Europeans found far fewer obstacles to their organizing politically in behalf of their interests than was the case with Africans.

The elevation of Europeans to high caste positions did not mean, however, that they acted as a monolithic corporate group. Indeed, there were many interests that divided the Europeans in a given territory. Administrators who were attempting to introduce cash crop agriculture to provide a better tax base in this area and who needed manpower for roads, bridges, and other public works were in competition with the European miners, planters, and others who wanted an available pool of cheap labor. Missionaries who sought converts and youths to fill the places in mission schools found themselves at variance with the labor recruiters, as well as with the colonial administrators who wanted to limit proselytizing in order to reduce certain kinds of conflict. Their diverse national origin was another factor hindering the potential unity of the European minority. In many British colonies, for example, membership in European clubs was denied to Greeks and Italians—despite the fact that their ancestors over two millennia ago had laid the foundations for European civilization, while ancient Britons were still running around using woad to paint themselves blue! The extreme example of fissions within the European minority group is South Africa, where the conflict between the Afrikaners, who were basically of Dutch, French, and German origin, and the English-speaking element has been a feature of politics for close to two centuries. One of the consequences of the apartheid program as well as the rural to urban movement of the Afrikaners has been a blurring of the distinctions between these two competing nationalist groups and a reduction of the public visibility of dissension within the white ranks.

The transition to Black rule during the anti-colonial struggle posed many problems for the nationalizing elite with respect to the continuing role of the formerly privileged white class. Independence, after all, affected the magnitude and quality of relations between the members of the two races in areas far beyond the political. The nature of these altered relationships, however, was not always predictable. At one extreme, the liberation struggle led by the MPLA in Angola and FRELIMO in Mozambique witnessed a mass exodus of Portuguese who feared that the long years of colonial oppression and the atrocities committed during the independence struggles would lead to massive retaliation against those whites who remained. Whether this exodus was desired by FRELIMO or by the MPLA regime is a matter of debate. In any event, the departure of planters, industrialists, bankers, and other whites left the nationalizing elite without many of the essential skills needed for modernization. Since the Portuguese had also tended to monopolize even semi-skilled positions, the flight of mechanics, masons, crane operators, and others brought the economy to a virtual halt. Eventually Cubans, East Germans, Romanians, and other socialist-bloc technicians came in to fill the void, but for a variety of reasons these were not always satisfactory replacements. Ironically, by the early 1980s the Mozambican and Angolan leaders were calling on the Portuguese to provide technical and other skills needed to get their economies working again.

At the other end of the spectrum, the governing elite in a number of Francophone states have actually maintained or even intensified their linkages with France since independence. The number of Frenchmen in the Ivory Coast, for example, is estimated to be four times as great as at independence in 1960 (50,000 vs. 12,000). To a lesser extent the expansion in the French presence also applies in Senegal, Cameroon, Gabon, and others of the nineteen states which enjoy a special relationship with France. These include Zaire, Rwanda, and Burundi, where the French have stepped in to assume the economic and financial positions once occupied by Belgians. Ironically, it even has come to include Guinea despite the bitter history which followed that country's independence in 1958. Throughout Francophone Africa, French businessmen, doctors, engineers, educators, and bankers supplement, if they do not take the place of, Africans who might have been trained for these roles. Although generally the French resident does not participate directly in the politics of the new state, Frenchmen are associated with the maintenance of political authority. In Djibouti, for example, 4,000 men of the French Foreign legion serve as a guarantee against this smallest of the former French colonies being absorbed by one of its two neighbors—Somalia or Ethiopia. Roughly 7,000 white officers and noncoms serve in the armies of Senegal and several other African states. Many of the key ministries in the Francophone states rely heavily on the expertise of French consultants in embarking on any new programs. Generally speaking there seems to be less overt resentment of the European physical presence by local nationals in Francophone Africa than is true of other states. Indeed, the manner in which the Francophone African elite prize their French diplomas and their ability to speak Parisian French creates special interracial bonds not found elsewhere in Africa.

Intermediate between the Portuguese and the French colonial experience, whites in many former British territories have also increased in numbers. The national origins of the new expatriates called in by the nationalizing elites, however, are very diverse, with West Germans, Americans, Scandinavians, Canadians, and Western-associated Japanese outnumbering the British. The new expatriates tend to be more short-term in their tenures and limited to business or technical roles. Hence they pose no political or even long-term vocational threat to the nationalizing elite or to the general upward mobility of the Nigerians, Ghanaians, and Tanzanians within their own societies. In the former settler territories in east, central, and southern Africa, the numbers of white farmers has diminished steadily since independence, but a substantial core in Kenya, Zambia, Swaziland, and Zimbabwe have elected to remain in what for them is their birthplace. The policy of racial reconciliation pursued by a remarkably forgiving Jomo Kenyatta immediately after Kenyan independence was significant in this regard. Despite the ferocity of the Mau Mau struggle, Kenyatta recognized the continued contribution that whites could make to the country's economic development. As long as whites regarded themselves as Kenyan citizens, they have continued to occupy significant posts in the administration and the military as well. One white politician, a son of L.S.B. Leakey, has actually competed successfully for a seat in the Parliament, and other whites enjoy prominent posts in education, the arts, and cultural life.

Taking a leaf from Kenyatta's book and following the advice of Samora Machel of Mozambique, who regretted the mass departure of European skills, Prime Minister Robert Mugabe of Zimbabwe has also pursued a policy of reconciliation. The efficiency of the European agricultural sector both in terms of feeding the Zimbabwe population and providing tobacco and other export earnings was not lost upon Mugabe. Hence, white farmers as well as those Europeans involved in the development of the industrial and mining sectors who could accept a political system dominated by Blacks were encouraged to remain. And although Mugabe has wanted to move to a one-party state, there seems to be no premature move to remove the guarantees with regard to the 20 out of 100 seats in the legislature being reserved for Europeans until 1987. Although the proportion of whites to Blacks in Zimbabwe has been diminishing, there was nothing at this stage that resembled the predicted "white flight." Considering, moreover, the bitterness over the land issue and racial discrimination, the degree of interracial harmony in Zimbabwe is far more significant than the scattered incidents of racial discord.

The Political Fate of Intermediate Groups

As noted previously, conflict between whites and Blacks was not the only type of racial tension under colonial rule. The social stratification system in most territories also witnessed the introduction of intermediate racial groups between the white pinnacle and the broad Black base. In a few instances, such as the use of Arabs and East Indians by both the British and the Germans in East Africa, the Europeans utilized the talents and experience of indigenous non-Africans in carrying out administrative and other tasks.[8] In other cases non-Africans were imported from Asia or the Middle East to provide support to the limited cadre of European colonial officers. Thus, in West Africa the Syrians and Lebanese and in East Africa the Hindus, Muslims, and Christian Goans from the Indian sub-continent (see Table 4) provided the artisan and supervisory skills required by the colonial bureaucracy, the private mines and plantations, the banks, and other European-directed enterprises.

In many cases it was the Asians who were the main purveyors of European and other externally produced consumer goods to the people in the African interior. Working long hours, surviving at a considerably reduced standard of living compared to Europeans, and willing to accept a smaller margin of profit, the small rural Asian shopkeepers became well entrenched in the retail and eventually the wholesale trade. Much of their accumulated wealth left the country after retirement to maintain them and their families in more comfortable circumstances in their countries of origin. Since Asians came into contact with Africans on a day-to-day basis and were the intermediaries in terms of European objectives, they often became the social scapegoats or "pariahs" whenever the Europeans and Africans sought explanations for friction within the colonial system. Their presence, moreover, made it less necessary for the European administrators to press forward in training Africans as clerks, masons, auto mechanics, and other skilled and semi-skilled artisans. Hence, the first nationalist hostilities on the part of Africans were often directed against the more vulnerable and visible Asians. The Asians were not entirely innocent bystanders. Many came to Africa voluntarily, in search of wealth not otherwise obtainable. They participated in self-serving political activities in Kenya, Tanganyika, and Uganda, as well as in South Africa. Ghandi's crusade in Durban, after all, was directed not against the pass laws in general but their application to Asians. In East Africa, as political representation was extended by the colonial authorities to Europeans, Asians demanded a voice for themselves as well. Various postwar reforms extended

TABLE 4
Racial Categories in East Africa
on the Eve of Independence

Racial Group	Tanganyika	Kenya	Uganda
African	8,662,684	6,171,000	6,449,558
Indian-Pakistani	71,660	169,000	69,103
Goan	4,757	—	2,830
Arab	19,088	37,100	1,946
European	20,534	66,400	10,866
Colored (Mixed)	2,257	964	1,334

SOURCE: Elizabeth Hopkins, "Racial Minorities in British East Africa," in Stanley Diamond and Fred G. Burke, eds., *The Transformation of East Africa: Studies in Political Anthropology* (New York: Basic Books, 1966) pp. 83–153.

representation and suffrage to Asians that, although not equal to that enjoyed by the Europeans, was superior to what was extended to the African majority. In Dar es Salaam, an Asian even served as mayor during the last decade of dependency.

In East Africa independence brought varying fates to the Asian minorities in the four territories. Most devastating of all was the January 1964 slaughter on Zanzibar of roughly 30,000 Arabs within one month of independence, precipitated by memories of the pivotal role Arabs had played in maintaining the East African slave trade. Rather than having the privileged position enjoyed by the Sultan and other Arabs under the British protectorate continue after independence, the Black majority rose up against its Arab ruling caste. While the coastal Arabs in Kenya and Tanganyika did not suffer a similar fate, the uprising on Zanzibar was a factor in the subsequent military mutinies in Tanganyika, Uganda, and Kenya.

It is the Indians, Pakistanis, and other south Asians in the intermediate group who have drawn the bulk of the attention of the nationalizing elites. Asians have been far more numerous than Arabs and their treatment has typically been far more harsh in terms of limiting their prospects of full participation. Tanzania, however, has until recently generally stood out as an exception. Asians at the time of independence were given a choice of taking out Tanzanian citizenship, and many chose to do so despite the complicated procedures. During a good part of Nyerere's administration, moreover, the contribution of the Asians had been publicly acknowledged; indeed, an Asian Member of Parliament, Amir Jamal, long served in a key cabinet position, that of Minister of Finance. It was not until the anti-corruption drive of 1983 that the small but prosperous and industrious Asian community in Tanzania was singled out for harassment.

Uganda during most of the period since independence has stood at the opposite end of the spectrum. In 1972 Idi Amin, seeking a scapegoat for his miserable failure to generate economic growth, escalated what had been minor discrimination against Asians and seized the properties of Asian shop-keepers and other entrepreneurs. All Indians and Pakistanis, including those who had taken out Ugandan citizenship, were ordered peremptorily to leave Uganda. Since neighboring countries were reluctant to accept more Asians, untold thousands were forced to seek refuge in Britain, India, Pakistan, or any other place that would open its doors to them. The departure left a dramatic void in the commercial, banking, and skilled artisan sectors of the economy, for the Kakwa and other troops that were given properties or positions by Amin were totally lacking in the skills and resources necessary to make a success of their opportunities. It was only a decade later, with the restoration of civilian rule under President Milton Obote, that the Asians were invited to return to resume ownership of their confiscated properties and run them in partnership with Africans. Since many of the small shops could not be profitably run with a co-owner, few small shopkeepers were prepared to take the risk. Some of the major investors, merchants, and landowners, however, have returned.

The Communications Factor in Nation-Building

The ability of all members of a national society to speak a common language is not an absolute requirement for nation-building, as the survival of Switz-erland and other multilingual states will testify. Conversely, if the use of a single language over a vast area was sufficient in itself to generate the bonds of national community, then Simón Bolívar's dream of constituting much of Latin America as one great Spanish-speaking republic would have mater-ialized over a century and a half ago. Nevertheless, the relationship between effective communication and successful nation-building efforts is not a casual one. The formulation of a rational language policy in a pluralistic society must have almost as high a priority as economic planning itself if the lead-ership of a new African state is to forge the unity required for survival of the state community and to accomplish the goals of overcoming poverty.[9]

In its own self-interest, a nationalizing elite in a plural society must ensure that its orders, policy directives, and programs are understood quickly, in relatively the same fashion, with the same nuances of meaning, by all major segments—or at least the leadership of these major segments—within the new state society. Equally important is the establishment of emotional bonds which create a sense of national community. Some of these bonds may be established through visual means (parades, flags, monuments) or through joint activity, such as participation in an integrated armed forces. Many of the symbols of unity, however, are verbal and are reflected in literature, song, poetry, and nationalist slogans. Thus, a rationalized language policy is essential if the society as a whole is to accept new myths of common origin and destiny; the selective reinterpretation of disparate histories that emphasizes unifying rather than divisive factors; and the new panoply of sainted national heroes and sacred events that must be memorialized in holidays and civic speeches. All of the preceding depend upon the creation of an effective system of social communication. Without it, the legitimacy of the nationalizing elite is at stake: it cannot hope to secure an almost automatic, unquestioning response on the part of the broader citizenry to its leadership commands.

Quantitative factors are, of course, significant in formulating a rational language policy in a plural society. How many speakers of how many languages are key questions. Given the pluralism of most African states, combined with the general poverty, it is apparent that some rationalization of language policy is absolutely essential if the governing elite is to maintain the integrity of state boundaries. Nigeria with anywhere from 250 to 300 distinct languages, Zaire with 6 major language groups and 35 distinct languages represented among its population, Sierra Leone with 12, Kenya with 40, and Cameroon with 100 languages have to arrive at reasonable formulae in dealing with situations of extreme multilingualism.[10] The complexity of communications for the continent as a whole is revealed in David Dalby's estimate that there are over 2,000 distinct languages in Africa, each with its unique vocabulary, syntax, and ways of organizing thought. Dalby notes that the estimated number can be reduced to a thousand if one groups interintelligible languages, but even that figure includes fifty major languages, each with over one million speakers.[11] Many, if not most, are tonal: the same sounds may produce entirely different meanings depending upon how they are sung. I have encountered many Africans who have a working knowledge of eight or nine languages; there are, however, cases in which even immediate neighbors have difficulty in making the transition from one African language to the next. Resort must be had to a third language or lingua franca for mutual comprehension. The typical African situation is far more complicated than that in Europe, where a speaker of one of the Romance languages—say, Portuguese—can move with relative ease to Spanish, French, or Italian, and a German speaker can swiftly gain a working knowledge of Dutch or a Scandinavian tongue. Within Nigeria or Zaire, moving from one area to the next can mean a transition from one major language family to another, and the number of such families within a single country is often considerable. The problems, moreover, associated with tone in most African languages and with clicks in the Khoisan languages of Southern Africa serve as further impediments.

The costs of multilingualism are prohibitive for most Third World states. Translating and printing textbooks or publishing the legal code and proceedings of the legislature in each of the major languages of the country would exhaust resources better allocated to health or agriculture. When it comes to radio and television broadcasting, no country has an unlimited number of broadcast bands available to it, or an unlimited number of hours into which it may break up the effective broadcasting day. There are other arenas as well, such as commercial transactions and religious discourses, where a reduction in the scale of multilingualism is essential in the accomplishment of goals.

Costs are not, however, the only consideration. The rationalization of language policy in a multilingual society must take into account qualitative factors as well. As experience elsewhere has demonstrated, the emotional appeal of—or hostility toward—particular languages must be taken into account in shaping a national language policy. In the new state of Israel, Hebrew had to take precedence over Yiddish, a more widely spoken language but one with bitter memories of the diaspora. Similarly, although it has had largely symbolic value, Gaelic as an alternative to the language of the "English occupation" has been important to the self-esteem of the Irish as citizens of a self-governing liberated republic. In Africa as well, these emotional or affective qualities have had to be taken into account. In Somalia, for example, acceptance of the Somali language rather than Italian, English, or Arabic has had certain costs in terms of reducing easy access to external education. Yet, it has been essential in maintaining the Somali irredentist myth that requires the five segments of the Somali nation to be rejoined within a common political state. Conversely, the potentially divisive consequences of opting for a particular language are also considerable. The selection in Nigeria of Hausa, Yoruba, or Igbo would most certainly have aroused immediate hostility on the part not only of speakers of the other two languages but others as well. The north/south conflict in the Sudan stems in part from the efforts of the northerners shortly after independence in 1956 to make Arabic the official language of the national administration. English or one of the traditional languages (Nuer, Dinka, Shilluk) had been used in the south during the British administration in a calculated effort to reduce Islamic influence in that region.[12] Finally, we can point to the crisis created by a decision on language in South Africa. Even though there were other factors involved in the Soweto riots of 1976, the spark that ignited the demonstrations was the decision of the South African government that instruction and testing of African students must be in Afrikaans rather than English. This decree was politically and psychologically repugnant to many African youths since it would educationally orient them to that sector of the European population which had been most strident in the application of apartheid legislation. Of equal importance was the fact that it would make it more difficult for Africans completing secondary schools to find places in the four white English-speaking universities. These four institutions had permitted entry of Blacks (roughly 11 percent of total enrollment) who wanted to pursue courses of study not available in Black universities. The successful imposition of Afrikaans would also have hindered African prospects for overseas education.

Affective or emotional considerations also were involved in Tanzania in Nyerere's decision to find a substitute for English. Realizing that the speakers of any one of its 120 traditional languages did not constitute even 10 percent of the population, and that giving official status to one or even a few traditional languages would arouse the hostility of many other language groups, he opted for Swahili. The latter is not particularly identified with any one of Tanzania's 120 ethnic groups but is rather the language of the coastal people whose political systems were undermined and whose culture and institutions were long ago subjected to the influence of the Arabs of Zanzibar. Although the language was formerly associated with the Arab slave trade (because the Arabs employed Swahili-speaking porters from the coast in their caravans to the interior), it was also used by the Germans and the English in administration, commerce, the legal system, and the schools of Tanzania long before independence. Since for the most part Swahili lacks tone, it is one of the more easily learned African languages.[13] While Swahili has also received official status in Kenya (along with English) and is spoken in Mozambique, Zaire, and other areas in East Africa, efforts to establish it as the national language in Uganda encountered greater resistance. The major ethnic group, the Ganda (Baganda), long regarded their language, Luganda, as superior to Swahili since the latter had strong associations with the Arab slave trade. Under Amin, Swahili was literally imposed upon the country as the national language.[14]

Despite the hostility which memories of the recent colonial past evoke, the language of the former colonialists often continues by default as the national language in many new states. Sometimes the European language will share with an African language the status of an official national language, as is the case with English and CiChewa in Malawi or English and Swahili in Kenya. Occasionally hostility toward major ethnic groups within the society or a seemingly unlimited number of languages from which to choose has left the national leadership with no other acceptable choice than the language of the colonialists. Remarkably, this has been the case in both Angola and Mozambique, in spite of the depth of animosity towards Portuguese colonial rule during the closing phase of the liberation struggle. The use of Portuguese not only continued the special links among former Portuguese colonies in Africa, but it has also resulted in maintaining special links with Brazil.

Aside from convenience or political expediency, there are other reasons for the persistence of European language use in Africa. For one thing, it was often their ability to master a European language that gave the governing party elite a claim to preeminance during the anti-colonial struggle. Thus, they have had a vested corporate interest in preserving a privilege which had put some social distance between themselves and the masses and had justified their elite status. This attitude is most pronounced in Francophone Africa, where the Ivoiriens, Senegalese, and other elites seem more snobbish than the Parisians themselves in insisting upon French being spoken "properly" even in informal discourse. A leader like Léopold Senghor prides himself upon writing poetry in French and being a member of the exclusive Academie Française. The assertion that French as a national language is a form of elite corporate "property" is reinforced by the fact that in Senegal roughly three-fourths of the population speak Wolof, while only a small minority speak French.[15] Beyond elite status, however, there are pragmatic considerations in giving official recognition to a European language. As both Somalia and Tanzania are discovering, resort to a European language is required at some point in the educational process if African states are to continue to have easy access to the information explosion which is occurring at the global level. Scientific and other data are presented largely in English, French, German, Russian, and other major European languages. This dependence upon a European language was acknowledged by Ministry of Education officials in Tanzania in 1984 when it was announced that English would continue to be encouraged as a medium of instruction despite heroic efforts in making Swahili a vehicle "for cultural emancipation and national unification."[16] Mastery of a European language is also essential if African diplomats are to be effective at the U.N. or even in communicating with their African neighbors about economic and other forms of cooperation.

Even when a European language is given official status as a national language or shares this with a major African language, concessions inevitably have to be made to some form of multilingualism.[17] Traditional languages may continue to be used in the home, the local market, and the church. In Muslim areas Arabic is the medium of instruction in Koranic schools, and it is used in the mosque. Indeed, there is a far higher literacy rate in Muslim areas than the official statistics reveal, inasmuch as literacy in Arabic is often ignored or downgraded in census data.[18] In a number of states, both for the purposes of effective instruction of the very young and as a concession to local pressure, a multi-tiered educational system has emerged either officially or informally.[19] In that case, a local or regional language serves as the language of entry and continues through primary school, then either the regional or the "national" language is phased in at the secondary school and university levels. This in effect is the practice in much of Nigeria. In some instances it is the arena of politics itself that must be sensitive to pressures regarding language use. A local candidate for the Malawian Parliament, for example, must be fluent in both English and CiChewa, and also might be expected to address campaign rallies in Yao, Ngoni, or one of the other traditional languages of his constituency. In Zambia fifteen years after independence, certain key documents such as the Constitution and the Party Charter were belatedly translated and published in seven of the major traditional languages.[20] Liberia, a country with at least sixteen traditional languages as well as a modified version of the English language (pidgin), in 1984 published the draft of its proposed Constitution in both standard English and pidgin in order to facilitate comprehension on the part of the widest possible pool of voters. Finally, the concession to informal multilingualism is apparent in the fact that there are few restrictions placed by government on any private effort to preserve or strengthen communications in a particular language. If one has the means and the audience, one is free to publish a newspaper, the Bible, or even leaflets on health in any of the traditional languages of a country.

Much of the preceding commentary on the relationship between effective communication and nation-building is further compounded in Africa by widespread illiteracy. Obviously the existence of a written form of a language is not essential to the survival of a political community over a considerable period of time. There were relatively few written languages in Africa at the time of the European arrival, (Hausa and Swahili had written forms using Arabic script). Yet some large-scale political communities emerged, particularly in West Africa. The maintenance of political control from the center, however, was intermittent. The unity of traditional society, moreover, was often maintained by encoding the legacy of political and cultural unity in various art forms—such as the recitation of heroic founding epics by *griots* in Mali, the telling of folktales and proverbs by elders, or the weaving or painting of pictorial representations of significant personages or events in the community's history, such as the Abomey appliqué cloths or the Ethiopian religious paintings. Intermediate messages from the existing leadership were transmitted by word of mouth. While traditional approaches are still relevant to the contemporary problem of nation-building, these are not the most precise means for getting specific or relatively novel messages across. They are also time-consuming in terms of making an immediate impact. Time is not what many African leaders possess in abundance when it comes to maintaining the stability of the new state community. More modern means of communication, such as radio and television, of course, can occasionally be used to reach mass audiences, and they do manage to capture some of the more significant aspects of traditional face-to-face communication. But the costs of television installation and maintenance are prohibitive for most African countries, and television remains largely the expensive leisure toy of the urban elite. Even with the far less expensive radio, the cost of transmission, training of personnel, and distribution of cheap, maintenance-free receivers are still problems in many societies.

Ultimately it is the written word that constitutes the most effective means for a nationalizing elite in communicating with a large and highly diverse population over an extended period of time. The precision of the message, the possibility of constant repetition, and the ability to provide more detailed information and nuances of meaning are enhanced with written forms of communication. Unfortunately for most African countries, the ability of the population to read—and to read in the language or languages which serve as the vehicles for nation-building—is highly limited. When the European missionaries arrived, they took on the primary burden of transcribing many of the continent's numerous languages as a proselytizing mechanism.[21] They also assumed the primary responsibility for spreading literacy in both African and European languages—recognizing that it magnified the impact of their efforts if converts could read the Bible and spread the divine message to the yet unconverted. Itinerant Muslim holy men had the same objective in mind in using Arabic as the medium for literacy in the Koranic schools. Colonial governments in areas under British, French, and Belgian control did take on some of the responsibilities for education. These were, however, limited to the achievement of a specific goal, such as the training of chiefs or securing vocational skills or administrative and other talents not provided by a mission education. In most cases, it was not until the pressures for independence had escalated that colonial governments began to supplement or displace the mission efforts with direct government funding of education.

In view of the late start, and despite the heroic efforts of independent governments to set a high priority upon education, the literacy rates in Africa generally remain quite low. Even counting the five north African countries where 50 to 60 percent of the population are literate, the African continent as a whole in the early 1980s lagged considerably behind the other world regions in terms of rates of illiteracy (Table 5).[22] Although the statistical data are not uniform in terms of dates and reporting methods, by the 1980s in twenty-five of the forty-one countries reporting, a majority still had illiteracy rates of over 50 percent, eighteen of them in excess of 70 percent and eight with 90 percent.[23] In addition to overall deficiencies with respect to illiteracy, there were extreme imbalances by sex (roughly 51 percent for females, only 30 percent for males) and by region (Ethiopia and Upper Volta, for example, had 15 times higher rates of illiteracy in rural areas than in urban areas). There were also age discrepancies, with the highest rates of illiteracy in the age 15 and older category. In only a few countries such as Tanzania have there been dramatic assaults on the problem of illiteracy. In colonial Tanzania the illiteracy rate remained around 90 to 95 percent. By the early 1980s as a result of a mass drive in basic literacy in Swahili, roughly 85 percent of the population has now become literate. Elsewhere in Africa, one cannot depend upon there being a literate minority in the rural area that will communicate the substance of national directives to their unlettered countrymen.

The lack of a substantial literate population is further reflected in the paucity of indigenous newspapers and magazines and the high cost of imported reading materials from abroad. For Africa as a whole there are only 11.2 newspapers per 1000 readers, which is the lowest for the Third World.[24] Most newspapers are government-owned or controlled; have only the briefest coverage even of national, let alone international news; and are largely

TABLE 5

Illiteracy at the Global Level in 1980

World as a whole	21.8%
North America	.5
Europe	.6
Oceania	4.8
Latin America	7.3
Asia	31.5
Africa	40.6

SOURCE: Based on Andre Lestage, *Literacy and Illiteracy*, UNESCO Educational Studies Document No. 42 (Paris: UNESCO, 1982); and UNESCO Division on Education, *Estimates and Projections of Illiteracy* (September 1978).

limited in readership to the urban elite. Private newspapers which are not subsidized by a religious organization must depend on subscriptions and advertising for income, and seldom survive beyond a few weeks or months of publication—if they do not earlier run into conflict with the government censor!

The Religious Factor in Nation-Building

There is ample contemporary evidence on the global level of the political relevance of membership in religious structures. Indeed, the evidence is not limited to the Third World, as revealed in the manner in which the issues of school prayer, abortion, and other moral questions have intruded on the American political scene in the 1980s. Of even greater significance in the Western world, membership in the Roman Catholic Church and the Anglican and other Protestant sects in Northern Ireland has come to be viewed as a kind of primitive tribal badge which provides sufficient reason for shunning, discriminating against, or even committing primitive acts of violence against other citizens of the same political community who differ in their religious affiliation. In Poland the Roman Catholic Church plays a role in keeping the spirit of Polish nationalism alive and in preventing the Communist party from monopolizing loyalties within the state. The Christian faith, of course, is not alone in becoming a factor in politics. In the Middle East, Islam has undergone a resurgence as a result of its efforts to counter the encroaching secular norms of modernization associated with Western colonialism and capitalism. The Islamic fundamentalist reaction is not limited to Iran and Pakistan, but has become a political issue in Sudan, northern Nigeria, and other African countries. From time to time, moreover, the ideological or theological schisms within the Islamic fold in the Middle East as well as the conflicts between nationalism and religion are set aside in favor of a broad pan-Islamic *jihad* against Israel and Zionism, Western secularism, and other challenges to Muslim faith and unity.

Despite efforts in many states to find an effective formula or series of mechanisms for separating the questions of religious affiliation, forms of worship, and religious ideology from the arena of politics, religion inevitably plays a role whether or not there is conflict among religious faiths. Religion or religions provide the underlying moral code for the members of a society, determining right from wrong and differentiating correct and ethical behavior from immoral and improper conduct. Religion often sanctifies the particular organization of individuals into kinship groups. Religious beliefs provide moral props for rules about pursuit of a marriage partner, responsibilities of individuals toward kinsmen, descendants, or the aged, and acquisition and use of whatever is regarded as property by that group. For members of pastoral, fishing, and other societies, religion determines what type of economic activity is properly pursued. There is an assumption, even in Western, secularly oriented societies, that God is politically on one's side during times of war or economic crisis as well as in less important situations such as the outcome of an athletic contest. Religion, moreover, sets limits on the definition of the political community by providing a set of rules with regard to those you may kill or steal from with impunity (because they are members of an enemy society) and those to whom you must pay moderate or extreme penalties for having violated their person or their property.

In traditional African societies the feeling is even more pronounced than in Western societies that the community actually consists of more than just the living members of the society who can be counted and seen by all. People in a traditional society operate on the assumption that their actions are controlled and observed by gods, nature spirits, ancestors, or more vaguely defined forces. These extra-human elements are associated both with the founding of the community and with its continuing fate and good fortune.

Observable political figures in traditional society, moreover, frequently are reputed to have mystical or magical qualities that place them above the rank of ordinary mortals. This myth of divinity seldom approached the ideal type of divine kingship set forth by Sir James George Frazier in his *Golden Bough*, but vestiges of that syndrome persisted in Africa through the colonial period and into the post-independence era among many African ethnic groups, even in areas where Indirect Rule was not applied. I witnessed this behavior in the Cameroons in the early 1980s among supplicants seeking some political, legal or economic favor from their *fon*, or chief. The petitioner approached the *fon* on all fours in order to avoid looking him directly in the face, and then only addressed him through an intermediary speaker. Such social distancing reinforced the notion of spiritual superiority of those who held political office. In the Sukuma area of Tanzania in the 1950s, the chiefs in many of the autonomous political units I studied were central to the performance of the annual rituals associated with the agricultural cycle.[25] The physical body of the chief or *ntemi* was identified with the spiritual body of the community. At the commencement of the cycle, in a public ceremony, the head of the chief was shaved to simulate the clearing of the fields. At various times during the growing season there was a ritualistic inspection of the chief's head by the royal councillors, with the growth of hair being related to the successful growth of the crops. Finally, when the chief once more had a full head of hair, it was a signal that the harvest was at hand. In other ways as well the body of a Sukuma chief was equated with the body politic in traditional times. In the event of the chief's senility or ill health, or conversely, if the chiefdom had suffered recurrent drought or defeat in battle, designated royal councillors committed the act of regicide while the chief slept. This enabled a young and more vigorous *ntemi* to be elected to replace the unfortunate incumbent. At death, the body of the late chief was buried with the skull of his predecessor which had been part of his royal regalia. This symbolized the continuity of the wisdom of the royal ancestors.

Similar examples from West Africa are depicted in Frank Speed's classic film, *Benin Kingship Rituals*, which notes the way the royal personage is insulated from the populace through enormous robes and other paraphernalia. The political and social rankings within society are graphically presented through the religious rituals associated with kingship and the agricultural cycle. Since the Bini *oba* has the most direct contact with the ancestors who are important to the entire Benin kingdom, an act of treason or disloyalty in the political sense becomes magnified: it is also an act of heresy.

The intertwining of religion with other aspects of life penetrates to the sub-community level as well. Each kinship group in traditional society has had its special set of ancestors who were the antecedents of the father (in the case of patrilineal groups) or the mother's brother (in the case of matrilineal groups). These ancestors were assumed to have continuing concern for the safety and progress of the living members of the kin group. Fear of offending these ancestors establishes and reinforces the moral order, with the ancestors of a chief or head of a major lineage being relevant to the health of the large political community. The successful relocation of communities in Africa to make way for development often hinges on the removal of graves of ancestors. This was the lesson of the Kariba dam in Zimbabwe, the Aswan dam in Egypt, and the Akosambo dam in Ghana. Hence religion, politics, and social relationships are intertwined in many traditional societies.

The same necessary interconnection of religious and other phenomena applies to economic activity in many traditional African societies. It thus differs from modern American society where economic roles are not only highly diversified but may be easily changed. In traditional society, by way of contrast, the economic activity pursued by the majority of the males is societal specific. That is, hunting, herding, cultivating, trading, or smithing is the prescribed activity for members of that society, with males and females having differing roles. The way in which one engages in this economic activity is at crucial points assumed to be controlled by ritual rather than by technology and learned skills alone. Often ritual accompanies the use of technical skills and inculcates in young observers the notion that attention to prescribed procedures is essential to the economic health and survival of the community. For example, certain fishing communities have taboos with regard to sex before going out to sea. Divisions of labor within the community are also ritually sanctioned. This applies not only to the distinct roles based upon gender and age, but also to particular kinds of labor. Among the Margi of northern Nigeria, for example, smithing—dealing with metals from the earth—is an activity relegated to a lower caste group, whose members are not permitted to intermarry with members of the broader Margi society.

The intertwining of religious and other forms of activity could potentially be an asset in nation-building since it not only provides a significant sanction for political authority but also establishes a moral order. Kwame Nkrumah in Ghana recognized this, engaged in ritualistic ablutions on various state occasions, and made use of other religious performances associated with traditional Akan chieftainship as a way of buttressing his secular authority as a national leader. It was also evidenced in his adoption of traditional titles, including "Osagyefo" or Military Savior.[26] The new state takes on many of the attributes of traditional kingship and cements relations between state leaders and the masses through what David Apter has called "political religion." This consists of ritualist trappings as well as lightly sketched myths of common origin that seek to provide mystical bonds among citizens of a heterogeneous community. As Apter states: "the sacred is employed in many new nations to develop a system of political legitimacy and to aid in mobilizing the community for secular ends."[27]

There are a number of impediments to the use of traditional religion as an instrument in contemporary nation-building in Africa. Many of these religious systems, it must be noted, no longer prevail or have effectiveness. Politically, they were based upon chieftainships which have in many instances been officially dismantled, or upon ancestors who were parochially oriented to the welfare of kinship and ethnic units at a level subordinate to the broader state community. Traditional religions, furthermore, have been steadily undermined by the various sects of Christianity and Islam, which are increasingly winning converts away from them. Both of these world religious systems, moreover, transcend in membership particular political or social communities, thereby creating a competing allegiance. Indeed, to the extent that the traditional religion, which is linked to a surviving traditional political system, continues to survive, it poses a serious threat to the claims of the new nationalist leaders who seek a monopoly over state loyalties.

Second, secularization has accompanied the spread of Christianity (and to

a lesser extent Islam), breaking down the religious sanctions that supported
the particular kinship, neighborhood, or other social groupings, and reinforced particularistic economic roles. Included in secularization, of course,
is the tendency to separate the domains of church and state so that any
continuing ritual associated with divine kingship is largely ceremonial—a
form of public entertainment.[28] The skills required to get ahead in politics
and administration, moreover, are not always associated with religions; more
often success is achieved through participation in political parties, the military, or other structures. One major exception to this was the example of
Liberia prior to the 1980 coup, where the Americo-Liberian elite interrelated
political leadership with the leadership of the leading Protestant churches
and the Masonic Order.[29] In Uganda, as well, the interlinking of the Democratic Party and the Roman Catholic Church was apparent during the First
Republic, as well as before independence.[30]

Third, there are only a few instances in Africa today where the modern
state consists predominantly of individuals drawn from a single ethnic grouping whose members share a common moral code based upon religion, and
where religion supports a particular set of political leaders. One state on the
margin of sub-Saharan Africa—Morocco—approximates this condition. King
Hassan II is assumed to be a direct descendant of Mohammed the Prophet
and hence is the country's prime religious as well as political leader. The
late king of Swaziland, Sobhuza II, who died in 1982, also reinforced his
political authority by basing his claim to govern upon his descent from sanctified warrior kings and the popular equation of the health of Swaziland with
the continuing vigor of the monarch. He lived to the age of 82, and fathered
almost 800 children, a sure sign of physical and political health!

In all other instances the multi-ethnic nature of the state or the political
fragmentation of major ethnic groupings has meant that religious claims to
political authority are either irrelevant or actually counterproductive in terms
of building a modern nation-state. The late Seretse Khama of Botswana, for
example, was only regarded as a religious personage with claims to leadership
based on royal descent by one ethnic grouping within the multi-ethnic Botswana state. Indeed, in many instances successful political leaders such as
Léopold Senghor of Senegal and Julius Nyerere of Tanzania—both Roman
Catholics—have actually had to downplay their Christian affiliation within
political communities that are either predominantly Muslim or have a substantial and highly politicized Muslim minority. On the other hand, Somalia
represents an alternate case in which the religious solidarity of the society
as a Muslim state does not provide a particular advantage to any one political
competitor who would base his claim on religion. The fragmentation of the
Somali people into politicized clans has often been of far greater significance
than the purported unity which is based in part upon a shared Islamic faith.

The counterproductive nature of the persistence of particularistic religious
claims to political authority is well exemplified in the case of the role played

by the late Kabaka of Buganda within the immediate post-independent Uganda. Being members of the largest, wealthiest, and best endowed kingdom in Uganda and possessed to an unusual degree of modern education and modern administrative skills, the Ganda (Baganda) felt that they had a special role to play in an independent Uganda. Indeed, in order to forestall demands for a secessionist Buganda state, both the British and a coalition of Ugandan political leaders recognized the tactical value of having the Kabaka serve as the first president of an independent Uganda. The mounting rivalry, however, between Prime Minister Milton Obote, who based his leadership upon geographically broad-based secular support, and Mutesa II, who had a narrow geographic base and depended in part upon religious claims to authority, culminated in the forced exile of the Kabaka in 1966. This was followed by Obote's dismantling of the royal structures of power not only in Buganda but in the other Uganda kingdoms as well. Resistance to this secularization had been one of the major factors in the Amin coup of 1971 and the subsequent economic and political collapse of Uganda as a viable state.

The traditional religious sanctification of economic roles has also come into conflict with the efforts of nationalist leaders to develop viable national economies. The resistance of pastoralists to the efforts of President Julius Nyerere of Tanzania to rationalize agriculture and residence patterns of Tanzanians is a dramatic illustration of this. Both the ritually sanctified technology of herding and the social, religious, and political significance which the Masai, Gogo, and other pastoralists attach to the ownership of cattle have come into conflict with the sedentarization of agriculture, villagization, and de-stocking. The religious base of pastoralism is evidenced in the fact that skulls of important cattle often adorn the entrance to a kraal to ensure the health not only of the animals but also the human residents of the kraal. The religious implications of a pastoral economy are invariably not appreciated by the urbanized elite which have spearheaded the drive for independence and modernization. Feeding a population deficient in protein and overcoming the soil erosion which comes from overgrazing of cattle on the limited amount of arable agricultural land usually take precedence over religious sentiments.

The Political Role of Islam

In other ways as well, religion has served as a divisive force in African nation-building, often setting one religious leader against another or against the secular leadership of the state. Even before the inroads made by Christianity in Africa under the umbrella of colonial rule, Islam had provided serious challenges to traditional religious beliefs along the East African littoral and across the Sahara into West Africa.[31] Often, to save his people from Arab slave raiders, a traditional African leader would embrace Islam, knowing that the Koran forbade the enslavement of Muslims. Thus a weaker non-

Muslim community could escape being the victim of a *jihad* on the part of a more powerful Muslim neighbor. At other times itinerant Muslim merchants would coopt traditional African leaders along the main trading routes for economic purposes. In exchange for protection and freedom from extraordinary exactions the traders would make regular tribute payments. The traditional leadership in turn was exposed to the utility of new forms of wealth and convenience that came from trade, and to literacy via the vehicle of the Koranic schools, and ultimately became converts to Islam.

Great Islamic political communities, of course, emerged in the Sahara and its margins centuries before Christian missionaries arrived on the scene. The Mali, Songhai, and other empires spanned great stretches of Western Africa and encompassed millions of Africans within the political state during the thirteenth to the sixteenth centuries. Until the ninteenth century, however, Islam was largely the state religion in the surviving political communities; the Islamization of the masses remained a veneer that did not penetrate deeply into the social system. Many traditional chiefs in the Sahel region below the Sahara found it convenient in the interest of trade or political survival to embrace Islam to satisfy their external challengers while continuing to observe traditional religious rituals for the benefit of their internal constituents. As long as the adherents to Islam remained a minority in Black Africa, the subcontinent was largely spared the kind of doctrinal and ideological schisms that have pitted the Sunni and Shiite Muslims against each other in the Middle East or the conflicts between the competing Islamic *tariqa* or brotherhoods that have divided otherwise unified Muslim communities.

The European colonial administrators nominally preferred the spread of Christianity to that of Islam. Indeed, the British in the southern Sudan and the French throughout West Africa attempted vigorously to discourage Islam's penetration of non-Muslim areas. Despite this, the European colonial peace provided an umbrella that was as hospitable to the spread of the Koran as it was to the spread of the Bible. In northern Nigeria Lord Lugard positively discouraged the establishment of Christian missions, taking the view that missionaries undermined the authority of the Muslim emirs upon whom he depended for the success of his policy of Indirect Rule. Even without that official protection, the more relaxed rules of conversion, the fact that its religious message was carried by non-whites, and Islam's potential of serving as an implied challenge to white rule gave Islamic conversion a distinct advantage over Christianity in many areas of sub-Saharan Africa. Indeed, Ruth Schacter Morgenthau and others have pointed out the way in which the Manding traders (called Dyula) combined their economic, religious, and political roles while serving as couriers in the independence struggle in West Africa following the Second World War.[32]

The size of the Muslim minority in post-independence Africa has become a political factor affecting the consolidation of national power in the hands of those who won independence from the British, French, and other colonialists. As is shown in Table 6, the Islamic influence in sub-Saharan Africa has been strongest in the eastern coastal areas closest to the Middle East and in the Saharan and Sahelian states bordering on the Maghreb, Libya, and Egypt.[33] It is a negligible factor in southern and middle Africa other than in states such as Malawi, which was a terminus of the Arab slave and trade caravans. Islam has not automatically been a counterforce to nation-

TABLE 6
Islamic Penetration of Sub-Saharan Africa:
Muslim Percentage of Population, by Country

Northern tier (Sahara and Sahel)

Mauritania	96%	Burkina Faso	43	Chad	50
Western Sahara	80	Niger	85	Sudan	72
Mali	60				

West Coast

Senegal	82	Sierra Leone	30	Togo	7
The Gambia	90	Liberia	15	Benin	16
Guinea-Bissau	30	Ivory Coast	25	Nigeria	47
Guinea	65	Ghana	19	Cameroon	15

Horn, East African coast, and Indian Ocean

Ethiopia	40	Kenya	9	Comoro Islands	80
Somalia	99	Uganda	6	Madagascar	7
Djibouti	94	Tanzania	24	Mauritius	17

Middle Africa

Sao Tome and Principe	—	Gabon	1	Zaire	2
		Congo	1	Rwanda	.5
Equatorial Guinea	—	Central African Republic	5	Burundi	1

Southern Africa

Angola	—	Zimbabwe	.05	South Africa	1
Zambia	1	Botswana	—	Namibia	—
Malawi	15	Lesotho	—		
Mozambique	10	Swaziland	—		

SOURCE: Based on Richard V. Weekes, editor, *Muslim Peoples: A World Ethnographic Survey* (Westport, Conn: Greenwood Press, 1978), pp. 499–527.

alism, even when the task of nation-building had been directed by a Christian. Léopold Senghor of Senegal is a case in point. Although a convert to Christianity in a country with a Muslim majority, Senghor forged an effective coalition of Western-educated urban elites and rural Muslim marabouts (the leaders of the brotherhoods) that not only brought the country to independence but also dominated the first two decades of the post-independence era. It was only in 1982 that the voluntary retirement of Senghor brought a Muslim—Abdou Diouf—into the presidency of that country. Like his predecessor, in the elections of 1983 Abdou Diouf sought and received the blessings of the so-called grand electors—those marabouts who politically spoke for their constituents.

Increasingly, however, those who are committed to a more fundamentalist version of Islam are opposing the secularist changes which have accompanied and are in many cases prerequisites of modernization and nation-building. The example of successful fundamentalist resurgence in Iran under the Ayatollah Khomeini coupled with financial and ideological support provided by Col. Muammar Qaddafi of Libya has encouraged Muslim fundamentalists in West Africa to become a disruptive political force. The events of 1982 in the northern Nigerian city of Kano which left dead an estimated 4,000 citizens are testimony to the political virulence of Islamic fundamentalism. Even in countries like Senegal, where the forces of secularism under French prodding were exceptionally strong, revolutionary Islam has been gaining ground. Among the three leading tariqa or brotherhoods, conflicts are increasingly apt to deal with issues of piety and commitment to the basic tenets of the Koran rather than economic advancement.[34]

Christianity and Nation-Building

Of perhaps even greater significance than Islam with respect to African nation-building is the impact of Christianity in its various forms. Admittedly, the positive contribution of Christianity to African nation-building was not always an intended consequence of the purveyors of Christian beliefs. Certainly the European missionaries were concerned about the transformation of African societies, but their primary intent was for the new African converts to become members of either the broader worldwide communion of Christians of that particular persuasion or of the colonial empire in which they had unwittingly become participants. Nevertheless, the undermining of traditional political allegiances coupled with various other activities associated with mission activity did contribute to the later demands for independence within the state communities. Foremost among those mission activities was the introduction of literacy. Partly as a vehicle for spreading the word of the Gospel but also as a device for introducing the new converts to a Christian lifestyle, Christian missionaries transcribed many African languages (and translated the Bible into those tongues); established mission schools with instruction in a traditional and/or a European language; and provided the converts with reading materials that broadened their perspectives beyond their parochial villages. Literacy gave the Christian Africans an important new skill which permitted them to compete with Europeans and Asians for positions in government or the private sector. It gave them as well a mechanism for communicating with other Africans beyond their own villages or family networks.

As with Islam, the various Christian denominations in Africa have at times hindered political stability and the process of nation-building. Even in the colonial era, they provided two broad categories of problems for European administrators. The first was competition between rival Christian denominations, which in one extreme case actually led to bloodshed. This occurred during the conflict in Uganda in 1892 between adherents of the Anglican Church and the Roman Catholic faith. Pitched battles between "Catholici" and "Protestanti" took on all the aspects of intertribal hostility that the new converts had presumably left behind. The martyrdom of catechists testifies to the misguided enthusiasm of the converts and their mentors.[35] Even where the situation did not reach such intensity, there was competition among rival mission groups to win the allegiance of this or that chief. Competition in the siting of a new church or school and in the securing of government support for mission enterprises became part of Ugandan politics. Colonial administrations around the continent were compelled to use restraining hands in reducing the worst manifestation of competition. This was especially true after the informal agreement between the Roman Catholic Church and several of the major Protestant churches collapsed in the mid-1920s. Under this agreement, various areas within the colonial territories had been staked out as proselytizing preserves by each of the sects—the religious counterpart of the political partition of Africa.

Despite the collapse of this private agreement, colonial governments attempted to reduce tensions elicited by Christian missionizing efforts by restricting, if not positively excluding, certain religious groups or kinds of mission activities. In colonial Zaire, the Belgian government tried to avoid repeating in the Congo territory the kind of schismatic split that had plagued Belgium itself. Hence, preference was given to the Roman Catholic Church in terms of setting up churches, schools, and hospitals, making it the third pillar—in addition to the colonial administration and the major economic enterprise, the Union Minière du Haut Katanga—with respect to the modernization and exploitation of the Congo. Similarly, despite the long history of French republican hostility to the Roman Catholic hierarchy, it was an unwritten rule that "anti-clericalism was not for export." The Roman Catholic church thus became an adjunct to the French state in Africa in its so-called civilizing mission, which sought to create Black Frenchmen. The British government had to take a different course. It did attempt to avoid Christian-Muslim conflict by giving almost absolute preference to one or the other religion. Islam, for example, enjoyed a monopoly in northern Nigeria but was virtually excluded from the southern Sudan. But the British found it difficult to play favorites among the various "main-line" Christian groups. They nevertheless attempted to minimize competition among these denominations by requiring that no group could operate in an area unless it had officially been recognized by the territorial registrar of societies. For example, in Tanganyika they continued the previous German practice of giving the Lutheran Church a virtual monopoly on one side of Kilimanjaro, with the Roman Catholic Church having full sway on the other side of the mountain.

The other politically destabilizing aspect of Christian mission activity was the overt hostility of certain sects to the authority of government. Obviously this observation did not apply to the Anglican, Roman Catholic, Methodist, and other "main-line" churches, which tended to reinforce the role of government in maintaining a stable environment conducive to the spread of Christianity. It did apply, however, to the so-called breakaway churches or syncretistic movements, which found themselves engaged in a two-way conflict both with other Christian sects and with government itself. This conflict stemmed from the fact that the breakaway churches rejected the patronizing role of the white ministry or clergy. Their opposition to both colonial and nationalist government was sometimes based upon secular issues, such as the payment of taxes, and sometimes upon theological issues, such as the refusal of Jehovah's Witnesses to salute the flag or acknowledge allegiance to any temporal authority. Many of these conflicts have carried over into the post-independence era, frustrating efforts at nation-building. The controversy in Malawi over the Watchtower Movement and the pitched battles between government forces and followers of the prophetess Alice Lenshina in Zambia are contemporary examples of this syndrome.

It is apparent from the foregoing that the role of religion in the new societies of Africa is a complex one. Whether it serves as a cohesive or a divisive factor in many ways hinges on the ability of the nationalist leadership to develop strong institutions at the state level which manage to transcend religious affiliation and which provide cross-cutting loyalties among the members of ethnically heterogeneous societies.

Alternative Strategies for Nation-Building

It should be apparent from the preceding commentary that nation-building in Africa cannot be a uniform process. The variety of languages, religions, racial groups, and other factors presents what is essentially a unique situation for each national leadership group. Historic bonds of enmity or cooperation among the peoples included within a given state may preclude one option and facilitate another. The strength or weakness of the bonds with the former colonial metropole also influences the strategy of the leadership group, as do the ideological predilections of the leaders with regard to economic, religious, and other issues. There are nevertheless a number of discernible strategies of nation-building pursued during the twenty-five years of African independence. Several of the strategies delineated below may actually be pursued concurrently by the same leadership group. This is certainly the case in South Africa today. In other cases, successive leadership groups may pursue alternative strategies over time within a single state.

PAN-NATIONALIST STRATEGY. During the early phases of the liberation struggle in the 1950s and early 1960s, the commitment to pan-African unity had become almost an article of faith on the part of many of the nationalists who had successfully terminated European colonial rule.[36] This sentiment is accurately reflected in the commentary of one prominent American scholar, Immanuel Wallerstein, who suggested in 1961 that:

> The drive for larger African unity, pan-Africanism, is probably stronger than similar movements elsewhere in the world. It is not strong enough to assure immediate success, perhaps not even ultimate success. But pan-Africanism seems likely to loom large as an active issue in African politics in the near future.[37]

The origins of the concept, of course, are not strictly African. New World Blacks who were attempting to reject the subordinate status to which Blacks in the Caribbean, the United States, and elsewhere were subjected early took up the cause of pan-African unity. Liberation of Africans from colonial rule itself became a fundamental element in the restoration of self-esteem on the part of Blacks everywhere. The pan-African torch was passed to West Africans in the various congresses in Europe at the end of the Second World War. Under the direction of Kwame Nkrumah and other West Africans, the pan-Africanist ideology stressed that the conditions of colonial oppression and underdevelopment which unified Africans far outweighed the inherited differences of the traditional and colonial past. It was assumed that the objective of achieving independence was a continental goal, and therefore Africans should seek to achieve their post-independence objectives within a continental framework of nationalism. Thus, any steps which divided Africans into smaller political units based upon irredentist or secessionist claims were to be resisted. It was further assumed that interethnic and interreligious conflicts which loomed significantly within the politics of a small state would be reduced in importance once those conflicts were translated to the arena of a larger political community. In the latter circumstances, the chances of one ethnic group or a coalition of ethnic groups dominating affairs within the larger community would be diminished. The expanded pan-African state, it was argued, would better combine the natural resources and the labor force of the smaller territories, thereby providing a broader base for economic development. With the larger economic benefits derived from political unity, the linking of ethnic and economic rivalries would also be reduced. Not only would the larger pan-African state wield more influence in international affairs but it would be better prepared than a Balkanized Africa to resist the reimposition of some new form of colonial rule.

Although the Organization of African Unity has brought the leadership of the continent together for discussion of mutual problems—particularly regarding the continuing issues of Southern African liberation—it is a far cry from Kwame Nkrumah's vision of a "United States of Africa." Regional economic associations, moreover, have often remained stillborn, with further cooperation coming to a halt even before the ink has dried on the treaty of cooperation. Regional groupings such as the fifteen states in ECOWAS (Economic Cooperation Among West African States) have suffered from the absence of complementarity in production and the preponderance of competition among the members for a place in already glutted world agriculture markets. One of the great disappointments with respect to regional cooperation was the dissolution of the East African Common Market, which had sought to build upon the structures of cooperation forged by the British and fully integrate the economies of Tanzania, Uganda, and Kenya. Reluctant to accept Julius Nyerere's offer to delay Tanganyika's independence in 1961 until the three territories could achieve independence jointly as a single state, the Ugandan and Kenyan leaders did agree to extend the previous base of cooperation laid by the three British colonial administrations beyond the areas of customs, post and communications, transport, higher education, medical research, and a number of other fields. But ideological differences, the significant advantages that Keyna enjoyed relative to its two partners, and other factors soon undermined even the limited cooperation achieved under colonial rule. Ultimately the Common Market was dismantled and its properties crudely distributed among the three partners. The climate of hostility was such that the border between Tanzania and Kenya remained closed for close to a decade.[38] Although other efforts at cooperation in West Africa and Southern Africa may succeed where the East African Common Market failed, the results at this writing are still only tentative.

More modest efforts leading to the actual political integration of neighboring territories have been few in number and often ephemeral at best. Most of these cases of amalgamation actually occurred prior to independence, such as the unification of British and Italian Somaliland, the union of British Togoland with Ghana, and the division of British Cameroon, with the Muslim north being joined to Nigeria and the south uniting with French Cameroon. One further effort at a pre-independence agreement to integrate—the case of Senegal and Mali—fell apart within two months of the June 1960 independence. The solitary clear-cut instance of post-independence political integration came in 1964, with the union of Tanganyika and Zanzibar. After close to two decades, however, Tanzania remains an incomplete case of political, military, and diplomatic integration. There is still optimism regarding the proclaimed union of Senegal and Gambia, but as the 1981 Senegalese rescue of the Gambian elite in the face of a police coup fades into history, so does enthusiasm for the idea of fusion. It is apparent that despite the economic opportunities offered by territorial amalgamation, African leaders are reluctant to make the personal, institutional, and economic sacrifices which political integration entails.

OVERARCHING INTEGRATIVE STRATEGY. This strategy of nation-building, associated with the efforts of Julius Nyerere and other party leaders in Tanzania, seeks to evolve a national culture and set of institutions that are African in character and yet not identified with any of the 120 or more ethnic groups which were represented in the Tanzanian population at the time of independence. This strategy attempts to include all residents under a single national umbrella. Nyerere, for example, wanted to avoid two undesirable alternatives insofar as national language policy was concerned. The utilization of one or more of the major indigenous languages in education, government, and commerce was simply out of the question. Even with limiting consolidation to the ten major languages spoken in Tanzania, government programs would not reach over half the population. The costs involved, moreover, in the reproduction of textbooks, laws, newspapers, and other items in a multiplicity of languages were staggering to an already impoverished country. His second option, using English, had far too many emotional drawbacks associated with it since it implied a continuation of the colonial mentality. Hence, Nyerere hit upon Swahili—a language which was African in origin, was not associated with any particular ethnic group, and which had become the lingua franca of government, commerce, the schools, missions, and other structures under Arab, German and British colonial rule. Time, it was felt, had eradicated most of Swahili's association with the Arab slave caravans of the period preceding colonial rule. Although the experiment in a single language policy has not been without costs, it has been a significant element in forging Tanzanian national unity.

In addition to avoiding giving a cultural advantage to any one ethnic group, the Tanzanian government programs attempt to redress historic imbalances which have led to one area or ethnic group having advantages over its neighbors in terms of exposure to Western education or to government and private funding of economic development. Thus, Nyerere's policy of "betting on the weak" finds previously neglected ethnic groups such as the Ha and Gogo receiving a disproportionate amount of attention while the once-favored Chagga area of Kilimanjaro experiences reductions in government funding for education and agriculture. The government program of villagization has been applied uniformly throughout the country rather than focusing only on those areas where success might be achieved quickly.

A further aspect of the overarching integrative strategy has been the creation of a series of national institutions which are not related specifically to the political institution of any given ethnic grouping and which embody many of the assumed common denominator characteristics of Tanzanian traditional

societies. Before that could be accomplished, the particularistic ethnic institutions had to be suppressed. Hence, one of the earliest moves involved the
abolition of traditional chieftainship, with the chiefs being replaced by administrators who were primarily responsible to the central government and
the party rather than to the local sources of legitimacy. Furthermore, preceding the move toward a single-party state, political parties based upon
membership in a single ethnic group, such as the Chagga Union and the
Sukuma Union, were banned. The secularization of politics, moreover, led
to the proscription on parties based upon religion, thereby separating the
affairs of any religious structure from the state. The state further assumed
greater responsibility for education, reducing the role both of the Christian
missions and the Koranic teachers. In this way, Tanzania has thus far avoided
the kind of Islamic schism that has challenged secular authority in Nigeria
and situations such as that in Uganda where the Democratic Party was closely
identified with the Roman Catholic Church.

To displace the conflicting loyalties based upon ethnic group affiliation
and orientation toward a traditional set of rulers, Nyerere has attempted to
discourage any reference in public dialogue to ethnic membership. Even
the census enumeration in Tanzania has dropped any reference to "tribe"
in accumulating planning data. Administrative and electoral districts no
longer adhere strictly to ethnic boundaries, and central government administrators are scrupulously rotated and appointed to districts away from their
home areas.

Unlike most efforts elsewhere in Africa the Revolutionary Party (*Chama
Cha Mapinduzi*, the former Tanzania African National Union) has been able
to achieve its objective of becoming a mass based party capable of with-
standing the challenge of the military. Unlike other parties which have limited their impact to a small urban elite, the Revolutionary Party in Tanzania
is organized in a pyramidal fashion from the president on down to the residents of every rural hamlet. Each citizen is organized into a ten-family cell,
which is the building block of the rural *ujamaa* (family togetherness) villages,
the latter become the terminal points in a two-way communication system
linking the rural citizen with the central committee. In theory—and often
in practice—policies are formulated at the top of the pyramid and com-
municated on down to the *ujamaa* village, whereas criticism of the policies
and suggestions for improvements flow upward from the grass roots. Emulating the manner in which decisions were made in traditional society, the
end of debate is not a division of the house into "yeas" and "nays" but rather
the achievement of broad consensus. With respect to the national legislature,
the courts, the army, labor unions, and other major structures in Tanzanian
society today, legitimacy is based upon the relationship of these structures
to the dominant party and upon their responsiveness to party directives.

A considerable investment in social engineering in Tanzania attempts to
orient the heterogeneous Tanzanian citizenry to "common" national symbols.

The charisma of Nyerere himself was a unifying symbol, but it went beyond that. The Maji Maji Rebellion of 1905 is presented as the First Phase in the Struggle for Tanzanian Independence (despite the fact that it only affected those ethnic groups in southeastern Tanzania and had no historic linkages with the movement that Nyerere headed from 1954 onward). Saba Saba (Seven Seven) Day, the Seventh of July, has become the national holiday, commemorating the founding of TANU, the predominant party. The new capital at Dodoma in central Tanzania also is relevant, signaling a break with the colonial mentality which oriented economic development externally to Europe rather than internally to Tanzania itself.

The success of the Nyerere strategy is evidenced by the fact that—aside from the abortive mutiny in 1964 and a reported coup attempt in 1983—there has been no serious challenge posed by the military to civilian rule. There has, moreover, been no serious ethnic-based challenge to party leadership even though the blanket implementation of the villagization program has affected some groups more adversely than others. Despite the continuation of many economic and ideological problems and of the conditions of poverty, aggravated by the severe drought from 1980 through 1983, Julius Nyerere remains one of the most respected African leaders both at home and throughout the continent.

PLURALIST ACCOMMODATION STRATEGY. The overarching integrative strategy cannot be employed easily where leaders of one or more large ethnic groups have tended to dominate the politics of the new state; where the traditional leadership of one or more of those groups is well entrenched; or where the national structures are extremely weak, relative to the authority of the more localized cadre of elites. Milton Obote seemed never to have learned this lesson during his two attempts to govern Uganda. Nor was this situation appreciated by other leaders, such as General Ironsi of Nigeria during his brief tenure as military leader of that country following the January 1966 military coup. Ironsi sought to overcome the ethnic-based political impasse that had immobilized Nigerian national politics under the First Republic by creating a strong centralized political system which would have weakened all political units intervening between the citizen and the national state. Since there was no truly national elite—either civilian or military— that could establish its legitimacy in the months following the coup, the centralization of authority was quickly perceived by other groups as an attempt by the Igbo associates of General Ironsi to consolidate their hold on the Nigerian state. This was especially the attitude of the traditional Hausa-Fulani leadership in the north as well as among the Hausa officers in the military who saw Igbos being advanced in rank considerably more rapidly than the members of other ethnic groups. It was this situation which brought about the second coup, led by General Yakubu Gowon from the Middle Belt.

The strategy of General Gowon as well as that of Gowon's successors,

Murtala Muhammed and Olusegun Obasanjo, was one which I label the pluralist accommodation strategy.[39] This nation-building approach attempts to avoid frontal assaults both on ethnic membership and on the traditional prerogatives of ethnic based leaders, and attempts to give positive recognition to the benefits of cultural diversity within a heterogeneous national society. In Nigeria this applies even to the once rebellious Igbo, who were accorded a policy of reconciliation under the military regimes of Gowon and his successors. The ultimate symbolism of this policy was the decision of President Shehu Shagari during the Second Republic to permit former General C. Odumegwu Ojukwu, the military leader of Biafra during the civil war, to return from exile in 1982 and run for political office in the 1983 elections. Instead of consolidating power at the central level, an imaginatively devised federal system distributed some functions of government to the federal states while retaining foreign affairs, defense, and economic planning as national responsibilities. These federal states—twelve in number originally, later raised to nineteen—do not rigidly follow ethnic lines. Instead, the major ethnic groups are divided among several states in order to dilute the threat that they potentially pose to federal authority (four Yoruba, two Igbo, and four Hausa), whereas the smaller ethnic groups that are lumped together in the several other states have the opportunity of making some impact upon politics in the more localized state arena. The electoral system under the Second Republic attempted to reduce ethnicity as a major factor in politics by recognizing only those parties for both national and state elections that had a broad national base. The electoral formula for the presidency, furthermore, required that the successful candidate receive not only a plurality but 25 percent of the vote in two-thirds of the states. Although parties and elections have been set aside since the military reintervened late in 1983, many of the functions of government about which people feel the strongest, such as education and roads, are still delegated to the states, and the state bureaucracies continue to function. In addition to some local tax authority, the states are given a portion of the oil revenues. The latter was a significant contribution of the Gowon government in overcoming one of the root causes of the Biafran War. One of the immediate causes of the war had been the Igbo assertion that they should enjoy disproportionate benefits from the oil industry since it was largely located in their region of the country. Finding an equitable formula and then having both the military and civilian governments distribute the funds fairly has been significant in making Nigerian federalism work. Each state thus has the means to emphasize those aspects of life which are most important to its citizens. This includes the creation of a major national university within each state. The difficulty, however, is that the subsequent oil glut and consequent drop in the price of Nigerian crude oil have threatened the ability of the national government to continue to placate economically the disparate ethnic groups within Nigeria. Finally, the location of a new federal capital at Abuja was to be a significant unifying symbol. Abuja is in the center of the country, and just as importantly it is not located within the territory of any of the three major ethnic groups.

Given the transition from military to civilian rule and then back to the post–1984 military government, it may still be too early to pass final judgment on the success of the Nigerian pluralist accommodation strategy of nation-building. It must be acknowledged that it took thirteen years for the military to establish popular confidence in its efforts. Certainly, having oil revenues to distribute among the states has made it possible for both the national and the local levels of government to engage in positive programs in the fields of education, health, road building, and other areas which have reduced the level of dissatisfaction with the national government. In effect, oil bought the national government essential time to put the new federal system into effect.

STATIC TENSION STRATEGY. This strategy is a pragmatic recognition of the fact that the conflict among leaders of two or more major ethnic or racial groups in a heterogeneous state may delay the development of strong national loyalties and meaningful national institutions. On the assumption that over time positive nationalist attitudes will emerge, the governing leadership at the state level concentrates on rapid economic development—with the benefits of prosperity being widely distributed among both old and new economic groupings—as a calculated strategy to reduce tension among the dominant competitors. Moreover, the governing elite avoids making a firm commitment on language policy or other cultural matters that would favor one ethnic group over another. This was the unsuccessful strategy employed in Nigeria during the First Republic (1960–1966) in an effort to balance off the conflicts among the three largest ethnic groups: Yoruba, Igbo, and Hausa-Fulani. It has appeared to be more successfully implemented, however, in Kenya, where the competition among leaders of two of the largest ethnic groups, the Kikuyu and the Luo, was manifested in political party organization, economic development, education at all levels, and other arenas. These were the two groups that had the greatest exposure to Western education during the colonial era and that have reaped the greatest benefits from economic modernization. The tension between the two groups was kept within bounds during the colonial era and during the tenure of Jomo Kenyatta as president. Kenyatta's charisma as the primary hero of *national* liberation more than offset the distinct advantage which the Kikuyus enjoyed through their control of the presidency. A crude balance was maintained in terms of distribution of major offices among these two ethnic groups as well as other groups that were beginning to assert their claims to national office. The fortuitous succession of Daniel arop Moi, a Kallenjin, upon the death of Kenyatta, once again kept the interethnic conflict within bounds even though some leading Kikuyu politicians have asserted that the office of president should be in the hands of Kenya's largest ethnic group.

DOMINANT ETHNIC STRATEGY. Under this strategy the leaders of one ethnic group that has historically or by sheer weight of numbers dominated politics during the traditional, colonial, or liberation period assert a claim to continue to do so after independence. Through their monopoly over the instruments of coercion, their control over the major economic resources, and other manifestations of power, the leaders of the dominant ethnic group define national culture and goals in terms of their own value system and standards. For external considerations or to avoid frontal resistance on the part of minority ethnic groups, some concessions may be made to local autonomy or to token representation of minorities in national institutions. In the long run, however, the cultural norms of the dominant ethnic group are intended to prevail. Obviously the dominant ethnic strategy is one that has obtained in those few cases, such as Somalia, Swaziland, Lesotho, and Botswana, where the overwhelming majority of the citizens are members of one ethnic group even though clan, regional, and other divisions persist. Among the Somali, for example, while intra-clan rivalry persists, there is little disagreement over language, religion, folklore, economic priorities, and interpretation of major historic events. In Swaziland and Lesotho, the institution of the monarchy is a further validating symbol which unites the overwhelming majority of these respective kingdoms.

The dominant ethnic strategy is also the one that persisted over an extended period in the two African states that had enjoyed international recognition as independent members of the global community: Ethiopia and Liberia. In Ethiopia, the extension of control by the Amharic-speaking people over the neighboring ethnic groups took place simultaneously with the European partition of Africa. The success of Emperor Menelik II in fending off Italian designs in the 1890s resulted in the triumph of a political system based on the monarchy and military overlords, the feudal land system, the paramountcy of the Ethiopic Christian Church, the Amharic language, and other Amharic values and institutions. Amhara dominated the Somali, Oromo, Tigre, and other subordinated ethnic groups included within the empire. The restoration of the monarchy at the end of the Second World War ended the brief Italian occupation, and the peace settlement also resulted in the ceding of Eritrea to Ethiopia. Although the federal arrangement with Eritrea was supposed to guarantee local autonomy for the basically Muslim population, all pretense was abandoned in 1960 and Emperor Haile Selassie vigorously pursued a dominant ethnic strategy in attempting to deal with the festering dissidence in Eritrea. Similar resistance was presented by the Somali, the Oromo, and the Tigre people. The military coup of 1974, as well as the four civil wars which the central government has had to fight simultaneously, is evidence of the failure of the dominant ethnic strategy.

A similar stratification prevailed in Liberia from its founding as a refuge for freed persons of color in the 1820s until the military coup of 1980. The Americo-Liberian minority imposed its norms and institutions upon the members of the sixteen or more indigenous ethnic groups.[40] The political system was based on a Liberian version of English, Christianity, the American family system, and the political and economic institutions which the Americo-Liberians themselves had only observed from the sidelines in pre–Civil War America. A major status reversal has taken place since 1980: the soldiers and noncommissioned officers who carried out the coup were from the ethnic groups least exposed to Western education and institutions.

Other examples of the dominant ethnic strategy of nation-building abound. This includes the case of the Sudan, mentioned previously, as well as several abortive efforts, including the claim to supremacy made by the Ganda (Baganda) over their ethnic colleagues in Uganda and the ancient Arab domination over the Africans on Zanzibar which came to a bloody demise a month after the January 1964 independence of the sultanate. It also includes several examples in which the political domination by one group is more apparent than are the efforts to impose the cultural norms of that group upon the national society. Examples of the latter would include the Baule domination of politics in the Ivory Coast and the ascendancy of the Shona majority in the political system of Zimbabwe.

SELECTIVE ISOLATION OR EXCLUSION STRATEGY. Typically this is not a solitary strategy of nation-building, but one which supplements the primary strategy. It is applied against a group or groups which the dominant elite regard as incapable of integration into the national system because of radical differences in lifestyle, the persistence of violent interaction between the dominant and subordinate groupings, the external orientation of the latter, or some other factor. It may be a temporary or a long-term strategy depending upon the strength or weakness of the factors involved. A classic case (outside Africa, of course) is the American treatment of "Indians not taxed," who are assigned to reservations and are only to a limited extent involved in the national political system.

While this is normally a strategy applied to a minority ethnic community, it is the policy pursued by the minority Afrikaners of the Republic of South Africa against the Black majority. The former since 1948 have sought to establish a dominant Afrikanerdom nationalism that integrates the English-speaking sector of the white dominant minority while compartmentalizing and isolating the non-white majority from full participation in the national political and economic systems. Since this will be dealt with in Chapter 4, the South African case will only be noted here in passing.

Insofar as Black Africa is concerned, the most significant applications of the isolation strategy have occurred with respect to the pygmoid peoples of Botswana, Zaire, and other areas. Few efforts have been made to incorporate these minorities into the national political system or to require that their lifestyles, which are adapted to survival in rigorous physical environments, be altered in order to adjust to national plans for economic development.

Similar policies of selective isolation are pursued in many West African states with respect to pastoral nomads—especially those who cross international boundaries on an annual basis between Nigeria and Niger or between Burkina Faso and Mali.

Another general application of the isolation strategy comes with respect to the relegation of "alien Africans" to *zongoes*, or stranger quarters in trading centers of West Africa. In many cases residence in a zongo is a matter of individual choice, but in the past itinerant merchants and other migrants were obliged to reside in these quarters while engaging in their activities. Residents of a zongo were occasionally permitted to elect their own headmen and magistrates. In other instances leaders were appointed by the dominant political leader of the larger city. Even though the strangers rendered a necessary service which was not provided by the indigenous resident, the strangers became in most instances a despised pariah group.

Finally, there is the exclusionary treatment of migrant workers in many countries which results in many long-time immigrants being denied full participation in the politics of the society in which they reside. The seasonal laborers who migrate from Burkina Faso to the Ivory Coast and are a vital element in the economic success of the latter country represent a case in point.

SELECTIVE EXPULSION STRATEGY. The selective expulsion strategy is in many cases a more radical version of the preceding approach to nation-building. It consists of the targeting of "alien Africans" and other religious, ethnic, or social groups who are patently rejected or themselves refuse to accommodate to a dominant ethnic strategy of nation-building. The most extreme manifestation of this strategy is the physical extermination of the rejected minority. At the global level, the treatment of the Jews in Nazi Germany is the epitome of this extreme, but the physical harassment of the Cherokee and other Indian groups in the United States fits into the same genre even though the magnitude of the mistreatment was not of the same proportions. For Africa this extreme manifestation of the expulsion strategy in the post-independence era is exemplified by the situation in the two East African states of Rwanda and Burundi. As previously noted, both were examples of traditional societies in which there were sharp caste stratifications based upon differences in physical type, which was reinforced by an unequal distribution of the means of coercion, of ownership of wealth, and other indices of political, religious, social, and economic power. The relationship between the two major caste groups altered considerably during the colonial era, partly as a consequence of the involvement of Hutu in migratory labor experiences to other territories and the achievement of education, economic, and other benefits by the Hutu under Belgian colonial rule. Thus, in terms of modernization, the social advantages of the Tusi had considerably diminished. Shortly before independence the Hutu of Rwanda rose up against the privileged Tusi ruling caste and either killed or forced into exile an estimated 200,000 Tusi, roughly a third of the upper caste group.[41]

In neighboring Burundi the Tusi (who constituted roughly 16 percent of the population) in 1972 undertook what some regarded as preventive action, ruthlessly rounded up the leaders of the Hutu political organization, and carried out a massacre. Estimates of the numbers killed or forced to flee the country range from 15,000 to 150,000.[42] Subsequently, President Jean-Baptiste Bagaza, who as a lieutenant colonel and chief of staff led a military coup against the monarchy in 1976, has been attempting to bridge the gap separating the Tusi and Hutu. It is apparent that Bagaza, who is himself a Tusi, has only partially succeeded in his efforts to encourage the exiles to return from Tanzania, Zaire, and other neighboring states. Despite the removal of an odious head tax and the reform of the land tenure system which had given the Hutu ownership of the land they cultivate, the preponderance of military, political, and economic power still resides largely in the hands of the Tusi minority caste.

Rwanda and Burundi are not the only African examples of this extreme version of the expulsion strategy. The rising of the Afro-Shirzai majority in Zanzibar against the ruling Arab minority in 1964 was an earlier case of determining the definition of national membership by violent means. Similarly, in the Ogaden area of Ethiopia, once the Somali invading forces had been pushed back to the Somali border in 1977, the Ethiopian government has attempted to force the original inhabitants to seek refuge across the border. New non-Somali settlers have been brought into the area in order to find a "permanent" solution to the Somali irredentist claims.

The most routine application of the expulsion strategy has occurred when the political leadership—acting on its own initiative or in response to mob hostility—attempts to single out a pariah group as the source of economic failure or other problems within the society. West Africa has a long history of resorting to this strategy. Examples would be the expulsion of Guineans from Senegal in 1967, the Cameroonian action against the Igbo at the onset of the Biafran War in 1967, the forcible evacuation of Fanti fishermen from Sierra Leone in 1968, and the general hostility throughout Francophone African countries toward the Dahomeans (citizens of Benin), many of whom had been employed by the French in the administration of their West African territories.

Considering the role that Ghana's Kwame Nkrumah played in advancing the pan-African strategy of nation-building, it is ironic that the first systematic effort to legislate against "alien" Africans should have occurred in Ghana. During the Second Republic under President Kofi Busia, the Alien Compliance Order of 1969 was broadly applied to both recent and long-term migrants to Ghana from other West African states. The primary targets of the Order, which resulted in the expulsion of thousands of "aliens" and the confiscation of their properties, were the Nigerians who had fled to Ghana during the Nigerian civil war.[43]

In terms of sheer numbers involved, however, it was the actions in January 1983 of the Nigerian government during the administration of President Shehu Shagari that remain unprecedented. Virtually all alien Africans in Nigeria who lacked the proper immigration papers were put on notice to depart from the country within two weeks. The human tragedy, the forfeiture of property, and the strain that was placed upon transport and communications in repatriating the immigrants to Ghana and other countries was unquestionably a low point in terms of Nigeria's relations with its neighbors. Ironically, to that point Nigeria had been the primary advocate for the adoption by ECOWAS of reduced restraints on the flow of labor and trade among the fifteen states in the West African association. Many of those expelled from Nigeria had actually been encouraged to come during the period of the oil boom when Nigeria was experiencing dramatic economic growth. With the recession accompanying the drop in oil prices, the illegal immigrants became a convenient scapegoat for Nigeria's economic difficulties.

IRREDENTIST STRATEGY. The final strategy to be analyzed is one which few African nationalist leaders openly espouse, yet in many respects it is a latent source of crisis in many areas of the continent. The irredentist strategy seeks the reintegration into the historic "nation" of all people and territory currently under foreign rule. Irredentism is the polar opposite of the pan-Africanist position since it rejects the assumption that the mere accident of geographic location on the continent automatically establishes a natural sense of political community among all Africans. Advocates of irredentism do not necessarily reject the principles of the OAU Charter on this issue; they do reject the specific application of those principles to the cause they are advancing. Those principles of the OAU Charter are contained in Article II, Section 3, which pledges African leaders to adhere to the principle of "respect for the sovereignty and territorial integrity of each State and for its inalienable right to independent existence." The clause was further elaborated in the July 1964 resolution adopted by the OAU heads of state in Cairo. That resolution declares that "the borders of African States, on the day of their independence, constitute an intangible reality . . . . "

Thus, advocates of a specific irredentism devote their energies to the resuscitation and revitalization of a particular ethnic community which has its origins in the pre-colonial past. Instead of accepting without question the validity of the arbitrary geographic boundaries established during the colonial era, it seeks a major readjustment in those boundaries so that they coincide roughly with the boundaries of the traditional political community. Since this in-gathering of the particular "national" community into one political community conflicts with the geographic authority of leaders of neighboring countries, it does damage to harmonious relations among the countries involved where it does not actually lead to the shedding of blood in behalf of the irredentist objective.

One of the earliest manifestations of this position to achieve international attention never came to fruition. The Ewe people of West Africa demanded during the pre-independence era that they be incorporated within a single political community. The Ewe during the nineteenth century had been divided among German Togoland, British Gold Coast (Ghana), and French Dahomey at the end of the last century, and they were further divided when German Togoland was split into two Mandate (later Trusteeship) Territories, with the British and French bearing separate responsibilities for administration. Taking advantage of the mechanisms for petitioning under the U.N. Trusteeship System, a number of Ewe leaders had requested that a united Eweland be established prior to the achievement of independence by the two Togolands and Ghana. There was much jockeying back and forth, not only between the British and French Trust Authorities but also between the Ewe leaders and the Ghanaians under Nkrumah who sought to have the whole of Togoland annexed to the soon-to-be independent state of Ghana. This, Nkrumah argued, would not only achieve the objective of uniting most of the Ewe people within a single political community but would also constitute one further step in the direction of pan-African political unity. Ultimately, however, a U.N.-sponsored plebiscite led to the separate independence of French Togoland as the Togo Republic and the integration of British Togoland into the independent state of Ghana.

The one irredentist strategy that has in part succeeded but has also constituted one of the most destabilizing situations in post-independence Africa is the one pursued by Somali leaders. The Somali people lacked a centralized traditional political system, but the bonds based upon language, religion, and family, as well as a common economy, support the Somali claim to being a "nation" prior to the alien occupation in the nineteenth century. At that time their people and territory were divided among four European dependencies and the Empire of Ethiopia. The five-pointed star on the Somali flag is a constant reminder of the five remnants of the Somali nation. Two of those segments have been "brought home" through the arrangement in 1960 which permitted the Italian Trust territory and British Somaliland to become independent at the same time as a united country. Although the Somali claim on the former French colony, Djibouti, has been a tenuous one (given the mixed character of its population), efforts with respect to the other two irredentist segments have persisted. The designs on the Somali area of northeast Kenya have been carried out only intermittently and at a fairly low level during the past twenty-five years. Kenya and Somali have, however, reached an accommodation. Although the reconciliation with Kenya in the mid-1960s did not abandon Somali claims to northeast Kenya, the two countries in effect "agreed to disagree" over the ownership of the territory. No such attitude, however, has emerged with respect to the Ogaden province of Ethiopia. There the Somali both directly and through the Western Somali Liberation Front have attempted by force of arms to "liberate" the area from Ethiopian imperial control. The invasion of the Ogaden by Somali *shiftas* and subsequently by the regular Somali army not only presented a crisis for the two countries concerned and for the Organization of African Unity, but it intensified external intervention in African affairs. The Soviet Union and Cuba came to the assistance of their new Ethiopian client and drove the Somali back to the international boundary. It was not until they had reached that point that the United States agreed to provide military and other forms of assistance to its new ally, Somalia. Significantly, the OAU solidly rebuffed Somalia's actions in attempting unilaterally to alter the colonial boundaries by resort to violence.

Another complex case which has had continent-wide ramifications was, curiously enough, one which had the agreement of the leaders of the central government in the two countries concerned. This was the offer in June 1982 of the South African government to accede to the Kingdom of Swaziland's long-standing claim to the areas of northeastern South Africa where the Swazi constitute a majority of the residents. The cession of the KaNgwana Homeland and the Ngwavuma district of KwaZulu Homeland was openly acknowledged as an effort to provide a buffer for the rest of South Africa against the African National Congress freedom fighters who were infiltrating down from their sanctuaries in Mozambique. The residents of the areas affected, who had not been consulted about the switch in sovereignty, were not the only ones who voiced strong objections to the proposal. A broad spectrum of white and Black opinion within South Africa was for widely different reasons hostile to the dismemberment of the Republic of South Africa no matter how valid the historic claim of the Swazi kingdom may have been. Throughout the rest of Africa as well, the cession of territory before the African majority within the Republic had had the opportunity of making that decision for themselves was regarded as a violation of the OAU Charter. Several things ultimately led the South African government to abandon its proposal. The first was the South African Supreme Court decision that declared the action unconstitutional. More important, however, the Nkomati Accord of 1984, which forced the Mozambique government to terminate its support for ANC dissidents, made the establishment of a buffer territory no longer necessary.

Given the arbitrary nature of the geographic boundaries, it is not unlikely that other irredentist claims will be advanced in the future.

The conceptualization of at least eight relatively distinct strategies of nation-building reflects the complexity of the political task facing the present leadership of the more than forty-five states in sub-Saharan Africa. The ethnic, linguistic, religious, racial, and other forms of diversity with which they must contend is certainly more complicated than that faced by earlier nation-builders in Europe and North and South America. Commitment to the existing boundaries as the arena within which national loyalties are to be established requires heroic effort in "squaring the circle" of conflicting traditional symbols and contradictory guides for action in the pursuit of economic, social, and political development. The historic accidents by which certain peoples were included and others excluded from a colonial dependency, and by which one leadership group inherited the reins of power at independence, give a continuing reality to the colonial legacy. In societies with limited resources for coping with the problems of illiteracy, disease, and poverty in general an inordinate amount of human energies and physical resources must be allocated just to keep the national society from disintegration.

Emphasis on the crisis aspects of nation-building, of course, runs the risk of overlooking the way that African leadership groups are successfully coping with the task of nation-building. With the passage of time people are indeed coming to regard themselves as Tanzanians, Cameroonians, or Zimbabweans. Rationalization of language policies is beginning to have its impact on the successful functioning of educational, commercial, legal, and other institutions in society. However arbitrary their national boundaries, Nigerians, for example, are coming to interact more significantly in economic terms with each other than they are with residents of other African countries.

It would be naive, however, as well as doing a disservice to Africans, to gloss over the high cost that nation-building will continue to exact in terms of denial of liberties, erosion of previous cultural values, disruption of ancient familial and other bonds of affection, and human life itself. Even if the violence associated with nation-building were limited in its impact to the residents of a given state, it would be sufficient to elicit the concern of the broader continental or global community. Unfortunately the coercive aspects of nation-building invariably not only involve the immediate neighbors of the affected state, but also invite intervention by non-African blocs and superpowers. This broader involvement once more places Africans at risk of having their destinies shaped by external forces and actors.

IV

SOUTH AFRICA
Apartheid and the Clash of Nationalisms

The term *apartheid* has already earned its proper place in the lexicon of twentieth-century hate words alongside *Holocaust, genocide, lynch mob,* and other terms associated with racial and ethnic intolerance and with totalitarian dictatorship. The South African policy of racial discrimination has systematically enhanced the interests of the white minority at the expense of the Blacks, Asians, and Coloureds—as persons of mixed racial origin are called. Apartheid has created a tragedy of classic Greek dimensions which most directly, of course, affects the day-to-day lives of South Africa's 20 million Blacks as they struggle to come into control of their own lives. Apartheid legislation regulates along racial lines whom persons may marry, where they may live, what kind of jobs they may hold, how freely they may travel about their own country, and how they relate to fellow nationals in religious, political, and social terms. The anomalies of apartheid were well demonstrated in 1985 when Bishop Desmond Tutu, the recipient of the Nobel Prize, was elected as the first Black bishop of the multiracial Anglican Diocese of Johannesburg. In order to attend his investiture, he had to apply to the government for permission to travel to the white-designated area where the cathedral was located. In less dramatic but more persistent ways, the doctrine of white supremacy has placed a rigid ceiling on the ability of those who are not Europeans to realize the full potential of their talents and aspirations, and it has created a twisted social myth which ignores the substantial contribution of the Black majority in particular to making South Africa the most economically advanced state on the African continent. Ironically, apartheid has also become a tragedy for those well-meaning members of the English-speaking and Afrikaner minority of 4.5 million who find themselves physically and psychologically isolated from the civilized standards of the rest of the world community. These whites have increasingly become prisoners of the very political monster they have created—denied the opportunity of making their own full contribution to the development of South Africa and the rest of the continent.

The policy of apartheid is not limited in its impact to South Africa; it has ramifications far beyond its borders. The nine independent Black states to the north of South Africa, for example, find their efforts to realize the economic potential of political liberation from European colonial rule being frustrated at every turn.[1] The geographic and historic legacy which has effectively given South African whites a stranglehold over the course of economic development in the countries to the north has been further complicated by the calculated South African destabilization of the entire southern region through diplomatic, economic, and military action.

Since the founding of the United Nations in 1945–46, the racial policies of South Africa have remained a permanent action item on the agenda of the General Assembly, and the global implications have become dramatically complex. The persistence of apartheid pits West European states against Black independent countries, developed countries against the less developed, capitalist against socialist proponents of development in the Third World, and the Eastern bloc against the West. It has exacerbated, moreover, the international schisms within both the Western democratic and the Marxist blocs of countries. For American policy makers in particular, the actions and the rhetoric of our executive and legislative officials with respect to South Africa have increasingly become critical litmus tests whereby African leaders and others have come to judge American politics and intentions with respect to the entire African continent.

From the perspective of most African leaders outside the Republic as well as of many leaders of the 20 million Black South Africans within,[2] the struggle against apartheid and the closely related question of Namibian independence constitute the third and final wave in the dramatic termination of white supremacy in Africa. The third wave, however, differs substantially from the first wave, which achieved its zenith during the decade of the 1960s and witnessed the steady procession of African states throwing off the yokes of British, French, Belgian, and Italian colonial rule and becoming a substantial voting bloc in the United Nations. Although the 1952–56 rebellion in Kenya (popularly referred to as "Mau Mau") constituted an obvious exception, the transition to independence during the first wave was widely characterized by the orderly and even friendly passing of the reins of authority from white to Black hands. It was a common-sense acceptance by European political leaders of Prime Minister Harold Macmillan's prophecy about the nationalist "winds of change" blowing through the continent. Albeit reluctantly in many instances, Europeans realized that it was no longer possible or profitable to continue to oppose African nationalist aspirations. Socialist and other opponents to colonialism within the European states themselves as well as pressures from the United States, the Soviet Union, and Arab and Latin American states had systematically convinced the European governments to accept the inevitable.

In contrast to the first wave, the second wave of African liberation was marked by the acceptance of armed confrontation as the ultimate instrument available to African nationalists. It was indispensable in dislodging the small but determined settler minority from its enjoyment of near political and economic monopoly in Zimbabwe, Angola, Mozambique, Namibia, and Guinea-Bissau. With respect to all but the last named, South Africa regarded the neighboring settler territories as part of the southern "white redoubt." During the 1960s and 1970s, the apartheid regime provided economic as well as military support in helping the Portuguese and the white Rhodesians to resist African liberation. Namibia, of course, was defended directly as South Africa's colonial responsibility. The period since 1960 has become one of conflict marked not only by extended guerrilla warfare, with the attendant loss of countless African and European lives, but also by the overt and covert involvement of the superpowers in Southern Africa. Ultimately, however, independence did come to Angola and Mozambique in 1975 and to Zimbabwe in 1980. The second wave still has not fully run its course, inasmuch as the decade-old liberation struggle still continues in Namibia; it blends into the third wave, the liberation of South Africa itself. In contrast to the remoteness of the independence movement in the 1960s, the South African government now finds itself confronted on its broad northern borders by countries whose leaders are militantly opposed to the continuation of the doctrine of white supremacy in Africa.

The third wave of African liberation appears destined to be more violent in its ultimate resolution than the preceding waves. More ominously, it threatens to be a protracted struggle which will undoubtedly invite the direct and active involvement of the world's superpowers. The size of the European minority in South Africa and in its colony, Namibia, is only one of the factors differentiating the third from the second wave of African liberation. Whites number 17 percent in South Africa and 11 percent in Namibia, as opposed to roughly 5 percent in Rhodesia-Zimbabwe and fewer than one percent in Angola and Mozambique. It is the entrenched nature of the South African white minority, however, that complicates the issue of majority rule. Unlike the Portuguese in Angola and Mozambique and the white settlers in Rhodesia, the dominant Afrikaner element within the South African white minority (60 percent, by most estimates) has no residual homeland to which it can retreat. They long ago burned the colonial and emotional bridges which linked them to Europe as a consequence of the 1652 Dutch settling in Cape Town and the later arrival of French Huguenots. If anything, the present Dutch government is one of the most vocal critics of apartheid. Most white South Africans—both Afrikaners and English-speaking—are not only determined to stay in what they regard as their home, but they have the means to resist any alteration in their situation for a considerable period. Numbers alone, as Table 7 indicates, do not tell the whole story. The earnings from the development of the mineral wealth of the southern region have given the minority whites the ability to create an industrial economy which is second to none in Africa. It has not only underwritten the privileged style

TABLE 7
Population of the Republic of South Africa, by Race

Racial Group	1911	Percentage	1980	Percentage
African (Blacks)	4,019,000	67.3	19,555,000	71.9
European (whites)	1,276,000	21.4	4,500,000	16.1
Coloured (mixed)	525,000	8.8	2,554,000	9.2
Asians	152,000	2.5	795,000	2.8

SOURCE: Leonard Thompson and Andrew Prior, *South African Politics*
(New Haven: Yale University Press, 1982), p. 35.

of life for Europeans or whites, but provided them with the means to purchase or actually manufacture the tanks, planes, and weaponry needed to
engage in protracted combat against both domestic and external threats to
the regime. Indeed, in a perverse way, concerted opposition both internally
and at the global level has brought forth the traditional Afrikaner response
of "circling the wagons" or *laager* whenever the citadel of Afrikanerdom is
threatened. Afrikaners take almost a masochist pride—as self-annointed children of God—in closing ranks against the "forces of error and evil" which
historically have confronted them.

In more analytical and objective terms, the conflict between whites and
other racial groups in South Africa can be viewed as a clash of nationalist
strategies. By contrast with the other racial groups, the strategy of the white
minority appears to be relatively cohesive and clearly demarcated on the
questions of ultimate goals and means. This can be said in spite of the 150
years of bad history between the descendants of the earlier Dutch, or Afrikaner, settlers and the later English-speaking element that began arriving
in the nineteenth century. Apartheid has managed to force the closure of
white ranks with respect to who ultimately controls decision-making over
social and economic change and regarding what groups are to be included,
partially included, or excluded from participation in national affairs. The
approaches to nation-building on the part of the Black, Coloured, and Asian
communities are, on the other hand, fragmented, diffuse, and in many instances internally contradictory. Divisions exist not only between the various
racial groups but within each community as well.

Enthusiasm for an overarching South African nationalism which would
transcend race and ethnic differences in the pursuit of secular modernization
is perhaps being given its last test. The earlier commitment of the African
National Congress (ANC), founded in 1912 to pursue nonviolent, interracial
cooperation and progress, has been abandoned.[3] Since its official banning
in 1960, its membership has become almost exclusively Black, and with the
jailing of many of its leaders, it has largely operated from bases outside the
Republic. Reluctantly, in the face of concerted resistance on the part of the

white minority to meaningful change, the ANC has been prepared to resort to selective violence. Indeed, in 1985 the ANC's most famous leader, Nelson Mandela, who has been in prison since 1965, reconfirmed this position, refusing to accept release from detention if his freedom were to be made contingent on his signing a pledge renouncing violence as a political tactic. In the ANC's place as a multiracial effort, the United Democratic Front (UDF) emerged in 1983–84 as a political movement rather than a party. Its local affiliates include a wide range of over 400 religious, labor, youth, community, and other organizations that have a combined membership of roughly 1,500,000 South Africans of all races.[4] The UDF leadership includes not only many who have had strong ANC connections in the past but also leading churchmen such as Dr. Allan Boesak, president of the World Alliance of Reformed Churches, and Nobel Laureate Bishop Desmond Tutu, and some leading Afrikaner dissidents, including the Rev. Beyers Naude and Andrew Boraine.

Increasingly, however, more strident voices within the Black majority are looking to a Black-led revolutionary movement, as represented in the mid-1970s by the Black Consciousness Movement. The South African security police gave the movement its martyr in the form of the young Steve Biko, who was murdered while undergoing interrogation in 1977. The successor to Steve Biko's group is the Azanian People's Organization (AZAPO) which recruits members not only from the African majority but from the Coloureds and Asians who in current politics have sometimes been redefined as "Blacks." AZAPO recognizes a legitimate but subordinated force for "correct-thinking" whites, namely, convincing their more intractable white colleagues of the need to dismantle the structures of apartheid. Indeed, the hostile reaction of AZAPO demonstrators to Senator Edward Kennedy's visit to South Africa in 1985 is concrete evidence of that group's determination that only Blacks can properly speak for Black interests.

At the opposite end of the Black spectrum, however, are leaders who part company with both the ANC and AZAPO, at least for the time being. These are the people like Kaiser Matanzima of the Transkei, who are prepared to accept the reductionist strategy proffered to them by the Botha regime in the form of limited local rule within the Black Homelands framework. There are also serious fractures within the Coloured and Asian camps with regard to whether these two groups should accept the crumbs of political reform contained in the 1984 constitutional changes.

The program of apartheid was launched with the electoral victory of the Afrikaner-dominated Nationalist Party in 1948 which brought into play a multifaceted strategy of nationalist development. Over the long haul, the most significant facet of the strategy has been and will continue to be the selective isolation or selective expulsion of the Black Majority from full participation in national life. Although President P. W. Botha in 1985 promised some modifications, essentially the dominant whites have sought to deny

Blacks both the label and the substance of South African citizenship in favor
of relegating them to the rural ethnic Homelands for purposes of national
identity. Those urban Blacks who have in fact no Homeland to which they
can be assigned are given the dubious passport designation, "nationality
undetermined." With respect to the other members of the non-white majority—namely the Coloureds and the Asians—the earlier Afrikaner strategy
of selective isolation of Coloureds and Asians within urban ghettos has been
giving way during the early 1980s to a strategy of static tension. The so-
called constitutional reforms of the Botha regime attempt to associate the
Coloured and Asians with the white community as very junior partners in
a collaborative national effort.

The Roots of Apartheid

REVERSING THE ANGLO-BOER WAR. The electoral victory of 1948 effectively
settled one aspect of the Afrikaner strategy of nationalism. This was the
Afrikaner struggle for political, economic, and cultural dominance within
the European or white community itself. Indeed, during most of the period
since the initial establishment in 1652 of a victualing station at Cape Town
by the Dutch East India Company, the ancestors of the modern Afrikaners
have regarded themselves as a beleaguered people struggling to maintain
their distinctive way of life. The settlers had not only to tame an unfamiliar
environment but to confront the indigenous San and Khoi people at their
doorstep while maintaining good relations with the distant paternalistic company administration in Holland.[5] The intention of the latter was a limited
one: the settlers were to provide a reliable source of food for ships on the
lucrative East Indian trade route. The victualing mission was undermined,
however, when the expansion of the settlers inland brought them into conflict
with the local African residents over the issues of land and slave labor. The
cost of defending the settlers would cut into profits of the trading company.[6]

By the end of the Napoleonic Wars, the remote Dutch East India Company
and its successor, the Dutch Colonial Government, had been displaced by
British administrators. The British during the Napoleonic Wars had occupied
the Cape colony intermittently from 1795 to 1803 and again from 1806 onward. Great Britain, under the terms of the 30 May 1814 Treaty of Paris,
took full possession of the colony from the Netherlands.[7] With government
encouragement of British missionaries and farmers to settle in the Cape and
along the coast to Natal, the Afrikaners—or Boers (rural or country persons)
as they were then called—felt increasingly threatened on a number of levels.
The Anglican and other British Protestant churches, for example, were given
priority over the Dutch Reformed Church. The English language increasingly had become the vehicle for administration and commerce, displacing
the modified Dutch language, eventually called Afrikaans. Roman Law in

the courts, moreover, was given a lower status than English Civil and Common Law. Two issues were the last straws that propelled many Afrikaners to remove themselves from British jurisdiction by participating in the Great Trek of 1835–37. The first was the continued restrictions on farmers venturing beyond the established settled areas near the coast, intended to restrain the land hunger of the Afrikaners.[8] The second was the protective attitude of the British administration with respect to the interests of the Khoi and San people (formerly called Bushmen and Hottentots) and other Africans as well. The Afrikaners had long been disturbed by this, and were clearly outraged by the abolition of slavery in the British Empire in 1834. This action, it was felt, undermined the Boer economy and way of life. By removing themselves during the Great Trek of 1835–37 to what later became the Orange Free State and the South African Republic (Transvaal), the Afrikaners secured an additional sixty years in which to develop their distinctive culture.[9]

The peculiar Afrikaner way of life was again threatened, first by the discovery of diamonds and gold on the Transvaal, which brought an influx of "outlanders" from Europe and elsewhere in search of instant wealth, then by the expansion of British imperial interests in Southern Africa. The subsequent defeat of the Afrikaners in the Anglo-Boer War of 1899–1902 once more brought them under British colonial rule. Despite the British Act of Union, which went into effect in 1910, and the subsequent elevation of South Africa to the role of a self-governing dominion, the Afrikaners still felt subordinated to English-speaking politicians in the Cape province and Natal as well as to the British business interests which dominated the mining and industrial complex in the Transvaal. It was not until the victory of the Nationalist party in the election of 1948 that the Afrikaners felt that at long last their interests—including their language, their interpretations of history, and their version of the proper relationship between whites and other racial groups in South Africa—had triumphed over all internal competitors.

BLACKS, SPECIAL TARGET OF APARTHEID. From the perspective of the ten or more ethnic groups that make up the Black majority in South Africa, their struggle to achieve control over their own political, economic, and social destinies is also viewed as an effort to liberate themselves from colonial domination. Indeed, the Zulus, Tswana, Xhosa, Venda, and others have their distinct memories of the historic battles which whites celebrate as national holidays. Whites boast about their development of the country; Blacks view those deeds as the theft of their ancestors' land. White triumphs are seen by Blacks as wrongs that must be corrected.

There are some who question the labeling of the Black South African struggle as a case of colonial liberation. South Africa, after all, has been recognized as an independent state since 1910. Its leaders contributed troops to the Allied effort in both world wars and the country was a founding member of both the League of Nations and the United Nations. Yet to the overwhelming majority of its residents, South Africa represents not merely a case of colonialism, but a distillation of the worst manifestations of European efforts to dominate the lives of non-whites in the history of Africa. Thus, as historian Leonard Thompson indicates, South Africa under apartheid is a caste society.[10]

By no means, however, did the caste system which apartheid represents begin with the Nationalist Party's victory of 1948. Rather, apartheid constitutes the maximal efforts to perpetuate and further solidify the European domination of other racial groups which have characterized interracial contacts for over 300 years. Extermination of many Africans and enslavement of others were among the worst manifestations of white-Black contact in the early period as the Dutch and later the British subdued each of the ethnic groups in turn. There were other characteristics of the situation, however, which continue at the heart of the political subordination and economic degradation of Africans today. Monopoly control of the best land by the white minority and severe restrictions on the freedom of Africans to move about their own country are just two aspects of that relationship.

The 1948 electoral victory of the Nationalist party made the Afrikaners the unchallenged regulators of interracial contact, permitting them to close the legal and political loopholes that had enabled many Coloureds as well as a few Blacks to participate on comparatively equal terms with whites in the matter of suffrage, employment, acquisition of private property, and other matters. Apartheid provided a firm legal foundation for the segregation and discrimination which had in many respects been left to informal custom and usage. It was all-pervasive and designed to disengage the white minority from its contact with—and dependence upon—Blacks, Coloureds, and Asians in all phases of national life. In order to shore up its minority position vis-à-vis the subordinated majority, the policy of apartheid erected barriers which would limit cooperation across racial or ethnic lines within the subordinated majority.

The Afrikaners' justification of apartheid is both complex and shifting, depending upon the nature of the defender and the character of the audience addressed. Many pastors of the Dutch Reformed Church, for example, apparently sincerely believe that their literal interpretation of the Book of Genesis is sufficient justification for modern-day segregation of the races. The dispersal of the family of Noah following the return of the Ark to dry land after the biblical flood assigns each of Noah's descendants to a distinct role in human existence and represents the beginning of racial categories. Under this interpretation, segregation is theologically sanctioned, and is in keeping with the Calvinist view of an "elect of God" ruling over the "great unwashed." As Prime Minister Daniel Malan stated in defense of apartheid in the early 1950s, he regarded it as "founded in another act of Divine Creativity."[11]

Malan and other Afrikaner apologists in 1948 further attempted to dignify

apartheid in more secular terms as the embodiment of humanitarian emancipation and reform.[12] Pointing to the analogy of the 1947 partition of India
into a Hindu and a Muslim state, it was argued that apartheid in South Africa
would permit Africans to preserve their traditional cultures instead of having
their institutions corrupted through daily contact with the more dynamic
structures of European society. Whenever two societies of unequal technological advancement come together—it was alleged—the superior technology inevitably leads to the domination of those with the less advanced
technology. Thus apartheid was defended as not only protecting the African
ways of life, but preventing the whites themselves from falling victim to
their own inherent rapaciousness. According to this philosophy, the salvation
of white souls was also at stake in implementing the policy!

The so-called humanitarian and the pragmatic justifications attempt to
portray South Africa as a society which is headed for vertical stratification,
with the urbanized Coloureds and Asians and the ten rural African Homelands, or "Bantustans," maintaining economic and other linkages with the
white minority. Only the latter group has legitimately both a rural and an
urban component. Despite the move toward decentralization of power, however, no apologist has suggested complete independence or disengagement;
rather, the white minority would stand in a "guiding" role with respect to
foreign relations and the overall strategy of South African economic development.

Other justifications, of course, were more blatantly racist and ignored
historic realities by insisting that the present-day economic prosperity of the
Republic has been due exclusively to the contributions of the white racial
group, and that Africans, Asians, and Coloureds had little to do with mining
the gold, building the roads, and doing the other things which have collectively made South Africa the most significant industrial complex in Africa.
Reversing Marxist thought, which attributes all developments to labor, Afrikaner thinking denies completely the contribution of the laboring class.
Indeed, the extensive industrialization of South African society had been
going on for more than a century, and it had drawn the members of all racial
groups into the mining and manufacturing complex which has made South
Africa's prosperity possible. An objective history of the past century demonstrates the increasing economic interdependence of all racial and ethnic
groups rather than providing justification for separation. Ironically, until
very recently the capital, talents, and attitudes contributed by the English-
speaking element within the white minority have been far more significant
in this respect than the contribution of the Afrikaners.[13]

Still other Afrikaner justifications for apartheid were crassly opportunistic,
such as insistence that the rapidly increasing birth rate of the Blacks, coupled
with the declining birth rate of the whites, would soon threaten the benefits
that the white minority currently enjoyed. In almost a contradiction, moreover, of the argument that Blacks, Asians and Coloureds were inherently

inferior in technological skills, proponents of apartheid demanded that white privilege be given legal protection by reserving certain categories of employment as the monopoly of the white minority. A series of actions put a floor under the level of security to be enjoyed by whites in an effort to avoid the creation of a "poor white" class which would have to compete for jobs, housing, and other material needs with poor Blacks. Thus, the danger of the poor forming a cross-racial coalition against the white elite was reduced, if not eliminated.

While the effects of demographic changes and the application of apartheid laws have glossed over the previously rigid distinctions between Afrikaners and the English-speaking element, it is apparent that the white community is not a monolith. Fissures even within the ranks of the Afrikaner segment of society became glaringly apparent in the early 1980s when the hardline racists formally split with the relatively less doctrinaire followers of Prime Minister P. W. Botha. Urbanization, secularism, and materialism have begun to alter the thinking of many younger Afrikaners on race.[14] This was evidenced by the overwhelming victory which the white voters gave the Botha government in October 1983 on the issue of providing national representation to the Coloured and Asian communities. The subsequent constitutional changes of 1984, which purport to provide the status of junior partner to the Asians and Coloureds in national affairs, are an effort to reorient these previously rejected racial groups toward the whites and away from their emerging alliance with the Black majority. Since the whites would still retain ultimate political control in the new tricameral parliamentary arrangement without having deviated from their ideological program, the significance of participation of Asian and Coloured leadership in the new mechanisms at this stage remains unclear. There are some within the Coloured and Asian communities who point to possible short-term economic and political benefits with respect to management of their communal social affairs. Others have expressed hope that the enfranchised Asians and Coloureds may be permitted to pressure for African interests from within the national political structures. On balance, however, the appearance of having betrayed the suffering Black victims of apartheid is regarded as too great a risk for many Coloured and Asian leaders to take.

The Structures of Apartheid

No single government document adequately explains the policies and programs of apartheid. They are revealed, rather, in a series of statutes of the South African parliament which were enacted and subsequently amended following the 1948 Nationalist Party Victory. Administrative interpretations of the law are often more significant than the wording of the statute itself. Central to the institution of apartheid is the Population Registration Act of

1950 which attempted to classify every member of South Africa's population into one of four separate racial categories: white, Bantu (Black), Asian, and Coloured. Coming, as the law did, after so many centuries of interracial mingling for sexual purposes, it would have been a laughable exercise had its consequences not inflicted so much tragedy. Particularly troublesome were the instances in which members of the same family were differentially classified into two or more of the racial categories. An actual birth record was not the only evidence taken into account; in some cases appearance, style of life of the individual, or general reputation and acceptance with respect to race became more significant factors in classification.[15]

Even before every resident had been legally and permanently pegged into a distinct racial category, earlier laws and administrative dictates had attempted to determine many other aspects of the lives of whites, Coloureds, Asians, and—particularly—Blacks. The Prohibition of Mixed Marriages Act (1949) and the 1950 amendment of the earlier Immorality Act attempted to prevent the enlargement of the Coloured category, many of whose members might thus easily "pass" into the white category.[16] To further guard against interracial sexual contact and erosion of white cultural values and institutions, the Group Areas Act (1950) provided the legal basis for segregation in residence by laying out areas in the countryside and the cities reserved for members of specific racial groups. The hardship related to the forcible eviction of individuals under this act is still a feature of life today, as the government attempts to bulldoze homes and shops in the so-called "black spots," where Africans had for decades enjoyed the rights of private ownership. Further legislation led to the rigid racial segregation of hospitals, parks, and other services, and created an educational system which was predominantly segregated in terms not only of racial contacts but of the curriculum and the professional training available. A further series of acts denied Blacks the right to join political parties and limited their participation in churches, trade unions, and other voluntary associations. The fact that certain technical and supervisory positions within the industrial and agricultural sector were reserved for Europeans further segregated the workplace. The freedom for Blacks—and all non-whites—to move about the geographical domain of the Republic was severely restricted by the rigorous enforcement of the odious Pass Laws, which had been on the books long before apartheid (the effect of the 1986 ending of the Pass Laws has still to be determined).

To control this process of turning back the clock on interracial and inter-ethnic contact in South Africa, involvement in national politics became the monopoly of the white minority. The constitutional reforms of 1984 did not alter this insofar as Blacks are concerned. To protect that monopoly against challenge both from dissidents within the non-white majority and from critics within the ranks of the white minority itself, the Suppression of Communism Act of 1950 and later modifications have given the government of the day exclusive powers to determine the nature or pace of change in all phases of existence.[17] Unauthorized advocacy of social, political, or economic change can result in being labeled a communist. Being so labeled, a dissident can be imprisoned or put under house arrest with severe restrictions on visitors, reading materials, and even the mention of one's name or thoughts in print. The labeling, moreover, is an administrative act from which there is normally no legal recourse in the courts. One becomes, in effect, a "non-person" in South African society. Indeed, considering the title of the original statute, there is an ironic comparison with the treatment of dissidents in the Soviet Union. As an alternative to all of this, many accused have fled into exile.

While the whites are the prime beneficiaries of the policies of apartheid and the millions of Blacks the primary victims, Coloureds and Asians have also remained in a precarious position during the period since 1948. Until the 1984 constitutional changes which provided parallel (but smaller) houses of parliament to represent Coloured and Asian interests, no national political role had been contemplated for these two intermediate groups. They suffered many of the same restrictions on residence, enjoyment of social amenities, employment opportunities, membership in trade unions, and other deprivations that had been inflicted on Africans. Yet they were considered to be permanent legal residents of urban areas (which few Africans are) and to enjoy the legal privilege of South African citizenship.[18] The standard of living of both Coloureds and Asians is, on the average, better than that of Africans, and they will have greater opportunity for access to privileged employment when the legal restrictions on job reservation are relaxed. The limbo status of the Coloureds and Asians is amply demonstrated by the ambivalence which many of their leaders have displayed to the Botha government's efforts to "share" national power with them.

The epitome of apartheid as a form of internal colonial rule, however, comes in the day-to-day degradation of Africans. The lack of respect implicit in the use of such terms as "boy" or "Kaffir" (a Hebrew term meaning heathen or excluded person) is humiliating, but the denial of the right to participate in decision-making with respect to one's entire future is even greater evidence of this oppressive colonial situation. Any changes of the roles of Africans in South African society come not by the exercise of Black suffrage, but from paternalistic decisions on the part of white administrators; by the accident of a situation which gives Blacks strong bargaining positions; or by Black resort to violent confrontation. Given the capricious nature of the first option and the uncertainty of the second, increasing reliance is being placed upon the third alternative as the events since the fall of 1984 have demonstrated. Without confrontation Africans were destined to continue to be relegated to the lowest rungs of the economic ladder. Despite the existence of a few relatively prosperous businessmen, educators, and other professionals, most Africans participate in the modern economy as unskilled or semi-skilled laborers in industry, the mines, household labor, or plantation-type agriculture. Until 1983, Blacks paid income taxes at higher rates than whites, Asians, and Coloureds, yet they received the lowest percentage of the benefits in return—particularly with respect to education. In recent budgets, whites per capita got eleven times the amount of educational funding accorded Blacks. Decisions which dramatically affect the economic status of, Black urban workers, such as the 75 percent rent increase on housing in Soweto in 1981, are introduced with virtually no consultation with Africans.

The absence of legal political organizations for Blacks is paralleled by restrictions on Black trade unions and cooperative societies.[19] The segregated union structure does not permit Blacks to exert the same pressures for improvements in wages and conditions of labor that the white unions have secured for their members. Several recent decisions of employer groups notwithstanding, the strike is still regarded in most instances as an illegal weapon in the hands of Black unionists. The job reservation policy significantly prevents legal intrusion on white privilege.

The residential logic of apartheid, moreover, makes employment security impossible for most urban Blacks. Although the countryside has been demarcated (albeit in highly unequal proportions) into separate areas for Black and white residence, the cities are by law reserved for whites and the two groups that do not have rural Homelands—the Coloureds and Asians. Some begrudging and contradictory legal concessions have been secured by a minority of thoroughly urbanized Blacks in the form of the right to acquire ninety-nine-year leases on homes (but not outright ownership) or to permit families to live in the city with adult male workers who have been in the city for ten years. Concessions granted, however, may also be withdrawn, as was demonstrated in 1983 when previously desegregated parks and other facilities in Pretoria were once again placed under petty apartheid legislation. Contradictory action takes place simultaneously in such actions as removal of the "black spots," that is, pockets of Black settlement in the midst of a white residential area. In any event, the overwhelming majority of urban Africans are legally regarded as transient workers, who since 1968 have been required once a year to terminate their employment in the city and return to the rural homeland to register anew for work in the city. Whatever skills they have acquired, whatever semblance of seniority or job security they have earned, whatever neighborhood, church, and other associations they have made, must be sacrificed to the ideology of apartheid.

The Homelands Policy

The only citizenship that the government at this writing has recognized for the overwhelming majority of Africans is the dubious citizenship in one of the ten tribal Homelands—formerly called "Bantustans'" [see map 5]. These are the areas where the apartheid regime expects the Zulu, Xhosa, Venda, Tswana, and other African ethnic groups to respectively shape their

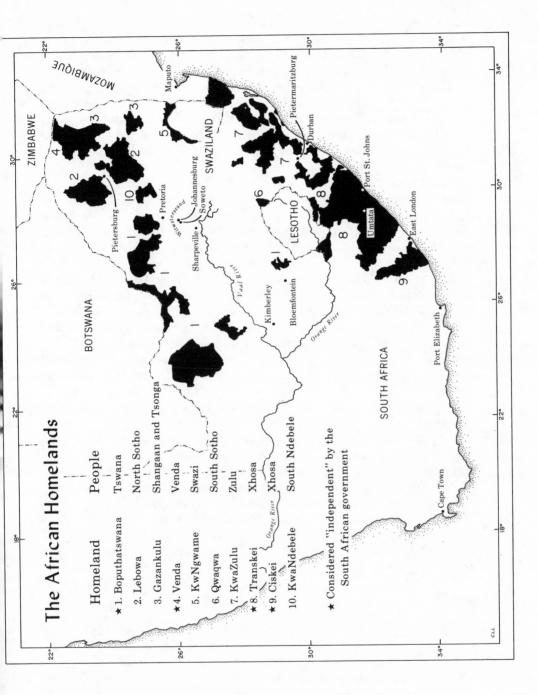

The African Homelands

Homeland	People
★ 1. Boputhatswana	Tswana
2. Lebowa	North Sotho
3. Gazankulu	Shangaan and Tsonga
★ 4. Venda	Venda
5. KwNgwame	Swazi
6. Qwaqwa	South Sotho
7. KwaZulu	Zulu
★ 8. Transkei	Xhosa
★ 9. Ciskei	Xhosa
10. KwaNdebele	South Ndebele

★ Considered "independent" by the South African government

independent cultures.[20] The political absurdity of the Homelands policy is revealed in the fact that the fragmentation of land holdings makes it impossible for any African authority to exercise effective control. KwaZulu, for example, consists of twenty-four segments separated by intervening white-designated areas. One of the seven fragments of Bophuthatswana is 200 miles distant from the others. It has been unrealistic, moreover, to expect that urbanized Africans would readily resubmit themselves to traditional norms of behavior or to indigenous leaders whose authority was long ago eroded by European administrators or by exposure to Western education and other aspects of modernity.

Thus far, only the leaders of the Transkei, Bophuthatswana, Venda, and Ciskei have opted for the status of independence within the Homelands framework. It is an independence, however, which no state other than South Africa recognizes. Thus, the commitment of the Organization of African Unity to the sanctity of the arbitrarily defined colonial boundaries is honored in this case as well. The international snub squares with political reality. Africans such as Kaiser Matanzima of the Transkei or Lucas Mangope of Bophuthatswana may have succeeded in extracting concessions from the white regime in terms of local politics and the management of minor economic and social affairs. There is no evidence, however, that whites have abdicated a scintilla of national power in critical areas such as foreign affairs, defense, national security, and the broad framework for the development of the South African economy. Indeed, Chief Gatsha Buthelezi, who has steadfastly refused to accept "independence" status for KwaZulu, has probably secured more concessions from the apartheid regime than the collaborating Africans.[21]

The economic travesty of the Homelands policy is equally apparent.[22] The almost automatic turnaround of Africans who return to the Homelands to reregister for new jobs in the urban sector demonstrates this. First, it provides evidence of the continued dependence of white employers upon cheap Black labor despite the myth regarding the commitment to economic disengagement. Second, it underscores the inability of the Homelands to provide meaningful employment for Africans. The 13 percent of the land which is reserved for African residence simply cannot sustain 77 percent of the population. Even if the agricultural bias of the African school curriculum had succeeded, the land can provide neither subsistence nor cash crop production. It constitutes the most overworked, overgrazed, and seriously eroded land in the Republic.

Third, the prospects of the Homelands for economic opportunity outside agriculture are also limited. Only Bophuthatswana contains any of the mineral resources that have made South Africa prosperous. Even there, however, ownership of the platinum, chromium, and vanadium mines is in white hands, and the corporation taxing power of the African authorities is limited.

Industrialization, moreover, does not provide an answer to the question of economic viability. Aside from some minor processing enterprises created by the highly publicized efforts of the Economic Development Corporation, most major industry remains the monopoly of whites in white-designated areas.[23] Cynically, white-owned industries continue to be set up along the borders of the Homelands. While Africans—it is argued—get the benefit of wage employment, the inconvenience of having to travel long distances from their home areas is a cost not calculated by their employers. The whites, moreover, have access to a pool of cheap labor without having either to provide proper housing and amenities or to endure the sight of the workers' slum residences which are the inevitable consequences of the marginal wages paid Africans. Thus the border industries further undermine the myth of the expendability of African labor in sustaining the Republic's economy.

Finally, with the exception of Bophuthatswana, the Homeland governments are largely funded by direct financial subventions from the Pretoria government or from the revenues generated from the operation of casinos. Apparently the puritanical Afrikaner government has no objection to whites gambling and enjoying pornographic movies in Bophuthatswana's Sun City and other casino resorts—as long as they do it in the Black Homelands. Casinos, however, hardly constitute the core of a well-balanced, viable economy which would benefit Africans. And the utter poverty of the Homelands and the dearth of electricity, adequate medical services and schools, and modern housing support this contention.

Prospects for Peaceful Change?

Despite the proclaimed intentions of the apartheid regime to achieve a kind of static relationship among the four racial groups, changes in the economic, social, and even political orders are in fact taking place. Whether they will take place fast enough and in ways which Blacks regard as significant in providing them with a meaningful stake in decision-making is subject to doubt. Increasingly, spokesmen within each of the racial groups seem resigned to the possibility that change will only come about through violent confrontation. The events of 1984–85—epitomized by the declaration of a state of emergency in July 1985—seem to confirm that prediction. As one critic has observed: "South Africa is a society no longer at peace, but not yet at war." What is the basis for this pessimism regarding the prospects for peaceful change?

In the long run it will undoubtedly be the Black leaders who will decide how fast and in what form change will come. In the short run, however, it is the entrenched power of the white community leaders that is crucial to the alternate scenarios of peaceful versus violent change. The White minority currently monopolizes power and wealth, and many of its leaders view race relations in terms of a zero-sum game. That is, every concession to non-whites tends to be regarded as a loss in privilege or power for whites.

Well-publicized fissures within the white ranks are often more apparent than real. As previously noted, apartheid has been extremely successful in closing white ranks since 1948, eliminating what had been regarded as radical differences in philosophy, attitudes, and practices between the highly reactionary Afrikaners and the more liberal English-speaking sector. The elimination of dual citizenship for English-speaking whites, the move to republican status, the withdrawal (or ejection) of South Africa from the Commonwealth, and the removal of the possibility of judicial appeal to the Privy Council in London have forced the English-speaking element in South Africa into a position far closer to the Afrikaner point of view. Of equal significance, many factors have contributed to the blurring of demographic and socioeconomic distinctions between the two European groups. True, until the depression of the 1920s, the Afrikaners had remained substantially a rural, agricultural *volk*. The depression compelled many of them to undertake the rural to urban migration in search of jobs—an experience which is sometimes referred to as "the second Great Trek." Even more recently, Afrikaner businessmen, investors, bankers, and industrialists have challenged what had been a British monopoly of the industrial sector of the South African economy. Urbanism, secularism, and industrialism have taken their toll on Afrikaner religious orthodoxy. Increasingly, both the Nationalist and the Conservative parties are making appeals which transcend the formerly rigid ethnic split within the white community.

Resort by the government to banning white dissidents, censoring the European-owned press, and taking other stands under the preventive detention and other security acts have forced the prospective white dissident—whether English or Afrikaner—to make one of three choices: remain silent, risk imprisonment or banishment, or go into exile. While it is true that the White Anglican, Methodist, and other clergymen associated with the English element have appeared to be more willing than their Dutch Reformed colleagues to criticize apartheid from the pulpit, there are limits to their open criticism. Similarly, the former *Rand Daily Mail* and other English language newspapers at first glance have appeared to be much more critical of government policies and practices than their Afrikaner counterparts, but through the years they have learned the art of self-censorship and seldom transgressed beyond the limits of what is acceptable to the censor. The English-speaking universities have also appeared to be more willing than the other white universities to open their doors to Blacks who cannot receive professional training in the Black universities. And a few highly prominent English-speaking parliamentarians, like Helen Suzman, have dared vocally and repeatedly to criticize the government on its enforcement of apartheid legislation.

On balance, however, the Afrikaner/English-speaking dichotomy has been substantially eroded as a source of division in the white fold.

If anything, the escalation in violence on the part of the African National Congress (ANC), operating from bases in neighboring countries, the growing diplomatic isolation of South Africa at the global level, and the war in Namibia seem to have intensified for the Afrikaner hardliner the spirit of "circling the wagons"—or laager—in the face of concerted opposition. The "laager" mentality has developed over centuries of having had to defend the special Afrikaner or Boer way of life against challenges from the Griqas, the Zulu, the British, and more recently SWAPO, the Cubans, and almost the entire United Nations. There are those Afrikaners who seem almost to enjoy being a beleaguered people—as if virtue will emerge from confrontation. Instead of capitulation, there is an attempt to shore up their position. The continued prominence of the Broederbond, a secret society of top Afrikaners formed in 1919, gives testimony that the government dare not stray too far from Afrikaner orthodoxy on the position of white supremacy.[24] The Dutch Reform clergy remain a key structure in the general determination to maintain white dominance, as is evidenced by frequent exhortations from the pulpit to whites to have more children in order not to be swamped by the growing Black population. The latter is a concern shared by the 1983 science committee of the President's advisory council, which concluded that the white birth rate has leveled off at less than zero increase while the birth rate for the other racial groups has been rising—in particular a 2.5 percent rate of increase for the Black majority.

The split within the Afrikaner camp between the hardliners (verkrampte) and the relatively more moderate (verligte) leaders came to a head in the early 1980s over the issue of power sharing with the Coloureds and Asians—a decision to which the Nationalist Party had committed itself in 1977. The formal defection in 1982 of sixteen parliamentary members, following the leadership of Andries Treurnicht, resulted in the formation of a new Conservative Party to challenge then Prime Minister (now President) P. W. Botha for allegedly opening the floodgates to non-white participation. Botha, however, appears to remain firmly in charge of the Nationalist party. If anything, the constitutional change of 1984, which replaces the prime ministerial system with a more powerful state presidency, has further strengthened Botha's authority. The victory in the October 1983 whites-only referendum on power sharing, moreover, was substantial (estimated at 66 percent) and seemed to discount the previous decline in electoral support for Botha's leadership among the Nationalists. The power sharing approach which has been presented as the beginning of genuine reform is in reality a strategy for augmenting the white-dominated coalition and permanently isolating the Black community from alliances with other racial groups in South Africa. Few white leaders prior to the 1985 state of emergency would have risked publicly suggesting that power sharing should ultimately be extended to the Black majority. Even though white businessmen and opposition parliamentary leaders met in 1985 with ANC officials in Zambia, the former refrained from endorsing the formula of "one man/one vote." One American scholar, Newell Stultz, has explored the possibility that genuine reform involving the Black majority may well be part of the Botha group's "hidden agenda." Stultz speculates that if this were the case, any public revelation of those long-term plans would result in the almost certain demise of the Botha government; hence, the leadership is obliged to engage in "reform by stealth." I would concur with Stultz, however, that it is a "fanciful" idea and more charitable to Botha than the facts to date warrant.[25]

Some look to the nonpolitical arena for potential sources of change. The judiciary, for example, has retained its role as an independent constitutional arbiter and has openly challenged the executive by guaranteeing the rights of Black workers with 10 years of continuous employment to residential and other prerogatives in the cities. The courts in 1982 also thwarted the efforts of the Botha government to cede the KaNgwane homeland and the Ngwavuma district of KwaZulu to Swaziland—without consulting the local inhabitants. The Botha government had hoped to rid itself of a troublesome Black area and at the same time build a geographic buffer zone between white areas in South Africa and the ANC sanctuaries in Mozambique.[26] The difficulty with judicial review is that the Constitution permits the parliament to override objectionable judicial decisions.

Some analysts argue that the most likely stimulus for positive change will come from the European and American business and investment interests in South Africa.[27] They note the recent concessions on recognition of Black unions and the pressure from both internal and external sources to relax the job reservations program. They point out that South Africa accounts for 40 percent of the African continent's industrial production, and expansion of South Africa's economy into its "natural" African market area requires reform in race relations. Indeed, even without reform and despite official boycotts, almost every state in Africa has some form of trade, investment, banking, and other economic linkages with the Republic.

Business-instigated reform is based on the premise that rigid adherence to apartheid carries a double risk: the flow of cheap immigrant labor from Black African states is curtailed at the same time that indigenous Black labor is either underutilized or actually alienated from participation.[28] Several factors, moreover, contribute to a shortage of white managerial skills. These include technological change in the economy, the dramatic drop in white immigration coupled with the emigration of skilled talent to Europe or America, and the drain of European talent into the military for combat roles in Namibia. Hence, it is argued by white economic interests that members of the other racial groups will have to be trained for the professional and highly skilled positions now reserved for whites, and that pay and other perquisites will have to be equalized across racial lines. Both educational and business groups within the English sector of white society, for example, have been responsible not only for the expansion in the number of non-white universities in the country but also for permitting the admission of non-whites to four English-language white universities when training in engineering and other critical skills cannot be secured at the non-white institutions. Eleven percent of the enrollment at Witwatersrand, Cape Town, Natal, and Rhodes Universities is non-white.

The political significance of the government's 1979 recognition of Black unions under the Industrial Conciliation Amendment Act was already being felt in the gold mine strikes of 1984. The unions are still severely limited, however, in terms of convenient resort to the strike as a legal weapon in bargaining. Nevertheless, many analysts point optimistically to the dramatic 1983 action of the main European mining employers' group, the Chamber of Mines, recognizing the right of Black mineworkers to organize and bargain collectively for better wages and conditions of labor. Previously the employers and the government on their own determined Black wages. Although the recognition of collective bargaining did not apply universally to all Black workers, it took place in a crucial area of an industry which accounts for roughly half of South Africa's export earnings and contributes almost a quarter to the Republic's gross domestic product. The mining industry is one in which white unions have most resisted Black demands; hence relaxation there is bound to have an impact upon Black workers generally. Ultimately union recognition could challenge the government's policy of requiring urban workers to return to their Homelands at the end of each year's contract.

Government Response: The Drive toward Self-Sufficiency

Despite having acquiesced to white business interests, Prime Minister Botha and his predecessors have long viewed so-called economic realities through different lenses. Instead of accepting the inevitability of racial economic interdependence, the government has steadily pursued a broad-gauged program for achieving economic self-sufficiency for the white community. First of all, it has viewed a favorable balance of trade not merely as a financial instrument but as a device which decreases South Africa's reliance upon foreign sources for those elements needed to maintain a diversified economy. With respect to food production, for example, South Africa is one of only eight of the forty-five states in sub-Saharan Africa that has over the past decade (with the exception of 1984) been able not only to feed its own population, but achieve a surplus. Indeed, the success of the white-managed, highly mechanized agribusiness is crucial to Southern Africa as a region.

South Africa is one of only four states on the continent that has exported surplus grain to its neighbors. It has also shipped significant quantities of oranges, grapes, and other crops to Europe, North America, and Israel.

Even more important than its self-sufficiency in food, is the maintenance of the industrial complex which provides the white minority with a standard of living comparable to that in Western Europe. And while the comparison is in most respects irrelevant and deeply resented by Black leaders, white South Africans point out repeatedly that the Republic's Black majority has a material standard of living better than that enjoyed by most citizens of other states in Africa. It is this industrial wealth that maintains the structures of apartheid. South Africa possesses within its borders most of the raw materials—given the present state of technology—required for industrialization: high grade iron ore; coal for both fuel and cooking purposes; cobalt, chromium, and other minerals needed for production of steel alloys; and both hydroelectric power and uranium as supplemental fuel sources.[29] In addition, it has the most significant pool of educated and skilled manpower in Africa, as well as a highly developed transport system for both internal and export purposes. The one element which is missing in this effort at economic autarky is oil, which is estimated to account for ten percent of its total import bill. Even before the Khomeini revolution in Iran cut off one of the Republic's most significant sources of foreign oil, South Africa had invested heavily in off-shore exploration for oil. More importantly, South Africa had developed the technology for converting its vast coal deposits into oil. The precise percentage of oil needs met from production at the Sasol conversion plants outside Johannesburg is a state secret. It is estimated, however, that Sasol provides about 40 percent of the Republic's requirements as of the mid-1980s. The rest of South Africa's foreign oil needs are acquired through purchases on the spot market or through complicated, surreptitious trading arrangements with Arab oil producers which circumvent the nominal oil embargo against South Africa. The latter is easily accomplished during the present oil glut when political pressure takes second place to "economic pragmatism."

At the same time that South Africa has become less dependent upon the outside world for the maintenance of its own industrial complex, the developed world remains dependent upon South Africa for many of the minerals needed for industrial growth. For many of these minerals the alternative source is the Soviet Union. Both the military needs and the economic health of the Western and Japanese economies require continued access to alloys such as manganese, chromium, and vanadium for the manufacture of high-grade steel. South Africa has many of the minerals needed in the production of jet engines as well as the platinum required for catalytic converters in anti-pollution devices. The country mines copper, uranium, and other minerals which have become essential to a technologically advanced society. By accidents of geography and geology, South Africa possesses a substantial share of the world's known deposits of these critical industrial minerals.[30] South Africa, moreover, contains a substantial share of the world's gold reserves (Table 10). Gold sales on the global market have historically been linked with the stability of the global capitalist economy. In 1981 South Africa was not only the largest producer of gold ore in Africa (655,728 kilograms) but its mining accounted for 53 percent of the world's total production that year—three times that of the next major producer, the Soviet Union.[31]

The Black states to the immediate north are also part of this "Persian Gulf of the mineral world" but are dependent upon South African transport, capital investment, marketing facilities, mining technology, and specialized personnel in the extraction of their own minerals. The strategic significance of South and Southern Africa is enhanced by the fact that the second most important source for many of these critical minerals is the Soviet Union. The West's dependence is one of the key factors in President Reagan's defense of his "constructive engagement" approach to the Namibian question and support of moderate reform of race relations within South Africa itself.

The foregoing is not meant to suggest that the white South Africans are fully in control of their own destinies with respect to international trade and investment. Over the period from 1982 to 1985 the price of gold experienced a dramatic decline, and the value of the rand against the dollar diminished by more than one-half. Although the government took steps to control the worst effects of inflation insofar as the white community was concerned, it was beginning to take its toll on the worsening economic condition of both the white minority and the non-European majority. Data on white emigration and immigration, moreover, although carefully controlled by the government, suggest that there has been a significant net loss of white professionals from South Africa. The events that had the most dramatic impact upon trade and investment, however, have been the series of strikes and mass demonstrations by Blacks and others following the 1984 implementation of the constitutional changes which had further isolated the Blacks in terms of national politics. The resulting instability, which has made almost daily headlines in the American and European press, has already had its impact on investment and emigration. The instability has also given a further impetus to churches, students, and others in the Western world who have been pressing businesses, governments, and other institutions to support divestment efforts. Their campaign, designed to discourage American and European investments in South Africa, in itself will probably be no more successful in accomplishing its ultimate goal than previous boycott and embargo efforts directed against the apartheid regime. It has nevertheless had a significant psychological impact both in South Africa and abroad that cannot be discounted.

Another area of self-sufficiency relates to the Republic's military defenses within the Southern African region. The Botha regime calculates that the environment is made less hostile to the whites through increasing the dependence of the Republic's immediate neighbors on South African trade, transport, investment capital, mining technology, and the employment of foreign migratory labor in the mines, industries, and plantations.[32] The lesson of Angola, Mozambique, and Zimbabwe, however, is that white minority regimes can be toppled by concerted guerrilla warfare mounted from sanctuaries in independent Black states. Hence the regime has engaged in a military buildup adequate not only for dealing with internal dissent but for carrying out military destabilizing activities in neighboring states as well. Some of South Africa's military needs have been externally secured, principally from Israel and from France during the period when the pre-Mitterrand governments quite blatantly ignored the U.N. mandatory embargo on military sales to South Africa. But cost as well as uncertainty regarding delivery has led the South African government to embark upon a substantial effort to produce its own weaponry, including tanks and military aircraft. This makes South Africa one of the top three producers of armaments in the Third World. It has also been engaged with Israel in joint research and testing of weapons, including the development of a nuclear strike capability and cruise missiles.

Finally, the effort at white economic self-sufficiency is apparent in the mechanization of industry and the move to computers and other forms of high technology. Since most of the jobs in this area are reserved for Europeans, there will be guaranteed employment for whites. And reduced dependence upon Black labor—particularly in the mines—makes the white employers less vulnerable to strikes, withdrawal of guest laborers from neighboring countries, and demands for improvement in wages, conditions of labor, housing, pensions, and other benefits. A similar lessening of dependence upon domestic servants is occurring as labor-saving devices are increasingly utilized in the home. Overall, this decrease in dependence upon Black labor accelerates the disengagement of the races and lends the appearance of credibility to the Afrikaner myth that South Africa's prosperity is attributable almost entirely to the work and genius of the white minority.

African Pressures for Change

Black attitudes and strategies toward political, social, and economic change in South Africa are—as suggested earlier—as diverse and sometimes mutually contradictory as the multiplicity of white justifications for apartheid. At the outset, moreover, it should be realized that South Africa is no different than many other societies at an early stage of what appears to be an era of revolutionary confrontation—whether it be Russia in 1917 or the American colonies in 1775. That is, there is a large segment of an oppressed people that is prepared to acquiesce in the status quo rather than to risk even further misery or the loss of what little privilege they have been able to gain amid the general system of oppression. In South Africa this would include, for example, the older generation of Blacks who have achieved a measure of security in the urban sector or on European-owned farms as a result of long residence. It would cover as well those Africans with positions in the civil service (including the police and local government) and those who have acquired seniority and perquisites in the clergy or teaching profession which they are reluctant to risk losing in a situation of political turmoil and uncertainty. Indeed, one of the largest Black religious groups, the Zion Christian Church, is so opposed to violence that it appears to acquiesce in, if not support, apartheid.

There are other Africans as well who do seek to change the system, but they are not necessarily concerned about the immediate political transformation of the society. Reference, for example, has already been made to the struggle of the Black trade unionists to achieve recognition of unions and the right to bargain collectively with management over wages and conditions of labor. These economic pragmatists often attempt to avoid political confrontation.

Also in the category of those willing to work for limited change objectives are those whom their critics have labeled "tribalists" or "cooperating opportunists"—the leaders of the Transkei, Ciskei, Bophuthatswana, and Vendaland who have opted for the uncertain status of "independence" under the Homelands program. Kaiser Matanzima of the Transkei and President Lucas Mangope of Bophuthatswana have attempted to take charge of local politics and to extract whatever economic and other concessions they can from the Pretoria regime. They reason, This is the only power that Blacks are going to get under the present regime, so let us make the most of it. They argue that it permits Africans to recapture some of their traditional past and is more meaningful than an artificial multiracial South African nationalism. A step apart is Chief Gatsha Buthelezi of KwaZulu, who, as the leader of an inchoate Homeland, refuses to recognize the validity of apartheid, the Homelands system, or the denial of South African citizenship to Blacks.[33] Buthelezi uses his position as a forum from which to criticize white racists on behalf of all Blacks in South Africa. Despite the fact that his Inkatha party has developed a distinctly Zulu version of African nationalism, Buthelezi remains popular with many leading white educators, businessmen, and others in Natal. Whites often join Zulu in calling for the creation of a multiracial (multistan) "homeland" for residents of Natal. Buthelezi, however, is viewed by many in the ANC and the multi-racial United Democratic Front (UDF) as a collaborator because he has not completely repudiated the Homelands formula. His Inkatha Party, moreover, effectively rivals other political movements in KwaZulu.

A growing number of Blacks in South Africa, however, are no longer prepared to acquiesce in apartheid or to accept limited functional or geographic changes in the national system. As noted earlier, the far longer history of opposition to the entire structure of white domination in the Republic is exemplified by the African National Congress. The ANC has moved steadily from a non-racial to a Black approach to nationalism as well as a reluctant acceptance of violence as a necessary tactic. Its banning in 1960 after the Sharpeville riots (which resulted in the deaths of 64 of the 300 Africans injured) and the subsequent arrest of its leaders forced it into exile. Until 1984, the ANC operated openly from sanctuaries within Mozambique and Lesotho. Its current president, Oliver Tambo, has been based in Lusaka. The ANC's popularity was considerably enhanced after the 1976 Soweto riots by its willingness to employ violence in attacking selective political targets. These included the daring 1980 attack on the Sasol plant, where coal is converted into oil; the several daylight bank robberies; and the car bombing at the South African Air Force headquarters in Pretoria in 1983. Even the retaliatory raids by the Pretoria government against ANC sanctuaries in Mozambique and Lesotho seemed only to enhance ANC's claim to being the legitimate vehicle for Black protest in South Africa. With the 1984 signing of the Nkomati Accord between South Africa and Mozambique, and the earlier secret agreement between South Africa and Swaziland, the ANC's ability to operate from sanctuaries in neighboring countries has been considerably diminished. Most of its exiled leaders have had to retreat, or be evacuated, to Tanzania, and to consider new strategies for maintaining their effectiveness, including affiliation with the United Democratic Front or infiltrating the ranks of the newly recognized trade unions.[34]

ANC, however, does not hold the stage alone. Leaders of organizations which are less patently political do nevertheless serve political purposes. Reference has already been made to the Black trade union leaders, who have been making significant strides recently in terms of more narrowly economic goals such as the right to be recognized, bargain collectively, and make demands for improved wages and conditions of labor. Union membership ranks have been swelling due to this recent success. Their leadership has seen no need to be overtly political, reasoning that economic concessions for Blacks might be the most effective way of undermining the structure of apartheid.

Even more vocally assertive in pressing for social justice for the non-white majority have been the Black clergy. The most famous is Bishop Desmond Tutu, who was awarded the Nobel Peace Prize in 1984. The Anglican leader had become an international cause célèbre because of his forthright remarks made at home and abroad regarding the system of apartheid and the resulting withdrawals of his passport. His actions have encouraged many other Black and coloured ministers such as Dr. Allan Boesak to daily test the limits of government policy in social and economic matters as well as religious affairs.

Within the more clearly political domain, ANC has various rivals for leadership in addition to the Inkatha party of Chief Gatscha Buthelezi. AZAPO, the successor to Steve Biko's Black Consciousness movement, has since its founding in 1978 been gaining considerable support, particularly among the young. The movement received a tremendous stimulation in the Soweto student riots of 1976, in which students were protesting the arbitrary substitution of Afrikaans for English in school instruction and testing. The Soweto riots themselves, besides creating a generational gap among Blacks, convinced many that they need no longer stand and suffer in silence or engage in the charade of accepting the small crumbs of reform passed out by the government. AZAPO is more clearly Black in its leadership than either the ANC or the UDF, and more willing to accept the legitimacy of violence. Its primary leaders have in many instances served prison sentences for their cause. AZAPO has capitalized upon the spontaneity of mass participation in demonstrations—particularly at funerals of slain Black leaders or demonstrators—and the predictable police brutality in putting down the protest. Africans in the period since Soweto seem more prepared to risk courting mass arrest through engaging in demonstrations or failing to carry passes; to making anti-government speeches from the pulpit or any other available forum; to boycott discriminatory firms; and to challenge apartheid in the courts. Protest reached a crescendo in the period since late 1984 when the constitutional changes intensified Black frustrations over their political isolation.

There are many factors that have made Africans in the Republic more assertive in behalf of their own interests. One is the achievement of independence by neighboring states in Southern Africa despite the hopes of white leaders in South Africa that the wave of liberation would stop short of Angola, Mozambique, and Zimbabwe. Thus the models of successful military (guerrilla) challenges to entrenched white minorities are available at South Africa's doorstep. Of equal significance, these countries until 1984 openly provided nearby sanctuary to the ANC and other dissidents who were prepared to engage in acts of violence. Many of the 1976 Soweto youth, fearing arrest and imprisonment, made their way across the borders to freedom.

Secondly, factors that have enhanced the white position or only marginally affected their economic status have increased the misery of Blacks, making them more susceptible to appeals for revolutionary change. Mechanization of industry and agriculture, for example, while decreasing white dependence upon unskilled and semi-skilled Black labor, has further swelled the ranks of the discontented unemployed. The capacity of the rural Homelands to absorb the displaced laborers has been further reduced by the 1981–83 droughts which have depressed Black income and raised the prices of foodstuffs. The obvious contrast between the spiraling African poverty and the still-comfortable lifestyle of the overwhelming number of whites increases the likelihood of an anomic demonstration. The logic of vocal dissidents urging the Black unemployed to act "now or never" is becoming more difficult to resist.

A further element in the new assertiveness of Blacks in challenging apartheid is the awareness that most of the rest of the world supports their cause. The condemnation of South Africa by the United Nations, various world church groups, and other international gatherings is being relayed to Blacks. While the implementation of programs like the Sullivan principles, which seek to liberalize employment practices of American and other foreign firms operating in South Africa, may not be making dramatic changes in the conditions of Blacks, their symbolic significance cannot be ignored. Equally effective as symbolic of external support have been the corporate divestiture campaigns in the United States and Western Europe.

Significantly, the escalation of violence itself is playing a role in raising the general level of awareness and expectations on the part of the Black majority; it is not limited to those directly associated with the bombings and other violent confrontations. An early example of this was the government-commissioned Schlemmer Report on the Soweto riots of 1976, which was replete with references to the "stupidity of government policies" regarding Blacks. The fortress of Afrikanerdom in the mid-1980s no longer appears to be impregnable, and even acquiescent Blacks realize that not everyone is passively accepting apartheid. The repressive action of the regime in retaliation for bombings and mass confrontations has actually escalated the level of violence. The brutal police action during the Soweto riots of 1976 was a critical turning point, for example, in convincing many young people to go into exile to take up terrorist training abroad. The government contributes to the drama of revolution by creating martyrs, as it did in the death of Steve Biko or the 1983 killing of Saul Mkhize, a farmer who was leading a protest against the regime's confiscation of over 5,000 Black-owned farms in one of the few remaining "black spots" inside white-designated areas.

Finally, there is the very real possibility that small, spontaneous incidents of violence can escalate and dramatically change all previous assessments regarding the relative power relations between the white governing class and the Black citizenry. Unless a government is prepared callously to ignore both domestic and international public reaction to the mowing down of unarmed multitudes, dead and mutilated bodies may count for more than bullets and tanks in a revolutionary situation. This was certainly the lesson of the Shah's overthrow in Iran.

External Pressures on South Africa

The "laager" mentality is not limited to domestic resistance to Afrikaner domination; it applies as well to external criticism of apartheid. There are some Afrikaner hardliners who appear to thrive on the more than three decades of condemnation by the United Nations toward apartheid, the mistreatment of Indians, and the reluctance to grant Namibia independence. Rather than folding its tent and withdrawing in the face of the further threats of quarantine of a diseased political system, the white government continues to take advantage of its membership in the United Nations and the specialized agencies; it continues to arrange exchange visits of soccer, tennis, and other sports teams; to flout oil embargoes by engaging in fake invoicing and third-party transactions with the very Arab states that engineered the boycott; and even to market Soviet-mined diamonds and to continue dialogues with Soviet officials regarding marketing of platinum. The government brazenly confronts American critics by funneling money into U.S. election campaigns, as it did in the 1978 defeat of Senator Dick Clark of Iowa. Almost relishing its role as one of the "pariah" states of the global community, the regime has eagerly pressed forward in creating linkages with states similarly categorized. This is particularly the case with Israel, which has been diplomatically linked in the U.N. with South Africa because of alliances between Arab states and Black Africa formed during the 1967 Six-Day War. (In return for Black African support on Palestinian issues, Arab states have joined in resolutions condemning South Africa.) South Africa's relations with Israel, however, are of its own choosing and are far-reaching. They go beyond trade and investment and include, for example, an exchange of advisors on military tactics and coping with terrorist attacks, and the development of nuclear energy for both peaceful and military purposes. Indeed, the "pariah" label spurs South Africa on toward greater efforts at economic self-sufficiency. Thus, in analyzing the prospects that external pressures will be effective in altering apartheid, it is apparent that the almost universal condemnation and the intensity of hostility will not necessarily budge the Pretoria regime to dismantle apartheid.

In considering the prospective effects of external forces and factors, one must be aware as well of the uniqueness of South Africa's situation. It has no parallel with other instances of white settler control in colonial Africa. In Kenya the Africans ultimately came into control because the British government in London reversed a half century of increasing white settler domination of Africans prior to withdrawing the colonial mantle. In Zimbabwe the white regime collapsed not only because of the increasing effectiveness of Black freedom fighters, but because the primary patron of the Rhodesian regime—the Republic of South Africa—saw continued conflict as a threat to itself and thus withdrew its support. Great Britain temporarily resumed its colonial responsibility in Zimbabwe (which had been in limbo since the 1965 Unilateral Declaration of Independence) in order to serve as a relatively neutral third party in bringing the various combatants to the negotiating table at Lancaster House in 1979. Even in the case of Namibia, South Africa stands technically as the outside third party. In the South African situation itself, however, there is no outside third party that can preside over a peaceable transition to majority rule. British colonial control ceased many decades ago, and South Africa lacks even the restraining role of membership in the Commonwealth of Nations, from which it withdrew (or was excluded) in

129

uld get beyond the delicate question of sovereignty, and
re desire to change, there is no single state or group of
Afrikaners would be willing to entrust their fate. Unlike
ya, Angola, and even Zimbabwe who could return home,
South Africa have few places to which they can emigrate and receive
enthusiastic welcome. The "laager" mentality during this period of extreme international censure of apartheid seems to compel the Afrikaners to dig in their heels and resist external interference. Convinced that they are in the right and possessing the military capability of resisting external intervention, they see no reason why they should permit others to determine the character of South African domestic institutions.

THE NAMIBIA QUESTION. A further complicating factor in the dismantling of apartheid has been the informal or implicit broader agenda of those pursuing African liberation. Discrimination in South Africa and the international responsibilities of South Africa with respect to Namibia have been on the agenda of the United Nations General Assembly since its first meeting in 1946.[35] Nevertheless, liberation priorities with regard to Southern Africa shifted following the completion of the first wave of independence in the 1950s and 1960s. The Portuguese in Angola and Mozambique seemed the most vulnerable at that point even though the Portuguese war actually brought more white settlers to Southern Africa. Indeed, those liberation struggles in Lusophone Africa did not come to fruition until 1975. The entrenched white Rhodesians were more difficult to overwhelm, but that, too, was accomplished in 1979 and early 1980. This left Namibia as the only clear-cut legal case of foreign domination on the continent, and it was South Africa that has been the colonial power—a role it inherited as its reward for South Africa's contribution to defeating Germany in Africa during World War I. German Southwest Africa—now Namibia—became a League of Nations Mandate under South African authority. Thus, the independence of Namibia appears to depend upon South Africa being amenable to a negotiated settlement under sponsorship of the U.N., which became the legal successor to the League of Nations. Namibian independence has been given an informal priority ahead of the ending of discrimination in South Africa. In any event, the major diplomatic efforts in Southern Africa of both the six African Frontline States (Tanzania, Angola, Mozambique, Zambia, Botswana, and Zimbabwe) and the five members of the Western Contact Group (United States, Britain, France, West Germany, and Canada) are at this point concentrated on Namibia.

South Africa is aware of the U.N. priority given the Namibian situation, which undoubtedly accounts for its more than three decades of resistance to settlement of the problem. From the founding of the United Nations, South Africa has refused to place Namibia under the Trusteeship System. The government has studiously ignored the many resolutions of the U.N. General Assembly and Security Council, the 1971 decision of the International Court of Justice, and exhortations from even friendly quarters regarding South Africa's obligations to set Namibia on the path to independence. The government at one stage attempted to "resolve the colonial question" by incorporating Namibia as a fifth province of the Republic. The eleven percent of Namibia's population that is white was given representation in Parliament, and the apartheid legislation of the Republic itself was being extended to cover the Blacks of Namibia as well. Although the government eventually backed off from this strategy, it has managed to forestall the independence question by attempting to set up a controlled multiracial party, by diplomatic maneuvering, and by a massive military campaign against the SWAPO (South West Africa People's Organization) forces that have been operating in Namibia from their sanctuary in Angola. The South African military has actually widened the geographic scope of the controversy by crossing into Angola itself to strike against SWAPO bases. The most recent delaying tactic has been to link Namibian independence to the withdrawal of the estimated 30,000 Cuban troops from Angola. Since the Cubans have been in Angola largely to assist the MPLA government in putting down the military challenge of the South African-supplied UNITA guerrilla forces, the circular nature of the linkage tactic only further delays the independence of Namibia. To the distress not only of the Frontline States but also of several members of the Western Contact Group, the Reagan administration supports the linkage demand. Thus, at this stage South Africa has not felt obliged to permit the U.N. to conduct a Namibian referendum—which SWAPO would almost certainly win. Not only does Namibia continue to be a military buffer for South Africa, but procrastination over the solution of that issue defers concentrated discussion of the more basic question of apartheid itself.

FRONTLINE STATES AND SADCC. The chances of other African states playing a significant military or economic role in altering South Africa's racial policies are at this stage remote. It is true that the independence of both Mozambique and Zimbabwe can be attributed in part to the sanctuary that Tanzania, Zambia, and Mozambique provided to guerrilla forces operating against the Portuguese and white Rhodesians. It is also true that the leaders of the Frontline States (Tanzania, Zambia, Angola, Mozambique, and Botswana, with the addition of Zimbabwe after its independence) have played a significant diplomatic role both directly and in liaison with the Western Contact Group in bringing about Zimbabwean independence and keeping alive the discussions regarding Namibia.

External support for liberation of South Africa's Blacks, however, is another matter. The differential in military power between the Republic and the combined Frontline States is formidable. Only a massive introduction of Cuban, East European, and Soviet troops and equipment could begin to equalize the military situation. In an attempt to forestall such buildups, the South Africans appear to have effectively closed out ANC sanctuaries in Mozambique and Swaziland.[36] The South Africans have also given military support to guerrilla operations in neighboring countries—such as the UNITA forces under Jonas Savimbi in Angola and the Mozambique Revolutionary Movement (MNR). These guerrilla units have successfully disrupted power lines and sabotaged the port and railroad facilities that are vital to the export and import trade of roughly ten states in the Southern African region. Disruption of rail links through Angola and Mozambique make these countries even more dependent on the alternative rail and road system of South Africa.

Direct military action by the Frontline States in support of South African dissidents would certainly bring about massive retaliation on the part of the white regime in South Africa. Nor could the Frontline States call upon non-African military support as occurred in Angola and Zimbabwe without fear of destabilizing action by South Africa. Soviet and Cuban military aid, in any event, is not a "free lunch," as the Angolan, Ethiopian, and other beleaguered African governments have come to realize. They have had to mortgage their coffee, sugar, and oil earnings to pay for the "fraternal" military assistance. Direct military action or even sanctuary support of ANC and other dissidents, moreover, complicates the Frontline States' attempts to disengage themselves from their economic dependence on South Africa. Since 1979 the six Frontline States—plus Malawi, Swaziland, and Lesotho—have been involved in a series of Southern African Development Coordinating Conferences (SADCC). Although nominally SADCC was launched to better coordinate economic development of the nine Southern African states, it is admittedly also designed to combat the long-standing political and economic aspirations of the white South Africans toward their "natural" area for expansion in Africa.[37] It is apparent that South Africa's hegemonic ambitions still include the proposed Constellation of States, which would economically link South Africa with its northern neighbors—building upon the already existing customs, currency, and other linkages with Botswana, Lesotho, and Swaziland.

Military action against the Republic by the Frontline States is also limited by the continued dependence of most of the SADCC states upon South Africa for foodstuffs, railroad transit for their mineral and agricultural exports, for investment capital, trade, and technical assistance in a wide range of areas. Despite Zimbabwe's successful victory over white racism at home, for example, the continued prosperity of its balanced economic development program depends upon the continuity of investment, trade, technical assistance, and other linkages with South Africa. Despite Mozambique's commitment to a radical socialist strategy of development, three of the principal elements in the funding of government programs are the revenues it receives from sending migrant laborers to work in the South African mines, from selling electrical power from Cabora Bassa dam to industries on the Rand, and from the transit fees it collects from South Africa for transport of goods by railway to Maputo and the use of the port facilities. Hence the rationale for the signing of the 1984 Nkomati Accord with Mozambique. Even Tanzania, which has made extraordinary sacrifices in behalf of African liberation, markets its diamonds through the South African–owned DeBeers Company. Sympathetic as they may be to the plight of their Black brethren in South Africa, the responsiblities of leaders of Frontline States to their immediate constituents have limited their ability to oppose the South African regime in either military or economic terms. As Robert Mugabe pointed out in 1980, an oil embargo against South Africa would undoubtedly disturb that country, but it could still secure petroleum on the spot market. For the countries that must import their oil through South African ports, however, the increased costs would be disastrous to their already fragile plans for economic development. One further facet of the dependency syndrome is the fact that—unlike the Western states, which are experiencing a shortage of capital for overseas investment—South Africa has surplus capital and is more than eager to establish further economic links with its neighbors.

WESTERN CONTACT GROUP. The formation of the Western Contact Group has been one of the few instances in which the United States has taken a positive leadership role with respect to Southern African issues. Hoping to reverse the negative image that the Ford administration had received from its CIA support of UNITA in the Angolan liberation struggle as well as to pursue a new human rights position in foreign policy, the Carter administration took the lead in getting together the four other Western powers—Britain, France, West Germany, and Canada—with substantial interests in Africa. Although the more immediate problems were Zimbabwe and Namibia, President Carter went beyond that by having both his Vice-President, Walter Mondale, and his U.N. Ambassador, Andrew Young, engage in direct dialogue with South African leaders in an effort to effect change within South Africa itself. Britain had additional reasons for participating in the dialogue, since its industries had even more substantial investments in South Africa than other Western states. And France was concerned that its continued military sales to South Africa might eventually undermine its continuing leadership role with respect to the Francophone states.

Although the Western Contact Group did achieve some of its goals in Zimbabwe and was the persuasive element in bringing South Africa to the negotiating table for the first time with respect to Namibia, its effectiveness has been extremely limited since the election of Ronald Reagan. The lofty declaration of Undersecretary of State Lawrence Eagleburg in 1983 denouncing apartheid as morally wrong came two and a half years after many words and deeds which indicated that Pretoria had little to fear by way of pressure from the United States. The policy of Constructive Engagement—as Assistant Secretary of State Chester Crocker labeled the American approach—seemed to make no moral distinction between the proponents and opponents of apartheid. Until President Reagan's denunciation of apartheid in 1985, his more characteristic comments were suggestions that the United States could not turn its back on a country that had been its ally in two world wars. This of course ignored the fact that many of the architects of apartheid in 1948 were the very South Africans who had opposed their country's involvement in the war against Nazi Germany.

Many of the arguments in favor of an even-handed, if not openly friendly, attitude toward South Africa by the Reagan administration have been based upon military or strategic considerations, frequently founded upon unsound premises.[38] Falling into this category is the argument that the United States needs a friendly regime in South Africa in order to protect the Cape sea lanes connecting the United States and the West with the needed oil resources of the Persian Gulf. If the oil tankers are to be protected, it is obvious that the real threat would come from an area much closer to the Gulf of Hormuz, and not from the remote south Atlantic. The strategic minerals argument is also flawed. Admittedly the United States does require cobalt, chromium, platinum, and other strategic minerals which are mined in South Africa or in adjacent states that must ship through South Africa. Several of these minerals are vital not only for defense directly but for maintaining a healthy industrial economy. And for several minerals Southern Africa is one of our most significant sources of supply, with the Soviet Union being the alternative source. But must this trading relationship tie the hands of political policy-makers in the United States? Even assuming that the United States cannot find alternative sources in the world or that technological advances cannot reduce dependence upon these specific minerals, must it be assumed that the West will be denied access to these minerals because of American official criticism of apartheid? The prosperity of the white community in South Africa will continue to depend upon its ability to market these minerals abroad in order to pay for the technology, goods, and services that it cannot itself provide. Denying these to the most logical customers—the United States and the West—would simply be counterproductive. The same argument would apply to any Black or majoritarian regime which might displace the Afrikaners. The desire to deny minerals to the United States because of its failure to support majority rule might be strong. Failure, however, to sell the minerals to the best customers would prevent that new government from delivering on its promise to spread prosperity more evenly among the population. The Soviet Union simply does not have the surplus resources to be able to stockpile, as a device for denying these minerals to the West, all that South Africa could export.

THE SOCIALIST STATES. Reference has already been made to the role of Soviet and other socialist states operating in Southern Africa. It would not be correct to speak of the socialist "bloc," since at various times socialist states work at cross-purposes. The prime case of this was the opposing roles played by China and the Soviet Union in the liberation of both Angola and Zimbabwe. In the case of Angola, the Soviet Union intermittently gave support to the MPLA, while a curious coalition of the United States, China, and South Africa gave support to the opposing UNITA and the FNLA guerrilla forces.

In the case of Zimbabwe, the Soviet Union and China split their support, with China backing the winner, Robert Mugabe's Zimbabwe African National Union, which operated out of Mozambique. The Soviet Union backed the rival Zimbabwe African People's Union of Joshua Nkomo, which was based in Zambia. As a consequence of its failure to support Mugabe, the Soviet Union was not even permitted to establish a diplomatic mission in Harare for almost a year following Zimbabwean independence.[39]

In addition to its direct military support to the MPLA, the Soviet Union has been providing military assistance to Zambia and, together with its East European allies, providing technical assistance to several states in the region. The most significant Soviet ally, however, is Cuba, which has some 30,000 troops in Angola alone. While in some respects it is a surrogate for the Soviet Union—for it surely could not financially or logistically support military operations in Africa of such magnitude without massive infusions of aid from the Soviet Union—it is pursuing its own ideological and other purposes as well. Cuban assistance does not come without cost to Angola, however, for the sugar crop has had to be mortgaged to support the Cuban forces. There is also an Alice-in-Wonderland quality to some aspects of the Cuban presence, such as the fact that Cuban troops guard the Cabinda oil refineries of Chevron Oil—an American firm whose own government does not recognize the MPLA government of Angola.

South Africa reacts to the presence of troops and advisers from Cuba, the Soviet Union, and other socialist states in an ambivalent fashion. On the one hand, it recognizes that if the numbers were substantially enlarged they could constitute a real military challenge to the apartheid regime, and that the Eastern bloc presence requires the South African state to devote an extraordinary amount of its resources to military expenditures instead of helping to further enhance the white style of life or placate potential Black dissent by engaging in programs of social improvement. It realizes, too, that the military raids which the South Africans feel are necessitated by the presence of Cuban and other Soviet bloc troops complicate South Africa's goal of creating economic linkages throughout the region.

On the other hand, the continued presence of Cuban troops has given the regime one further reason for delaying both Namibian independence and the dismantling of apartheid. The Botha government, moreover, is able to present itself to its own right-wing critics as the defenders of the fatherland against the "Red menace" at the gates. And to the Western critics, it is able to present a case—which it no doubt firmly believes—that it is the vanguard state in Southern Africa defending democracy and capitalism against Soviet expansion. There are some within the U.S. Congress and the present administration who accept that interpretation of South Africa's role.

For those who are pessimistic about the prospects not only of change, but of peaceable change, it must be remembered that politicians and scholars alike have been poor long-range predictors of politics in Africa. Few in the 1950s would have envisioned that over half of the colonies in Africa would be independent states at the end of the 1960s and that most would achieve their freedom without a single shot being fired. Even fewer would have predicted at the end of that decade that the "white redoubt" in Zimbabwe, Angola, and Mozambique would crumble. Few anticipated the success of concerted guerrilla warfare being employed against both the 400-year-old Portuguese empire in Angola and Mozambique and the intransigent white minority under Ian Smith's leadership in the former Rhodesia. Events can move very quickly in Africa, making yesterday's solid predictions amusing reading tomorrow.

For those, moreover, who analyze change completely in terms of comparative statistics, logical patterns of movement, and other sober assessments, it must be recognized that events—particularly where violence has been introduced—often have a logic of their own. The events at Sharpeville in 1960 and Soweto in 1976 dramatically changed all previous assessments of the prospects for peaceable change. A similar reassessment is taking place as a consequence of the escalation of both mass demonstrations and police violence which have followed the 1984 constitutional changes. While the extent of human tragedy involved should make one humble in predicting violence as the only instrument of change, there are circumstances in which the direct participants feel that this is the only avenue open to them. The American colonists in 1775 realized this in their dealings with a recalcitrant Parliamentary group in Great Britain; the African majority in South Africa feels that channels for peaceful accommodation are even more closed for them than they were for the Americans at the outset of their revolution.

V

THE CRISIS OF
ENDURING POVERTY

Famine in Africa can no longer be a remote and impersonal abstraction to Americans and West Europeans. The technology of satellite telecommunications in the mid-1980s has brought the immediate tragedy of the great Ethiopian famine directly into the living rooms of countless millions on the other side of the globe. Despite the distance involved, the viewer is visually only seconds away from the scores of emaciated men, women, and children being photographed as they stream into the refugee camps. The world has become instant witness to yet another child dying before our eyes as she clings to the shriveled breast of her mother. The outpouring of funds and sympathy in response to this tragedy has transcended all racial, national, and ideological barriers.

Yet, the utter despair and hunger of these refugee camps reveal only a portion of the greater, long-term tragedy of African starvation. Only gradually has the outside world come to realize the extent of malnutrition, the persistently high infant mortality rates, the obstinacy of endemic diseases which kill or cripple their victims, the mounting growth of urban slums with their teeming millions of unemployed or marginally employed migrants, and other aspects of African poverty. Even the World Bank, when it optimistically suggests that, with reforms in governmental policies and better coordination of donor assistance, "the quality of life in tens of millions of Africans can be significantly improved," also acknowledges that things will get worse before they get better.[1]

The euphoria of the 1950s and 1960s regarding Africa was marked by the belief that independence would bring not only political freedom but also the economic prosperity that many Africans felt the colonial system had withheld from them. Events have proved otherwise. Kwame Nkrumah's oft-quoted admonishment to his fellow Africans to "Seek ye first the political kingdom, and all else will be added unto you . . ." has a hollow ring now that independence is a reality. Instead of being automatically transferred from the European and Asian minorities to the African majority, as had been expected, wealth either continued to remain in the hands of non-Africans or was reluctantly shared with the few African political leaders who augmented the ranks of the former privileged colonial elite. Independence did not unleash massive forces and resources thought to have been consciously suppressed by European administrators and businessmen during colonial rule. Indeed, economic growth in many instances only marginally increased, if it did not in fact retrogress.

The cold, hard economic statistics confirm what the television coverage of the Ethiopian famine has suggested: the African crisis of poverty is a deep and enduring one. Each year the World Bank categorizes the 150 or more countries of the world on the basis of their economic development. The numbers in each category vary from year to year, but roughly forty states in the past two decades have been designated as low income countries. These are the countries popularly known as the "Fourth World," where the per capita income in 1982 was $410 or less.[2] The poverty of these nations is confirmed by other basic indicators, such as production capacity and performance; trade imbalances; aid, debt, and capital flows; food and agricultural production; fiscal data; and various social indicators pertaining to longevity, infant mortality, and medical services. These are the states that exist at or below the margin of economic viability and persist as national economies in often the narrowest sense of the term, as in the case of war-torn Chad. Unfortunately for Africa, of the thirty-six states which the World Bank in 1984 designated as "Fourth World" or low income countries, twenty-three are in the sub-Saharan region (Table 8). Many African leaders and their people fatalistically accept the fact that a substantial portion of the citizenry each year will die either of starvation or disease. Countless other Africans will survive in only the marginal sense—substantially undernourished, underclothed, and inadequately housed. Those African leaders who have refused to accept fatalistic determinism are nevertheless often compelled to accept massive relief and developmental assistance from the more fortunate countries of the world in order for their people to survive. Only a few African leaders are in the fortunate circumstances of being able to undertake heroic efforts to stimulate both the people and the leadership cadres to view poverty as a challenge which can be met and overcome.

A. W. Clausen, President of the World Bank, in January of 1982 said that the world could be divided into eight distinct poles of development. Of the eight groupings of interrelated economies—four in the industrialized areas and four in the developing states—Africa ranked at the bottom of the list.[3] Eighteen of the forty-five states in sub-Saharan Africa had actually suffered declines in per capita income during the 1970s. Thus, the indices of poverty and underdevelopment apply not only to the twenty-three African states in the Fourth World category, but to several of the others as well. Only eight, for example, of the forty-five have established records over the past decade of having achieved and sustained self-sufficiency in food production. Only three of the latter category—and that includes the Republic of South Africa— have had sufficient food surpluses over the past decade to be able to share their prosperity with their African neighbors.[4] Indeed, the World Food

TABLE 8
World Bank Ranking of African Countries by GNP, per Capita, 1982 (in Ascending Order)

Low Income Semi-Arid

1. Chad
2. Mali
3. Burkina Faso
4. Somalia
5. Niger
6. The Gambia

Low Income—Other

7. Ethiopia
8. Guinea-Bissau
9. Zaire
10. Malawi
11. Uganda
12. Rwanda
13. Burundi
14. Tanzania
15. Benin
16. Central African Republic
17. Guinea
18. Madagascar
19. Togo
20. Ghana
21. Kenya
22. Sierra Leone
23. Mozambique

Middle Income Oil Importers

24. Sudan
25. Mauritania
26. Liberia
27. Senegal
28. Lesotho
29. Zambia
30. Zimbabwe
31. Botswana
32. Swaziland
33. Ivory Coast
34. Mauritius

Middle Income Oil Exporters

35. Nigeria
36. Cameroon
37. Congo People's Republic
38. Gabon
39. Angola

NOTE: Not included for lack of data: Cape Verde, Comoros, Djibouti, Sao Tome and Principe, Seychelles.

Council paints a dismal picture of diminishing capacity of the continent to feed its population as the century draws to a close.

In those countries which are self-sufficient in maize, sorghum, and other staples, malnutrition may still be a problem due to unbalanced diets. Tsetse fly infestation has affected protein intake by preventing the raising of livestock in more than half the continent's arable regions. Even in those areas which have livestock, as noted earlier in Chapter 3, cultural attitudes toward cattle as an element in the prestige economy have exacerbated the problem of protein deficiency. Changes in traditional dietary preferences that have accompanied modernization have also been a factor. In the face of a severe famine in 1984, for example, Zambians—who had become used to eating white maize—complained bitterly about having to eat the yellow maize which came in as food relief from America. Either variety of maize, however, is less nutritious than the sorghum and millet that had served as their staple until the colonial administration persuaded Africans to switch to maize. Unfortunately for Africa, much of the success of the Green Revolution in Asia and elsewhere has been with respect to rice and other grains which are not the typical staples of the African diet.

In addition, the African population generally finds that its productivity and enjoyment of life are considerably diminished by the prevalence of both endemic and epidemic diseases. Africa has not only most of the respiratory diseases and other illnesses associated with the temperate zones, but also all those now considered "tropical" diseases because sanitation, research, and public health measures have largely reduced their incidence in temperate zones. They include malaria, yellow fever, schistosomiasis (bilharzia), dengue fever, and onchocerciasis (river blindness). Research and facilities for dealing with health problems are clearly limited in sub-Saharan Africa. The crude birth rate per thousand for Africa as a whole in 1982 was 17, compared to 8 for upper middle income countries and 9 for industrial market economies.[5] Although the infant mortality rate has declined considerably in the past two decades, the death rate for children aged 1–4 in Africa is 23 per thousand compared to 5 for upper middle income countries and only 2 per thousand for the industrialized states. Africa is also one of the world regions most poorly served by hospitals, physicians, and nurses despite the herculean efforts of Tanzania, Malawi, Kenya, Guinea-Bissau, and Zambia to provide rural clinics and paramedics in even the most remote areas. On the average, there is only one physician for every 21,234 persons in sub-Saharan Africa, compared to one for every 2,021 in the upper middle income countries and one for 554 in the industrialized states.

The problem of securing a healthy population is in part, of course, limited by environmental factors and the absence of marketable resources to sustain improvements in the field of health and development. It also relates to governmental policies that discourage rural economic and social development and that misdirect limited national resources to military expenditures, prestige projects, and official corruption. The most critical policy failure in the area of human resources, however, has been the failure to contain the population explosion, which threatens further to immerse the African continent in the throes of poverty. Sub-Saharan Africa's population growth rate is not only eight times greater than that of the industrialized countries, but it is twice the average of all the least developed countries combined. Kenya alone had a 4.4% annual growth rate in 1982 compared to 3.3 for the continent as a whole and less than 2 percent elsewhere. Much of this population increase in the sub-Saharan region ends up in the mushrooming cities. In addition to slums and other social problems, rural to urban migration means fewer producers of food in the countryside and more mouths to be fed in the non-producing cities. Yet few national leaders in Africa have had the courage either to launch effective programs to limit population growth or to stem the rural to urban exodus. Indeed, the leaders of arid Mauritania, unable to support its existing population of 1.6 million, are actually encouraging the citizenry to have larger families. In part difficulties in limiting population stem from traditional African attitudes toward the family as the basic economic unit. Religious attitudes are also involved, since Islam and various streams of Christianity are opposed on principle to abortion, contraception, and even family planning. Moreover, since much of the "conventional wisdom" regarding the dangers posed by Africa's population explosion has come from Western demographers and economic planners, many African leaders perceive the warnings as racially motivated or as an effort to prevent Africa from pursuing the same course of industrial development followed earlier by the West. Finally, some African leaders reject family planning since they naively tend to regard population size as a relative index of a country's political importance in continental or world affairs.

The Pursuit of Industrialization

As noted above, while Kwame Nkrumah of Ghana is often credited with having led the struggle for political independence, he is also blamed—rightly or wrongly—for having miscued his fellow Africans with respect to economic development. This criticism stems from his untested assumptions that a socialist strategy of development could bring about a dramatic transformation in both traditional and colonial economies in Ghana, and that African development required instant industrialization. Nkrumah's efforts to establish a steel mill in Ghana—despite the absence of appreciable quantities of either iron ore or coking coal—were typical of this mentality. Robert H. Bates in an insightful volume has adequately documented the dire consequences of a too-rapid plunge into industrialization for societies that are basically agricultural. Inevitably, Bates argues, the costs of that instant industrialization are placed largely on the backs of the diminishing pool of agricultural producers.[6] Nkrumah furthermore went counter to Ghana's own basic economic interests in having the Akosambo Dam built, mostly as a prestige project symbolizing Ghanaian industrialization. In a lopsided agreement Kaiser Aluminum, with whom Nkrumah negotiated the project on the Volta River, extracted terms which gave Kaiser the lion's share of the power produced by the dam in refining bauxite ore with little left over for Ghana's domestic use. Kaiser Aluminum, moreover, was not required to process bauxite mined in Ghana or even in the neighboring African countries of Guinea and Sierra Leone, so most of it was mined in Jamaica and transported across the Atlantic.

Thus the value of the dam to African employment and development was negligible.

While the results of this desire to achieve instant industrialization in Africa have been discouraging, the motives for choosing that route as a quick passage to modernity are at least understandable. Modernization and modernity relate not simply to changes in the environment; but to alteration in human attitudes about the possibility and the desirability of beneficial change in one's surroundings and personal relationships. Modernization assumes a commitment to science rather than magic or religion as the appropriate vehicle for effecting change. It also assumes popular involvement and acceptance of the consequences of change.

There are numerous assertions in the literature on development that modernization is not to be equated with industrialization. Nevertheless, most of the societies that have successfully changed their physical environments in terms of improved transport, modern buildings, and hospitals as well as changing attitudes toward the innovation itself have been industrial models. There are a few cases of states having in abundance one commodity the rest of the world needs. Those states are able thereby to purchase the end products of industrialization without having to put up with factories, slums, industrial strife, and other side effects of industrialization. The oil in Kuwait and the high grade *arabica* blending coffees in Costa Rica offer cases in point. There are also countries, such as New Zealand, which have so mechanized agricultural production that they have been able to import many of their required consumer and capital goods.

Fascination with industrialization as the key to modernization, however, conveniently neglects much of history. As John Kenneth Galbraith has pointed out, the growth of industry in the United States followed, rather than preceded, the growth of agriculture:

> In the last century, when public minds in the United States turned to economic development, it was chiefly to agriculture: to the best design for the tenure and use of public lands; to the establishment of rural schools and agricultural experiment stations; to a transportation system that was very largely in the service of agriculture. . . . Some thought—but no comparable thought—was given to industrial development. It was not that industry was believed unimportant; rather, at that stage in the development process, agriculture was rightly seen as having the higher claim.[7]

Conversely, in examining the contemporary development problems in the Soviet Union, one cannot but be aware of the difficulties posed by neglecting agriculture at the expense of heavy industry.

African political leaders, moreover, fail to see the contradiction in their political commitment through the OAU to the maintenance of the existing arbitrary political boundaries and their economic commitment to instant industrialization. Given tariff barriers, subsidies, and other restraints on international trade, a country hoping to modernize through industrialization must either possess the needed ingredients within its own borders or have worked out reliable exchange agreements with other countries. Few states in Africa are able to export in sufficient quantities and variety those goods the rest of the world desires, in order to purchase those ingredients of industrialization they currently lack.

What are the ingredients needed for industrialization? Certainly the list is not a static one. New factors are always entering into the picture, such as uranium as a fuel source in the period since World War II and, even earlier, petroleum as the essential energy source at the end of the nineteenth century. In the future solar energy could certainly be a factor which might alter Africa's industrial potential. Changes in technology can further alter the requisites of industrialization. Since we are currently in the "Age of Steel," the present state of industrial technology at a minimum requires access to high grade iron ore, coking coal, and the alloys used in tempering and hardening the steel. Industrialization also requires oil, not only for lubrication and fuel purposes but for a myriad other uses related to industrialization. Table 9 reveals the relative poverty of sub-Saharan Africa with respect to these essential ingredients of industrialization.[8] Some of the deficiencies could be overcome by use of supplemental sources of fuel—hydroelectric power, wind and solar energy, or uranium, a resource which Africa has in great supply. Finally, industrialization requires not only a substantial pool of relatively mobile unskilled and semi-skilled labor but also the technical, managerial, and other highly trained skills essential both directly to manufacturing and to the banking, transport, and other enterprises associated with a modern industrial economy.

In assessing Africa's potential, several items work in favor of an optimistic attitude toward modest industrialization as a long-term goal. The first of these is the expanding knowledge base regarding Africa's resources. Only South Africa, the Shaba region of Zaire, and much of Zimbabwe have been thoroughly surveyed by geologists. In most countries—particularly those where European investment and commercial interests were minimal during the colonial period—the systematic task of geological mapping has only just begun. Twenty years ago, for example, it appeared that only Nigeria had substantial exploitable deposits of oil. In the interim Angola and Gabon have become leading producers and Cameroon, Congo Republic, the Ivory Coast, and other countries have also entered the list. Even desperately poor countries like Niger and Chad have had their prospects for economic development considerably altered as a result of uranium strikes.[9]

Second, Africa's prospects for industrialization would brighten instantly upon dismantling of the arbitrary political boundaries that now limit the possibility of rational, integrated use of resources. As long as tariff and other trade barriers persist and as long as the transport network serves only narrow national interests, the potential for producing high grade steel outside South-

TABLE 9
Production of Basic Minerals for Industrialization, 1980
(in thousands of metric tons, unless otherwise noted)

CRUDE PETROLEUM

World Total	2,975,228

Sub-Saharan African Producers

Nigeria	104,190
Gabon	8,895
Angola	7,428

URANIUM *(metric tons)*

World Total	44,734

Sub-Saharan African Producers

South Africa	6,146
Niger	4,100
Namibia	4,042
Gabon	1,033

HARD COAL

World Total	2,729,892

Sub-Saharan African Producers

South Africa	116,587
Zimbabwe	3,134
Zambia	569
Mozambique	400
Botswana	371

IRON ORE

World Total	525,450

Sub-Saharan African Producers

South Africa	25,300
Liberia	19,540
Mauritania	8,270

Steel Alloys

CHROMIUM ORE

World Total	4,480

Sub-Saharan African Producers

South Africa	1,571
Zimbabwe	266
Madagascar	61
Sudan	15

COBALT ORE *(metric tons)*

World Total	33,432

Sub-Saharan African Producers

Zaire	15,500
Zambia	3,309

MANGANESE ORE

World Total	10,425

Sub-Saharan African Producers

South Africa	2,355
Gabon	1,172
Ghana	120

SOURCE: Europa Publications, *Africa South of the Sahara, 1984–85* (London: Europa Publications, 1984), pp. 107ff.

ern Africa is limited. Given the rigidity of Latin American political boundaries for the past 160 years, one might be pessimistic about the prospects for
successful regional or continental economic cooperation in Africa. On the
other hand, taking the analogy of events in Western Europe during the past
four decades, there might be room for encouragement. It may be that
SADCC, ECOWAS, or a revived East African Common Market will, in the
final analysis, provide viable vehicles for economic cooperation.

Third, there is a rhythm to development, so that progress with respect
to one commodity or one part of a country or the continent has unforeseen
consequences in neighboring areas. If, for example, the continent could
begin to put to work at least some of its vast potential in hydroelectric
power—approximately 30 to 40 percent of the world's total—the question
of an energy shortage in Africa might be dramatically reversed. Multinational
corporations, moreover, could begin to process more of Africa's mineral and
agricultural materials *in situ* if cheap power were available.

The present political boundaries, however, are still part of the economic
realities. That being the case, there are very few countries in sub-Saharan
Africa which have within their boundaries the natural resources that stand
at the core of industrialization. As Table 9 indicates, only three states have
substantial quantities of two or more of the basic raw materials: the Republic
of South Africa, Zimbabwe, and Nigeria. Only the first has become an industrialized state in the full sense of the term, on the basis of its possession
not only of iron and coal, but also chromium, cobalt, vanadium, and the
other alloys needed to produce high grade steel. The one commodity that
it lacks is oil. Even there, however, it possesses significant coal reserves
which can be converted into petroleum, and has the earnings from its store-
house of other minerals to be able to afford the expensive technology associated with this conversion. In addition to having roughly one-half of the
world's total gold production—as indicated in Table 10—South Africa has
vast reserves of tin, phosphate, uranium, platinum, manganese, copper,
diamonds, and chromium.[10] The revenues from these minerals—which have
earned Southern Africa the label of the "Persian Gulf of the Mineral
World"—have subsidized education and training in the technical, managerial, financial, and other skills needed for industrialization. Unfortunately,
the full impact of development potential is limited by South Africa's racial
policies. The kind of economic help which South Africa can provide its
neighbors is resented as a manifestation of neo-colonialism and efforts are
being made to disengage economically from South Africa. The countries
within the region fear that exogenic links with the Republic contribute to
the maintenance of the structure of apartheid. They find themselves, nevertheless, in a more insidious dependency relationship since independence
than had existed under colonial rule.[11]

A second country having industrial potential could serve as an economic
counterweight to South Africa for states in the Southern Africa region. I

TABLE 10
Production of Other Key Minerals, 1980

GOLD ORE (*kilograms*)

World Total   1,191,419

Sub-Saharan African Producers
South Africa	672,786
Zimbabwe	11,446
Ghana	10,980
Zaire	972
Zambia	932
Ethiopia	289
Liberia	225

UNCUT DIAMONDS, Gem and Industrial (*ooos metric carats*)

World Total   41,449

Sub-Saharan African Producers
Zaire	10,235
South Africa	8,420
Botswana	5,101
Namibia	1,560
Angola	1,500
Ghana	1,258
Sierra Leone	602
Central African Rep.	350
Liberia	298
Tanzania	274

TIN CONCENTRATES (*metric tons*)

World Total   204,700

Sub-Saharan African Producers
South Africa	2,811
Nigeria	2,383
Zaire	2,346
Rwanda	1,287
Zimbabwe	1,157
Namibia	850

COPPER ORE (*ooos metric tons*)

World Total   8,223

Sub-Saharan African Producers
Zambia	530
Zaire	503
South Africa	207
Namibia	49

PHOSPHATE ROCK (*excluding guano*) (*ooos metric tons*)

World Total   138,707

Sub-Saharan African Producers
South Africa	3,282
Togo	2,933
Senegal	1,408

SOURCE: Europa Publications, *Africa South of the Sahara, 1984–85* (London: Europa Publications, 1984), pp. 107ff.

refer, of course, to Zimbabwe. Unfortunately, Zimbabwe itself is still highly dependent upon South Africa for trade, investment capital, and transport links with the outside world. The major spurt in Zimbabwean industrial development, ironically, took place during the independence war, when the Ian Smith regime was attempting to achieve self-sufficiency. The victorious forces of Robert Mugabe have fortuitously inherited the industrial development, based on substantial iron and coal deposits; the accelerated exploitation of chromium, tin, and other minerals; and an economy that is reasonably self-sufficient in food production. The white minority, however, is still in control of the major economic infrastructures, and thus Mugabe is faced with mounting political demands to Africanize the economy.

The third state with demonstrated industrial capacity is Nigeria, which, with a population over 90 million, is—after the Sudan—the largest state in sub-Saharan Africa. It possesses coal and iron ore deposits in appreciable amounts, and its oil resources permitted it to become the first African member of OPEC. But its oil boom in the 1970s was a double-edged sword: it not only financed the substantial industrial development of the country, but also fueled inflation, a huge international debt, and rampant corruption among both military and civilian officials. Fortunately for the long run, however, the oil revenues also financed one of Africa's most ambitious programs of educational development at the university level. Each of the federal states of Nigeria has at least one university, and there are also a number of technical community colleges in major cities. Nigeria's vastly expanded pool of trained manpower can help sustain its economic growth and contribute to meeting the needs of other West African states as well.

There are, in addition to these three, a few other countries with limited populations that have been able to secure a modest level of modernization. This has been possible because they possess one or more of the critical minerals needed by the industrialized states of the West or Japan. The list includes Gabon (oil, uranium, manganese), Zambia (copper and cobalt), Botswana (diamonds), and Liberia (iron ore and gold). An additional tier of states have achieved a modicum of modernization based on a combination of light industry, processing of agricultural produce, and the export of surplus agricultural commodities. This group includes the Ivory Coast, Cameroon, Kenya, The People's Republic of the Congo, and Senegal.

The one country in Africa aside from the Republic of South Africa which has the greatest potential for prosperity based upon extraction of its mineral resources is Zaire. The Shaba (formerly Katanga) region of Zaire possesses some of the world's richest reserves of tin, gold, copper, diamonds, and cobalt. Unfortunately, the violence attending its independence in 1960 and the recurrent political instability of the country have diminished Zaire's prospects of reaping the same benefits from the Shaba resources that the Belgians did in the colonial era. The outrageous level of official corruption in Zaire, moreover, is legendary and has resulted in the coining of the term "kleptocracy"—government by theft—to describe Zaire's political system.

THE COLONIAL ECONOMIC LEGACY. There are a number of difficulties, however, which African countries face in basing their development plans on either the mineral or the agricultural extractive routes. For one thing, many of the colonial patterns of development have persisted after independence. The British imperial system, for example, called for each dependency to specialize in the production or extraction of a limited number of commodities. The dependencies were usually not competitive with each other, and the production of raw materials was complementary to the industrial needs of the European metropole. Production was usually sufficient to provide both a revenue and an employment base for the particular colony. Thus, Ghana specialized in cocoa; Tanzania in sisal; Zambia in copper; the Sudan in cotton; Malawi in tea; Uganda in coffee and cotton; Sierra Leone in iron ore; and Nigeria in peanuts, palm oil, and rubber. Once the imperial net was removed, however, each independent African state was clearly exposed as virtually a single commodity economy. The prices for these commodities were set in global markets, rather than in Africa. Since producers of agricultural products and most minerals have never been able to forge OPEC-like agreements on production and price, the African economies have been extremely vulnerable to recessions in the industrialized countries. As long as the world price of copper was on the rise in the 1960s and 1970s, Zambia's development prospects seemed excellent. Once the glut had produced a decline in world prices for copper, Zambia's ambitious development schemes had to be considerably scaled back. Ghana similarly has been so locked into cocoa production as its primary source of income that it has never been able to diversify its agricultural production. Cocoa was to have paid for Nkrumah's grandiose schemes for instant industrialization. The steady decline in cocoa prices during the past two decades, however, is one of the factors accounting for Ghana's disastrous economic situation.

A further hindrance is the fact that many African agricultural exports are either items that are not indispensable to the outside world or there are cheaper and more readily available alternatives if the price of the African product rises dramatically. Cocoa as a beverage, for example, may easily be replaced with coffee and tea. Synthetic rubber and plastic rope during the period after World War II seriously challenged the natural rubber market in West Africa and the sisal market in East Africa.

There are three additional factors, however, which have limited the African countries' ability to establish viable industrial economies or even to engage in the mechanization of export agriculture. These factors may be temporary impediments, but they are significant. The first is the lack of petroleum products at reasonable prices. To the chagrin of most African states, the tradeoff which they developed in the 1960s and 1970s with the Arab bloc in the United Nations has not worked to their advantage. In return for African support of the Arab bloc on Arab-Israeli issues in the U.N., the Arab bloc had pledged itself to support African diplomatic and other efforts directed against South Africa. The cost of this cooperation to African states was considerable, since Israel, prior to the African states' breaking off of diplomatic relations during the 1967 "Six-Day War," had been an important source for investment capital, technical skills, and favorable trade exchanges in the sub-Saharan region. When the Arab-inspired escalation of OPEC oil prices began during the 1970s, the damage that was done to the economies of resource- and revenue-poor African states was drastic, even though it was

not they but industrialized states of the Western bloc which were the targets
of the action. To offset some of the undermining of development planning
that resulted, the oil-producing Arab bloc set up a fund to provide either
outright grants or low-interest loans to the poorer African states. But the
Arab aid is relatively sparse compared to that which continues to come from
the West, and tends, moreover, to be heavily oriented to those African states
with preponderant Muslim populations. Without some concession on oil
prices, the cost of transport alone has further impoverished even some of
those African countries which in the early 1970s had reasonable prospects
of development.[12]

THE MANPOWER CRISIS. The second factor limiting industrial development
is the shortage of skilled manpower. One of the harshest indictments of
colonial rule is the failure of the European powers to permit Africans to
acquire the skills needed to manage their own economies once independence
was achieved. The record of the Portuguese, who ignored African education
at all levels, makes the other powers look good only by comparison. The
Belgians, who did an outstanding job of education at the primary and secondary school level—particularly with respect to many of the technical skills
needed in mineral extraction—had a shameful record in terms of higher
education. At the time of the independence of Zaire (the former Belgian
Congo), there were reputed to be only a dozen Zairois college graduates in
a population in excess of 16 million. The management of the huge mineral
enterprise in the Shaba (Katanga) region remained a European monopoly at
independence.

The British and the French have more creditable records in terms of the
number of Africans sent abroad for university training. Indeed, the British
by 1948 had established respectable universities in Ghana, Nigeria, and
Uganda, and even a century earlier had launched Fourah Bay College in
Sierra Leone. Both the British and the French approaches, however, had
quantitative and qualitative shortcomings. Few African territories, for example, had achieved literacy rates of 20 percent on the eve of independence,
and most hovered around the 5 percent mark. Few Africans who attended
universities in Europe or Africa received degrees in fields other than the
classics, law, history, theology—the usual subjects associated with a European university education. The schools of agriculture in African universities
were underfunded and poorly staffed, and agronomy, veterinary sciences,
and forestry enjoyed low prestige among African students. Engineering,
commercial education, communications, industrial management, and other
fields common to the American land grant university system were considered
by the European mentors to be suitable only for technical or trade schools.

Not all African leaders are content to accept the legacy of colonial education
as a permanent barrier to development. Since independence Tanzania has
provided an outstanding example of what can be done in terms of achieving
basic literacy in a brief two decades, and Nigeria, emulating the American

model, has invested heavily in skill-oriented higher education. Unfortunately, the resources of most African countries are too meager to make much progress even when education is at the top of the national priority list. Deficiency in skilled manpower means, in most states, continued reliance upon expatriate personnel, a delay in the training and employment of Africans in managerial and other skilled positions, and a greater outlay in salaries that will be spent elsewhere. Hiring expatriates also involves the added burdens of overseas transport, subsidized housing, interest-free car loans, dependent schooling, home leave, and other perquisites needed to attract expatriate personnel to Africa. Since few African states enjoy an advantageous position in bargaining for skilled personnel, multinational firms are often able to resist or delay the implementation of laws requiring the phased-in training of host country nationals.

TRANSPORT AND DEVELOPMENT. The third factor which limits a development strategy based upon instant industrialization is the absence in most African countries of an efficient, low-cost transportation network. The movement of goods and people, after all, is at the heart of the modernization process. If people are to change their basic approaches to securing better food, housing, and clothing as well as improving their health, education, recreation, and other aspects of living, mobility of goods and people is essential. Development requires the expanding of horizons beyond the parochial village and region so as to include ultimately the entire global community. Since many of the materials and skills needed for this transformation in the quality of life are not actually present in Africa, they must be brought in from outside the continent. Conversely, if Africans are to be able to purchase those needed materials and skills, they must be able to export to the rest of the world those things which are desired in exchange.

In intercontinental trade, Africa is at a severe disadvantage with respect to other major continents, and this situation increases the cost of development. To begin with, water transport is still the cheapest and most efficient means for hauling goods and people. However, as was noted in the discussion of colonial rule, the relatively smooth coastline of Africa—and hence the absence of natural harbors and shelter for ships—limited the ability of Europeans to establish effective beachheads for the conquest of the interior. Although it has now been possible to build artificial harbors at Monrovia, Abidjan, Takoradi, and other points along the coast, the cost of maintaining these man-made ports has been considerable, and berthing space at most ports is still limited. Other continents possess great river systems such as the Rhine, Danube, Mississippi, and Yangtze that provide easy avenues of access to the interior; Africa's river systems, by contrast, pose problems to navigation. Many of the rivers are dry except during the few months of the rainy season; transit is complicated by the series of falls or cataracts along the course of a river; and the mouths of many rivers are often obstructed by sandbars, vegetation, and other barriers to navigation. The limited river system further compounds the problem posed by Africa's smooth coastline and compact shape. As noted earlier in Chapter 2, the ratio is 1 mile of coastline to every 107 square miles of land mass in Europe, compared to 1 mile of coast for every 510 square miles of land mass in Africa. Consequently, a series of random points in the interior of Africa are potentially five times more distant from the coast than a similar series of random points in Europe. This ratio means that transport costs in Africa are considerably greater.

The alternatives to water transport are also more costly in Africa than in Europe or North America. Due to the absence of known oil resources and established refining capacity, most of the petroleum needed for road and rail transport must be imported at considerable cost and aggravation of the balance of payments situation. Railroad ties in Africa, moreover, must be made of iron or creosote-impregnated timber; otherwise termites would destroy a rail bed in less than a year. Rock slides, swamps, and washouts caused by torrential downpours further complicate the task of constructing and maintaining an effective road and rail system.

In addition to geographic and natural impediments, political considerations have also limited the construction of an effective transport network. The colonial administrations were seldom interested in developing a well-integrated domestic economy in a given territory, and they had even less interest in maintaining economic links with neighboring territories under the control of another European power. They were mainly interested in the exploitation of mineral and agricultural resources which would benefit the metropolitan economy. Hence, the roads and rails frequently went from the coastal port to the area of exploitation and no further. Roads and railroad lines normally stopped considerably short of international borders, with the expectation that goods and labor would largely remain within the individual territories. The only major exceptions to this rule occurred in Southern Africa. There, the value of the minerals being shipped from the Katanga (now Shaba) area of Zaire, and the demands of settlers in Rhodesia for shorter links to the sea, did result in railroads being built across the neighboring Portuguese territories of Angola and Mozambique. In Africa generally, once independence came, the patterns of colonial transport networks have proved to be ill suited to the tasks of national unification or the development of national or regional integrated economies.

Prospects for Agriculture

LIMITS ON AGRICULTURAL INNOVATION AND TRANSFER. Given the restraints on industrial development as well as the problems posed for mineral development and export agriculture, the best that most Africans can hope for is the improvement in lifestyle that comes through an improvement in subsistence or localized agriculture. But before examining the prospects for improvement in agriculture, it would be well to explore the problem of technological innovation and transfer as it applies to African development generally. Hazards and liabilities often outnumber gains in efforts to industrialize as well as in the arena of agricultural innovation. Some of the difficulties arise from the misreading of gross data. To begin with, African statistical information is sparse and often of questionable validity, since the accumulation of reliable data has not been a high-priority area for either the colonial or the independent governments. The conclusions drawn from the data, moreover, are often misleading, if one applies the experience of temperate zone areas in making estimates for development in the African tropics. Take the case of national average annual rainfall figures, or data on the percentage of land mass covered by surface water during the year. Such data are meaningless for a country like Botswana, where the rain and surface water are limited largely to the vast Okavambo Swamps—several hundred miles away from the greatest concentration of Tswana citizens along the semiarid corridor adjacent to South Africa. A figure of 35 inches of rainfall per year for a district in Tanzania, moreover, will have substantially different consequences than a similar statistic for a Midwest American state. Instead of being spread out over many months, rainfall in Tanzania may occur during a period of only a few weeks. Indeed, much of it may occur on just a few days, or even during a few hours of that limited period. Thus, the land may be parched a few days after a torrential downpour so intense that it destroyed young crops and carried a good percentage of the topsoil down to the Indian Ocean. Similarly, data on population densities are meaningless unless that population is considered in relationship to availability of arable land or the existence of industrial or mineral extractive enterprises. Arable land is a changing concept. Land which has the proper soil for growing crops and which was once subject to human occupation and settlement may be removed from production as a consequence of the variations in rainfall patterns or the encroaching of the desert sands. The land in Ethiopia, for example, may take more than a decade to recover from the effects of the early 1980s drought. Man's ability, resources, and persistence in coping with the incidence of disease vectors and other pests may further affect—positively or negatively—the amount of arable land available within a country. Tsetse fly, the vector for sleeping sickness, is a special limiting factor in expanding the areas of cultivation since roughly one-third of the continent is afflicted with this scourge.

Some techniques for dealing with health or agricultural problems are more appropriate than others for poorer countries in the tropics. In Malawi, for example, developers have worked with rather than against nature in carrying out development programs. During the past five years, for example, clean water has been provided to a million or more Malawians who previously did not have a nearby source of uncontaminated water during the dry season. Water developers in Malawi rejected the option of using expensive imported pumping equipment, which breaks down and requires spare parts, or drilling bore holes, which may lower the water table. Instead, by inserting pipes into the mountain streams—above the pollution level—that flow year-round, they simply utilized gravity in bringing water to the rural inhabitants of the lower altitudes. Malawi has also used appropriate technology by breeding oxen to take the place of imported tractors in agricultural production. The oxen are less costly than tractors, require no imported petroleum or spare parts, and the plows they pull do less damage to the soil. In addition, the oxen can be used for transport purposes and their manure used as a natural fertilizer.

Perhaps the most interesting misapplication of technology comes in the case of dam construction, a frequent manifestation of the desire for instant industrialization. The many cataracts in African rivers that limit their utility for navigation in theory could provide the continent with close to 40 percent of the world's hydroelectric potential. In a continent that is still deficient in oil and other sources of energy this is significant. Thus, it is not surprising that over the years many African official visitors to the United States had a mandatory stopover at Muscle Shoals or some other installation in the Tennessee Valley Authority complex. TVA has a special significance with respect to rejuvenation in the 1930s of one of America's most depressed areas. The watershed of the Tennessee River was a Fourth World area within a First World country. The general poverty of Valley residents, the tragedy of annual flooding, and the deep scars of soil erosion were a national disgrace. Building a series of hydroelectric dams along the various tributaries of the river provided the area with low-cost electricity to light homes and power for new industrial growth. Of equal importance, the dam construction contributed directly to other improvements in the region as well as providing additional revenues to local and state governments that enabled them to carry out related development projects. Harnessing the river, for example, virtually eliminated the annual flooding and halted the destruction of valuable topsoil. Regulating the seasonal flow of water—complemented by the construction of locks adjacent to the dams—restored the Tennessee River to its previous role as a navigable waterway, giving farmers and industrialists a cheap form of transport for the regional goods which ultimately entered world commerce. The recreational potential of the lakes behind the dams provided a new source of tourist earnings for the region, but more importantly in several ways the lakes improved the health of the local inhabitants. The protein intake of the population, for example, was enhanced through the ready supply of fish, while the reservoir provided a reliable source of drinking water for municipalities along the river system. The water plus the electricity, made possible the establishment of new industries in the valley. Hence, from the one plus—namely, electricity—came a substantial number of positive direct and indirect byproducts.

The TVA model, however, cannot be applied indiscriminately to African situations. Prior assessment of the full consequences of dam construction is essential, as is further research on coping with the negative side effects. The results otherwise can be disastrous.[13] In the first place, the production and utilization of electricity in Africa may be only a partial accomplishment. In addition to limits on the distance electricity can be transmitted, the lag in parallel development of industrial users of electricity within a country may find a hydroelectric scheme operating at far less than full capacity. Indeed, during the drought of 1984 in Ghana the low level of retained water prevented the Akosambo Dam from being used in generating any electrical power for the refining of bauxite. Moreover, instead of augmenting the economic productivity of a region, construction of a dam may actually cause retrogression. The Egyptians, for example, found that the Aswan Dam had the unanticipated consequence of retaining in Lake Nasser a good portion of the nutrients which, together with the water, had for millennia made the Nile the "fertile valley." Only through the importation of expensive chemical fertilizers could agricultural production be maintained in Egypt. Nutrients in the flooded Nile, moreover, had provided natural nutrition for the crustacean industry which had long flourished at the mouth of the Nile; this industry was virtually wiped out. The retention of the Nile's water in Lake Nasser also changed climatic conditions in southern Egypt and northern Sudan, requiring a major shift in agricultural technology for the people of the area. Elsewhere in Africa the construction of dams slows down the pace of the river, permitting the growth of vegetation which clogs previously navigable rivers. The greatest negative consequence from dam construction in tropical Africa, however, comes in the field of health.[14] The lake behind each dam and the slower moving rivers and streams provide additional breeding grounds both for the mosquitos that are the vector for malaria and for the snails that are the intermediate host for bilharzia or schistosomiasis.[15] The incidence of these two diseases increases dramatically with dam construction, particularly as we now appreciate the negative consequences of using insecticides and molluscicides in eradicating mosquitos and snails. In addition to the threat of health posed by the lake behind the dam, the highly oxygenated water flowing over the spillway provides the ideal conditions for the breeding of the black fly (*simulium damnosum*).[16] The latter is the vector that transmits onchocerciasis or river blindness throughout West, East, and Central Africa.

The difficulties in transferring technology and experience from one area to another are not intended to discourage innovation. Rather, they suggest that innovation must be undertaken cautiously with due regard for the unintended by-products of technological transfer. They also suggest that far more funds have to be allocated to research in controlling these negative side effects than has been the case to date.

Given the limited number of states in Africa that have the immediate potential for industrialization, what are the prospects for agriculture alone providing the expected good life for Africans? Here, too, the evidence is not promising. It has already been noted that recurrent famine and the inability of more than eight states to achieve self-sufficiency in food production over the past decade demonstrate that the problems are both short range and long range in their impact. The Food and Agriculture Organization in early 1985 noted that twenty-one countries in Africa were in urgent need of food, with six being acute cases of starvation. An estimated 30 million Africans in those countries were affected by the famine.[17]

The prospects for non-food production, which includes mostly items intended for export, are somewhat better, but only in relative terms. In fact, there has been a dramatic decline during the decade from 1972 to 1982 in the annual average growth rate for many of the beverage and other non-food commodities that African states depend upon for earnings to purchase imports and pay off the mounting debts. This applies to coffee, cocoa, tea, timber, cotton, rubber, and sisal. Only palm oil, tobacco, and hides and skins have experienced even modest gains.[18] The entry of new producers of these commodities elsewhere in the world as well as the development of synthetics and other substitutes have begun to take their toll. The slowdown in the economies of the major industrial states during the decade from 1974 to 1984, however, must also be taken into account.

The obstacles to African agricultural development are very complex. Notwithstanding the neo-Marxists, who comfortably explain African underdevelopment in terms of the rape of Africa by European capitalism, there are a multiplicity of factors which enter into the analysis of why African agriculture is in bad shape and getting worse.

HERITAGE OF TRADITIONAL ECONOMIES. One serious impediment to the rapid expansion of wealth in Africa is the persistent impact of traditional institutions and values. Several words of caution, however, are appropriate at the outset. First of all, economic patterns of behavior which appear to be obstructive to the modern exchange economy have played positive roles in sustaining life and accomplishing social, political, and other purposes in traditional society.[19] One of the frequent targets of criticism is the extended family networks, which cover many more individuals than are normally included in the family unit in Western society. They are cited as impediments both to innovation and to the accumulation of capital on the part of talented, upwardly mobile members of contemporary African society. Operation of the extended family means that the economic success of the individual innovator often brings forth more claimants on his wealth in modern society, rather than permitting the individual to accumulate capital. Some critics have labeled the system "family parasitism." Yet in most traditional societies the extended family served as the vital unit not only in production but in providing social security for the very young, the elderly, and the unfortunate. Membership was not a "free lunch," inasmuch as social pressures imposed by other family members made everyone a contributor to the success of the corporate enterprise. No slackers were permitted. And in societies that lacked the formal structures of political leadership, family heads and lineages doubled as economic, social, and political units.

A further problem arises in generalizing about the nature of African traditional economies. There were in excess of 800 distinct ethnic societies in Africa at the outset of colonial rule, and each to a certain extent represented a unique collection of economic institutions and values. Production systems ranged from simple hunting and gathering communities, such as the !Kung people of the Kalahari Desert, that seldom extended beyond the basic family and others who had established marital links with that family. At the other end of the spectrum were complex trading societies scattered across the Sahel, which were in contact with both Europe and the Middle East.[20] Cities such as Timbucktu, Ouagadougou, and Kano served as the focal points for vast networks of markets, with a high degree of monetization rather than reliance upon barter alone. Gold dust, cowry shells, twisted bars of iron, and other forms of money served in lieu of actual coins. Within the broader social community in these more complex societies, there was a specialization of labor based upon crafts, including the making of leather products, clay pots, metal objects, and other commodities. Intermediate to the hunters and gatherers and the large city-state economies, there were a number of pastoral societies located around the continent with political, economic, and social systems based upon the ownership and exchange of cattle.

Most economies in pre-colonial Africa, however, were based upon subsistence agriculture, supplemented by hunting and gathering. There was little by way of surplus for exchange internally or externally. The work unit consisted of the immediate members of the extended family and neighbors who engaged in some cooperative enterprises relative to cultivation, hunting, or housebuilding. The basic work unit largely consumed what the unit itself had produced, and—given limited techniques of storing and preserving crops—most of the foodstuffs were exhausted before the next harvest had commenced. There was only a limited amount of economic role differentiation within most agricultural societies other than the distribution of tasks by age and sex categories. Production was based in most instances upon the limited technology of the digging stick or the hoe, and that technology was transmitted largely in oral form or by imitation. Some societies, it should be noted, were more ingenious than others in constructing elaborate irrigation systems, coping with loss of soil fertility, and devising ways of adjusting to a very unpredictable environment.

Although cultivators had a good working knowledge of the nature of the soil, the prospects for rainfall, and other basic data, this practical knowledge was supplemented by a heavy reliance upon magico-religious performances as a means of ensuring success in cultivation. Rituals, which involved political leadership, played a significant role in each stage of the cultivation cycle from the preparing of the fields to the gathering of the harvest. Rational innovations in technology, of course, did occur from time to time as new crops were discovered and introduced, but since most communities were living at the margin of survival and faced with recurrent drought, there was little enthusiasm for taking risks in experimenting with new techniques of production.

The ownership of land stood at the center of economic decision-making in traditional African society. With few exceptions among agriculturalists, the ownership of land was vested in the community, with an individual and his family having only claims to the land they cultivated on the basis of usufructory right of occupancy. Each family was assigned land sufficient to meet family needs. As the family size increased, so did the allocation of land. Conversely, land claims diminished as old age, marriage, or death of family members reduced need. One could, however, personally own the products of the soil, as well as any trees which were planted by the family or any structure built on communally owned land. As an aspect of social justice in the land tenure system, land was frequently parcelled out in widely scattered fragments rather than being assigned as one compact block. In this way, each cultivator had plots of varying soil quality and varying proximity to a water source or the village settlement. Shifting cultivation was the conventional means for restoring the fertility of the soil: the community had to have under its jurisdiction three or four times more land than was actually being cultivated at a given period.

Although those who exercised political authority in the allocation of land might be able to claim some portion of the crop and a portion of the hunt as tribute, agricultural surplus was limited. In times of hardship, moreover, tribute paid to political leaders in the form of grain and other produce was redistributed as a form of welfare to those in need. Any tendency to abuse political power would be partially inhibited by the prospect of discontented members of the community picking up their limited material possessions and striking out into the wilderness in search of unoccupied land, or joining a neighboring community. "Hiving off" was a popular form of political protest in areas where unallocated productive land was abundant.

While some of the social aspects of traditional economic behavior may appear to be in line with the modernization objectives of nationalist leadership intent upon either a socialist or a capitalist strategy of development, this may be only a superficial observation. For certainly the dramatic transformation of agriculture under any strategy of development is impeded by the excessive acreage needed for shifting cultivation; by the inefficiency of fragmented land holdings; by the ritual control over agriculture; and by other traditional values, institutions, and techniques. The new social collective, moreover, tends not to be the family or the parochial village, but the national state itself, or producers' cooperatives. In addition, the persistence of settlement in isolated and scattered rural homesteads is not conducive to the more efficient use of human and other resources for expanded production.

Scattered patterns of residence make more difficult and costly the provision of schooling, health facilities, and other human services. For those intent upon modified capitalist development, collective ownership of land limits prospects that the innovative cultivator will have collateral for a loan to improve the land.

Even more aggravating to the modernization process is the stance many nationalist leaders have had to take with respect to pastoral societies within their midst. As noted in Chapter 3, pastoralists in East, Central, and Southern Africa tend to view the ownership of cattle as socially and politically significant within their respective societies, rather than as a source of protein on the hoof, designed to meet nutritional needs. Thus, instead of contributing to improving the living standard of members of that society, the raising of cattle largely contributes to the further erosion of the limited soil resources of the society and engages a significant portion of available labor and water in a largely uneconomic enterprise. Modern veterinary science only aggravates the problem by increasing the size and vigor of the herds. Efforts to restrict herds, erect fences to limit their grazing areas, and encourage both the sedentarization of pastoralists and the sale of cattle to abattoirs are resisted by what proves to be the most traditional of all people in Africa. In countries like Botswana and Cameroon the pastoralists exercise significant political power at the national level.

PRE-COLONIAL SOURCES OF ECONOMIC CHANGE. Not all change is necessarily for the good, as is certainly apparent when we examine some of the pre-colonial sources of economic transformation in Africa. Certainly one of the most dramatic factors in change was the slave trade. Although slavery as a domestic institution existed in many societies in Africa long before contact with non-Africans took place, it was the external slave trade which made the greatest impact upon traditional economic systems. Much attention has been focused on the dehumanizing treatment as a form of property to which most of these captives were subjected in the New World, as well as on the appalling loss of life during the journey to the African coast and at sea. Less attention has been paid to the impact of the extrication of over eleven million young adult males and females from their rural villages upon African agricultural productivity and development in general. Many Marxist critics argue that it prevented Africans from having the same early responses to economic innovation that led to the transformation of some of the less developed areas of Europe during the same period. Instead of remaining in Africa and responding to European trading demands for palm oil, rubber, and other crops which could be grown there, the African slaves contributed to the development of the cotton, tobacco, and other agricultural activities in the developing economies of the Americas. Not on the same scale, perhaps, but over a longer period, the Middle East slave trade found Arab caravans raiding villages far into the interior of West, East, and Central

Africa. An estimated million were pressed into doing domestic and other menial tasks in the Sudan, Zanzibar, the Arabian peninsula, and far beyond.

Curiously, the religious belief system and other factors associated with the societies which produced both the West Atlantic and the Middle East slave trade had a positive impact upon economic change in African society. The Arab slaver, for example, was invariably accompanied by itinerant Muslim traders. In addition to exposing cultivating societies to woven cloth, metal utensils for cooking and eating, and other commodities, the Arab trading centers became future cities, which altered the exclusively rural patterns of African residence. The use of various forms of currency, moreover, provided a cash economy which complemented what had been basically subsistence or barter economies. Although it had largely a religious purpose and consisted of rote learning in an alien tongue, the establishment of Koranic schools by Muslim traders did introduce a form of literacy into societies which—with only a very few exceptions—previously lacked written forms of their own languages. This was an unintended stimulus to modernization, altering the role of the convert in his traditional community.

An even more significant impact upon traditional economies was made by Christianity.[21] Missionaries brought not merely a different belief system which undermined the ritualistic basis of society—including traditional agriculture—but a new form of social organization which disrupted the economic work units of traditional society. The nuclear bilateral Christian family has gradually replaced the extended family based upon plural marriage or polygamy. The education system of the Christian missionaries, moreover, had a transformational impact upon social, economic, and other relationships far beyond that of the itinerant Muslim Koranic teachers, even though literacy was at base a vehicle for spreading the Gospel. The missionaries transcribed many African languages, thus providing reading skills in a language familiar to the African reader. Education furthermore provided the catechist with technical skills which allowed him or her to pursue a livelihood independent of his extended family and neighbors. Thus, the bakers, masons, carpenters, clerks, and other roles needed for the running of the mission churches and schools became readily available to the broader society beyond the church. A particularly relevant feature of the Protestant variety of Christianity was the emphasis placed upon individual responsibility with respect to one's action leading to salvation. This is central to secular innovation, and it contributed to undermining the collective nature of traditional economic organization.

COLONIAL RULE AND ITS LEGACY. The formal imposition of colonial rule, however, constituted the most pervasive factor in undermining traditional economies as well as ushering in—for good or evil—those institutions, values, and behavior patterns associated with modernization. No African society was immune from the prospects of externally directed change, including the dominant ethnic minorities within the nominally independent states of Ethiopia, Liberia, and South Africa. Internally each of these three states, as noted previously, represented another form of colonial dependency.

Under European colonial rule no community or its citizens were free to pursue unimpeded all the kinds of economic activities that had characterized traditional society. Although the formal institutions of slavery and the slave trade came to an end just prior to the concerted political scramble for territory during the latter half of the nineteenth century, human beings under imperial rule became in effect the property of the colonial state. As noted in Chapter 2 Africans could be conscripted into European armies; required to give a number of days free labor in behalf of road construction and other European government purposes; forcibly recruited to work in the European-owned mines or plantations; or pressured to leave their homes in search of wage employment in order to pay European-imposed taxes. Tax obligations could no longer be satisfied by labor or produce in kind, and this compelled those Africans who did remain at home to enter the monetized economy by planting cash crops, which could be sold within the territory or exported abroad. It could be argued that the surplus cash did provide Africans with the means to purchase consumer goods that would otherwise be denied them, but nevertheless, it was European administrators and private associates who determined the wages of laborers as well as the prices of cocoa, palm kernels, and other crops, and it was the European merchants who decided what consumer goods should be provided and determined the country of origin of these commodities.

The imposition of colonial rule, at the same time that it expanded African participation in an economy or economies beyond the parochial village or regional colonial rule, also limited the way in which Africans participated in economic transactions at the continental or global level. That is, the territorial taxation system, the network of roads built within a colony, the European-controlled marketing arrangements, and other factors did translate the African economic participant to a larger geographic plane of activity. On the other hand, the use of specific territorial currencies, the erection of tariff duties on goods crossing the international borders, and other factors largely restricted African participation to a colony or grouping of colonies controlled by a single metropole. Indeed, from the broader perspective, the particular crops or minerals which were produced and exported from a specific colony often only made sense in terms of the overall interests and needs of the imperial power concerned. As noted earlier, instead of permitting each British colony to duplicate and compete with the others in terms of production there was a specialization with respect to agricultural and mineral extraction. Development was in many cases, moreover, intentionally deferred for specific countries such as Sierra Leone, Tanganyika, and Malawi, and information regarding known mineral resources was suppressed if it upset the imperial plan by creating competition for already established markets. As a consequence of all of this, there were few colonies—other than the white settler territories—which had diversified and balanced economies. One or a limited number of export commodities were developed in each colony. This meant that the colony after independence became extremely vulnerable to price fluctuations, to the development of synthetics, and to diseases which might destroy the principal crops. With respect to the last, for example, the economic health of colonial Ghana was threatened in the early 1950's by the root-shoot disease which hit the cocoa crop—the mainstay of the economy.

It was clear in many ways that, despite references to "taking-up the white man's burden," the primary purpose of the colonial administration was to serve the interests of the local whites or the European metropole. This meant, first, that pre-existing patterns of economic interaction persisted only on sufferance, if at all. Hence, indigenous long distance trading, the grazing of cattle over great areas in West Africa, and other transactions were substantially altered. Secondly, as noted previously, the overall thrust of colonial production concentrated upon the export of crops and minerals needed by European industries, to the neglect of domestic food production. Very little of the processing of these extractive commodities was done in Africa unless the high costs to local Europeans became a factor. This meant generally that there was less opportunity for African employment in the significant stages of processing and manufacture. Canning factories or even shops for producing simple agricultural equipment were not established in colonies other than the settler territories. Most of the earnings from the extractive industries were exported in the form of company profits or used to pay the high salaries and perquisites for the expatriate European personnel who monopolized the skilled positions.

There were many ways in which the colonial bureaucrats put themselves at the service of private European entrepreneurs: the forcible recruitment of labor, the statutory setting of wages and conditions of labor, setting prices for consumer items, and designing the transport and communications networks to serve the direct interests of European entrepreneurs. It was not until the Second World War that the British and the French began to commit significant public funds to African economic development per se.

The impact of colonial rule upon individual Africans as economic entrepreneurs was in many respects idiosyncratic. Whether exposure to European enterprises was a plus or a minus, it tended to affect most significantly those who by accident of residence were located near a port, a mining center, or a transport route that was of primary interest to Europeans. The colonial administrators were not interested in all regions of a dependency to the same degree. The location of a mineral, the existence of conditions favorable to plantation agriculture, and other factors led the European colonial interest to be concentrated in clusters. Despite the dramatic development of long-distance labor migration throughout the continent, those Africans who were located near an enterprise were normally pressed into employment earlier than those in more remote areas. When schools and clinics were estab-lished—because employers needed a healthy work force with a certain level of skills—then the Africans in adjacent areas or those who migrated to that center tended to receive a disproportionate share of the benefits of contact. Hence, by the end of the colonial era the uneven regional patterns of de-velopment left the nationalist leaders with some difficult problems in terms of equalizing participation in, and benefits from, modernization. Not only was there regional imbalance, but most of the developments took place within the urban centers as they emerged, creating the current urban/rural conflict.

It was not only in the agricultural realm that African involvement was qualitatively limited. With respect to the expanding network of commerce, Africans could be consumers and engage in petty trade, but the large trading houses that monopolized exports and imports were owned by Europeans or even by Asians and Lebanese. In mining and industrial development, too, Africans were largely excluded from ownership and participated only at the lower ends of the employment spectrum. As a case in point, in the vast Katanga Province of the former Belgian Congo, the Union Minière du Haut Katanga did perhaps the best job of any industrial group in training Africans to run heavy equipment and occupy other skilled positions. At the time of independence, however, not a single African served in a significant mana-gerial position in the UMHK, and there was not in 1960 a single trained economist among the dozen or so Zairois college graduates. Economic control was intended to remain in Belgian hands long after political independence had been achieved.

Inasmuch as the overwhelming majority of African producers were (and still are) involved in agriculture, it was in that field that colonialism made the greatest impact upon traditional economic systems and African entre-preneurs. In those colonies which were attractive to European settlement, the colonial impact upon African agriculture was tragic in the extreme. As noted in Chapter 2, colonialism removed from African hands and transferred to Europeans the ownership of the most productive land. Africans were in many cases forcibly evicted from land that had been the property of their community for generations and that held the graves of their ancestors. Al-ternatively, they were permitted to remain as tenants or squatters working as part of the pool of cheap labor on the new European estates or plantations. In the case of South Africa, the 72 percent of the population that was Black had been reduced to legal occupancy of roughly 13 percent of the land area. In Zimbabwe the 5 percent of the population that was white owned 50 percent of the land. Similar quantitative racial disparities emerged in Kenya, Zambia, Angola, Mozambique, and other settler territories. The disparities in quality of land were even more revealing. In very few instances, for example, was land containing significant mineral deposits left in African hands. A clear case of travesty occurred in Kenya where the European-owned agricultural land was in the more comfortable and salubrious high-lands; had the greatest prospects of a reasonable rainfall each year; was mostly free of tsetse flies, mosquitos, and other organisms that transmit the debili-tating diseases that affect humans in the tropics; and was relatively sparsely populated. Alienation of land to Europeans in Kenya, Zimbabwe, and other settler areas not only accelerated the creation of a landless proletariat in the new urban centers, but it provided the focal point for armed hostility to European colonial rule.

Agricultural systems and the lives of peasant cultivators were also dis-rupted for those Africans who were left on land still held under communal tenure. Instead of being limited to subsistence cultivation, cultivators were encouraged if not actually compelled to engage in cash crop farming. Indeed, the element of coercion was a recurrent aspect of the contact between African cultivators and European administrators and agricultural technicians. In-novation was to come not by persuasion or example but by threat of a fine or even imprisonment for failure to innovate. Africans, for example, were told to plant those crops which were needed in Europe or for processing industries in the colony. Conversely, Africans were forbidden to plant crops—such as coffee in Kenya—where doing so would compete with Eu-ropean plantation agriculture. Africans were told how and when to plant not only the introduced crops, but their own traditional food crops as well. This often had disastrous consequences, since the orders of the European agri-cultural officer were often based upon imperfect knowledge of local growing conditions. In British Africa each rule about soil conservation, planting tech-niques, cutting and planting of trees, grazing of cattle, and protection of water sources carried a fine or other penalty for failure to comply. Agricul-tural education and demonstration took a far distant second place to coercion in achieving agricultural change. As a consequence, there persists in many countries a continuing antipathy toward agricultural innovation.

Another recurring aspect of the colonialists' desire to bring about changes in peasant cultivation was caprice on the part of European administrators. My micro-study of the Newala District of colonial Tanganyika documented the way in which innovation in natural resource management reflected more the whims, prejudices, and preferences of the current British commissioner rather than the broad interests of African cultivators. Seldom did the ad-ministrators take into account African "conventional wisdom" about the promise and limitations of the physical environment regarding cultivation. As each new commissioner was posted to the district, the Africans had only to wait patiently to discover the latest version of what they called in Swahili "the white man's madness." As soon as the new madness was evidenced, one could adjust accordingly, forgetting all the innovations of the preceding commissioners.[22]

The coercion and arbitrary actions of the colonial era have left a legacy of negative African attitudes toward agriculture. Leaving the farm to find work in the city or the mines was a way of escaping the harassment of the rural administrator. In interviews this author conducted in Tanganyika during the 1950s, very few school boys indicated that they desired a career in agriculture, and hence it is not surprising that the implementation of Julius Nyerere's program of development based upon agriculture has had ultimately to resort to a measure of coercion. These negative attitudes are also reflected throughout Africa in the low prestige of schools of agriculture in the many new universities. To a great extent, disdain for agriculture has been responsible for the rapid rate of rural-to-urban migration in Africa. This has left more and more mouths to be fed in the cities, with fewer and fewer hands in the rural area to produce the food. Women and children did have critical roles to play in traditional agriculture, but the burden imposed upon them in the entire range of agricultural activities was intensified with the absence of young adult males who had migrated elsewhere in search of wage employment. Since women continued as well to have their traditional roles to perform, this inevitably made cultivating and marketing of crops a less efficient enterprise.

This is not meant to suggest that the colonial impact upon agricultural practices was all bad for the African cultivator. Traditional agricultural technology, after all, was survival technology at best. European contact supplemented this with information about the value of natural and chemical fertilizers, the utility of crop rotation and diversification, and the use of plows and other instruments that were helpful but not destructive of the fragile African soils. Many cultivators were encouraged to plant yams and other food crops in the same field with the cocoa and coffee trees. The income provided by export agriculture did, moreover, put cash into the hands of cultivators so that they could pay school fees, build better housing, and invest in petty training or transport. The horizons of the African producers were considerably widened as a consequence of their involvement in the global economy. Marxist critics to the contrary, such involvement was not always destructive of African interests.

POST-INDEPENDENCE POLICIES AND PRACTICES. It is apparent from the preceding that the institutions and values of the traditional and colonial eras have had a mixed impact upon the development of both food and export agriculture in the period since independence. Many of the negative attitudes toward agricultural innovation and patterns of global economic dependency are difficult to alter. Evaluation of post-independence performance is further complicated by the catastrophic droughts that have afflicted various sectors of the continent during the 1970s and 1980s. However, as Carl K. Eicher, one of the leading agricultural economists working on African problems, has concluded, "the current dilemma is not caused by the weather." While recognizing the impact of colonial surplus extraction strategies and the faulty advice from many expatriate planning advisers, Eicher further concludes that "post-independence corruption, mismanagement, repressive pricing of

farm commodities, and the urban bias in development strategies" are significant factors. He asserts that "the crisis stems from a seamless web of
political, technical and structural constraints which are a product of colonial
surplus extraction strategies, misguided development plans and priorities of
African states since independence. . . ."[23]

Most African states have now enjoyed twenty-five years of independence,
yet the colonial powers and international capitalism still serve as convenient
scapegoats to mask the fact that much of the responsibility for failure must
be placed at the feet of African political leaders themselves. Take the case
of refugees, which is tied in with the manifestation of famine in many parts
of Africa today. A good portion of the refugees are victims not of the drought
alone, or even simply of the drought combined with politics, but of political
policies and programs exclusively. Idi Amin's expulsion of the Asians from
Uganda in 1975, for example, was a significant factor in the famine and
economic dislocations that occurred there in the decade that followed. The
famine in Ethiopia has been exacerbated by the political and economic chaos
arising from the unwillingness of the Amhara dominant minority in the central government in the regimes of both former Emperor Haile Selassie and
Lt. Col. Mengistu Haile Miriam to accede to the legitimate demands of the
Eritreans, the Somali, the Oromo, and the Tigre people for either autonomy
or independence. To the shock of Western donors and the distress of the
people in the rebel areas, the Dergue refused during the 1985 famine to
permit foreign relief agencies to distribute food on a non-political basis.
Finally, however well intentioned or long overdue, the action taken by the
revolutionary regime in 1975 against the feudal patterns of agriculture in
Ethiopia, as well as the timing of this ideological program, must be counted
as a major factor in the subsequent agricultural crisis.[24] The estimated
100,000 or more refugees from Rwanda and Burundi in the 1970s were also
victims of politics, not the drought. Finally, the decision of the Nigerian
civilian government of Shehu Shagari in 1983 to deport roughly a million
West Africans certainly had a disruptive effect upon Ghana and the other
host countries of the deported aliens; the returnees could not quickly be
absorbed into the agricultural sector, yet they constituted additional mouths
that had to be fed.

The difficulty with political and other refugees is that the rhetoric of pan-
Africanism of the 1960s has virtually disappeared now that the nation-building within former colonial boundaries has become more firmly entrenched.
There are few African leaders like Jaafar al-Nimeiry, the former president
of the Sudan, who have been courageous enough to suggest that, in keeping
with the principles of the Koran, his country must welcome all strangers in
need. Nor are there many with the vision of former Tanzanian leader Julius
Nyerere, who creatively followed the traditional African pattern of hospitality
toward strangers: "After three days, the guest is given a hoe." That is, Nyerere offered land to the refugees from neighboring states and provided

them with the opportunity to be absorbed into the new Tanzanian society. Tanzania is a society in which specific ethnic identities have been subordinated to a broader national identity. Far too many African leaders prefer to keep the refugees in their midst as temporary residents even when they are of the same ethnic origins. Somalia, for example, has not resettled the roughly one and a half million refugees from the Ogaden region of Ethiopia on its territory. To do so would constitute a forfeiture of the irredentist territorial claim to the Ogaden itself. Thus, like the Palestinians, the Somali refugees seem destined to constitute a permanent refugee population, requiring massive external relief efforts to sustain them.

Another political source of poverty is the urban bias—if not outright disdain for the rural sector—that is manifested by many African political leaders in various ways. A disproportionate share of a typical African national budget, for example, goes to meet the health, educational, and other needs of the urban minority. The paving of streets in the national capital takes a higher priority in most states over the creation of even modest feeder roads to the rural villages where the domestic foodstuffs and other agricultural commodities begin their journey into national and international markets. Only a few countries like Nigeria, Tanzania, and Malawi have substantial and respectable schools of agriculture or forestry in their new national universities, and research on agronomy, crop diseases, and the general field of natural resource development is grossly neglected in favor of more esoteric subjects.

The bias in favor of urban over rural interests is probably most dramatically revealed in the series of policies which give the national governments of many African states extraordinary control over the agricultural production. As Robert Bates has persuasively pointed out, the earnings of the African grower are substantially reduced as a consequence of the monopoly which government marketing boards attempt to assert over the distribution of seed and the purchase of crops, the conscious setting of prices at far less than world prices, the taxing of export crops, discriminatory import tax structures that penalize farmers at the expense of city dwellers, and other mechanisms.[25] The African farmers, according to World Bank estimates in 1981, in at least thirteen states were short-changed by as much as half the value of the crops that they grew for export.[26] Producers of domestic food crops were similarly undercompensated or found the currency they received in payment was considerably inflated. The receipts, moreover, could not be creatively employed since the shops in rural areas were severely limited in terms of available consumer goods. Rural schools and clinics were equally in short supply.

The reasons for this urban bias are twofold. In the first place, the leadership of a state that has a very fragile political system is alert to the anomic potential of a dissatisfied urban mob. The Rice Riots in Monrovia in 1979, for example, set the stage for the coup one year later. Similar riots occurred in Ghana and the Sudan following increases in the price of sugar and other commodities. Placating urban mobs so as to keep the current governments in power requires extraordinary measures. Second, as Bates has pointed out, it is the proceeds from the one sector that is not politically organized and that has demonstrated some growth—however modest—that are expected to pay for the instant industrialization sought by the leadership, on the assumption referred to earlier: that most modernizing societies tend to be industrializing societies. Thus, rather than curbing consumer and other expectations of the urbanites at the doorstep of the national elite, the latter puts the squeeze on the more remote rural producer. Sometimes, as in Senegal, this takes place with the acquiescence of a privileged rural elite that has been coopted into the national coalition as a tradeoff for placating the rural constituents politically.[27]

The response of rural cultivators to the policies of urban bias vary. Some, for example, elect to throw in the towel and join the ranks of those who have gone to the city in search of better income, if not a partially subsidized way of life. Others, reluctant to abandon their rural roots, turn to domestic black market operations or to smuggling their produce across an international boundary where they can get a higher price. Still others stay in the countryside but either revert completely to subsistence farming to ensure a steady source of food for the immediate family or turn to the production of crops which are not purchased by the government marketing boards. Whatever the options, however, the decline of African agriculture continues.

The Quest for Ideological Solutions

Faced with the mounting poverty of their people and their own politically precarious position within society, many African leaders have turned to ideology as the answer to their problems.[28] This applies whether the leaders are civilians or military leaders who have come to power in the midst of an economic crisis. Often the ideology is simple and unrefined. It consists of identifying the culprit responsible for the present economic or political misery and reminding the public constantly who or what that enemy is. As often as not, it is the "heritage of colonial rule," "neo-colonialism," or "international capitalism" that is identified as the source of African poverty. Or the ideology may consist of a few convenient slogans which are supposed to serve as guides for overcoming the economic crisis. A lot of rhetoric and energy, for example, went into the campaign, "Operation: Feed the Nation," which the military under General Obasanjo in the late 1970s mounted to deal with Nigeria's rising food imports.

One of the more simplified ideological slogans actually makes a lot of sense, but has unfortunately been more honored in the breach: the demand for "self-reliance" as the preferred antidote to the disease of "neo-colonialism." This means recognizing that reliance upon external skills, sources of capital,

trade relationships, and other economic linkages only delays the development of national institutions, economic relationships, and habits that are of
direct and primary benefit to the African society. "Self-reliance" sometimes
takes the form of creating modest local industrial efforts which result in
import-substitution activities. These activities not only provide jobs for Africans but alleviate the balance of payment problem faced by every African
country. In a country like Malawi the leadership has embarked upon a whole
range of pragmatic answers to external dependency situations.[29] They include
greater diversification in the production of crops for export; cutting the
external transport costs by having a shorter rail link built to connect land-
locked Malawi to the sea; relocating the capital in an effort to stimulate
greater economic interaction among the three regions of the country; mounting an impressive reforestation program which diminishes Malawi's need for
imported fuels and building materials; and exploiting largely untapped domestic resources—such as the fish from Lake Malawi—in meeting the nutritional needs of its people. In addition, by foresightedly storing surplus
grain during periods of bountiful harvests, Malawi has managed to save for
subsequent years the one-third of the crops that would otherwise fall victim
to predators, rot, and mildew.

Unfortunately, the slogan of "self-reliance" in many countries has remained largely an instrument for placating dissident political challengers to
existing regimes or for persuading a potential external donor that the assistance sought will be short-term in nature—that is, sufficient to get internal
forces to take over and assume the momentum to sustain further development. Ironically—as will be discussed below—the popularity of the "self-
reliance" slogan has proceeded at about the same accelerated pace as the
African states increased reliance upon external grants, loans, and other forms
of assistance. Probably no single country demonstrates this anomaly more
than Tanzania, whose leader, Julius Nyerere, was one of the more eloquent
apostles of "self-reliance." The external public debt of Tanzania (eighth highest in Africa) went from 248 million dollars in 1970 to 1.6 billion dollars in
1982. Its share of development assistance to all of Africa from overseas donors
went from 267 million dollars in 1976 to almost three times that figure in
1982.[30]

THE LURE OF SOCIALISM. Many African leaders, not content with slogans,
have gone on to formulate broader ideological programs of development.
These programs range in sophistication from a series of scattered, isolated,
and frequently contradictory pronouncements by the national leadership to
the kind of elaborate philosophical party manifestos issued by Julius Nyerere
of Tanzania over the years, which constitute a formulated action program
for translating the ideas into a functioning reality. Some leaders attempt to
give modern expression to traditional norms and institutions, while others
attempt to integrate the principles of Islam or Christianity into the program

for economic modernization. What many of the ideological programs have in common, however, is some kind of commitment to socialism.

Within the broad category of socialist strategies for African development there is a considerable range of diversity. Some programs regard the achievement of socialism as an end in itself; others view it as an intermediate stage preceding that end phase of history which Marx called communism. Some leaders like Nyerere and Kaunda have insisted that socialism is to be achieved by voluntary means, whereas the Ethiopian Dergue accepts the utility of coercion. There is a difference of approach with regard to mass involvement; Tanzania and Zambia have insisted on it, while Ethiopia's position is that the masses are to be led to this new stage by a vanguard party of enlightened elites. Finally, the programs differ considerably with respect to the appropriate role of the military in carrying out a socialist strategy.[31]

How do we explain the fascination for a socialist approach to development in Africa? In part it can be viewed as another phase of the anti-colonial struggle. Since each of the six West European states with colonies in Africa represented some form of capitalist development (even though Spain and Portugal varied considerably from the others), one could attack the evils of colonialism by attacking capitalism.[32] Moreover, it was argued by the neo-Marxists, continuation of the links with the global capitalist markets was a major factor in keeping Africa underdeveloped. The most privileged white and Asian elites in colonial Africa were those who owned land on a freehold basis, participated in the market economy, and advocated freedom of enterprise in the use of physical and human resources. Thus, in attacking local colonial privilege one must also attack the capitalist principles on which the privilege appeared to be based.

There was also the question of models of development available to African leaders. The industrial capitalist models of the United States, Britain, or even France seemed to be inappropriate to the rural and backward conditions of most African states. These models were years beyond the grasp of the African states, and in order to remain in power the new nationalist elite had to move quickly if Africa was not to fall even further behind economically. Traditional models (whether agricultural, commercial, or pastoral), moreover, provided few guidelines. Given not only the lack of dynamism in these models but also the multi-ethnic nature of most states, which traditional model was to be chosen? The fascist models of Spain, Portugal, and prewar Italy were also inappropriate given the racism and elitism associated with them.

The Soviet and Chinese experiments in socialist development, on the other hand, appeared promising. Both states were relatively backward at the time of revolutionary change, were predominantly rural, had not been identified with the colonial partition of Africa, and were the primary challengers to the capitalist states that dominated African external economic relationships.

The USSR and China as potential friends lacked the conflicts of international loyalties, moreover, which made it difficult for the United States and the West to be unequivocally committed to the termination of European colonialism and of white racism in South Africa. Of even greater significance, the USSR and China had both demonstrated the ability in a remarkably brief period of time not only to bring order out of politically chaotic situations, but also to accomplish feats of economic advancement which were unthinkable a decade before the experiments in socialist development were launched.

Not all advocates of socialism felt that emulation of the Soviet or Chinese models was desirable. Nyerere, for example, saw the transition from traditional to modern norms and institutions more easily accomplished within a socialist framework, but he rejected the inevitability of class conflict as a necessary instrument in achieving socialism. A Roman Catholic, he also saw an appropriate role for religious and other non-economic values. This rejection of economic determinism was also evident in Kenneth Kaunda's "Humanism."

Finally, it must be recognized that some African leaders opportunistically flirted with socialism in order to attract attention and funds from both East and West by giving the appearance of charting a course independent from the colonial past.

Whatever the motivations for opting for socialism over capitalism, however, few African leaders who were demanding "self-reliance" seemed to be aware of the irony of their rejecting one Western model for development— capitalism—in favor of another—socialism—which also had Western credentials. Nor did those who opted for "scientific socialism" or a rigidly Marxian path to socialism acknowledge the inappropriateness of applying Marx to African economic conditions. The Marxian dialectic explicitly assumed that in the age-long quest for abundance, mankind must pass through several phases of economic development. Industrial capitalism, of which Marx was but one of many nineteenth-century critics, was nevertheless regarded by Marx as a necessary prior stage to the achievement of socialism and the end stage of history called communism. Without capitalism, Marx had argued, there could be no socialism or communism. Despite this, Lenin and his Soviet colleagues in post-Czarist Russia attempted not only to leap over the stage of industrial capitalism but also to supplement the revolutionary role of the industrial worker with the ancillary support of the peasantry. (Marx, ironically, had only contempt for the peasant and his parochial mentality.) Mao Tse-tung in China went even further than Lenin in assuming that the socialist revolution could commence in a society which was still basically rural and agricultural, and in assuming that the worker and peasant shared an equal responsibility in bringing the revolution about. Thus, in opting for a socialist strategy, most African states are not only considerably removed from the original Marxian thesis, but they lack even the modicum of urban-

ization, commercialization, and industrialization that China had evidenced
in 1949. Few Africans outside Southern Africa could be labeled industrial
proletariat in the original Marxian meaning of the term. Nyerere therefore
argued that African socialism had to be something different than Marxian
socialism since classes of any significance did not exist in traditional society,
and those class differences introduced during the colonial era disappeared
when the rule of white colonialists was terminated. Moreover, even as theoreticians realized that Africa did not easily fit the amended Soviet and
Chinese versions of the Marxian dialectic, in a strange twist of fate, leaders
in these two latter models have suddenly rediscovered the need for some
belated endorsement of capitalist principles such as price mechanisms, wage
differentials and incentives, sectoral autonomy, an element of choice in use
of human talents, and even some limited private ownership of property. This
turn of events, frankly, has left the African socialist theoreticians "twisting
slowly in the wind."

Even before the 1980s shift in thought in China, however, there was a
realization in many African states that socialist principles were simply not
working. In Tanzania, Nyerere had to forswear his objections to coercion in
order to get more people associated with the *ujamaa* villages. Under the
ujamaa (literally, "family togetherness") program every Tanzanian was to be
identified with a rural village and to participate not only in the transformation
of agriculture but in the restructuring of Tanzanian society along socialist
lines.[33] Similarly, Mugabe in Zimbabwe found that in the early stages of land
redistribution after the liberation war the demobilized troops preferred to
acquire land on a freehold basis or to return to a traditional form of ownership
rather than farming collectively with their former comrades-in-arms.[34] The
more successful cases of meeting the goal of self-sufficiency in food production were those states whose leaders rejected socialist panaceas. Other indices of development also seemed to favor pragmatic and eclectic rather than
strictly ideological programs.

THE ASSUMPTION OF EGALITARIANISM. Before leaving the issue of ideology,
it should be noted that much of the socialist thinking and strategy in Africa
has been based on a dual assumption: basic equality was not only characteristic of traditional society, but it was what Africans desired and demanded
in the future. Given limited resources and the slowness of economic growth,
anything short of egalitarianism—it was argued—would leave many people
in an aggravated state of misery while a few elites reaped the benefits of
whatever growth did take place. The insistence on egalitarianism also meant
that the potential talents needed for development would be denied the
society as a whole if regional, sex, ethnic, or other ascriptive factors led to
the unequal distribution of educational, health, and other services of government.

The evidence that egalitarianism was a feature of traditional African society
is based upon a selective analysis of economic, social, and political norms

and institutions. In the economic category, egalitarianism was clearly manifested in the communal ownership of land, reinforced by the principle of
distribution of fragments in terms of their varying quality. Those who assigned rights in land were highly localized in their authority and thus prevented from constituting themselves as a landowning class. Egalitarianism
could also be found in the fact that much of the work in agriculture was
performed collectively by members of the extended family or the neighborhood. Moreover, the environment limited the accumulation of great
stores of wealth, and even the manner in which cattle were distributed within
pastoral societies reinforced bonds of solidarity between the patron owners
and the clients who tended the cattle, with the clients getting some of the
benefits in terms of milk, manure, and social protection. It was also argued
that the exchange of cattle at the time of marriage, divorce, and other ceremonial occasions distributed this form of wealth more widely among pastoral
societies.

The "leveling" tendency of the extended family has also been referred to.
While the size of a kinship group did have social and political significance
in traditional society with respect to relative power, a large kin group meant
a large number of individuals who could make claims for support against the
more fortunate members of that group. Generally, as Nyerere suggested,
there was a tradition of charity within the group as well as hospitality toward
strangers. The other social traditional groupings based upon sex and age
categories in a community were also equalizing factors inasmuch as they cut
across kinship lines. Thus, these groupings in many societies established
bonds of horizontal solidarity that transcended any claim to higher social
rankings on the part of the "founding" clans or families. This tendency toward
egalitarianism was even more pronounced in societies such as the Zulu under
Shaka, where young men were physically removed from their families and
remained in regiments for a period of several years. The peer group relationship within Zulu society, therefore, was a counterbalance to the prestige
of particular families within Zulu society.

Finally, in terms of political relationships, egalitarianism was manifested
in the many traditional societies in which political power was situational
rather than the continuous monopoly of one person or one family. The rules
regarding how and when people fought each other within headless (acephalous) political societies such as the Nuer or Masai limited the kind of
relationship between and among kinship segments. The rules actually
achieved "peace in the feud." Foes in one situation would have to be relied
upon as allies in a subsequent conflict. On the other hand, in those societies
which had institutionalized political offices, there were also egalitarian mechanisms. For example, the payment of tribute was often viewed as a social
security measure, with grain and other commodities only being collected by
leaders in time of good harvest and being redistributed to the people in
times of famine or other misfortune.

The painting of traditional society as typically egalitarian in thrust is, however, a highly selective analysis which ignores much of the countervailing evidence. In Tanzania, for example, Nyerere acknowledged the low status of women in traditional society in his country, but he conveniently overlooked the existence of rigid caste systems among the Haya, the Ha, and other societies.[35] He ignored as well the fact that slavery was an indigenous institution long before it was exacerbated by the Arab slave trade. The political egalitarianism Nyerere described was not a feature of those societies in which kingship was ritually protected from challengers except in extreme situations. The option of "hiving off" into the forest when political leadership became abusive of property and other rights only existed when pressures on arable land were not severe. Finally, the picture of economic sharing—while reasonably accurate for many traditional societies—could not ignore the added prestige and power as well as command of limited resources that accrued to those who controlled the allocation of land or who owned the largest herds of cattle.

The egalitarian argument based upon tradition, however, may soon became academic. The period of colonial rule created new kinds of ethnic and regional privileges and distinctions based upon disparities in education and exposure to modern economic enterprises. New forms of property emerged to challenge the traditional wealth based upon land distribution or ownership of cattle. Although the discrepancies in wealth between Africans on the one hand and Europeans and Asians on the other may have been more distinctive than discrepancies among various categories of Africans, the latter distinctions were of significance in shaping the nationalist movements. As independence came, moreover, Africans displaced many of the departing Europeans and Asians, and at that point the differences in status and wealth among classes of Africans became increasingly more pronounced.

Evidence is lacking that the post-independence realities match the pre-independence egalitarian rhetoric of the governing elite. This applies whether that rhetoric emanates from civilian or military proponents of egalitarianism. Class differences are increasingly in evidence. As a corporate group, for example, the military has emulated the lawyers, educators, businessmen, and other civilians it displaced by enhancing its control over the limited resources of the state wherever it has assumed power. The military has not been averse, moreover, to individual cases of flagrant corruption. The first Rawlings coup in Ghana, after all, was directed against the corruption of senior military officers; it was the second intervention that was concerned with civilian abuses of power. Instead of correcting the urban/rural or regional imbalances of wealth, there is a tendency for both civilian and military political elites to amend the general urban bias only slightly by giving extraordinary preference to development or even meaningless prestige projects in the rural areas from which they themselves emanate. Leaders ranging from Houphouet-Boigny and William Tolbert to Idi Amin and Emperor Bokasso have been guilty of this behavior. Few national leaders follow the example of abstemious living pursued by Julius Nyerere in his long presidency of Tanzania. In representation of African countries abroad or at the U.N., moreover, there is nothing to distinguish the lifestyle of a Fourth World African diplomat from that of an emissary from a wealthy, highly industrial state. The kind of bureaucratic elitism that Milovan Djilas criticized in the allegedly classless Yugoslav society in the period following World War II is emerging today in even the most committed socialist governments in Africa.[36] The actual extent of the turning away from egalitarianism among the nationalist elite and its consequences with respect to development in Africa are still subjects of vigorous debate.[37]

ASSESSING THE LURE OF SOCIALISM. Despite the optimism and enthusiasm that have marked their pursuit of an alternate strategy of development, socialists in Africa at this stage have had little to show for themselves by way of successful models. Many concur with Carl Eicher's assessment that "Agrarian socialism is now under fire throughout Africa: after 20 years of experimentation, there are presently no African models which are performing well."[38] Whatever success, for example, Zimbabwe has experienced in economic development, cannot be attributed to the socialist rhetoric of Prime Minister Mugabe and his ZANU party politburo. It is traceable rather to the continuity of many of the structures and programs created under the previous white regimes when the predominant agricultural, mining, and industrial sectors were substantially in private hands. None of the other African economies which are experiencing reasonable success in food production, the growth of medium range industrialization, successful exploitation of previously unknown mineral resources, and a manifestation of other indicators of growth have leadership cadres that espouse socialism. The closest Kenya came to socialism was the brief flirtation under the Kenyatta regime in the mid-1960s. The Kenya state paper on socialism, however, sounded remarkably like capitalism under a new label. The other models of economic growth in Black Africa, such as the Ivory Coast, Cameroon, and Malawi have leaders who are avowedly anti-socialist.

On the other hand, successful examples of economic growth do not represent capitalist models either. Indeed, when we include the most successful case of economic growth on the continent, namely South Africa, we can hardly present that as a capitalist model of balanced development of industry and agriculture. Three-fourths of the population in South Africa are denied access to significant private property, and freedom of enterprise in the use of human talents and physical resources is a monopoly of less than 20 percent of the society. The South African government intervenes at every level of economic activity, and it establishes prices for a wide range of goods and services. Instead of many sellers, there are only a few who control the production and sale of the minerals which have made South Africa economically successful, as with DeBeers in the case of diamonds.

Whatever the political value derived by an African regime from a rhetorical espousal of socialism, the economies which have fared the best in post-independence Africa are those in which the leadership has deliberately downplayed an explicit, integrated ideology in favor of pragmatic solutions to a diversity of problems. Indeed, in analyzing the historical antecedents of various norms and institutions operative in the more successful cases of African development, we find a strange ideological mix.[39] Traditional communalism, for example, manifests itself in the persistence of land tenure based upon usufructory right of occupancy and in the organization of work through kinship and neighborhood groupings. Feudalism is evident in the many patron-client relationships which persist among pastoral people and in the economic bonds existing between Islamic religious leaders and their followers. The great trading networks which have continued to thrive throughout West Africa represent a pre-European commitment to a form of commercial capitalism. Under the colonial umbrella, the introduction of the notion of private property as well as freedom of enterprise in the use of human and other resources encouraged an acceptance of some aspects of laissez-faire capitalism. At the same time, colonial rule witnessed the introduction of the large European trading companies. Those companies, together with the subsequent multinational corporations, in the fields of mineral and agricultural extraction represent monopolistic capitalism. The national governments' ownership, moreover, of railroads, communications, and other facilities, as well as the intervention by political leaders in most aspects of the economy which have persisted from the colonial days to the present, could be identified as state capitalism, if not socialism. Similarly, many of the new cooperative societies, credit associations, and trade unions launched in the later phases of colonial rule are comfortably accommodated within a socialist strategy. This diverse mixture of institutions and norms exists side by side in states such as the Cameroon, Malawi, Kenya, and—most significantly—Nigeria. However diverse their origins, they operate concurrently and mesh remarkably because the leadership is not immobilized by fruitless quests for ideological purity.

The need for a less ideological approach to development is justified on other grounds. As was pointed out elsewhere in this volume, African political elites have in general lacked training in economics, finance, agriculture, forestry, natural resource management, and other skills needed for development. They have in many cases long been physically divorced from the very rural areas where much of this development is to take place. Given the lack of direct experience, a dogmatic approach to development has been the last thing Africa needed. Africa had more than its share of that under the colonial attitude, "Auntie Knows Best."

Those leaders who have succeeded in economic development recognize at least tacitly the diversity of the cultural attitudes toward economic activity incorporated within the post-colonial state. Rather than insisting upon a lockstep approach to improvement in the material condition of their people, they have appreciated the value of a multi-pronged approach to development. Some people are good at one kind of activity, some at another. Some people are recognized by their neighbors as having more entrepreneurial skills than they themselves possess or as being more willing to undertake innovative risks in agriculture. Although this may constitute a form of ethnic stereotyping, appreciation of the different cultural attitudes represented within a state may be put creatively to work in behalf of the broader society.

The biblical parable of the wise and foolish virgins to the contrary, perhaps what the dogmatic ideologues lack most of all is confidence in the ability of people at the mass level to maximize their own material well-being if given the opportunity to do so. This means recognizing two things. First, despite their poverty, people do have some basic understanding of the environment in which they and their ancestors have operated, and they have established preferred routes for coping with that environment. Second, development should start with the base of what the people already know and proceed from there. Ancillary to that, as the experience of the colonial period should have more than demonstrated, innovation that is done *to* or *for* people never succeeds as well as innovation that is accomplished *with* people.

The practical application of the preceding is that the primary emphasis at this stage of development ought to be on improving African agriculture (because that is what the majority of Africans are still involved in) while moving gradually in the direction of modest industrialization (because that is what ultimately will make a substantial difference in the quality of life for Africans). Within agriculture, the emphasis on government support ought to be oriented to the smallholders, who traditionally operate on three- to six-acre plots. This is so not because of any ideological preference for capitalism or communalism but because most African cultivators are smallholders who would prefer to remain so, despite adverse governmental policies or the vagaries of the weather. As noted in Chapter 6, the preference of many—if not most—urban migrants is to retain one's standing in his or her rural homeland. Finally, it was to retain their rightful place in agriculture that Africans in Kenya and Zimbabwe—to cite two cases—were prepared to take up arms against those who had dispossessed them of their traditional land holdings. The hostile attitudes of the dispossessed Africans in those two countries toward collectivization of agriculture in favor of the restoration of smaller farms should serve as evidence to leaders in other countries who are embarked upon the untried course of socialist development. Added to that is the lesson of the failure of Nyerere's program of *ujamaa* villagization to increase agricultural productivity and to sustain even the progress that had been made in export crop production under colonial rule.[40] Good intentions and incorruptable leadership—while desirable—prove to be no substitute for taking into account the knowledge and aspirations of the people who are the alleged beneficiaries of development.

Belatedly, many African leaders themselves have come to the realization that the ideological commitment to central planning, nationalization of resources, and collectivization of agriculture have had disastrous results. Evidence of this is found in the decisions of committed socialists such as Samora Machel of Mozambique and Julius Nyerere of Tanzania to allow the reentry of free enterprise as a supplement to collectivization. Even more telling evidence is found in the December 1984 U.N. General Assembly resolution on Africa's economic crisis. The Resolution was the culmination of a series of discussions within the OAU, the U.N., and other arenas in which African leaders not only recognized the shortcomings of their policies but indicated their intentions to accept some of the basic tenets of Western capitalism in overcoming their economic crises.[41] Echoing some of the recommendations of the World Bank, the IMF, and others, one key to economic progress was a reemphasis on the crucial role of the African smallholder—and particularly women cultivators—in meeting food and agricultural needs on the continent.

Self-Reliance versus Foreign Aid

One issue that has persisted throughout this analysis of African poverty is the source of the energy, capital, and creative talent needed to spur economic development. One answer, provided by Kwame Nkrumah of Ghana in the 1950s, was that the problems of poverty would almost automatically take care of themselves once Africans came into control of their political destinies. Less persuaded of the automatic nature of this transformation, a few leaders such as Julius Nyerere, H. Kamuzu Banda, and Ahmadou Ahidjo (first President of the Cameroon), felt that a more deliberate commitment on the part of Africans themselves was required. Any course other than "self-reliance," Julius Nyerere argued, would spell continuing dependency upon external forces and factors.[42] As noted previously in this chapter, the fragile nature of post-independence states has made it difficult for most leaders consistently to espouse "self-reliance," including the demand for necessary sacrifices on the part of both leadership cadres and the masses in curtailing consumer appetites, deferring industrialization in favor of radical changes in agriculture, and dispensing with the major prestige projects that added little to basic development.

A far easier route for most to pursue was to demand external aid as an obligation which was due Africa and other developing areas. Precisely who owed the debt was not always clear. The neo-Marxist scholars, such as the late historian Walter Rodney, assumed that the debt was owed by the capitalist world in general for having "underdeveloped Africa."[43] Indeed the case is a strong one, given the export of labor during the slave trade, the confiscation of land in the white settler territories, the rampant exploitation of mineral and agricultural resources, and the iniquitous global price mechanisms that pay low prices to Africans for their exported commodities while charging high prices for the manufactured goods they import in exchange.

Others would more specifically hold accountable for the debt those West European colonial powers—capitalist or otherwise—who had politically subjugated the continent during the last century. Indeed, several of the colonial powers themselves acknowledged this obligation even before the neo-Marxists brought it to their attention. The explicit commitment by Britain, and subsequently by France and Belgium, came during the Second World War when those states were themselves struggling for their own national survival. The Atlantic Charter of August 1941 and the subsequent Colonial Welfare and Development Act committed the British Conservative-Labour wartime coalition to an extensive program of building roads, ports, and other physical infrastructures in the colonies as well as launching major agricultural and other development schemes designed to transform traditional and colonial economies. Parallel with economic changes, colonial governments in Africa (and elsewhere in the Empire) would assume the primary responsibility for expanding health and education facilities, encouraging trade unionism, and setting colonial peoples on the path to self-government. After the liberation of France and Belgium their governments followed Britain's lead.

The conversion of the specific debt of the colonial powers into a more general obligation on the part of the industrialized states was signaled more than a decade before Africans started to throw off the yoke of colonial rule. One key event in this drama was the 1949 Inaugural Address of President Harry S Truman; his Fourth Point was a pledge on the part of the U.S. to provide technical assistance to the less developed states. Within the next few years similar commitments were made by other non-colonial powers including the Scandinavian states, Japan, and even many of the more fortunate among the Third World states themselves, such as Brazil, Saudi Arabia, India, Israel, and China. It was inevitable, moreover—given the fascination of many African leaders with a socialist strategy of development—that the Soviets, East Germans, and other members of the Second World would begin to provide investment funds, personnel, and other forms of aid, while still insisting that capitalism was the root cause of Africa's misery.[44] While the contributions of others have been significant, it has been the West Europeans, both unilaterally and collectively through the European Economic Community (EEC), that have shouldered the main burden of providing aid to Africa.

By the mid-1960s the acceptance by the developed states of their moral and economic debt became translated by the Third World states themselves into a set of specific demands that the transfer of wealth from the industrialized states of the northern hemisphere to the raw material producing states of the southern hemisphere had to be accelerated if the latter were not to fall even more desperately behind in providing food, clothing, and shelter to their people. From the U.N. Conference on Trade and Development (UNCTAD) in 1964 emerged an ideological position referred to as the North/South Dialogue, which sought a more equitable distribution of the world's wealth. Unfortunately for the developing states the Dialogue became a casualty of the oil embargo crisis of the 1970s and the recession in the industrialized world during the 1980s. Africans and other Third World leaders still continue to press for global agreements or for the funneling of aid through multilateral channels, such as the U.N. or the EEC, where the national identities of the donors are obscured and the ideological strings attached to aid are limited. Most aid nevertheless continues to come in the form of bilateral agreements.

The forms of assistance to African and other developing states are highly diverse. The general public is most aware of emergency relief during times of famine, flood, or other natural disasters. On a more continuing basis donor assistance includes outright grants, interest-free or low-interest loans, student scholarships, exchanges of technical advisors, and the provision of technical information and research findings in a wide range of areas. Assistance also includes more complex arrangements such as the preferential trade access which the ten members of the EEC have given to the agricultural, mineral, and other products from sixty-six African and other Third World states under the series of Lomé Pact agreements between 1975 and 1984.[45] The American government under the guaranteed loan program encourages private American investment in high-risk countries.

The constant flow of African students to Europe, the United States, and Asia as well as the physical changes in the African landscape itself in the form of new universities, ports, office buildings, and roads attest to the impact of foreign aid over the period of the last three or four decades. The value of the relationship between foreign aid and African development, however, is a hotly debated issue. There are some who recognize the *growth* in economic activities and the changes in the quality of life of many Africans in the midst of poverty, but insist this is not *development*. That is, the growth has not been accompanied by basic changes in local economic institutions and there has not been the development of human attitudes and habits or the technical and administrative talents required to sustain economic growth once the foreign assistance has been withdrawn. This was the conclusion of the Northwestern University economic task force in Liberia in the early 1960s.[46] Others view foreign aid as most effective when dealing with a crisis situation—such as the outpouring of funds in response to the Ethiopian famine of 1985—but lacking in the kind of donor government support required for dealing with less dramatic long-term problems.

Even less charitable are those critics who insist that foreign aid, on balance, is a negative element in African development. This, it is argued, is particularly the case when the loans/barter arrangements are utilized to enhance the military capacity of an African dictatorship instead of being used to create new educational and health facilities or agricultural programs. As Ali Mazrui has suggested, ultimate power in Africa increasingly resides not in those who control the means of production—as Marxists would argue—but in those who control the means of destruction."[47] The relationship is also negative when foreign aid is directed largely toward grandiose airports and other prestige projects or into the pockets of corrupt officials rather than toward alleviating poverty.[48] Development, moreover, is not advanced when the conditions of private foreign investment in mining or agribusiness do not result in significant training of local personnel, where no arrangements are made for in situ processing of raw materials, where there are few regulations on the expatriation of profits, or where the host country is denied access to the commodity produced. The most negative aspect of foreign aid, however, has been the debt servicing problem with respect to the high interest loans contracted with private Western banks. While the African debts are not of the magnitude of those of Brazil, Peru, or Mexico, they nevertheless divert scarce foreign exchange earnings from the creation of new enterprises and the development of talents that can be used in the creation of new sources of wealth. Difficulties in meeting interest payments and other problems of administrative management have increasingly involved the African states in a relationship with the International Monetary fund (IMF) which many leaders equate with the external dictation of the colonial era. The conditions for fiscal stringency which the IMF imposes with regard to refinancing of loans and other financial matters strain the political relationship between the leaders and key segments of their constituency directly affected by the IMF assistance.

While the global markets within which the African economies operate put serious constraints on development, in the final analysis many of the issues which frustrate development relate to the issue of self-reliance. No external group can be more effective than African leaders themselves in dealing with the questions of population explosion, deforestation, desertification, rapid exploitation of natural resources, the low priority of agriculture in African society, the character of the African educational curriculum, attitudes toward cattle as a source of food, and the relentless migration of Africans from the rural areas to the cities. As the World Bank analysts in 1984 predicted:

> Unless these long-term issues receive continuing and increased attention, whatever the short-term problems, development in Africa will continue to be frustrated, leading to what the Economic Commission for Africa (ECA) has called a political, social, and economic "nightmare" by the turn of the century.[49]

VI

THE DILEMMA OF POLITICAL COMMUNITY IN THE URBAN CONTEXT

The bleak horrors of famine and rural poverty which the television cameras have so vividly portrayed in the Sahel region during the 1970s and in Ethiopia, Uganda, and Mozambique during the 1980s exceed any description that the written or spoken word can provide. Yet alongside the dramatic assault inflicted by drought and human failures upon the lives, health, and hopes of millions of rural Africans is a less startling but related tragedy: the mounting poverty of the African city. The mass exodus of survivors from the impoverished countryside leaves not only fewer hands to grow the nation's food but more urban mouths to feed. Admittedly the ills of the city are slower to take their toll than the stark specter of rural famine. Food relief supplies—in the face of inadequate transport and ineffective organizations for distribution—invariably reach the undernourished urbanites long before they reach the dispersed starving rural peasants and nomads. Living in a more concentrated pattern of residence and being at the doorstep of politically sensitive national leadership, the residents of the capital cities—and other cities as well—are more effective claimants for international relief supplies and the other scarce resources of the society.

Yet in the long run, after the rains return and rural hunger diminishes, the problems of the city continue inexorably to grow. Many analysts view Africa's urban unemployment, uncollected garbage, carbon monoxide- and lead-polluted air, and growing crime rate as time bombs soon to detonate, destroying the lives and dreams of those who expected a better existence after the achievement of independence. The population explosion in Kenya and other states which so alarms the demographers is essentially an urban problem. Much of the natural population increase—2.9 percent per annum for Africa, compared to 1.7 for the rest of the globe—has been accompanied by a dramatic shift from the rural to the urban sector.[1] Unless new resources are located, new methods of technology perfected, and courageous political leadership emerges, the wants of that increased population will go unfulfilled. And the explosion, when it does occur, will come in the cities.

A cursory glance at the gross demographic data for sub-Saharan Africa, however, makes it difficult to appreciate why African urbanization is a problem. In contrast with other global regions, Africa in 1980 had one of the smallest percentages of urban as opposed to rural population, as is revealed in Table 11.[2] For certain African states, the percentage of urban population is well below the world average: Burundi (2.3%), Rwanda (4.4%), Uganda (8.7%), Mozambique (9%), Malawi (9.6%), Burkina Faso (10.6%), and Tanzania (11.8%).[3] Of the forty African states reported on by the International Bank for Reconstruction and Development (IBRD) in 1980, half had less than 20 percent of their population living in urban areas. Given the fact that a certain level of concentrated population is needed to sustain even a modest level of industrial development, overurbanization would not appear to be one of Africa's problems. Concentrated settlement, moreover, is to be expected when the transformation of underdeveloped economies requires co-ordination of transport, banking, and other facilities as well as centralized direction in the provision of educational, health, and other public services for the new states.

Overurbanization, however, does become a real problem in the face of two other factors.[4] The first of these is the *rate* of urban growth in states that not only lack many of the basic ingredients of industrialization (iron ore, coal, oil, raw materials, and skilled manpower) but that are not able to produce the food required to feed their growing urban population. Africa's annual rate of urban growth (5.3%) is almost twice the world average of 2.7 percent and actually increasing, while most of the world (other than South Asia) is tapering off. For particular countries and particular cities, the data on urban growth rates are staggering. The population of Zambia, which was still basically a rural society three decades ago, went from 23.1 percent in urban areas in 1960 to 43.9 percent by 1980.[5] Close to half of Zambia's residents live in Lusaka and the stretch of towns along the Copperbelt in the eastern part of the country. Also rapidly approaching the 50 percent mark are Mauritius, South Africa, Congo Republic, Ivory Coast, Ghana, Gabon, Cameroon, and Zaire. In Zaire the Belgians encouraged systematic migration from the rural sector to speed the exploitation of that country's mineral resources, and political turmoil has intensified the process. Zaire went from 15.7 percent urban in 1960 to 35.8 percent in 1980. For twenty-four of the forty states covered in the IBRD data, the percentage of urban residents more than doubled in the two decades from 1960 to 1980. One extreme case was Botswana, which went from 1.8 percent urban population in 1960 to 20.2 percent in 1980. In several of the states, such as Malawi and Tanzania, urban growth continued despite government policies discouraging rural to urban migration.

The same dramatic rates of growth are found in many of Africa's other cities. Abidjan, which was only a small fishing village of 30,000 people at the beginning of World War II, became the fastest growing city in Francophone Africa after a channel was cut through the sand bar and the port

TABLE 11

Percentage of Urban Residence, by Global Region

Global Area	1950	1980
World, Total	28.9	41.1
North America	63.9	76.9
Oceania	61.2	75.8
Europe	55.4	70.5
Latin America	40.8	65.4
USSR	39.3	63.2
East Asia	16.8	32.7
Africa	14.8	28.8
South Asia	16.2	24.8

SOURCE: United Nations Department of International Economic and Social Affairs, *Demographic Indicators of Countries: Estimates and Projections* (1982), p. 39.

and railroad development to the north made it an important transport entrepôt. Its population today exceeds half a million. The figures for Lagos and Kinshasa are also startling, with the former going from roughly 1 million to 3.5 million in two decades. The oil boom, the influx of migrants from neighboring countries, the disruptions associated with the Biafran War, and the Sahelian drought of the 1970s have made Nigeria's capital one of the world's fastest growing—and most poorly organized—cities. Even in South Africa, where government policies have been directed to restricting African migration to cities, the African sectors of the major cities continue to attract Blacks who simply cannot sustain themselves on agriculture in the impoverished Homelands. The million-plus Black population of the Johannesburg suburb of Soweto (an acronym for SouthWest Township) roughly rivals in numbers that of predominately white Johannesburg.

The second factor which is relevant to overurbanization in particular countries is the concentration of urban population in one large city (usually the capital) or in a series of a few cities having populations in excess of 100,000. If that same population had been distributed in many medium-sized communities it could interrelate more closely with relatives in the adjacent rural hinterland, which would reduce welfare demands and also make the governmental task of dealing with other urban problems more manageable. Nigeria by 1975 could reckon twenty-seven cities with populations in excess of 100,000 and four—Lagos, Ibadan, Kano, and Ogbomosho—with populations numbering more than 400,000. Other countries having several cities in excess of 100,000 include South Africa (16), Zaire (11), and Zambia (7).[6]

In the face of the general poverty of the African states, most large and expanding cities simply cannot cope with the management problems associated with garbage collection, disposal of human wastes, the provision of clean water, the regulation of traffic, and the orderly development of roads, lighting, and other services for a burgeoning population. In Lagos, for example, a journey that would take less than fifteen minutes if the streets were cleared of vehicles might take up to three hours through rush hour traffic. The mounds of trash in Lagos, even along the main thoroughfares, keep getting higher and higher, threatening epidemic disease outbreaks that would tax the resources of even one of the more prosperous Black African states. Urban crime in most African cities is escalating as the continuing influx of migrants—predominately young adult males—exacerbates the problems of unemployment and lack of school facilities for the young, as well as prostitution, homosexuality, and other phenomena related to the imbalance between male and female ratios in the cities. Latent hostility among competing ethnic groups for jobs and housing space, and the general volatility of the marginal bread-and-butter issues such as bus fares and the price of the food staple, leave many cities close to the social flashpoint. Riots, strikes, and boycotts have become recurrent features of urban life.

The Weakness of the Urban Political Community

In addition to the foregoing problems of urban growth, several factors are weakening the sense of political community within many of Africa's major cities. One of these is the very recency of the urban experience for most residents. This is not to suggest that cities did not exist in the pre-colonial period. Indeed, for a variety of purposes great concentrations of population appeared across the southern rim of the Sahara, along the East African coast, and in the interior of central Africa hundreds of years ago.[7] Some, like Bobo-Dioulasso and Kano, were great trading centers. Others, like Timbuktu, were founded as centers of religion and learning. Still others, like Begjho, Great Zimbabwe, Kumbi, and Tekrur, were the military and political capitals of great empires that came on the scene, lasted several hundred years, and then faded away. A few, like Old Oyo, Benin, Gao, Kumasi, and Jenne, have had a continued existence for several hundred years and in the case of Mombasa over a thousand years.

To a considerable extent the pre-modern cities of Africa differed substantially from the modern metropolises where the dramatic population explosion is taking place today.[8] The pre-modern city tended to be very much linked to its rural hinterland, with many of the inhabitants surviving as urban merchants, craftsmen, or religious and political leaders because they could also continue to have their families grow food in the adjacent countryside. Some actually had enough available land within the city to continue carrying on traditional subsistence agriculture. Admittedly, with some exaggeration, many of the older urban agglomerations resembled in terms of social structure, economic activities, attitudes, and other critical ways the lifestyle of contemporary rural villages of Africa. That is, the most significant social organizations were those based on the lineage and other face-to-face groupings; the economic activities centered around farming, trading, and crafts; and the social norms were those associated with the parochial, highly interdependent, and personalized way of life of a rural community. Many Yoruba families, for example, even today have weekday homes in Ibadan, weekend homes in the country.[9]

Most of the urban centers in Africa that are currently experiencing the explosive growth of the past two or three decades did not exist at all at the time of the European penetration of Africa a century or so ago. This includes Nairobi, Kinshasa, and Abidjan. Ibadan, which P. C. Lloyd described as a city-village and which for a long time was the largest city in Black Africa, was only a small Egba village at the beginning of the nineteenth century.[10] The burgeoning of Ibadan beyond its traditional core really only began with the advent of European rule in 1893 and the coming of the railway in 1901.[11] Many of the other cities which presently account for the rapid urbanization of the continent similarly existed a century ago only as small fishing or farming villages. This list includes most of Africa's largest cities, such as Johannesburg, Lagos, Douala, Kampala, Yaounde, Dar es Salaam, Lusaka, and Harare.

The recency of the development of Africa's cities with their mushrooming populations, however, cannot alone account for the weakness of the sense of political community. A more relevant factor is that cities were seldom established primarily to meet the needs of the Africans who have now come to inherit them. They were designed as European administrative capitals, ports for the shipment of goods between Africa and Europe, railroad termini, and headquarters for European mining operations or plantation agriculture. Some were planned as missionary stations, where the new converts to Christianity could be protected and provided with schools and clinics. Indeed, in all but the case of the Belgians—and to a limited extent the French—permanent African residence in cities was treated with indifference if not outright hostility by colonial administrators. The primary beneficiaries of urban residence were the European minority associated with colonial rule and with the economic exploitation of Africa. Secondarily, the cities served the needs of the ancillary populations of Indians, Lebanese, Malays, and others who assisted the Europeans as government clerks, bank tellers, masons, carpenters, and retail merchants.

The African city in the colonial era was not expected to develop as a meaningful community for its African inhabitants. It was designed to serve as an entrepôt between the European colonial metropole and the territorial hinterland beyond the capital or the port of entry. A few cities, such as Nairobi, Harare (Salisbury), Johannesburg, and Lubumbashi, had industrial or mineral processing operations that gave those cities economic activities which had at least some internal logic. The economic and financial activities of most colonial cities, however, made sense only within the larger framework of the worldwide capitalistic system. The orientation of the colonial city was Eurocentric rather than Afrocentric. The White enclave community which established the city and directed its affairs attempted to recreate in the African environment the European lifestyle and trappings that they had been accustomed to at home. Where this was not possible, the European residents sent their children back to England or France for some part of their schooling and themselves spent their annual holidays on "home leave" in Europe. The banking system, modern department stores, parks, and other facilities and amenities were either largely irrelevant to Africans or their use was actually prevented by law and custom.

From the perspective of developing an urban sense of political community, the foregoing did not abruptly change with independence. Although African leaders have inherited many of the homes and jobs once occupied by Europeans, and generally have come into control of the structures of political decision-making, other things remain constant. The economies of most independent states are still export-oriented; thus the national transport network still reflects the higher priority being given to getting minerals, agricultural produce, and other commodities into the world market rather than to developing a well-integrated and viable domestic economy. Port cities and capital cities in particular remain way stations. The successor African leadership often retains many of the attitudes and perquisites associated with the European expatriates. Indeed, the president of the Ivory Coast, Félix Houphouet-Boigny, emulating the typical Frenchman, prefers to vacation in France during the month of August. Many African leaders elsewhere felt that as a matter of right they should, at independence, inherit the entire list of the prerogatives enjoyed by their European predecessors— including "home leave." The international junketing that many African leaders engage in with respect to the United Nations, the OAU, and other organizations also perpetuates the external orientation of those who run Africa's capital cities.

In order to make the capital city more relevant to the development needs of the African state, a number of leaders have embarked on rather ambitious programs of relocating them closer to the geographic center of their respective countries. The precedent for such a move, of course, has earlier roots in national decisions made elsewhere regarding the location of new capital cities. One can cite the decision in 1789 to locate the American capital at the geographic center of the thirteen states, or the post–World War II decision to establish Brasília in the interior of Brazil. In the case of Botswana, of course, sovereignty demanded that the old colonial capital of Mafeking, which was actually located across the border in South Africa, be abandoned in favor of a well-planned capital city at Gaborone. Starting with the previous military government in Nigeria, that country's leadership has been attempting for nearly a decade to construct a new capital at Abuja, which would not only be more centrally located but would, it is hoped, avoid the chaos and congestion of Lagos. Julius Nyerere attempted to shift the thrust of national political development away from the coastal capital of Dar es Salaam to a more central location at Dodoma. The most successful example of this genre, however, has been the implementation of President H. Kamuzu Banda's plan (formulated while he was in political detention at Gwelo prison during the pre-independence era) to move the capital of Malawi from Blantyre to Lilongwe. This is discussed in greater detail below.

The Push and Pull of Rural to Urban Migration.

The problem of developing a sense of urban community is further compounded by the fact that only a small portion of the growth of Africa's major cities is attributable to natural increase. The demographic explosion of Africa's major cities is to a great extent a result of rural to urban migration. The imbalance between males and females and the higher percentage of young adults over children and the elderly in the demographic statistics reflects the fact that many of the young male migrants—regarding the sojourn as a temporary phenomenon—leave their wives and children behind in the rural homestead. If the migrant is unmarried, the informal liaisons which he establishes for sexual purposes in the city do not often lead to procreation. Many of the migrants to a city do not regard the urban milieu as a proper environment for the development of the whole gamut of social relationships and all aspects of one's personality.[12] The migratory nature of the population increase means that many of the urban residents have no particular stake in having the city function for them as a dynamic, integrated political community. This is even more the case for those migrants who come from other African states and are thus put in the tenuous legal category of "alien" Africans. As noted in Chapter 3 on nation-building, the vulnerability of the latter to the vagaries of African domestic politics was amply demonstrated in 1983 when Nigeria expelled over a million Ghanaian and other alien Africans. Thus, the "alien" migrants are restrained from making a long-term commitment to city life even where in fact they are second- and third-generation residents of that urban community.

The rationales for rural to urban migration (as well as the lesser phenomenon of migration from smaller to larger urban settlements) are extremely varied. Marxist scholars attempt to explain everything in terms of economic causation, and, indeed, evidence provided in interviews with migrants would seem to show that many of the "push" and "pull" factors do suggest economic motivation.[13] Among the "push" factors are the governmental pressures which insist upon the payment of taxes in cash, the escalating expenditures relating to the accumulation of bridewealth, and other economic needs that cannot be satisfied within the limited subsistence economy of the rural area.

Conversely, there are also economic "pull" factors, such as the availability of low-cost consumer items in the city markets, the prospects of enhancing cash resources by engaging in rural to urban trade, and the possibility of improving economic status through exposure to the educational facilities which are more readily available for oneself or one's children in the city. Curiously, the flight to the city continues even when the reports of returning migrants regarding employment prospects are dismal. The hope is still more important than the stark reality of rural poverty.

The Madisonian theory of Federalist No. 10 rather than the Marxian analysis, however, is probably closer to the African reality. That is, economic factors persist and are among the abiding causes of migration, but noneconomic considerations are equally valid in identifying precipitating ("final straw") causes as well as explaining the more general clustering of factors leading to an individual's decision to migrate. While most scholars agree with Phillip H. Gulliver in rejecting the "bright lights" theory as far too facile an explanation,[14] my own survey in 1955 of Chewa-speaking migrants on the Tanganyikan side of Lake Malawi revealed the significance of noneconomic factors. Long-range migration among young Chewa-speaking males had become a substitute for the more traditional initiation rites and a way of achieving social ranking. Those Chewa-speakers, for example, who had migrated all the way to Cape Town had higher social status than those who had only migrated to the mining operations in South Africa and the two Rhodesias.[15] My research in other parts of colonial Tanganyika suggests that young males often migrated to escape the enforcement of arbitrary and capricious rules on cultivation introduced by European officers who simply did not understand African agriculture.[16] Kenneth Little, in surveying the literature on West Africa, pointed out other noneconomic causal factors in migration, such as avoidance of harassment by local authorities and escape from an unhappy home life. For women in particular, Little identified a desire to seek greater independence in regulating their own lives plus the search for higher social prestige.[17] In this respect, African migrants are not unlike their Marxian analysts, who make decisions to change location or change universities for a complex of reasons, only a few of which are economic.

Whatever the causes or motivations, the fact that the increase in urban population is primarily the result of largely unplanned migration compounds the inability of city administrations to provide the streets, garbage collection, and other necessities of an expanding environment. The new services must be provided without the additional revenues being forthcoming. Since the migrants are only marginally employed, they contribute little to the revenue base. Even more serious is the fact that the heterogeneous nature of this migration—often originating in remote sections of the country or indeed from across an international border—intensifies at the micro level all the problems of nation-building that the political leadership must face at the state level. Indeed, the fact that people from heterogeneous ethnic backgrounds live in relatively close proximity complicates the many tasks of multilingual communication, adjustment to differing moral standards, and integrating divergent social, economic, and religious structures into a functioning whole. In urban areas, interethnic stereotyping and the prospects for resultant violence during times of crisis are far more likely than in the rural environment, where one's contacts with members of other ethnic groups are limited.[18] This interethnic mix is particularly exacerbated when there are more distant migrants as well as an urban ethnic majority that is drawn from the immediate rural hinterland. The conflicts between the indigenous and immigrant ethnic groups are well documented by Howard Wolpe in his seminal work on the Igbo minority in the Ijaw-dominated oil town of Port Harcourt. Wolpe often found multiple and reinforcing points of differentiation and conflict resulting from language, religion, educational attainment, degree of adaptation to modern economic norms, monopolistic tendencies with respect to certain kinds of occupations, and other divergent norms and facets of behavior.[19] Abner Cohen describes a similar situation with respect to Hausa migrants in Yoruba towns in Nigeria.[20] To the extent that there exist few cross-cutting loyalties among the two groups which transcend the differences, the potential for violence during times of interethnic conflict is magnified. The disregard for rights, property, and sensitivities of the minority were dramatically revealed in the mass hysteria associated with the treatment of Igbo immigrants in northern Nigeria at the onset of the Biafran War or in the mass expulsion of "alien" Africans from Ghana in 1967 and from Nigeria in 1983.[21]

At the personal level as well, the migratory nature and the recency of the demographic increase in urban population complicate the development of a sense of commitment to the city. The typical urban resident was probably not born or reared in the city where he or she currently resides, or indeed in any urban setting. Behavior patterns developed in rural areas ill prepare the individual for survival in the city. Coming from a pedestrian village, for example, it takes time to get accustomed to looking both ways before crossing streets or to refrain from walking between parked cars—let alone driving a vehicle properly. The rural pastoral residents of Botswana—to cite a further case—in the past were used to picking up their house poles and hide coverings when the garbage pile outside the homestead became too high. These same Tswana, when they move to Gaborone, find that they must develop different ways to dispose of trash and waste materials if they are to avoid being overrun by rats or subjected to epidemic diseases. The prospect, moreover, in a highly congested city of supplementing one's family food supply by putting in a front yard garden is foreclosed for many rural migrants to Monrovia and other capital cities.[22]

Three Types of Urbanites

The difficulty of establishing a sense of political community within many of the newer African cities is further aggravated by the fragmented character of the urban population. On any given day there are at least three relatively distinct categories of individuals represented within an urban population. The smallest of the three is the group of *ad hoc transients*, individuals who essentially retain their rural values and patterns of behavior but who have come to the city to obtain a specific object or a service not readily available in their rural homelands. Since they are only present within the city for a matter of days or even hours, the ad hoc transient needs to know only the minimum rules of participation required to accomplish his or her limited objectives. The Masai herdsman, for example, who comes into the provincial town of Arusha in northern Tanzania to exchange his cattle in the market must master a few basic procedures for survival. To avoid conflict with the law, he must be aware that there are certain established routes of ingress and egress, and that he is not free to run his cattle down the main streets, interfering with automotive traffic. To negotiate the sale of cattle, he must be aware of the rudiments of a cash economy, including the possibility that at one stage in the transaction he must temporarily accept a paper chit as a representation of money due him for the cow he has just sold. Beyond learning a few additional rules and acquiring a few other skills, the urban experience is one that the herdsman can view with curiosity while remaining detached and unpersuaded that it is superior to the values and behavior patterns of the Masai herdsman's rural life.

Two other categories of individuals can be identified in the city. They differ from the ad hoc transient as well as from each other with respect both to the time period individuals are resident in the city and to the degree of their acceptance of urban attitudes and modes of behavior. One group, who are referred to as *situational urbanites*, may actually be far larger than either or the other two categories of residents. Situational urbanites are individuals who have either a cluster of goals or one significant goal which can only be accomplished by an extended period of residence in the city. The longer residence of necessity involves some form of temporary employment; acquisition of the skills needed to secure food, shelter, and other basic means of survival; and the ability to neutralize potential threats or demands from officials, temporary neighbors, and even one's own kinsmen. The situational urbanite tends to expect something far less than a full set of social relationships in the city, since typically he is not accompanied to the city by his wife, children, or aged parents. In many cases, the position of situational urbanite may be primarily a state of mind in which the resident continues to retain the notion that he is an immigrant despite long years of residence and intense involvement in urban affairs. The psychological attitude that at some future point he is obligated—or actually prefers—to return to his rural roots prevents him from making the full acceptance of urban life. The organization "Igbo Sons Abroad" in Nigeria is representative of this mindset that holds that a return to the rural homeland is the ultimate objective of the situational urbanite. Even such an urbane and sophisticated individual as the late Dr. Kenneth Dike, the noted Igbo historian and educator, manifested this syndrome. After decades of residence in urban centers in Nigeria and America, Dr. Dike carefully planned for the day when he would retire to his rural village in southeastern Nigeria. Similarly, F. Gervaise in a survey conducted in the 1950s noted that many migrants to mining areas in the Katanga (Shaba) Province of the Belgian Congo (Zaire) continued to associate themselves in concrete ways with their rural heritage after two to four decades of residence in the mining centers.[23]

Situational urbanites differ from individuals in the third category—*committed urbanites*—in a number of ways. The committed urbanite, who has both physically and psychologically severed his rural roots, tends to reduce his kinship obligations to a nuclear, monogamous family that lives with him or her in the city. In contrast, situational urbanites, who tend predominately to be male, remain committed to polygamy as the ideal marital form but normally leave wives and children behind in the safer rural hinterland. The situational urbanite establishes short-term rotating liaisons with concubines and prostitutes in order to satisfy his sexual needs. The search for material and other forms of security, moreover, leads to a redefinition of kinship linkages for the situational urbanite. Distance from what he considers home does not reduce his kinship obligations to a nuclear family (husbands and wives and their offspring); on the contrary, the rural extended family continues to claim a hold on him. Indeed, within the context of the city this extended family is redefined, and frequently includes within its network individuals as well as obligations not normally taken into account in the rural setting.[24]

The committed urbanite and the situational urbanite differ as well with respect to a number of other relationships, norms, and behavior patterns. This was graphically illustrated in Sembene Ousman's classic film *Mandabi* (*The Money Order*). As depicted in the film, the committed urbanite, for example, tends to be more pro forma in his religious observances, and may even abandon many of the prescriptions and proscriptions of his faith. He accepts, moreover, all of the implications of an exchange economy including the use of cash, the significance of money orders and other representations of money, and the value of written deeds to property. The committed urbanite, in addition, tends to be linked to other individuals on the basis of formal written contracts; accepts the secular pace of modern life, including adherence to time factors in regulating behavior and the use of the automobile and other mechanical devices. The committed urbanite tends in the direction of accepting achievement rather than ascriptive norms in relating to others—particularly women.

In contrast, not only does the situational urbanite in the Senegalese film remain faithful to his or her religious performances, but religious structures serve as receiving institutions which insulate the migrant against the cultural shock of urban life and provide the stranger with a whole set of potential friends. The situational urbanite still organizes his life in terms of face-to-face rather than impersonal relationships. He accepts a man's word as being his bond, and his concern for the fate of others is as important as his own self-advancement. Relationships with others are established in terms of sex, relative age, kinship, and other ascriptive factors, and the spoken word is the primary if not exclusive form of communication. The only partial entry of the situational urbanite into the cash economy is reflected in the fact that a backyard garden or an occasional trip to the country supplements his cash income and many transactions are carried out in an informal credit arrangement or even on a goods-for-service barter exchange basis.

THE PERSISTENCE OF SITUATIONAL URBANISM. In the long run, as African cities continue to absorb population from their rural hinterlands and acquire a momentum and dynamism of their own, committed urbanites will eventually outnumber situational urbanites. The miserable condition of African agriculture and policies of government may accelerate this process, making even a risky existence in an African city seem increasingly preferable to rural life.[25] As one continues to reside in a city, one tends increasingly to acquire a vested stake in new friends, the cluster of urban family relationships, and membership in a host of urban associations. One acquires, moreover, some form of property rights in a job, a lease to a house, a driver's license, and other privileges which were initially secured with difficulty and which one is unwilling to surrender lightly. The urban ways eventually come to seem more natural than rural ways, and the resident begins to acquire over time a sense of community and belonging toward his or her neighborhood, if not toward the city as a whole. This comes to rival the pull of the old rural community, which in any case will have been substantially transformed— and not for the better—in the migrant's extended absence.

For the short term, however, the situational urbanite continues to be more typical of the population of many African cities. Why is this so? While it is questionable whether the colonial experience should continue to be blamed for all the current ills of Africa, it is the case that the policies and practices of colonial governments did in fact contribute to the African sense of insecurity regarding urban life. The extreme case is that of the African areas under British rule (and in South Africa today) where white settlers tended to have a privileged position. Thus, in British East, Central, and Southern Africa housing not only was rigidly segregated along racial lines, but the African majority were made to feel that they were in the cities on sufferance. That is, they were there to provide household help for European officers and cheap unskilled labor for European mining or industrial enterprises, or to secure the cash needed to pay colonial tax collectors who would no longer accept produce in lieu of money. The anti-urban bias of officials in settler territories was epitomized by the existence of pass laws, which required urban Africans to carry identity cards indicating, among other things, the nature of their employment in some European-related economic activity. An African who could not produce a valid pass could be fined, imprisoned, or forcibly repatriated to the rural homeland. This calculated effort to make Africans feel insecure in colonial Lusaka, Salisbury, or Nairobi was reinforced in other ways. Africans in those cities, for example, could not acquire land or houses on a freehold basis or even a long-term lease. The crude housing provided by the government-owned railroads and other parastatals for the male employees seldom had accommodations for wives and children. Hence, the demography of most cities in the former settler territories (and in South Africa today) reveals a disproportionate sex and age ratio among Africans, with young adult males predominating. It was, moreover, only marginally easier in the colonial era for an African to acquire seniority and some kind of permanent stake in government employment than it was in the private sector.

In British West Africa, where settlers were few in number, the situation was only slightly better. Putting things in their most favorable light, Margaret Peil suggests that the British "*laissez faire* policy let the local people build a town that suited them." Europeans did not dominate all economic and other activities.[26] Modifications of traditional land tenure rules permitted many Africans to acquire long-term stakes in housing. Nevertheless, official expenditures in colonial Ghana, Nigeria, Sierra Leone, and The Gambia on public housing, sanitation, road construction, and crime prevention were minimal at best. Little official effort was taken to make cities in Nigeria or Ghana attractive places for African family life.

By way of contrast, the policies of the French tended to be more receptive to African urban residence even though they, too, tended to separate French residences from those of Africans with a buffer zone (*cordon sanitaire*), to protect the French minority from outbreaks of epidemics and crime emanating from the African quarters. In keeping with their philosophical goal of cultural integration, the French argued that it was in the city—where the migrant was detached from the counterpulls of kinship, tribal languages, Islam, and other traditional norms—that he could best achieve the status of évolué and become, in effect, a Black Frenchman.[27] The problem was that most urban Africans in Francophone countries did not achieve this privileged status. The contrasts in amenities, lifestyle, and access to privileges which separated the European and African sectors was dramatic, as Aristide Zolberg pointed out in his analysis of colonial Ivory Coast.[28]

The only colonial administrators that had a distinctly positive attitude with respect to African urban residence were the Belgians. They wanted to encourage the growth of a long-term, modernized African work force not only to provide unskilled and semi-skilled labor, but also to fill the many skilled positions required for the sustained exploitation of the mineral wealth of the Katanga (Shaba) Province of the former Congo. The Belgian administration is credited with providing the évolué class with well-designed family housing, medical services, facilities for primary and secondary education, and various amenities not enjoyed by Africans in other colonial areas. The consequences of the Belgian attitude are reflected in the fact that Zaire, which had none of the traditional trading and other pre-modern cities found in West Africa, has already surpassed the 35-percent mark in 1980 in terms of urban residence. Its eleven cities with populations in excess of 100,000 give Zaire a third-place ranking, behind Nigeria (27 cities) and South Africa (16).[29]

Belgian efforts to convince Congolese (Zairois) of the benefits of a permanent shift to an urban lifestyle were, unfortunately, limited. Until the eve of independence, modernized Africans were denied the opportunity of university education and the right to participate in either local or national politics. The planned orderly growth of cities in the Katanga area, moreover, did not extend to African quarters in cities elsewhere in the Belgian Congo. Indeed, it was the squalor and unemployment of Leopoldville (Kinshasa) which sparked the demands for independence in 1958.

Aside from the negative role that colonial governments generally played, private European employers during the colonial era similarly discouraged Africans from making a long-term commitment to urban life. Africans were recruited to work in the mines, on the plantations, or in other enterprises for only a limited period of time. Although the Union Minière du Haut Katanga in the Belgian Congo encouraged Africans to advance into skilled positions, this was not the case elsewhere. Africans were a cheap source of unskilled or semi-skilled labor at best, and constituted no challenge to the European, Asian, and other third-party employees. The turnover in the labor supply meant that wages did not have to be based upon seniority and longevity in the job, and the employer was not required to provide retirement and other long-term benefits or even housing for families. It also helped limit pressures for African unionization to a few areas, such as Guinea or the mining compounds in the Rhodesias and South Africa. The division of the African work force along ethnic lines, moreover, provided a barrier to Africans' developing cross-ethnic linkages which might have contributed to the broader sense of political community. Africans were assigned to mono-ethnic work groups, and various stereotypes were developed by employers with respect to what kinds of jobs were suitable for members of particular ethnic groups.

Insulation from the Full Urban Commitment

The reluctance of many Africans to make a full commitment to urban life, during the colonial era as well as today, is partly explained by the fact that they have seldom been required to throw in their lot fully with the growing urban sector. Many African males, for example, found that migration was not the only means of securing the cash needed to pay the tax collectors or acquiring the consumer goods that were beginning to appear in rural shops. They could do so by turning to cash crop farming on land which they held under customary tenure. Admittedly, in some dependencies they were prohibited from competing with European production of certain crops, for example coffee in Kenya. Generally, however, Africans were encouraged—to cite a few cases—to grow cocoa in Ghana, peanuts in Nigeria, coffee in Uganda, and cotton in Tanzania and the Sudan. Alternatively, African cultivators could continue to maintain largely without interruption their familial and other rural linkages by working on nearby European plantations.

For those males, moreover, who were recruited for labor in the cities or who went voluntarily in search of employment, it was not always necessary or desirable to burn one's rural bridges. As J. van Velsen has pointed out in his study of the Tonga in Central Africa, a change in living style does not automatically require a permanent change in one's basic value systems and preference. The migrant Tonga is as easily reabsorbed into his rural environment as American soldiers were reabsorbed into civilian life following a full immersion in and exposure to military life during World War II.[30] Unlike the seventeenth to nineteenth century immigrants from Europe to the Americas, moreover, African migrants were not distanced from their roots by a great ocean. Indeed, in the case of the African migrant workers who travel from Burkina Faso (Upper Volta) to the Ivory Coast, it was only necessary to be gone for part of the year. The migrant could go down to plantations owned by Europeans or Ivoiriens to pick the coffee and cocoa and still return home in sufficient time to cultivate and harvest a subsistence crop.[31] Of more general application, the typical African system of land tenure encouraged only a temporary commitment on the part of the male to work in urban employment. Since land claims were based upon the principle of usufructory right of occupancy, a migrant could leave his wife and children behind to maintain a claim which might otherwise have to be forfeited if the land went uncultivated, say, for two years in a row. Leaving the women and children behind had other advantages: they were not exposed to the "corrupting" influences of urban life, and the worker could maximize his meager earnings by not having to pay for food and housing for the members of his family.

Beyond land claims, maintaining one's standing in his rural village and among his extended family had other payoffs in the form of social security. The migrant worker who maintained his rural links could be guaranteed support in time of illness, old age, persistent unemployment, or arbitrary dismissal by his European employer. An absentee in good standing could return home to acquire a suitable wife or send his minor children back to the countryside for education in the traditional ways peculiar to the migrant's ethnic group. The expectation of full reciprocity in his rural homeland is earned as well by the urban migrant who has provided hospitality to other migrants on their initial arrival in the city; paid visits to the rural homestead for funerals and other important occasions; joined urban ethnic associations which were dedicated to the improvement of the rural community; or periodically dispatched money orders and gifts to persons crucial to the maintenance of his rural ties.

RECEIVING INSTITUTIONS. There are a number of groups both formal and informal that, in assisting the newly arrived migrant with his adjustment, help to insulate him from the strange ways of the city and thus render it unnecessary for him to make a full commitment to urban life. The most important of these "receiving institutions," of course, would be the extended family—assuming that kinsmen have preceded the migrant to the city.[32] As noted previously, deciding who are counted as members of the extended family and defining the nature of the reciprocal obligations existing among them may be substantially different in the urban than in the rural context. People who were only distant kinsmen in the country are regarded as close relatives in the alien city. Kinsmen who have preceded the migrant are expected to provide food, lodging, and other limited forms of hospitality until the newcomer has had a reasonable time to adjust. Therefore, in terms of such matters as language and diet, the immigrant is on familiar ground during the introductory period. The earlier arrival, moreover, is able to provide information about the job market and to instruct the "greenhorn" in the art of coping with the new social relationships, the expectations of authorities with regard to proper urban behavior, and other aspects of survival in the new environment.

Beyond the family linkages, various voluntary associations based upon ethnicity also serve to integrate recent arrivals into the urban milieu and to recreate in the novel urban context many of the values and relationships that were familiar to the migrant in his rural homeland. As is true of the family, the definition of who can be counted as a co-ethnic differs substantially in the urban context, with even members of neighboring ethnic groups accepting a common ethnic designation. This phenomenon of "supertribalism" is a recurrent one. In my studies of the Sukuma of Tanzania, migrants from the closely related Nyamwezi and the Sukuma groups in Dar es Salaam both accept the generic label "Sukuma." Inasmuch as Sukuma have long been regarded as excellent porters or carriers, using the Sukuma label makes it easier for a Nyamwezi to secure employment.[33]

Ethnic associations are important everywhere in Africa for insulating the new arrival against the shock of full immersion into the culturally heterogeneous urban life. As Sandra Barnes has pointed out in her study of Lagos, however, the very recent immigrant normally does not have immediate access to many of these associations since he lacks the initiation fees, the demonstrated commitment to residence and employment in the city, and other qualifications for formal membership.[34] Even without full participation, however, the very existence of the ethnic association has a "halo effect" with respect to the socialization of non-members. The ethnic association provides a readily identifiable cluster of people who speak the same language, share the same attitudes, provide opportunities for friendship with co-ethnics, and organize sporting events and other activities which reduce the tensions of adjustment for the new arrivals. The efforts of the association to collect funds for a new clinic or school or provide other improvements in the rural home-land also assist the members collectively in maintaining linkages with the ethnic base in the countryside.

Another receiving institution for the situational urbanite is the church or mosque, which provides not only spiritual and psychological reinforcement but also a whole set of social relationships. Two studies of colonial Ghana presented by Kofi A. Busia and D. K. Fiawoo point out that Christian churches as well as cults played a vital role in easing the adjustment of immigrants to city life even where the affiliation was only temporary.[35] In some instances a religious association draws almost exclusively upon migrants from one ethnic group or region. This is comparable to the role of the Catholic Church in Chicago which has distinct parishes appealing to the descendants of Polish, Lithuanian, and Czech immigrants.

There are other voluntary associations, such as sports and dance groups, which also ease the adjustment of the situational urbanite. In the case of South Africa, where the government attempts both ethnically and racially to divide the Black population that is temporarily resident in the urban sector, many of the dance groups are subsidized by the government in an effort to encourage the retention of ethnic linkages by urban Africans and sustain competitive tensions among the various corporate groups. In other areas, however, these ethnically oriented recreational groups emerge out of the Africans' own desire to relate to their co-ethnics.

Some associations, such as the credit and savings societies that abound in Sierra Leone, Liberia, and other parts of West Africa, assist the situational urbanite in adjusting to the predominantly cash nature of the urban economy.[36] Since banks are frequently viewed as alien institutions, housed within forbidding marble walls and often staffed by aliens, the credit societies provide the useful function of safeguarding a portion of the migrants' money earned in wage employment, market transactions, and other activities. The existence of credit associations partly overcomes the risks of loss of cash through theft, destruction of bank notes by termites or other insects, or undesired demands made upon surplus funds by less fortunate family mem-bers and friends. The credit groups have also permitted a migrant to ac-cumulate larger amounts of capital needed to purchase a high-cost item, such as a bicycle or a sewing machine. A frequent pattern in credit societies has been for every member to put in a fixed amount each week or month, with the members in rotation receiving the full contribution for that meeting.

Kenneth Little and others have pointed out the endless diversity of the

African imagination in producing new forms of voluntary associations which assist in the psychological adjustment of the migrant to the potentially hostile urban environment. Many of these associations have roots in traditional society; others, such as local chapters of the Red Cross and the YMCA, have decidedly modern origins. Some are based merely on the demonstrated need to form an affinity group. In colonial Zaire, where trade unions and political parties were outlawed by the Belgians and other modern associations were suspected of having covert political goals, many Congolese formed literary societies, and even name societies, which linked all persons with the first name of Jacques or Pierre.

Ethnic associations among the many forms of voluntary societies have been central to this manifestation of receiving institutions assisting the individual's adjustment and integration. They have nevertheless had negative repercussions in terms of delaying the development of a broader, more cohesive sense of political community within many of the newer African cities. Ethnic associations divert the attention of the situational urbanite away from the city and toward his rural roots. In the case of the rural improvement objectives of such groupings, they have actually drained the city of resources and talents that could have been contributing to making it a more viable economic and social community. The very vitality of ethnic associations has fragmented the city in a vertical fashion, since residential patterns frequently have tended to follow ethnic lines. Segregated housing patterns have occurred by preference even where they were not actually required or encouraged by the central government. The latter, of course, is still the case in South Africa today and it was the case even before colonial rule in West Africa, where "alien" Africans were expected to reside in that section of the zongo (stranger quarters) reserved to members of their particular ethnic group.

It is acknowledged that segregated residence, whether in racial, ethnic, or other forms, is not in itself a necessary cause of social conflict within a larger urban community. Nevertheless, the potential for interethnic conflict is exacerbated when segregated housing reinforces other forms of ethnic stereotyping based upon occupational monopolies enjoyed by certain groups, assumed personality characteristics (aggressiveness, competitiveness, or exclusiveness), discrepancies in wealth and educational attainments, and so on.[37] Thus, the Igbo migrants from eastern Nigeria in the mid-1960s tended to live in the Igbo sections of Kaduna, Kano, and other Hausa-Fulani cities in the north, and they predominated in the taxi business as well as in certain kinds of retail trades. When the interethnic crisis within the first Nigerian military government at the national level came to a head in July of 1966, the pent-up hostilities between the Igbo and the indigenous Hausa-Fulani again came to the surface. The patterns of segregated housing facilitated the assault on Igbo lives and property. But even when ethnic differentiation in housing, occupation, and other matters does not facilitate actual conflict, it does serve as a barrier to the early development of broader cross-cutting loyalties that transcend ethnicity.

Conflicts between Urban and National Politics

A further factor in the failure of many African cities to develop a cohesive sense of community is that national leaders are as reluctant as their colonial predecessors to permit the capital city or even secondary and tertiary cities to become political entities distinct from the national society. The closest analogy in Western experience was the long delay in the United States before granting home rule to residents of Washington, D.C. Until very recently, the U.S. Congress tended to serve as the city council for the nation's capital. In theory, Congress is still constitutionally empowered to withdraw most of the localized authority it has delegated to Washington's elected city officials.

Similarly, in Africa the budgets for education, health, and other government services in many capital and other cities are included as part of the national budget. Only a few African cities possess independent taxing authority. Most have to rely instead upon grants from the national governments. The planning for economic growth of cities is invariably an integral part of the national plan for development. In many cases the national ministries run programs normally associated with city government in Western societies, and lines between national and local civil servants are blurred. Where separate elections of local councillors and mayors are permitted, in many instance the positions are honorific or advisory, with real power being reserved to executives appointed by the national government. The reserved powers of the national constitution often permit the central government to replace the local officials when it suits the purposes of the national leadership.

This does not mean that the needs of the urban residents—particularly those of the capital city—are ignored. On the contrary, as Bates has pointed out, they are often given higher priority than those of the rural residents who provide the subsidized food for the urbanites and underwrite the efforts at industrialization which help reduce urban unemployment.[38] More often, however, the needs of the urbanites are addressed in a capricious rather than a systematic fashion, as responses to strikes, boycotts, and other anomic disruptions over issues such as a rise in bus fares or the price of rice. Decisions are made *for* the urban residents rather than *by* them since there is only minimal popular involvement in city politics.

Thus, the national political leadership distributes resources for development and monopolizes the use of legitimate force to maintain itself in national office. It is not often part of the national elite's mission to create a sense of political dynamism within the capital and other cities. Like the urban masses generally, the national leaders who control urban development have no particular loyalty to the urban centers in which they reside. They were probably born in a rural area and educated at boarding schools away from the "corrupting" influences of the city, or perhaps even abroad. Their attention is directed away from the cities where they reside to the spheres of national and even international affairs.

The foregoing comments should not lead one to the conclusion that cities are without government and public services or that the situation verges on anomie. Even in those colonial areas where the government was hostile to permanent African participation in city life, the long arm of government was extended. If nothing else, the administration was interested in collecting head and hut taxes and in reducing the level of crime and disease which might affect the European and Asian residents of towns. In more positive terms, the British and other colonialists realized that minimal direction of the affairs of African urban residents could secure positive results in terms of improvement in housing, marketing, and other activities, reducing the burden of attention and expense on the part of the administration. When urban growth and the problems associated with a particular city reached a critical point, some rudimentary form of local government was introduced even if this only involved the creation of African advisory councils lacking any real powers of government.

Long before colonial governments acted, however, Africans in the new cities had on their own undertaken to establish informal political institutions. In some instances these institutions were simply an effort on the part of the traditional chiefs, emirs, obas, or other authorities in the surrounding rural area to extend their influence and political jurisdiction into the urban areas.[39] This would augment the pool of citizens who could be called upon to pay taxes or provide labor for road construction and other communal works projects. On the other hand, the extension of jurisdiction may have been initiated by the heterogeneous urban residents themselves, who sought to improve their relationship with the original inhabitants of the area or secure an impartial adjudicator in the disputes that arose over uses of land, personal injuries, and relationships outside the bounds of traditional marriage.

In some instances, such as in the squatter communities which form beyond the legal boundaries of cities, an informal kind of urban political organization often arises in response to the felt needs of the residents themselves. As David Wiley describes these cities along the Copperbelt in Zambia, the informal squatter organizations often come into existence in the face of a crisis—such as the threatened demolition of the shanties or cancellation of bus service to the area. Once the crisis has passed, various leaders in the squatter area continue to be influential in settling disputes or in representing the interests of the squatters to the national government and to the formally organized local government council.

Despite the uncertainties of city life, most studies of African urban communities concur with Leonard Plotnicov's assessment of the Nigerian city of Jos as being "neither a 'sick' nor anomic community."[40] The heterogeneous immigrant population does manage on its own to create institutions which are viable and durable even though they only have relevance to the migrant while he or she is resident in the city. Despite the complexity of the situation, social life in the new communities does get organized and is systematic. There is, after all, a streak of pragmatism combined with adventurism which led to the decision to migrate in the first place, and this pragmatism permits the migrant to survive in an otherwise hostile, alien environment.

Unfortunately for the development of a city-wide sense of political community, this individual adjustment to city life and reduction in personal tensions come through identification with ethnic, religious, neighborhood, and other particularistic associations. Given the general weakness of political parties and their total eclipse in many of the states governed by the military, there are few institutions which operate between the levels of national elite and the urban masses that can regularly and systematically aggregate the demands and interests of urban dwellers within the context of the broader community. The attention of the national political elites is directed to the solution of all-absorbing national and international problems, leaving little time or energy for addressing the concerns of the city. Even where there are political parties, city branches seldom operate independently from the national organization. Leaders from the urban branch cannot take issue with positions which are at variance with national policies and plans. Thus, few African cities have a situation comparable to that in cities along the eastern coast of the United States during the nineteenth century and even today in which political party bosses and their local representatives ("ward heelers") greased the entry of the rural migrant into urban life by finding him jobs, socializing him, and serving as the intermediary among the family and ethnic groupings which had emerged. National leaders in Africa, moreover, have often failed to capitalize on the informal leadership structures which arise in squatter settlements, referred to previously. Squatter leaders and organizations could serve as effective bridges were they not looked upon with suspicion by the fragile national leadership and the urban planners.

Significantly, two of the best organized political parties in office, ones with genuinely mass-based strength, have officially adopted policies which attempt to thwart urban growth and make the cities less attractive to rural migrants. One of these is the villagization program of President Julius Nyerere and the Chama Cha Mapinduzi (the former TANU) in Tanzania—an effort to provide an intermediate residential pattern between the isolated rural homeland and the congested city. In addition to a posture of "benign neglect" in repairing city streets and in making other capital city expenditures, "rustication" efforts are launched from time to time in Dar es Salaam to round up the urban unemployed and send them back to the villages where they can be productive. The symbolic value of rustication is apparently regarded as far more important than the results, since many of the same vagrants drift back to Dar es Salaam within a matter of a few weeks or months.[41] With the dual objectives of discouraging further growth of the capital city and shifting political development attention away from the externally oriented capital port city of Dar es Salaam to the rural interior, Nyerere has long been engaged in developing a new capital at Dodoma, near the geographic center of the country. It has been his hope that Dodoma would remain a small, non-industrialized, pedestrian city, thereby retaining its rural image. Difficulties of finding a reliable water supply and other logistical problems—to say nothing of the costs involved—have delayed the move of many ministries and headquarters staffs to Dodoma. Foreign embassies and companies are also reluctant to move to a location which lacks schools, clinics, and other amenities.

Although often regarded as politically the polar opposite of Nyerere, Malawi's President H. Kamuzu Banda has also attempted to control the rate and pattern of urban growth in Malawi. His development of the small settlement at Lilongwe as the new centrally located capital city has already helped to shift the patterns of economic development away from the former capital of Blantyre in the south. Blantyre's location was a reminder of the colonial origins of Malawi (formerly Nyasaland) as an extension of European interests in South Africa and the Rhodesias. The orderly planning of the new capital has thus far avoided many of the problems of squatter development elsewhere in Africa. Malawi has also extended construction of schools, roads, markets, and other manifestations of development into the "Dead North," the once-neglected northern third of the country. Instead of emphasizing the deterioration of existing cities, Banda has attempted to make rural life more attractive by building schools and clinics in rural areas and by nation-wide efforts to provide year-round sources of water for every village by the end of the 1980s.[42] New developments, moreover, are—whenever feasible—distributed geographically around the country instead of being concentrated in the major cities.

The Impact of Urbanization on the Rural Sector

Before leaving the subject of the weakness of the urban sense of political community in Africa, it must be noted that the counterpart to this development is the negative impact of rural-to-urban migration upon the rural sector of African society. Complementing severe age and sex imbalances of the cities, the rural sectors have a disproportionate share of an African society's females and of its very old and very young. More and more, the female head of household becomes a typical feature of the rural African family, with responsibility for organizing the economic life of the children and carrying the entire burden of parenthood. The absence of a crucial group of males in the society may also mean that the initiation rituals for young males are not performed in an appropriate manner, and that neighborhood and other corporate activities—such as communal house building and care of widows and orphans—are neglected. Add to this the economic consequences of migration discussed in Chapter 5, and it becomes understandable why an increasing number of women and whole families are throwing in the towel and joining their menfolk in the inexorable march to the city.

Finally, the vitality of rural politics has been similarly eroded by urban migration as a consequence of the absence or only partial commitment of many key male members of the rural community. In those states where traditional political leaders are still recognized, the failure to observe many of the annual rituals that bind the community together and buttress traditional authority has taken its toll. The ability of traditional as well as appointed rural leaders to present the case of the peasantry to a remote urban national leadership is highly limited. Even where the political party has not been displaced by the military, with its own narrow agenda, the political parties tend to be creatures of their urban roots. Only in a few cases such as Tanzania, Malawi, the Cameroon, and Senegal are the national parties effectively organized in the rural countryside. Hence, the absence of an effective sense of political community is a national phenomenon, which is exacerbated by the character of African urbanization.

VII

POLITICAL PARTIES
The Quest for Popular Government

Politicians, journalists, and even scholars tend to formulate observations about political behavior in terms of the thoughts and actions of leading personalities associated with particular societies and particular historic eras. In certain instances this may be justified. Obviously the impact which Gandhi, Hitler, Joan of Arc, Genghis Khan, or Catherine the Great had upon political outcomes in their respective days was far out of proportion to the impact made by other individuals operating during the same periods. In the words of the philosopher Sidney Hook, these were "event-making" individuals.[1] For good or evil, they were able effectively to focus attention upon the critical needs and issues of the day, to communicate with the members of the politically relevant strata of that society, and to marshall both the human and physical resources needed to accomplish significant goals.

The tendency to concentrate on dominant personalities in explaining political behavior is even more prevalent in the case of recent African history than it has been for many other areas of the globe. Partly this emerges from a desire on the part both of external observers and of actual participants to make sense quickly out of situations which are novel and therefore relatively incomprehensible given our previous mindsets regarding predictable human behavior. In the face of weak institutions and political scenes that are kaleidoscopic in nature, the extended tenure of certain African leaders gives one a somewhat stable hook on which to hang political analysis. Africanist scholars themselves have contributed to this phenomenon through the abuse or at least overuse of the concept of *charisma* to explain political situations which differed substantially from the analytical models developed to explain politics in Western societies.[2]

Politics is normally more mundane. While there are those heroic leaders who are "touched with grace," most political leaders are merely "eventful" persons no matter their longevity or ability to exclude more meaningful political actors from the scene. That is, the overwhelming majority of British kings and queens and elected American presidents and the steady procession of Bolivian military dictators just happen to be at a particular place at a fortuitous point in time. Political outcomes during their "watch" tend to depend less upon their genius or force of personality than they do upon circumstances of the time, the conditions of the environment, challenges to the status quo, or the continuing impact of the special cultural and institutional arrangements of the leader's society.

Even those Hook identifies as "event-making" leaders manage to make their mark in history because of their ability to organize and sustain activities which lead to the implementation of their ideas and programs. Without denigrating the role of individual creative leadership, politics is at base group behavior rather than the consequence of actions of isolated individuals. The nature of the crucial political group (or groups) varies from society to society and within a single society over time. In the modern process of nation-building, for example, structures that were essentially religious in nature played critical roles both in Poland during the long partition prior to World War I and in Cyprus as it emerged from British colonial rule. The military as a corporate structure had much to do with the formation of Turkey as a modern state following the collapse and dismemberment of the Ottoman Empire. In most of the new states of Africa, it has been the political party, at one stage or another in the transition from colonial status to independence, that has been one of the crucial institutions in politics. In a number of those states the party that waged the battle for independence has continued as the dominant structure, governing the heterogeneous society in the decades following the withdrawal of the colonial power.

Despite the efforts of party leaders at independence to monopolize all forms of legitimate political participation and communication, the party has remained only one among several forms of social organization in sub-Saharan Africa having political relevance in the post-colonial era. The military most obviously became a significant competitor, since in a majority of states it has successfully displaced political parties. In some instances the military takeover has appeared to be permanent; in others the leaders of the armed forces have attempted to determine the new rules for party competition once it has withdrawn to the barracks. While less powerful than the military, religious leaders in Africa have also challenged party leaders with respect to certain aspects of behavior. These rivals include not only those associated with Christianity or Islam but also traditional secret societies, such as the Poro Societies of Sierra Leone and Liberia.[3] And, of course, the traditional African family—albeit sometimes modified to adapt to modern purposes— has continued to play a key role in recruitment to political office, the distribution of patronage, and controlling political dissent.

The Concept of the Political Party in Africa

African political parties have enjoyed a somewhat checkered history in the period since the achievement of independence. A few, such as the dominant parties in Tanzania and Malawi, have actually gained in strength during the past two decades; others have either fallen victim to military intervention or have become moribund political groupings which exist largely in name only, and which come to life every few years to conduct uncontested plebiscitary elections in behalf of the entrenched governmental elite. Yet, despite their uneven history and the great disparities in the organization and tactics, political parties in general can rightfully claim significant credit for having brought many of the new states to independence. They did so in many cases in the face of the combined opposition of colonial administrators, European settlers, co-opted traditional rulers, Asian merchants, and others who enjoyed a vested interest in the colonial status quo. While not suggesting that political parties accomplished the task without assistance from both external and other internal forces, nevertheless some mark of their success is the fact that in the space of roughly twenty-five years all territories in Africa with the exception of Namibia and South Africa witnessed Africans coming into control of their own political, economic, and social fortunes. The political party—regardless of its form—was one of the earliest social instruments which not only effectively uprooted Africans in considerable numbers from their localized environment but also permitted them to identify emotionally with the larger geographic entity created by the colonial powers. All parties in a sense contributed to this breakdown in parochialism—for even the parties which attempted to organize upon an ethnic basis were forced to break down some of the lesser parochialisms of clan, village, and chiefdom.[4]

As is true in other sectors of the globe, the term political party in the African context covers a wide range of structures, differing in their goals, their tactics for achieving and retaining power, their recruitment of members, and their relationship to other groups in society. In some Western countries it has been convenient to differentiate between interest groups, which are the *articulators* of interests, and political parties, which serve as *aggregators*.[5] That is, the aggregators attempt to consolidate groups with similar or complementary goals into a cohesive political force and to gloss over or cancel out the points of conflict that emerge over the articulation of diverse interests. In the West the purpose of constructing a coalition of groups is to win an electoral victory over similarly organized opponents and earn thereby the right to organize a government.

This distinction between parties and interest groups has not always been relevant to the analysis of African politics.[6] During the latter days of the colonial era, for example, overtly political African movements were often banned, and where they were not banned, they could not electorally compete in a political system that was monopolized by European administrators and others. The best most political groupings could hope for was to be articulators of interests. They could petition the administration for the implementation of a new program of benefit to their members or seek the rejection or modification of programs regarded as inimical to their basic concerns. In those rare instances where African political parties could compete in elections under colonial rule, the cards were stacked against their gaining control of the colonial state.

The Western distinction between articulators and aggregators of interest has also been less than helpful for analyzing post-colonial politics in Africa. Most political parties—and particularly those that survived into the post-independence era—tended to become both articulators and aggregators of interests. That is, the party leadership recognized that the low level of political, social, and economic awareness on the part of the illiterate masses made it necessary for the party leaders to tell the people what they should actually expect from the new political community. Still tied to traditional ethnic groupings or intimidated by the restrictions of the colonial administrators, the African peasantry was not aware of how it should actually go about achieving a better way of life. It was assumed then to be the task of the party leaders to instruct them. While there were other structures that were equally prepared to share in the task of articulating new interests and demands, party leaders tended to regard them as rivals for popular support. These included not only the traditional chiefs but also leaders of trade unions, cooperatives, religious groups, and schools that had served as "co-conspirators" with the party leaders in challenging colonial rule.[7] By one means or another, these competitive articulators of interests were either coopted into the party structure or suppressed or brushed aside. The party then assumed the dual role of articulator and aggregator of interests, assuming that it had an uncontested mandate to undertake the restructuring of post-colonial society and the achievement of various political, economic, and social goals in behalf of the new nation-states.

ORIGINS OF MODERN AFRICAN PARTIES. The difficulties of dealing with the concept of the political party in the African context are reflected in the almost erratic way in which this structure has been handled during the past three decades by European, American, and—most recently—African scholars. In the first phase there was almost an implicit assumption that the formation of territorial or supra-territorial associations was a temporary aberration from the norms of African political behavior. Lord Hailey and George H. T. Kimble, for example, in their early 1950s compilation of data for their monumental surveys of African affairs gave parties only the most cursory attention.[8] Even many of the political scientists and social anthropologists who recognized the growing role of parties in territorial politics nevertheless focused their research attention on international relations or community-based politics at the ethnic level, ignoring the territorial parties in between. Only a few, like Thomas Hodgkin, Jacques Lombard, James S. Coleman, and Ruth Schacter Morgenthau, ventured to provide in depth studies of political parties.

Having discovered the existence of this phenomenon, the next phase of scholarship was marked by a vigorous effort to make African parties more intelligible to a wider audience. Parties were classified into patron versus mass-based, ethnic versus nationalist, modern versus traditional, monopolistic versus competitive, revolutionary versus conservative or syncretistic, and other matching pairs to facilitate comparative analysis. In the process Africanist scholars may have been guilty of giving many of these movements or associations more concreteness than the facts warranted and to ignore other forces which were already active or—like the military—waiting for their time on stage. It may be, too, that scholarly enthusiasm for the subject may have persuaded European parliamentarians and colonial administrators to transfer authority to party leaders before a viable territorial alternative to the colonial administration had actually materialized and taken shape. Whatever the criticism of scholars, administrators, journalists, and others on this count, the fact is that in the late 1950s and early 1960s as the struggle for independence was shaping up, the political party in most territories was "the only game in town." In terms of formulating demands and mobilizing energies of a broadening spectrum of Africans regarding the evils of colonial rule, the political party was far in advance of other structures.

The realization that the case for political parties may have been overstated by scholars came in the third phase, as the succession of military regimes displaced party leaders in the governing of African states. The extent of this disillusionment is registered in the proportionate tapering down in volume of political studies dealing with parties as opposed to concentration on a far broader range of issues.

It is difficult to pinpoint with certainty the origins of political parties in modern Africa. Liberia, as the first Black state to achieve self-rule, had inchoate party organizations even before its independence in 1847. The 1980 military coup in that country witnessed the demise of Africa's oldest political organization, the True Whig Party, which had been in existence since 1870. For colonial Africa, however, the process was long delayed. But there are historic events which evidence the early stirrings of African leaders seeking a political role in the new colonial territory superimposed by Europeans upon the traditional African societies. One early event was the formation in 1912 of the African National Congress in South Africa, bringing together a coalition of Blacks, whites, and Indians committed to the nonviolent reform of the white supremacist system.[9]

A second event was the formation in 1917 of the National Congress of British West Africa under Joseph Casely-Hayford. Western-educated Africans in Nigeria, the Gold Coast, Sierra Leone, and The Gambia sought political rights for themselves analogous to those extracted by European settlers in Southern, Central, and East Africa from the British Colonial Office This included control over internal political affairs and a greater say in taxation and the expenditure of revenues on education and other social services.

In analyzing the popularity of the political party as the chosen instrument for realizing African aspirations for freedom, it is important to remember that Africans did not monopolize this form of modern association. In territories such as Kenya, Zimbabwe, and Zambia, which had substantial immigrant populations, the white merchants and miners as well as the Asian merchants had organized political parties at a much earlier date. Given the economic strength of these minority groups, the associations were far more effective than African interest groups in pressuring the colonial bureaucracy to respond to their needs and to do their bidding. They did, however, serve as role models for Africans.

In territories where African political associations were legally permitted, parties turned out to be among the few modern structures of significance in colonial society in which both the leadership and the rank-and-file members were predominantly African. The Christian churches, for example, recruited Africans at the mass level, but the clergy still tended to be overwhelmingly European or tightly controlled by Europeans. In the colonial military, the officer class and even significant noncommissioned posts in Francophone Africa were monopolized by Europeans. In the area of commerce, although Africans could engage in petty as well as long-distance trading, the major economic structures in colonial society were also under European or Asian ownership and control. The same barriers to significant mobility applied with respect to the educational sector, trade unions, the professions, and other modern activities.

Another facet of the popularity of political parties as vehicles of African mobilization is that the requirements for leadership and membership alike were far less demanding and less prescribed than was true of other associations, whether traditional or modern. In areas where the British and others relied upon traditional political authorities to carry out their rule, ascriptive conditions such as ethnicity, sex, relative age, or birth into a particular "royal" family limited participation in traditional politics at both the mass and the leadership levels. Compared to other modern structures, moreover, which required a period of tutelage or apprenticeship prior to full admission to membership, political parties normally only required an expression of intent, attendance at rallies, voting (where this was available to Africans), and occasional payment of dues. The last named requisite was often honored more in the breach, since the leadership seldom kept accurate records (which could be confiscated by the authorities to harass dissidents), and there was a tendency to inflate membership figures for the purpose of commanding greater attention from the colonial authorities or from external critics of colonial rule. By way of contrast, the Catholic Church, for example, required baptism, catechism, regular attendance at mass, and confession for its bona fide members, as well as a drastic revision of lifestyle, abandonment of polygamy, and other departures from traditional values and practices. Church membership required the dual act of acceptance of the new and renunciation of the old value system. Islam similarly presented a set of demands upon converts to attend Koranic school, reduce the number of legal marriages to no more than four, pray five times daily, and ideally to make the pilgrimage to Mecca. Membership in structures such as teachers' associations and other professional organizations also placed as a minimum the requirement of training and experience requisite to that occupational skill.

Conversely, expulsion from party membership did not carry the ritual, economic, or moral sanctions associated with excommunication from a church or the withdrawal of one's trade union work card. Indeed, party membership imposed few demands for outward and visible signs of commitment on the part of the political faithful. One was merely expected to lend one's body and voice to a mass demonstration or boycott, take vicarious pleasure in seeing colonial or traditional chiefs confronted and harassed for their sins of omission and commission, and in other ways identify with the party leadership.

Even taking into account the existence of mono-ethnic and mono-religious parties or movements, the political party in many colonial territories was attractive to a mass following because it tended to be one of the few structures with a modern "world view" that transcended the limited perspective of an ethnic group, a church, or a trade union. Unlike the traditional chiefs (where they had not been deposed, forced into exile, or stripped of power), the political party leaders were not ascriptively limited in their appeal to the ethnic group into which they were born, nor were they unduly restricted by traditional values and conventions. They were free to break new ground in terms of behavior patterns and establishing social relationships across ethnic lines. They came to accept the artificially created colonial territory as the logical arena for action instead of being limited to the parochial confines of a "tribal" reserve.

Many of the early parties emerged from groupings which were not necessarily intent upon controlling the colonial state but rather had limited objectives of an economic, cultural, or other nature. Gradually their leaders realized that to accomplish their more narrow purposes they had to pursue the broader route of contesting the authority of the colonial group in general. Thus, for example, in Nigeria the National Convention of Nigeria and the Cameroon (NCNC) in 1944 grew out of a congeries of trade unions, literary societies, professional associations, social clubs, and tribal unions.[10]

Some parties were outgrowths of voluntary associations. In other cases the leaders were graduates of a particular school or of Western-type schools in general. For example, the National Unionist Party emerged in the Sudan in 1949 from among the alumni of Western-type schools.[11] The William Ponty school outside Dakar served a similar role as the training ground for the future nationalist leaders of Francophone states in West Africa.[12] There were also parties in East Africa such as the Kabaka Yekka Party of the Baganda in Uganda which were organized along ethnically exclusive lines.[13] More typically, leaders of political parties attempted to achieve cooperation among those diverse people who were arbitrarily included within a single colonial territory or were residents of a regional grouping of territories under a single colonial power, such as British West Africa or French West Africa. Furthermore, although political protest often drew strength from colonial authorities' harrassment of religious groups (such as the Watch Tower Movement in Central Africa) or the agitation of trade union and cooperative leaders for a better economic deal for Africans, political party leaders were less restricted in their agenda. They could capitalize upon—and yet at the same time transcend—such narrow clusters of concerns as improvement in urban wages, removal of planting restrictions, and missionary opposition to polygamy or clitoridectomy. Initially a party leadership might concentrate on narrow "bread and butter" issues of direct interest to a localized constituency of peasants or urban unemployed, particularly when the illiterate masses did not respond well to more abstract, universalistic issues such as "freedom" and "justice." The most successful movements, however, were those which were not geographically or ethnically limited and which accepted a broad mandate by taking on all aspects of individual concerns from the cradle to the grave. Successful parties had to be prepared to probe any and all of the weaknesses of a colonial administration.

PARTY LEADERS. Political parties also had certain advantages over other contemporary traditional structures in terms of leadership requirements. Party leaders, for example, were often accused by the colonial authorities of being "unrepresentative" of the people. (Implicit in this charge was the paternalistic notion that the Europeans themselves were the true representatives of African interests.) Or it might be suggested that Africans who collaborated with Europeans and governed under the mandate of the colonial umbrella were better judges of the true interests of the African masses. Curiously, however, this collaborating group included not only those traditional chiefs who had been co-opted under the colonial policy of Indirect Rule, but also the artificially created warrant chiefs—Africans who had been arbitrarily posted to areas where the traditional political system either had been eroded if not destroyed during the conquest, or was not readily adaptable to European purposes.[14]

In any event, the charge of being "unrepresentative" is irrelevant. A political elite—and particularly a counter elite which is opposing the entrenched establishment—seldom constitutes a broad cross-section of its own society.[15] That, indeed, is what makes a group an elite: the possession of prized skills and other qualities not widely found among the general population. A potential elite controls attributes which are scarce but admired and which give it a claim to preeminence over others in society. Not only does the elite enjoy a sense of corporate identity, based upon its own awareness of the value and relatively exclusive nature of its gifts and characteristics, but it is convinced that its preeminence establishes a set of rights, entitlements, duties, and behavior patterns that properly set it apart from the mass of society. When this claim to superiority is acknowledged by the masses, it takes the form of acts of deference or respect and efforts to imitate those aspects of elite behavior which are subject to emulation.

There were several distinctive qualities which set the African party elite apart from the masses during the anti-colonial struggle. Most notably, the elite tended to have an urbanized life style within societies where the majority of the population was still rural. It was this urbanized group that had been early exposed to Christianity or Islam rather than continuing to participate in traditional forms of religious worship. In societies, moreover, that not only were predominantly illiterate but lacked written forms of indigenous languages, the party elite that sought control of the colonial state had for the most part been educated at Christian missionary schools, and its members were articulate in a European language or in a dominant African lingua franca beyond their mother tongues. Members of the party elite were accustomed to a monetary exchange economy and the values associated with it, whereas the bulk of African society was still committed to subsistence and barter economies.

The foregoing does not suggest that the aspiring governing elite in any territory was a monolith. Indeed, there were marked differences in ideology, in orientation to tradition or to specific ethnic groups, and in commitment to the pace and manner of confronting the colonial presence. What the independence-seeking political elite generally shared was the firm conviction that they were the legitimate representatives of the masses in the new Africa and that they could simultaneously restore the values of the past and combine them with the best that was provided by the sustained contact with Europeans. The party leaders were often characterized as being modernists who opposed the chiefs, elders, and other representatives of traditional authority. In fact, the most successful party leaders were those who were eclectic in their appeal and in their personal traits. Instead of being hostile to traditionalism, the party leaders had to woo away support from the chiefs by convincing the masses that traditional values and institutions would be better preserved and invigorated under party leadership. Politicians had to convince the more traditionally oriented masses that the leadership's embrace of Western education, religion, and lifestyle was not a rejection of African culture per se. It was the colonialists and colonial rule—through the imposition of the color bar and other racial restrictions—that constituted a rejection of African values and institutions. To make the argument more convincing, a Western-educated leader like Sékou Touré had to stress his ancestral linkage with the great warrior-chief Almany Samoury Touré, one of the last effective challengers of French imperial rule in West Africa.[16] The same factor was implicit in Nkrumah's decision to rename the Gold Coast after the ancient African kingdom of Ghana, situated much further to the northwest than the present-day state bearing its name. The tendency to blend contemporary and traditional symbols of authority also manifested itself in the adoption by party leaders of the umbrella, *kiboko* (hippo-hide swagger stick), ornately embroidered robes, formalized salutation, ornamented stool, and other manifestations of traditional royal authority.

There was general agreement among the members of the party elite, moreover, that their own corporate interests were being poorly served under colonial rule. Even in those cases where the French, Belgians, and Portuguese offered the legal status of évolué or assimilado to a minority of educated and Christianized Africans, there was the cruel realization that these semi-Westernized elites had become virtual strangers in their own societies, looking on from the sidelines at what was essentially a European show. Despite the promise that education and a transformed lifestyle would bring them enhanced status and greater material rewards, their gains never quite matched those accruing to the European and Asian immigrants in their midst. They became in effect almost "non-persons," caught between two worlds. Both the quantity and quality of significant African participation in the new society were painfully retarded, as the London-educated Jomo Kenyatta protested upon his return to colonial Kenya. Hence, what was required was a frontal assault on colonial privilege in order to accelerate the timetable of African self-government—if not independence—and reverse the contradictions of colonial society.

As was true of the rank-and-file membership, requirements for leadership roles in the emerging political parties were far less vigorous than those imposed upon officers in the military, the established Christian churches, the colonial bureaucracy, the professions, significant economic structures, or ethnic-based associations. Leaders of political parties were in a few instances elected by the broader membership. More often than not, however, recruitment took place either by self-selection or co-optation. That is, a particularly gifted organizer with oratorical and other skills would organize a party or a branch unit of an existing party, and his leadership role depended upon his success in attracting a following. Most frequently, the existing leadership would recognize a young man of talent and energy and co-opt him by giving him a position of responsibility in the party. The training required for more advanced posts within the party hierarchy was acquired "on the job," with the specifications for each job being determined in a flexible fashion—tailored to the talents of the incumbent. Success in securing and retaining a party following ultimately depended upon the ability of the leaders both to satisfy the felt needs of their members and to identify the points of vulnerability and egregious errors committed by the colonial administrators, settlers, missionaries, and others associated with colonial rule. African party leaders had to capitalize upon popular hostility to a new tax, an increase in the bus fares or market fees, or some other irritant in the relationship between Africans and the colonial power structure. Europeans often accused African party leaders of duplicity, in that many of the very policies which a nationalist leader opposed while seeking power were vigorously enforced once he had been given the responsibility of governing. In Ghana, for example, Kwame Nkrumah gained the support of the cocoa farmers by opposing the recommended technique for dealing with the root shoot disease—namely destroying not only those trees which were already infected, but healthy ones which had probably been exposed to the root virus.[17] Ghanaian farmers objected to seeing apparently healthy trees, their source of prosperity, destroyed. It was thus a logical issue for Nkrumah to seize upon in gaining support for the Convention People's Party in its campaign against both the British and the rival, more conservative United Gold Coast Convention. Once Nkrumah was given the responsibilities of First Minister, however, he quickly moved to support the British policy of destroying the exposed trees as the only available method for protecting the cocoa crop, which had become the mainstay of the Ghanaian economy. Julius Nyerere did a similar reversal after having first opposed the British for introducing an agricultural bias into the middle school curriculum. Once in power, Nyerere was even more rigorous than the British in elevating the status of agriculture within the school curriculum in Tanzania.[18]

The strategies of the party leaders were not entirely based upon opposition tactics. Indeed, with respect to their potential following they lacked the negative sanctions available to church, military, and other authorities. If expelled from the party, for example, dissidents might form a rival organization to challenge the original party. Parties had to present positive programs to potential members in terms of the "good life" that would be available once the Europeans had been deposed. Parties often secured a broad membership by becoming surrogates to the extended family. In the tradition of nineteenth-century America, immigrants to the city who were seeking jobs, companionship, lodging, or entertainment often turned to the party bosses for assistance. (See Chapter 6.)

In many respects, party leaders during the colonial period could operate without being precisely accountable to their members or to the broader society. Their appeal to the rank and file was in many instances their oratorical skill in identifying problems and promising miraculous solutions once the colonial authorities had been ousted. Hence, they were not to be held responsible for their performance in the way that a union leader or the manager of an agricultural cooperative society would have been. Since they often lacked official recognition and were not eligible to achieve elective office within a parliamentary structure, it was difficult as well for the colonial administration to hold them accountable for their performance. The latter could, it is true, establish requirements regarding fiscal accounting of dues, the conduct of meetings, and recruiting practices. Often, however, the colonialists lacked the supervisory personnel to enforce such standards.

Ironically, a rigorous effort on the part of colonial administrators to control the words and actions of party leaders was often a guarantee of success to the movement and its officials. Indeed, there were calculated efforts on the part of aspiring leaders to provoke the colonial authorities into banning an organization and imprisoning its leadership. The drama associated with conspiratorial action served to swell the ranks of the party rather than diminish them. Boycotts and strikes not only secured popular participation and identification, but they significantly tied up the resources of the colonial bureaucracy and increased the costs of colonial rule. More importantly, the creation of "living martyrs" sharply focused attention upon the issues of discontent and "separated the men from the boys" among rival claimants to national party leadership. The term "prison graduate" acquired positive connotations, and achievement of this status became almost a rite of passage in anti-colonial politics. The list of those who went from the jailhouse door to new or enhanced responsibilities in the pre-independence governments included such famous leaders as Julius Nyerere, Kwame Nkrumah, H. Kamuzu Banda, and, of course, Jomo Kenyatta. The last named, a Kenyan nationalist, spent close to a decade under preventive detention in the brutal environment of the Northern Frontier District before being called by the British Governor to head the new transitional government.[19] Indeed, the willingness of African leaders to undertake such personal sacrifice was a key factor in changing public opinion regarding the immorality of colonial rule among not only Africans but opinion leaders in the European metropole and at the global level as well.

Leadership of party movements in the pre-independence period was marked by a high premium on the ability to manipulate words and symbols, with lesser attention being placed on actual experience in government, knowledge of economic affairs, or even demonstrated skills in mass organization. Thus, most movements were at critical junctures headed by teachers, lawyers, editors, and African clergy. Jomo Kenyatta, for example, was a teacher and author of an important book, *Facing Mount Kenya*. Julius Nyerere resigned in 1954 from his post as principal of a Catholic school in Tanzania to devote himself fully to the task of revitalizing the Tanganyika African National Union. Two of the four competitors for leadership of the Zimbabwean independence struggle were ministers: Bishop Abel Muzorewa and the Reverend Ndabangi Sithole. Only occasionally were the other professions represented in key party roles—obvious exceptions being two medical doctors, Sir Milton Margai in Sierra Leone and H. Kamuzu Banda in Malawi (Nyasaland). The latter had a successful medical practice in London for many years before ultimately returning to Malawi to assume the leadership of the campaign against the white-dominated Federation of Rhodesia and Nyasaland. During Banda's self-imposed exile in Britain he had befriended and given financial support to Nkrumah, Seretse Khama, Kenyatta, and other future leaders of Africa.

Verbal skills unfortunately far outweighed skills in the organizational tactics needed both to create genuinely broad-based political movements and to accept the responsibilities for governing an independent African state.

Indeed, the weakness of the former Tanzanian Africa National Union in post-independent Tanganyika led Julius Nyerere to resign from his post as prime minister in 1962 in order to revitalize the party's organizational effectiveness in the countryside. A year later, having accomplished this task, Nyerere returned to office.[20] Sékou Touré of Guinea was perhaps the only African head of state who had served as a leader of a trade union organization before accepting the mantle of leadership in the Parti Démocratique du Guinée (PDG).[21] As the historian Lansine Kaba has pointed out, the trade union base of the PDG not only broadened its popular support but gave the movement access to external funding and provided the party with models for political action—strikes, boycotts, discipline—borrowed from the struggle for economic justice in the industrial order. More readily than other political parties, the PDG was able to capitalize upon complaints about conditions of employment in Guinea and thus enlist a more committed mass membership.[22] The only other African parallel approximating this is the experience of Tom Mboya, the Luo trade union leader who kept Kenya-wide politics alive during the ban on Kikuyu participation at the height of the Mau Mau emergency. Mboya might have succeeded Jomo Kenyatta had not an assassin's bullet earlier terminated that possibility.

What hurt the pre-independence party leaders most, however, was their lack of training in economics and finance. This was in some respects the fault of the colonial powers, who saw no need to establish universities in Africa with solid programs in economics and finance or to provide scholarships for study abroad in these disciplines. On this score, the British and French educational heritage turned out to be only moderately better than the disastrous course pursued by the Belgians, Portuguese, Italians, and Spanish with respect to African education. Indeed, the Belgians in Zaire (Congo) were quite prepared in 1960 to surrender political power to the Zairois as long as Belgians remained in control of the vast economic resources of the Katanga, or Shaba, area. The European monopoly in this area is demonstrated by the fact that the ministries of finance and economic planning were among the last of the three or four portfolios which the British, for example, would surrender as they incorporated Africans into the transitional governments on the eve of independence. Hence, the admonition of Kwame Nkrumah to "seek ye first the political kingdom" was a recognition of a deficiency in economic skills among African leaders as well as a realization that Africans could not do much about economic planning until political power had passed into their hands. Nevertheless, their lack of skills in economics and finance proved to be a critical deficiency in their attempts to overcome the twin threats of poverty and neo-colonialism.

THE COLONIAL POWERS AND NATIONALIST RESPONSES. It is difficult to generalize about the attitudes and policies of the colonial powers with respect to the formation of political parties and the demands of Africans to participate in effective decision-making regarding their own economic, social, and political fate.[23] Not only did each of the major powers differ from the others, but within a single imperial system practices varied from country to country and even within different sections of the same territory. The British, for example, acceded far earlier to the demands for self-government and African participation in politics in West Africa then they did in East, Central, and Southern Africa, where the pressures from highly vocal European settler minorities slowed the pace of African political advancement. In East Africa, concessions to African political development in Kenya amd Uganda lagged behind those made in Tanganyika, which was a League of Nations mandate and later a United Nations Trusteeship Territory. The trusteeship system created a supervisory apparatus of annual reports, triennial visiting missions, and the possibility of Africans petitioning directly to the U.N. regarding grievances. There was also an explicit commitment to independence. These mechanisms did not exist in non-Trust territories. Even within a single territory, such as Sierre Leone or the Gold Coast (Ghana), moreover, demands for representation in quasi-parliamentary institutions were recognized earlier on the coast then in the less developed interior.

Despite the foregoing, it is perhaps legitimate to say that the colonial powers differed largely in the degree of their hostility toward African demands to participate in parties and to engage in electoral politics. Even the British and the French, who have better records than the others, had to be coerced into making concessions. They did not go about actively encouraging opposition to their virtual monopoly over political decision-making. The British only conceded when the costs of not doing so became prohibitive, constituting a drain on the British taxpayer or creating a barrier to the full exploitation of the trade and investment opportunities that Britain expected from its colonies. Strikes and other forms of instability, moreover, lessened the strategic value of colonial bases. Timely concession to vigorous local demands thus was a means of guaranteeing a continuity of the cultural, economic, diplomatic, and other linkages within the Commonwealth of Nations. Since the national political institutions forged by the British administration in the closing decades of colonial rule were based on the Westminster parliamentary model, it was only logical that parties and electoral machinary should eventually become available to Africans. It was, however, a slow process. As noted in chapter 2, in the early stages in British territories representation was by administrative selection rather than popular election. In some instances, reversing previous trends, the least developed— and "more loyal"—areas of the interior were given greater representation than those areas which had experienced more rapid change. This was a calculated effort to slow the demands for drastic reform. Representation of rural traditional authorities in national institutions was encouraged as a barrier to the quick takeover of territorial power by the more urbanized, western-educated party elites.[24] In the later stages of development, executive power was shared with Africans, but even here the initial ministerial responsibilities offered to Africans were in non-sensitive areas such as tourism. Defense, foreign affairs, finance, and justice were often retained by the British until the eve of independence.

Despite the emergence of political interest groups in the early decades of the century in West, East, and even Southern Africa, the history of political party development per se in British Africa was a checkered one. If parties were not banned outright in particular territories or districts, their leaders were subjected to a variety of legal and extra-legal forms of harassment. The Registrar of Societies in a territory would often set up unreasonable pre-requisites for recognition of a party; would require district-by-district formation of a political group rather than permitting it to be launched at the territorial level; would establish rigorous rules about recruitment techniques, accounting procedures for dues collection, membership rolls, and filing minutes of meetings; and would engage in other delaying or harassing tactics. When concessions did come at the end of the Second World War regarding African participation in modern politics, the British preference, for example, was to have Africans compete for seats on local councils rather than allowing electoral politics at the territorial level. Moreover, the ban, in the United Kingdom upon active involvement of civil servants in domestic politics was carried to absurd extremes in Africa. Since most educated Africans were employed by the government, it effectively disenfranchised the most articulate segment of the community.

Superficially at least, the French appeared to have a more relaxed attitude.[25] After all, the évolués of the four communes around Dakar in Senegal had participated in local elections under the Third Republic (1870–1940). African participation, moreover, in French political parties and in the parliamentary institutions of France itself was permitted under the constitutions of both the Fourth (1946–1958) and the Fifth (1958–present) Republics following World War II. Future leaders of independent African states, such as Léopold Senghor and Félix Houphouet-Boigny, were regarded as more than token participants in French national politics. Many of the leading parties of metropolitan France organized branches in the African territories.[26] The reality, however, was that party activity in French colonies was permitted or encouraged as long as the parties were allied to parties in metropolitan France itself or straddled a large region—such as French West Africa—rather than focusing upon control of a single territory. The effort was to divert active African political participation away from the individual territories which were ultimately to become the future nation-states. It was not until the loi cadre of 1956 that serious attention was given to constructing meaningful territorial political institutions in each of the French colonies.[27] Excluded from the list of legitimate aspirations of African politicians, moreover, was the notion of independence from France itself. The harsh treatment which de Gaulle meted out to Sékou Touré and the PDG when Guinea voted not to accept the Constitution of the Fifth Republic was intended to serve as a warning to other prospective defectors from the French Community. Indeed, it was only the steady procession in 1960 of former British, Italian, and Belgian colonies joining the ranks of independent states in the United Nations that compelled the French as well as the Ivoiriens, Senegalese, and other Francophone leaders to accept the inevitability of independence.

With all their limitations, the British and French were leagues ahead of the Portuguese, the Spanish, the Belgians, and the pre–World War II Italians. The Portuguese under Salazar, the Spanish under Franco, and the Italians under Mussolini did not permit competitive political groups to challenge the monopoly of the fascist party in their respective countries. It should not have been expected, therefore, that the situation in Angola, Fernando Po, or Eritrea would be more liberal than it was in the European metropole. Elections, where they did occur, were confirming plebiscites conducted to give the regime the appearance of legitimacy. African participation was token where it was permitted at all.

In contrast with the fascist regimes, the Belgians had a long history of multi-party democracy at home, but until roughly two years prior to independence they denied this form of government to the citizens of the former Belgian Congo (Zaire).[28] The Congo was governed in a paternalistic fashion by a troika: the colonial administration, the Roman Catholic Church, and the industrial corporation known as the Union Minière du Haut Katanga. The Congo was destined neither for independence nor incorporation into the Belgian state; rather it was to have an association with Belgium (in a subordinate status) "for a hundred years"—as the Minister of State for the Colonies said in this author's presence in 1952 during a speech at Harvard University. Educated Africans could achieve the status of évolués, with special economic and social benefits accruing to them. Politics, however, was specifically proscribed. Literary, social, religious, and other associations were permitted, but no political party as such was officially sanctioned until the mid-1950s. ABAKO, which had been recognized officially in 1953, was initially presented as a voluntary association interested in the spread of the Kikongo language.[29] The Belgian Socialist government elected in 1954 moved in the direction of reform, but it was not until 1959 that it hastily created a national parliament for the Congo and authorized party elections. These fledgling institutions never had a chance to function, however, before they were effectively destroyed in the chaos attendant to Zaire's independence in 1960.

Given the variations in official policy and practice from one colonial territory to the next, and the wide range of development and modernization within particular territories, the goals, strategies, and tactics of each political party tended virtually to be *sui generis*. Some parties, such as the Kabaka Yekka Party in Uganda, the Chagga Union in Tanganyika, and the Ashanti Union in Ghana, were centripetal in character, seeking independence or special political status for a particular region or people within a colonial territory. Many parties excluded traditional chiefs from leadership roles; on the other hand, the Action Group in Western Nigeria and the Union Progressiste Sénégalaise (UPS) in Senegal represented a coalition of traditional and western-educated leadership. Some parties, such as Nkrumah's CPP in Ghana or Nyerere's TANU, were centrifugal in nature, seeking not only independence for the primary state in which they operated but political independence and unification of all African states within a region or on the continent as a whole. Most parties in British Africa tended implicitly if not explicitly to have independence as a goal, whereas many Francophone parties would have been content with some continued form of association with France. Some groups, such as Banda's Malawi Congress Party, took a pragmatic incremental approach to economic development strategy; Tourè's PDG in Guinea attempted to embark immediately upon a course of radical socialist development. Some parties, such as Kenneth Kaunda's United National Independence Party, (UNIP) in Zambia, relied upon petitioning, mass demonstrations, and other largely non-violent forms of confrontation in achieving the goal of independence. Others, conversely, were directly engaged in massive street demonstrations, strikes, and other forms of non-compliance with unpopular laws. Some attempted to disengage from Europeans through the creation of schools outside the established framework of government and mission institutions, the withholding of crops and services from the marketplace, or boycotts of European goods. Many of these tactics literally begged for a violent reaction from the colonial authorities that would create martyrs and heroic events to spur the movement along. This is what occurred in Kenya in the 1950s.[30]

In most cases, the rather amorphous political parties and relatively non-violent confrontational tactics proved sufficient to move the colonial authorities along to the critical decision to fold up their tents and go home. The more extreme tactics of peaceful electoral challenge and outright resort to violence seem to have been less representative of successful efforts at termination of colonial rule. With respect to elections, for example, most colonial territories denied Africans suffrage until *after* the decision to withdraw had been made. Among the exceptions was the victory of Nkrumah's CPP in the 1956 Ghanaian election, in which not only the colonial government but Nkrumah's primary rivals, the UGCC and the Ashanti NLM, were thoroughly repudiated.[31] Similarly, Nyerere's victory in 1958 found TANU not only sweeping the designated Black seats in the so-called multiracial partnership government, but also winning seats reserved for whites and Asians. Nyerere's victory effectively ended the British delaying tactic of insisting on a multiracial partnership instead of majority rule as well as blocking the creation of an Upper House in Parliament for traditional chiefs. And, of course, the third significant election in this category was the *"non"* vote cast by Guineans in the plebiscite on de Gaulle's 1958 constitution, which resulted in Guinea's immediate independence from the French community.

Equally few in number are the cases in which an anti-colonial movement achieved its goal of independence as a direct consequence of sustained military confrontation. The earliest case of this, insofar as sub-Saharan Africa is concerned, is Kenya. Although the Kenya African Union and its successor the Kenya African National Union stood organizationally apart from the guerrilla organization which waged the so-called Mau Mau rebellion of 1952–56, KANU was the direct beneficiary of that activity: its leader, Jomo Kenyatta, was asked by the British in 1961 to form the pre-independence government. In the case of Zimbabwe and the three Portuguese territories of Angola, Mozambique, and Guinea-Bissau, there was a much closer relationship between the political parties and their respective guerrilla forces. In Zimbabwe, for example, ZANLA was the fighting arm of Robert Mugabe's Zimbabwe African National Union (ZANU) which was based in Mozambique, whereas Joshua Nkomo's ZIPRA army operated under the political aegis of ZAPU, headquartered in Zambia.[32] The other two major political groupings under Bishop Abel Muzorewa and Rev. Ndabangi Sithole also had their respective military arms. Although there were some leaders who occupied strictly political or strictly military roles, there was an overlap and fusion of roles at lower echelons. As was true of the MPLA in Angola and FRELIMO in Mozambique, Mugabe's political operatives emulated the Chinese Yenan experience (1934–1949) in acquiring the experience of governing while they were actually engaged in the military phase of the liberation struggle.

In each of the cases where military confrontation was involved, the successful political party leadership had to engage in a three-way struggle against the colonial bureaucracy, an ideologically or ethnically divergent African opposition, and an entrenched European settler minority. In the face of a dogged determination by the settlers to deny Africans political and other rights, military confrontation was the only way to tie up the resources of the settler group. Such action focused international attention on the plight of the disenfranchised Africans, and ultimately compelled the primary external supplier of the whites (Britain in Kenya; the Lisbon government with respect to the three Portuguese colonies; and South Africa with respect to the Smith regime) to cease their support of white privilege.

Africa and the the Single-Party System

When the British and the French—and ultimately the Belgians—were pressured into creating parliamentary deliberative bodies at both the territorial and the local levels, they assumed that at the initial stages party politics could be avoided. If the colonial administrators could appoint or co-opt the "right" Africans with the appropriate kinds of experiences, those selected could be expected to carry out their duties in a "responsible" fashion.

At the subsequent stage of political reform, it became apparent that the African point of view did not necessarily coincide with that of the Europeans. Africans wanted to choose their own people to represent them in these parliamentary bodies. At that stage the European administrators naively assumed that politics would be conducted along European lines, with either a two-party or a multi-party system. African political leaders, however, had other intentions. Even before independence had been achieved, nine of the territories witnessed the emergence in each of a single party as the sole political representative of the African masses in opposition to European interests. In each case the dominant party tended to monopolize political expression to the exclusion of divergent African points of view and competing leadership groups. Once independence was achieved, this process accelerated, with seven more states being added to the list of single-party regimes by 1965.[33]

In Kenya the dominant party, KANU, demonstrated particular skills in rewarding its friends and punishing its rivals through the use of patronage, government control of the radio station, the ability to provide government loans, and legislative manipulation of electoral district boundaries. As other parties were to do elsewhere in Africa, KANU used against its opponents the same coercive apparatus created by the colonial administration in suppressing African political expression prior to independence. This included retention of restrictive registration requirements, limits on public meetings, curbs on fund-raising mechanisms, and the use of preventive detention measures.[34] By 1984, twenty-five of the forty-five states in sub-Saharan Africa had experienced some form of single party government, and there were many near-misses as well.

Developments during the latter part of the 1970s and early 1980s seemed to suggest optimistically that the movement toward single-party rule had been halted. Leaders of civilian-dominated states such as Senegal and the Ivory Coast were attempting to orchestrate multi-party competitive systems, and leaders of military regimes in Ghana and Nigeria had designed civilian governments which appeared to guarantee party competition. Furthermore, the constitution for Zimbabwe, forged at Lancaster House in 1979, committed all participants to make no change in the status of its multi-party system prior to 1987. Optimism regarding the continent-wide prospects of multi-party competition, however, was dealt a severe blow as a consequence of the re-entry of the military in Ghana at the end of 1982 and in Nigeria on New Year's Eve, 1983. Equally disturbing has been legalization of one party rule in Sierra Leone and Kenya and the pressures leading to the de facto establishment of a single-party system in Zimbabwe.

What has been the source of this long-term tendency toward single-party rule? It must be made clear at the outset that the rationale that justifies the move to and retention of a single-party system may differ substantially from the objective conditions that facilitate it. Various factors, for example, have contributed to the concentration of power in the hands of one among various competing groups. One such factor was the use of the winner-take-all "list" system of voting employed in various Francophone West African states, including Togo. This electoral device gave all the seats in the national parliament to the official slate of the one party which won a majority of the votes or even a plurality. Even without this electoral mechanism, the old maxim that "nothing succeeds like success" served to convince those who were interested in patronage in its various forms that they must stick with or switch to the winner. Hence, not only were there rank-and-file defections to the party that was victorious in a pre-independence election, but the leaders of the smaller associations often agreed to being absorbed into the dominant party as a way of sharing in the stakes of governing. In Tanzania, the leaders of the Sukuma Union, the Chagga Union, and other ethnic-based parties, for example, were voluntarily absorbed into TANU after the latter's overwhelming victory in 1958. The 1962 formal ban on ethnic- and religious-based parties in Tanganyika merely formalized reality. Similarly, in Uganda many of the parliamentarians elected as members of the Ganda-oriented Kabaka Yekka Party had "crossed the aisle" and given Obote's UPC a legislative majority before Obote made his 1966 frontal assault on Buganda separatism. In some territories an invitation by the colonial administrators to the leadership of one party to form a transitional government virtually guaranteed the demise of all other competing groups. This was certainly the case in colonial Ghana in 1951, where the electoral results demonstrated the strength of Kwame Nkrumah's Convention People's Party. The call to Nkrumah (who was still in jail) proved to be the death knell not only to the older, more conservative United Gold Coast Convention of Dr. J. B. Danquah but to the Ashanti-dominated National Liberation Movement and other ethnic and regionally based parties in the north.[35] Similar developments occurred in Kenya and Tanzania.[36]

The justification of a governing party in the outright banning of or placing of severe restrictions upon opposition parties was often presented in lofty terms. More mundane considerations, however, were often the real rationale. Most parties, as was suggested earlier, were very weak and were often prisoners of their own histories. Many were limited in membership to the urban sector—which meant in most instances the capital city—and sometimes to the particular ethnic group or religious affiliation of the founding leadership, and thus lacked broad-based support. When the solidarity that enabled a coalition of parties to present a united front against the European colonial oppressors had accomplished its primary purposes, old ethnic rivalries or the divergent interests of the urban versus rural residents once more presented themselves. Meanwhile, the pool of leadership of the dominant party—when it had been entrusted with the task of governing—had been further drained by the need to fill administrative, diplomatic, and other posts previously filled by Europeans or Asians. It was invariably the less talented and ambitious of the party cadres who were left to maintain the less attractive party apparatus. Without the struggle against the colonial enemy, the formal party organization often became moribund, only surging to life every few years to organize uncontested national elections or referenda. There were only a few countries in which the party retained a vital structure following independence. Most prominent in this category were those states where the dominant party had forged its organizational structures, recruited its membership, and thought through its future governmental programs while it was still fighting a guerrilla war against the colonial authorities. This would include FRELIMO, the MPLA, and the PAICG in the three Portuguese colonies and Robert Mugabe's ZANU party in Zimbabwe. The only other exceptions were those instances in which the primary leader recognized the role that agriculture would play in economic development and took extraordinary steps to organize the party throughout the countryside. Ironically, the two examples which come most readily to mind had leaders who were ideologically distant—Nyerere's Revolutionary Party (Chama Cha Mapinduzi, formerly TANU) and Banda's Malawi Congress Party.

One explanation for the failure of multi-party competition is the brevity of the experiment in parliamentary democracy during the colonial era. As noted previously, the introduction of party politics, elections, and representative assemblies was long delayed even in the British and French areas. Colonial rule, moreover, was hardly an apt environment for the proper functioning of a parliamentary system. Democracy requires debate, negotiation, compromise, and a willingness to tolerate unpleasant dissent. Colonial rule, on the other hand, survived by command, maintenance of rigid hierarchies, and the attitude that "Auntie Knows Best." Colonial systems, as Coleman and Rosberg have indicated, were "highly centralized, even quasi-military [and] everywhere tended toward bureaucratic authoritarianism, even though it was paternalistic in motivation."[37]

It was not merely the heritage of the colonial experience, however, that made dominant political parties intolerant of formal opposition. The weakness of the party cadre as a governing group was also a major consideration. With very few exceptions Africans had not been permitted to exercise significant ministerial responsibility until the last year or two preceding independence. African party leaders understood their own insecurity and lack of training in key areas—such as economics—which would be vital if they were to live up to the very popular expectations that they themselves had created regarding the good life that was awaiting the masses once colonial rule had come to an end. Some party leaders found it difficult to make the adjustment from being vigorous harping critics of the colonial government to the acceptance of full responsibility for positive programs of an African-controlled government.

THE CRISIS JUSTIFICATION FOR THE SINGLE-PARTY STATE. Unwilling for the most part to publicly proclaim their own insecurity and inexperience, advocates of the single-party system sought other justifications for their actions. The most frequent justification was "The Crisis We Face." During the anti-colonial struggle, for example, it was argued that Africans could not afford the luxury of a division within their ranks while facing a far better financed and organized colonial bureaucracy with arms as well as other means at its disposal in enforcing its will. The settlers and other private Europeans were similarly well organized to contest African demands. In some cases the greatest competitors of the party nationalists were other Africans. The early imperialists had established their rule by playing off traditional rulers against one another. They maintained colonial authority (in British areas, at least) by keeping Africans divided geographically into "Tribal Reserves" and ethnically and ideologically by the policy of Indirect Rule, in which the British utilized the services of traditional chiefs. Hence the dominant party leaders found themselves appealing for solidarity in the face of a heterogeneous but relatively coordinated enemy.

Once the anti-colonial struggle ended, a new series of crises presented themselves which also required a common front. The task of nation-building, for example, demanded that parties based upon ethnicity, religion, region, or other divisive factors be banned in pursuit of a higher Tanzanian, Ghanaian, or Ugandan nationality. Any political opposition organized around such divisive factors threatened the very existence of the new state. The problem of poverty also required unified action: raising the GNP, achieving greater production, creating a more effective system for distribution of goods and services, and bringing Africans into control of their own economic destinies. The limited pool of educated talent had to be put to work in behalf of the common prosperity, not frittered away on competitive politics. Regional politics, which often focused on the interests of the most productive regions of the new state, such as Buganda in Uganda, the oil-rich Igbo area of Nigeria, or the mineral-wealthy Shaba or Katanga area of Zaire, led to secessionist demands which threatened further to impoverish the remainder of the former colonial territory. An additional threat to the fragile economy posed by opposition politics was the danger that better organized international economic forces as well as the entrenched European and Asian immigrant community could take advantage of the vulnerability of the new government. Hence, the argument was made for restricting debate on competing ideologies and strategies of development.

The crisis-oriented apologists for the single-party system were quick to point out that the leading critics of African politics—including officials in the Western democratic nations—had set the example: Western democracies have often denied themselves the luxury of structured debates in the face of crises that affected the very survival of the state. They noted that Britain had had coalition governments during both the Great Depression and the Second World War. Indeed, the British government went from 1935 to 1945 without holding a national election. Similarly, the United States during the first hundred days of the New Deal virtually ignored the constitutional provisions regarding separation of powers and checks and balances. The executive branch under the New Deal assumed the full task of governing. Indeed, the early history of the American republic had many parallels with contemporary Africa.[38] This stream of justification for single-party rule suggested that when the crises had abated in the new African states, they too would return to multi-party competition and the other niceties of democracy. It was in this spirit, for example, that Senegal in the mid-1970s reintroduced a multi-party system.

JUSTIFICATION FROM TRADITION. A second strand of justification for the single-party state is based upon African tradition. Instead of apologizing for the single-party as a temporary aberration from the norms of Western democratic behavior, this stance boldly asserts that it is a modern adaptation of traditional African political behavior.[39] In those traditional societies where broad popular participation was permitted and encouraged, politics was directed to the achievement of consensus rather than a continued bipolarization and proliferation of opinions and groupings within the society. In the search for an elusive truth, the Western political model encourages a continued division of society, with the possibility that those who lose an election or a crucial vote over policy may be permitted to continue their criticism. At the same time, the losers in a Western election risk being temporarily or even permanently excluded from the effective act of governing. This exclusion leads to a sense of alienation and potentially creates enemies of the state. In contrast, the African forum (baraza, pallaver, Kgotla, etc.) encourages the fullest discussion of all aspects of any problem until community consensus is reached. Even if one does not wholly accept the final solution, each individual was a party to the ultimate decision, and had an opportunity to present his point of view. The final outcome frequently incorporates the ideas of the minority into the majority position. Indeed, in most traditional societies there is no permanent minority, and no feeling that politics is a zero-sum game with every gain for one group being a loss for another. Extended discussion, moreover, has a cathartic or healing effect, bringing every dissident back into the fold. Unlike Western democratic thought, which places a heavy emphasis upon individualism, the interest of the collectivity in many African societies is paramount; the interest of the isolated individual is secondary.

This striving for consensus in African politics was also noticeable in customary court procedures and in the penalties meted out. In the traditional society the objective of the court seemed to be less a desire to punish the guilty than to restore harmony or a measure of equilibrium within the community. The issue of justice as well as the extent of restitution was the subject of elaborate discussion. During the protracted deliberation, which was often open to the public, the participants considered the "sociology" of the case and the impact which various solutions or settlements might have upon the broader community, not merely upon those most directly affected by the dispute.

Unlike Anglo-Saxon jurisprudence, moreover, which is concerned with specific rights and obligations and which demands that the data presented in court be strictly germane to the case at hand, an African customary court takes a much more cosmopolitan view. Although the case involves a specific situation, it also serves as a vehicle for the discussion of wider grievances and the settlement of a broad spectrum of outstanding questions. Thus, again the emphasis is upon the community and the general restoration of equilibrium rather than on the punishment or rewarding of individuals.

Procedures for recruitment to office in traditional society were also consensus-oriented, and the community was never left long in doubt regarding the rightful claimant. Where ascriptive rules did not identify a specific successor, the range of choice among possible contenders was still limited. In reducing the field to the one successful claimant, various devices were employed to lessen the possibility of the emergence of permanent cleavages within the community. The very fact that a succession struggle was taking place was often kept from the public. The process of selection, moreover, resembled a papal election in that it permitted the partisans of particular candidates to indicate their support in symbolic ways, which could be re-interpreted after a solitary victor had emerged from among the contenders. With respect to the Banyankole of Uganda, unanimity was secured through resort to a succession war among the possible claimants.[40] The struggle physically eliminated all but the one candidate whose cunning had permitted his survival. In like vein, the institution today of an unopposed Life President reduces cleavage within the modern nation-state by eliminating any discussion of succession to the most crucial national office.

Finally, the traditionalist defenders of the single party system in Africa point to the greater degree of consensus which might be expected because of the more genuine strain of egalitarianism which ran through African traditional society. As pointed out in Chapter 5, this was especially true in the realm of distribution of wealth. Westerners from James Madison to Karl Marx have assumed that the substance of politics is the unequal distribution of property and that this is the primary cause for class conflict. Although the African leadership borrows heavily from Marx both in French and English-speaking areas, Nyerere and others explicitly rejected the notion that class warfare was indispensable to revolutionary change in Africa. It was argued that there were few great disparities of wealth prior to colonial rule, and colonial rule did very little to upset this basic egalitarianism insofar as Africans were concerned. Aside from white settler areas, land rights were left largely intact. And where the notions of private property and large scale economic enterprises were introduced, the African was, statistically speaking, affected in only a marginal fashion. It was the alien immigrants—the Indian or Lebanese merchant, the European mine operator or planter—who constituted an upper economic stratum in the community. And this group was already being eased out during the last throes of colonial rule, with the establishment of cooperative societies, marketing boards, and other mechanisms. Once independence was achieved, the aliens either departed or were placed under rigid restrictions so that they remained in the community on sufferance and have been largely depoliticized.

The difficulty with the justification of single-party rule based on an egalitarian tradition, however, is that it borrows some, but ignores much. It overlooks the many instances in which sharp stratification based upon religion and differential political power existed—particularly in northern Nigeria, Niger, and other areas north of the Sahel. Although the cleavages even between slave and king might not have been as great as they have been in Western society, it is doubtful whether the argument of relativity is very comforting to one who finds himself at the bottom of the heap. The egalitarians, moreover, ignore the fact that the missionary, the colonial administrator, the European or Lebanese merchant did bring about an erosion in the value system of the African population, particularly in the urban areas. Even though Africans were not permitted to participate in a meaningful way during colonial rule, this does not mean that the aspirations to do so were not firmly implanted. Finally, the notion of traditional egalitarianism overlooks the fact that the consensus and egalitarianism that nationalists stress were manifested within the confines of parochial ethnic societies. Consensus within each ethnic group differed somewhat, if not radically, from the consensus in a neighboring ethnic community. How can one emphasize an aspect of traditional society without breathing new life into the sub-national community, thereby complicating the party's already difficult task of nation building?

THE VANGUARD JUSTIFICATION. A third broad category of justification for the single-party system is oriented neither to coping with the present conditions of crisis nor to the restructuring of modern African society along traditional lines. Its orientation is to the future, to the creation of an African society which will at a minimum address the material demands for better food, housing, and clothing. Even more importantly, however, it will also establish radically new linkages between leaders and the led, as well as among citizens without respect to differences in language, race, religion, or culture. Since the masses, according to this theory, only dimly perceive their true interests, it is required that an enlightened vanguard elite lead them out of the wilderness and confusion of the traditional and colonial past into the brighter tomorrow. There are many entrenched resistors to the required change as well as an absence of a consensus among the masses regarding the nature of this future society. Hence, the vanguard elite must be free not only to resort to whatever means are required—including violence—but also to approach the task of governing and to fashion a coherent ideology without the impediment of a legalized opposition.

There are, of course, qualitative differences among the range of vanguard parties which have emerged at the global level in the twentieth century. Fascism constitutes one variation; religious messianic movements constitute another. The most persistent form of vanguardism in post-independence Africa, however, is of the socialist variety. While some early manifestations of African versions of socialism appeared in Tanzania and Zambia, increasingly socialism has come to mean the Marxist-Leninist version of this ideology as represented by FRELIMO in Mozambique, the MPLA in Angola, and the series of Marxist-oriented military regimes which are attempting to transform themselves into vanguard civilian parties in Ethiopia, Benin, Congo-Brazzaville, and Ghana. The central thrust of the ideology is the more equitable distribution of the fruits of production in a basically classless society. The African Marxists do in many cases part company with the Leninists on the need for the prior existence of classes in bringing about the revolution. African Marxists also reject the absolute need for urban industrialization as a necessary stage in the historical process leading to socialism. But they seem to have concurred with the Leninists in their insistence that an elitist, exclusivist, and conspiratorial vanguard party is required to hurry the revolution along to its desired goals. Voluntarism, pluralism, popular spontaneity, and other aspect of the "open society" have been rejected in favor of the direction of society from the top by a gifted vanguard elite.[41]

The Future of the Single-Party System

Not all civilian political systems in post-independent Africa have been characterized by the efforts of a single party to monopolize power. There are a limited number of cases in which multi-party competition has prevailed in a virtually uninterrupted manner since independence, and, opposition parties both openly contest elections and have their votes counted fairly. This would include Botswana, the Gambia, and, of course, Mauritius. The latter is the only instance in Black Africa of a peaceful transfer of power from the incumbent party to its principal civilian challenger in a freely contested election. Sierra Leone experienced a near miss in 1967, only to have a series of military coups frustrate the apparent popular will. In 1968, however, the victorious opposition party did ultimately assume office. There are a number of other experiments, moreover, in which either civilian governments (Senegal, the Ivory Coast) or military regimes (e.g., Ghana and Nigeria) have engaged in political engineering, hoping to reestablish some form of multi-party competition. Despite these exceptions, civilian regimes in most African

end to be characterized by the exclusive exercise of power by a single
al group. What evaluation can we make of the performance of single
party systems in Africa?

PARTY GOVERNMENT VERSUS THE LEADERSHIP CULT. The legitimacy base of
party leaders contrasts with that of the colonial administrators whom they
displaced and with the military leaders who tend to be the recurrent challengers to the African leaders of a single-party state. Party leaders claim to
be the only true instruments of popular government in Africa and the only
group responsive to the democratic will of the people, basing this claim to
legitimacy on the purported role that they played in ending colonial rule
and in setting the new society on the course toward nation-building, overcoming poverty, and securing respect for Africa and Africans at the global
level. To what extent can this claim to legitimacy be substantiated?

One of the most significant mechanisms for determining legitimacy in
Western democratic societies is the requirement that political leaders must
submit themselves to periodic elections in which the electorate is free to
extend the mandate of the incumbent party or to terminate it by opting for
an alternative political group. Inasmuch as legal opposition is foreclosed in
African single party states, to what extent can carefully orchestrated elections
(such as the 1985 elections in the Ivory Coast in which Houphouet-Boigny
received 99 percent of the vote) be considered as a mechanism for extending
the popular mandate of the governing party? In a few cases, leaders of some
African single-party states have decided that the element of choice and
expression of discontent are, after all, essential aspects of the democratic
process. Hence, as long as all of the candidates presenting themselves for
election are bona fide members of the fairly broad-based dominant party,
the electorate in either a primary election (Zambia and Kenya) or in the
general election (Tanzania) can make its choice from among two or three
candidates for an office.[42] In both Tanzania and Kenya these intra-party
elections have led to the rejection by their local constituents of cabinet
members and other candidates backed by the central organ of the party.[43]
In national elections in Kenya during the two decades since independence
the rejection of incumbent KANU parliamentarians has ranged from thirty
to sixty-two percent. In one election all but one of the candidates who were
identified with the central organization of the party were defeated. The
latitude of electoral choice, however, is limited to legislative offices in the
national parliament or in local councils. The head of state, who is often styled
"President for Life," is either exempt from having to stand for reelection or
runs unopposed. Hence the office which is most crucial to the functioning
of the party and the government is precluded from systematic public scru-
tiny.

Most single-party states, however, do not even permit choice at the legislative level.[44] Elections become routine plebiscites in which the public is
asked to ratify the personnel and programs of the dominant party. Only the

bravest of souls register their disapproval by absenting themselves or by casting negative ballots under the watchful eye of the election supervisors. Rather than providing a genuine choice, plebiscitary elections are viewed as mechanisms for mobilizing the public in favor of the new society, the government, and the party. In the process, people may become identified with the nation rather than with their ethnic, religious, geographic, and economic sub-groups. Depending upon how carefully orchestrated the electoral campaigns are, the government party may actually employ this forum for the purpose of informing the public about personnel and programs and for soliciting popular reactions at rallies to existing and proposed policies. The ritual of the election, moreover, may become a formalized occasion in which at least some of the personnel of government are rotated out of office or unpopular programs are discarded without loss of face on the part of the national party leadership. Elections may, furthermore, become instruments for expanding or at least altering the base of patronage to include previously excluded groups. Finally, the ritual of electioneering may be a useful way of identifying energetic young party workers who might be groomed for future leadership roles. Useful as these consequences of plebiscitary elections may be, they are no substitute for genuine electoral choice among competing governing groups in meeting democratic expectations.

A further strand of criticism of the single party as the instrument of the popular will is the extraordinary role of the party leader in the single-party system. Although the label "charismatic" might aptly be applied to a few of Africa's leaders who enjoy the continued respect and adulation of their people, in far too many cases the attributes of charisma have been self-applied as a device for placing an autocratic leader beyond popular criticism and even beyond accountability to the very political party which brought him to power. However useful the personification of political authority might be in terms of transferring the emotional commitment of the masses from their ethnic or religious sub-group to the new national community, it has taken its toll.

One of the problems associated with charismatic leaders is that they and their followers tend ultimately to believe in the myth of invincibility and of the ability of the leader to continue to perform political, economic, and other miracles. There is a tendency to hold on to power long after their own charisma has become—as Weber noted—routinized. This complicates the evolution of a mechanism for orderly, nonviolent succession to leadership. Only a few leaders, such as Léopold Senghor of Senegal in 1981, have had the courage to recognize that, having accomplished the tasks which they set out to perform—or, conversely, having outlived their effectiveness as national leaders—it is time to step down.[45] Julius Nyerere of Tanzania, who had been promising to follow the Senghor example for years, only released the reins of presidential power to Ali Hassan Mwinyi in 1985. Significantly, Nyerere chose to remain as party Chairman of the CCM until 1987. Siaka

Stevens of Sierra Leone also voluntarily resigned in 1985. One other leader who voluntarily gave up the presidency subsequently tarnished his statesmanlike image by attempting to undermine the effectiveness of his own designated successor; I refer to the transfer of power in Cameroon from Ahmadou Ahidjo to Paul Biya.

Whether the reputation of a charismatic leadership is genuine or contrived, the costs of the sycophancy associated with it, as Carl Rosberg and others have pointed out, are enormous. I do not mean only the economic costs, significant though these are, given the general level of poverty in most African societies. Undoubtedly the present desperate straits of Ghana can be attributed in part to the early outlay for monuments, parades, high-cost prestige development projects (such as the ill-fated steel mill and the little used-superhighway from Accra to Tema), and to the costs of the foreign representation required to sustain Kwame Nkrumah's image internally as the "Asagefo" and externally as the apostle of Pan-African political unity. Leaders of single-party systems, of course, are not alone in this depletion of scarce resources, as the examples of President (later Emperor) Bokasso in the Central African Republic, Colonel Muammar Qaddafi of Libya, and other military autocrats will testify. The scale of ostentatious living by civilian autocrats, however, is often greater since it tends to be spuriously justified in terms of "popular will" or doing what the impoverished peasantry have allegedly wanted and expected their leaders to do.

The political costs of the cult of leadership, however, may be even more significant in the long run. The case of the late Sékou Touré of Guinea aptly demonstrates this.[46] Undoubtedly Touré's dramatic stance in urging his fellow countrymen to run the risk in 1958 of severing their links with France generated popular support of heroic dimensions. This adulation gave Touré the breathing time to consolidate his rule, establish new external linkages, and find new sources of aid to replace the almost total loss of French personnel, capital, and other forms of assistance. In the early period, there was substantial evidence that the populace supported Touré's efforts to equate his personal fate with the fate of the Guinean state, the PDG, and indeed the entire Guinean society. Although a Muslim, he is quoted as having once said "I am of all faiths . . . as president, I am everybody."[47]

This adulation turned into self-adulation that effectively put Sékou Touré above public or even private criticism of his actions, his policies, and his leadership of the party and the state. The number of dissidents who were forced into exile, imprisoned, or killed is difficult to assess with any degree of accuracy, but Amnesty International estimated that it exceeded several hundred thousand. The intolerance of dissent even within the inner circles of power led to the physical elimination of over thirty-five of his own close political associates and cabinet ministers during the latter years of his reign. Although his fears of being toppled were in some instances based upon concrete evidence of internal or external challenges, his paranoia led him to assert that Guinea was faced with a "Permanent Plot" to overthrow his government. The suspension of civil liberties over the years eliminated the possibility of even constructive criticism being raised with respect to his actions or programs. In the process, the party became an empty shell, devoid of real decision-making capacities and limited to leaders and the masses going through the motions of participation. Touré's all-absorbing egotism and his fear of sharing real authority with anyone else prevented him from dealing with the succession problem. Anyone who was identified as his heir apparent was quickly disposed of. Hence, within a week of Touré's death in March 1984, a military group took over the governing of the country. The top civilian cadre of the PDG had been so emasculated that it was powerless to resist.

THE ASSAULT ON PLURALISM. A further factor in the evaluation of the performance of single dominant parties is their role in encouraging or inhibiting the growth of stable political, economic, social, and other structures in society. These structures could supplement or displace those institutional groupings which were destroyed or eroded under colonial rule and during the transition to independence. The critical institution in this new schema, of course, was the dominant political party itself. Although the experiences varied widely, most dominant parties suffered a decline in vitality or actually stagnated as the top leadership was diverted from the tasks of party organization to the responsibilities of governing. The urban bias and ethnic imbalances in membership (which had in many cases been falling during the independence struggle) became increasingly pronounced as the lower echelon cadre recognized that the real power of the new society was concentrated in the urban capital. Instead of collective leadership, or at least the discussion of issues by party councils or conventions, decisions regarding the direction and programs of the party tended increasingly to be made by the charismatic president or prime minister and his immediate coterie of political associates. Mass participation was perfunctory and carefully orchestrated during elections, national crises, or other situations which called for a display of sycophantic support for the leadership.[48] Not all parties followed this course, as the example of the Tanzanian Chama Cha Mapinduzi (the former TANU) testifies. But it was the general trend.

With respect to the new political system, even leaders like Nyerere attempted to discourage the notion that the development of an efficient autonomous bureaucracy, charged with the day-to-day administration of the country, was a healthy thing. The party and the bureaucracy were to be fused, in order to prevent the bureaucracy taking on a conservative, self-serving class attitude which would divorce it from the more revolutionary objectives of the party. A similar concern emerged regarding the claims of the judiciary to operate independently of the political system in support of more universal principles of law and justice. Obote, Nkrumah, and other party leaders often found themselves at loggerheads with jurists who had learned their Western constitutionalism well.

The absence of sharp boundary maintenance was even more evident between the party and government bureaucracy, on the one hand, and what in other societies would be regarded as the private sector, on the other. Despite the role that trade unions, churches, cooperatives, and other structures had played in the liberation struggle, they eventually came to be viewed as competitors of the political party, particularly when coalitions of economic and religious groups challenged the supremacy of the party. In many instances the complaints of these private structures against government restrictions or regulation did not cease when the reins of government changed from European to African hands. Indeed the heightened expectations regarding improvements in the economic standing of members of cooperatives and trade unions could not be met by the party elite unless there was to be a dramatic change in the base of production following independence. And that was not the case. In a systematic way, unions, churches, cooperative societies, the Boy Scouts, and even traditional ethnic associations became subordinated to the dominant party. This took place in various fashions: through the co-optation of the leadership of these groups; through the continuation of colonial controls; or through outright banning or elimination of competing groups. Many of these structures, such as youth groups or women's associations, became wings or branches of TANU under Nyerere. Thus, the distinction in Western society between interest groups as articulators of interest and the parties as aggregators was virtually eliminated as the party cadre consolidated its grip on the new society—as it attempted to do in Milton Obote's Uganda under his Uganda People's Congress (UPC). It was the party that strove to take on the role of socializing all elements of society with respect to the new post-colonial world. It was the CPP under Nkrumah that attempted to monopolize the press, radio, education, and all other forms of communication in the new state of Ghana.

The consequences of this elimination or, alternatively, the absorption of other groups into the party behemoth, were disastrous for the society and the party itself. There was, first of all, a loss both of creativity and of differing perspectives regarding alternative courses of development. This pluralism is vital to the solution of the complex problems facing the heterogeneous post-colonial society. The over-burdened party cadre did not possess the answers to critical problems, yet they were unwilling to listen to others who might. During both traditional and colonial eras, many of the social service, economic self-help, educational, and spiritual needs of Africans were performed by private groups. Given their limited talents and the revenues available to modern party leaders in Africa, these services could not be assumed by the party cadre even if they had wanted to. Thus a situation of anomie prevailed, particularly in the new urban centers. Instead of leaving these social tasks to be performed well or badly by the private groups, the presumptive attitude of the party meant that it alone had to bear the burden of failure, thereby further contributing to the demise of its own legitimacy.

The significance of the erosion of pluralism in African society became disastrously apparent when the party cadre was ultimately confronted by its sole effective challenger for political power: the military. As Chapter 8 points out, in the early stages of the liberation effort party leaders tended to view the colonial army with disdain. It was an institution under alien control, unmodern in its tactics and recruitment, and irrelevant to the liberation effort. Once in power, however, the party leadership increasingly came to rely upon the military to sustain itself in office. Faced with ethnic and religious challenges to its nation-building efforts and unable to deliver on its promise of a more abundant life, the party leaders almost instinctively called upon the military to deal not only with ethnic secessionist threats but with labor strikes, student protest, and other manifestations of unrest. In the process, the military quickly perceived both its own strength and the weakness of the civilian leadership. Meanwhile, the political field had been effectively cleared by the party leadership of all other pockets of influence or authority in society. There were no intervening and interlocking structures whose leadership may have ameliorated the emerging contest between the party and the military for control of the state. At that stage, the absence of a pluralistic base to post-colonial society tipped the scales of power in the direction of the military.

Those parties that did succeed in holding onto the reins of power in the post-colonial state were normally those that genuinely attempted to broaden the base of popular participation and identification of the citizenry within the new society. The "overarching integrative" strategy of Nyerere's TANU, the "static tension" strategy of Jomo Kenyatta's KANU, and the "pluralist accommodation" strategy of Kaunda's UNIP, seemed to be better calculated to win support from either depoliticized or even previously hostile groups than were many of the other strategies of nation-building referred to in Chapter 3. Obote's UPC in Uganda, for example, exacerbated latent conflict by simultaneously attacking rival parties, the leadership of the traditional kingdoms, the wealthy cotton growers, the Catholic Church, and other structures. By contrast, KANU's policy of reconciliation and ethnic and racial balancing under Kenyatta was broadening the base of participation and identification. Not only many of the white settlers and those Africans who had fought as "loyalists" alongside the British during the so-called Mau Mau struggle, but others as well were made to feel that they shared a common goal in a more prosperous Kenya. The trade unions, the growers' cooperative societies, white and Asian businessmen, and other economic groups were encouraged to function outside the party framework. Similarly, the various Christian and Muslim sects under KANU's policy of reconciliation appreciated their joint benefits of participation in a state that remained secular and neutral with respect to religion. While politics in Kenya has on occasion been turbulent, KANU has succeeded in many arenas where other more ideological parties have failed to win a broad base of support. Thus, it is apparent that some charismatic leaders were able to infuse a measure of vitality into the political institutions which would survive them. In other cases the ego of the leader and his own uncertainty prevented his charisma being "routinized" and becoming a stable feature of the newly created political system.

VIII

MILITARY INTERVENTION
Aberration or Way of Life?

There was great optimism in the late 1950s about the strength both of African political parties and of the parliamentary institutions through which they would operate following independence. Events have since eroded that euphoric prognosis. Considerably diminished is the ideal of an African public being regularly permitted to hold its political leaders accountable at all levels through a series of open, freely contested, and fairly administered elections. Instead, the military coup d'état has become the recurrent instrument for changing top political leadership and for effecting dramatic changes in foreign and domestic policies in Africa. Some surviving single-party states have, indeed, permitted an element of electoral choice at the legislative level or have used the ritualistic occasion of an uncontested election as an opportunity for making significant changes in executive personnel and in national politics. Single-party states, however, are increasingly in the minority in Africa today, and states which permit legal opposition parties to function are an even smaller fraction of the whole.

Contrary to the earlier expectations of both practitioners and scholars, the majority of African states have now experienced at least one successful military coup since independence; a majority of that number have fallen victim to their second, third, or successive coups. The citizens of roughly half of the states have endured more years with some form of military intervention than periods of patently civilian rule. Despite early storm warnings, scholarly reluctance to forecast military intervention as a recurrent feature of African political behavior persisted until the Nigerian and Ghanaian coups of early 1966. Until that point, the 1958 coup in the Sudan, the Zaire mutiny of 1960, the assassination of president Sylvanus Olympio of Togo in 1963, and the rash of military mutinies in former British and French territories in 1964 were viewed as aberrations, which did not affect the long term trend. It was indicative of the state of the scholarly art that neither the early single country studies by James Coleman, David Apter, and others nor the several comprehensive surveys of African politics edited in the early 1960s by Gwendolen

This chapter is based on my essay, "The Military Factor in African Politics," in *African Independence: The First Twenty-Five Years*, ed. Gwendolen M. Carter and Patrick O'Meara, © 1985 by Indiana University Press.

Carter, James Coleman and Carl G. Rosberg, and William Lewis made more than fleeting reference to the African military.[1] Even my own writings on Liberia in those edited volumes hardly suggested that the military would be a major challenger to the civilian elite who had governed that state since 1847.

Hoping to make amends for the absence of prescience with respect to the politicization of the military, Africanist scholarship has produced a virtual flowering of both broad and narrow gauged theories about the African soldier's role in politics. In analyzing more than fifty cases of successful intervention and a greater number of abortive coups, one is struck by the idiosyncratic nature of civil-military relations in Africa. The conditions and identifiable causes of intervention are considerably varied, as is the level within the military which provides the coup leadership. Despite the unique nature of African coups, some excellent studies based on single cases do suggest a more generalized pattern of behavior. Included in this category of studies would be Michael Lofchie's analysis of the 1971 coup in Uganda, which hypothesized that General Amin was acting as the agent of an economic class that saw its own corporate interests threatened as the meager resources of the society were dissipated on socialist experimentation.[2] Another case study, Robert Price's analysis of the 1966 Ghanaian coup, theorized that defense of military professionalism—as determined by the military itself—was a key factor in the army's turning against a civilian regime that had overstepped the bounds properly separating the civilian and military spheres of responsibility in a modern society.[3]

Two scholars with in-depth African experience early attempted to formulate theories of broader applicability to the sub-Saharan region. An intriguing causal explanation based upon an analysis of eleven African coups that occurred between 1963 and 1972 was proffered by Samuel Decalo.[4] He suggested that although general societal instability had to be taken into account, one of the strongest factors for military intervention was, directly or indirectly, the personal ambitions or fears of specific key officers relative to civilian authorities. While it provides excellent post hoc analysis, the sui generis nature of the circumstances makes the Decalo thesis a difficult one to apply for predictive purposes.

A more thoughtful exploration of the various factors which have contributed to military intervention has emerged from the work of Claude E. Welch, Jr., over the past two decades.[5] Welch has made a significant contribution to our understanding of the multiple "causes" of intervention as well as making preliminary efforts at establishing typologies for comparative analysis of civil-military relationships both in the Third World and in the more industrialized states. He has provided some particularly significant insights regarding the place of the military in the modernization process of African states.

It is increasingly apparent that the data on military intervention in Africa are not peculiar to that world region, even though there are many factors differentiating sub-Saharan African politics from politics in Latin America, the Middle East, and Asia. Africa, for example, has lacked the class linkages among the politicians, military leaders, and the landed aristocracy that have characterized many Latin American states. The persistence of colonial rule in Africa until the 1960s, furthermore, precluded significant African participation at the officer level and thus reduced in significance the issues of military professionalism, career mobility, and divergent ideologies that have marked civil-military relations in the Middle East and many parts of Asia. Nevertheless, Africanist scholars and comparativists with rich experience in the studies of the military in both the more developed societies and the Third World have attempted to formulate theories of global relevance. One of the most persistent in this effort has been Morris Janowitz, who early assumed that organizational and professional characteristics of the military as an institution were crucial to our analysis of the causes of military intervention or non-intervention into the political arena.[6] Janowitz focuses on organizational format, skill structure and cadre lines, social recruitment patterns, professional ideology, and social cohesion within the military as factors of primary significance in our understanding of the politicization of the armed forces. Often posed in opposition to Janowitz's emphasis (although Janowitz denies the existence of a conflict) has been the contention of Samuel Huntington that the most significant factors in military intervention are found in the nature of the broader political, economic, and social structure of society within which particular militaries exist.[7]

The frequency with which coup groups have succeeded in toppling either a civilian regime or their own senior military colleagues should attest to the difficulties faced by practitioners and scholars alike in making educated guesses about "who, when, where, and why" with regard to military intervention in specific African countries. It is often the case, as Decalo has suggested, that the coup is a highly personalized affair. And indeed, the evidence regarding the variations in coup leadership manifested in the 1980 coup in Liberia (a master sergeant), the abortive Kenya coup of 1982 (a private), and the 1983 New Year's Eve coup in Nigeria (a major general) suggests an even more highly capricious—and therefore unpredictable—quality associated with recent coup attempts. The "wild card" factor is all too persistent in African military interventions.

Rather than formulating a predictive theory of intervention, the purpose of this chapter will be fourfold. First, an effort will be made to explore the evidence from the past quarter of a century regarding the political role of the military in order to elucidate broad trends that can account both for the general failure of civilian regimes and, equally important, the continued acceptance of military regimes by the African masses, inasmuch as many of the conditions that encouraged earlier military intervention persist in Africa today. Second, it will explore some of the basic problems confronting the

African military when it attempts to assume a governmental role in nation-building, directing economic development, and undertaking other political tasks. Third, it will attempt to evaluate the performance of military as compared to civilian regimes in carrying out the essential tasks of government in the new African countries. Finally, the recent Nigerian experience notwithstanding, an analysis will be made of the elements which must be addressed in making a successful transition from military to civilian regimes in Africa.

Factors Leading to Intervention

THE WEAKNESS OF PARTY GOVERNMENT. Among the many factors that have contributed to or encouraged the intervention of the African military in post-independence politics, a primary one is the weakness of political parties. African militaries, as we shall note shortly, are weak; but parties—as noted in Chapter 7—have inherent weaknesses as well. In state after state, the civilian politicians who inherited the mantle of authority from the departing colonial administrators tended to overestimate their own strength as well as the role that parties had played in the demise of European colonial rule. There were cases, such as Kenya, Mozambique, Angola, Guinea-Bissau, and Zimbabwe, where massive and sustained armed confrontation by Africans against European settler minorities was the critical element in the success of the independence effort. However, these are not representative of what was generally a fairly peaceful transfer of power in the vast majority of cases. Violence or the threat of violence was not entirely absent in these cases, but without denigrating the efforts of African party nationalists, there were other factors that compelled the European powers to face the inevitable and to withdraw from their colonial liabilities on conditions most favorable to their own long-term economic, diplomatic, and other interests. Hence, I would suggest that the independence of African states is significantly related *inter alia* to the success of liberation efforts in India and Algeria; victories of socialist labor parties in the European colonial metropoles; the shrinking global military commitments of Great Britain; continuing pressure from within the United Nations; and the anti-colonial postures of the United States and the Soviet Union.

Not only did party leaders overestimate their own role in terminating the colonial presence, but they overestimated as well their organizational capacity in controlling the post-colonial state. Some parties such as the NCNC and Action Group in Nigeria did demonstrate organizational strength even though each was oriented to a particular region and cluster of ethnic groups. Elsewhere in Africa parties—as was noted in Chapter 7—generally lacked experience in organizing tactics; the obstructionist policies and practices of colonial administrators had in many cases prevented the emergence of well-oiled party machines. Membership rolls were invariably inflated, the payment of dues was honored in the breach, and party leadership tended to be unevenly representative of certain sectors of the population—the urban minority, one religious faction, or particular ethnic groups, for instance—to the detriment of others. While it is true that Pan-Africanism and anti-colonialism were unifying ideologies to the point of independence, they were of little value in instructing leadership about management of the new state apparatus.

In the post independence era the pool of talent available both to run the state and continue the vital role of the political party in galvanizing society with respect to nation-building, economic development, and the other tasks was dangerously shallow from the outset. Colonial educational policies had been marked by neglect where they were not characterized by positive hostility toward the concept of educating Africans to manage a complex modern society. The British and French only differed by degree from their Belgian, Portuguese, and Italian counterparts. The absence of people with skills in the fields of public administration, medicine, engineering, diplomacy, and the general areas of economics and finance was appalling. Added to this legacy was the lower priority given by African party leaders themselves to economics and other matters during the anti-colonial struggle. Kwame Nkrumah's dictum to "seek ye first the political kingdom . . . " meant that serious planning regarding the nature of the post-colonial economy was long deferred. In any case, African politicians were by force of circumstances unequal bargaining partners during the transitional period relative to the vested European economic actors.

These statements about the general weakness of political parties vis-à-vis military interventionists are further supported by counterevidence from the several categories of cases where the political party leadership has in fact endured almost continuously since independence, despite threats of military intervention. In the first category are those parties which took on a military posture during the anti-colonial struggle, whose leaders thereafter not only galvanized the society with respect to the legitimacy of the new polity and its goals, but took steps to politically subordinate the party's military wing. FRELIMO in Mozambique and ZANU in Zimbabwe are cases in point. In the second category are parties whose leaders, shortly after having achieved independence, took conscious steps to create a broad cross-regional, cross-ethnic, cross-religious, grass-roots party organization and to address the problems of economic—and particularly rural—development. Although the reasons and circumstances differ, there are parallels in the enduring success of party regimes in Tanzania, Cameroon, Malawi, and Zambia. Finally, there are a series of states—largely in the Francophone group (Ivory Coast, Senegal, Gabon)—in which the continuing presence of external military support early permitted African civilians to remain in control irrespective of whether the party had remained vital or moribund or whether the party and state bureaucracies remained separate or fused.

SOCIETAL PERCEPTIONS OF THE ROLE OF FORCE. Undoubtedly the counterpart to the political party leaders' over-estimation of the strength of their own party organizations was their tendency to underestimate the amount of force which had been required to maintain the colonial state. This led to the naively optimistic assumption that the use of military force would not be a significant sanction for authority in domestic politics or a significant element in the relations among African states once independence was achieved. The speech of Chief Obafemi Awolowo to the Calabar Congress in 1958—two years prior to Nigerian independence—was one of several instances in which a nationalist leader urged a policy of nonarmament for his country following independence.[8] Kwame Nkrumah of Ghana and Julius Nyerere of Tanzania (then Tanganyika) had also taken similar stances, as did Awolowo's long-time Nigerian adversary, Nnamdi Azikiwe—albeit in a less emphatic manner. They were convinced that the spirit of Pan-Africanism at the continental level and the unity forged during the nationalist struggle at the territorial level would permit the new states to direct their energies to economic development, expansion of educational and health facilities, and the other more positive tasks associated with nation-building.

Only a few African party leaders were prepared to take their own rhetoric literally and dispense with a national army altogether. David Jawara of The Gambia, for example, took into account his country's geographical position as a defenseless "Jonah in the belly of the Senegalese whale" and elected to provide paramilitary duties by means of a slightly expanded national police force. Even this step, ironically, did not spare him the indignity of an abortive police-orchestrated coup in 1981. The leaders of Botswana, Lesotho, and Swaziland, mindful of their similar encirclement or near encirclement by the Republic of South Africa, also attempted to reduce their national military establishments to ceremonial size and role during the early post-independence era. While leaders elsewhere in Africa assumed more pragmatic stances after liberation, realizing the need for some sort of military unit to serve both domestic and defensive purposes, the initial tendency was to give a far lower priority to the military than to other categories of expenditure in the national budgets. The neglected areas of health, education, natural resource development, and other programs had to come first. Soldiers, moreover, had not been accustomed to serving development roles in the colonial period, and thus they were viewed by the civilian nationalists as exhausters of scarce resources. When a budget crunch came, as it did in Togo in 1963, President Sylvanus Olympio's first instinct was to reduce the budgetary allocation for the military. Similarly the complaint of the mutinous armies in Tanzania, Uganda, and Kenya in 1964 and of the military leaders who toppled Kwame Nkrumah in 1966 was that the civilian regimes had drastically undermined military performance by failing to provide the army with satisfactory equipment, housing, uniforms, and other material.

The calculated efforts to minimize the political role that the military had played in maintaining civil authority in the European colonial state may be attributable to initial acceptance by African civilians and soldiers alike of the theory of the civilian supremacy model of civil-military relations. Military force in the context of West European parliamentary democracy was assumed to be at the disposal of civilian authorities and not an autonomous sanction available to the military directly. Curiously, the civilian supremacy model during the colonial era was not even strictly applied in Europe itself—as the de Gaulle intervention of 1958 should have demonstrated. In any event, it would be a radically distorted interpretation of Africa's distant as well as recent past to assume that the ideology of pacificism would find fertile ground in Africa. This argument would constitute the reverse side of the stereotype which viewed Africa prior to the European-imposed peace as a Hobbesian state of nature, with a "war of each against all." Historians, anthropologists, and others are providing evidence that the truth regarding the sanction of force in pre-colonial Africa lay somewhere in between. Africans did indeed, for example, engage in trade and participate in religious and social structures over great distances where cooperation prevailed over conflict as norms of behavior. On the other hand, there is a long history of interethnic combat waged on an intermittent if not a continuous basis, among many groups around the continent. Moreover, the social structure of entire groups, such as the Ashanti in Ghana and the Zulu in South Africa, were organized along rigid military lines with military values infusing all aspects of society.[9]

The pacifistic optimism of some nationalists also underplayed the role of force in subjugating Africa during the nineteenth and early twentieth centuries. While it is true that many societies capitulated without being conquered, a number of others over an extended period stoutly resisted the European imposition and were only subdued after the loss of countless lives and the destruction of the indigenous political, economic, and social systems. And it was in many instances African armies in collaboration with the small component of European offices and troops that were the real factor in the conquest of their fellow Africans.[10] In a number of cases, such as the Nandi of Kenya, full acceptance of European dominance came only after repeated punitive raids which involved a scorched earth approach as well as the near-genocidal liquidation of men, women, and children.[11] Such punitive expeditions and the convincing use of the Maxim gun and other superior weaponry by European-directed armies were frequently sufficient to convince other potential resisters of the futility of their actions.

The myth regarding the minimal role of force required in maintaining the European presence after the actual conquest may be attributable to the relative absence of major armed confrontation in the period following the First World War until the Kenya uprising called "Mau Mau," which began in 1952.[12] Around the continent the military units of the ethnic groups that had collaborated with the Europeans in imposing colonial rule were promptly divested of their junior partnership role once conquest of neighboring groups had been completed. Traditional armies and regiments of young warriors were quickly disarmed and reduced to ceremonial roles. In most colonial territories, the military forces that maintained order for the colonial administration were recruited from outside the districts where they served and hence had no conflicting loyalties with respect to local traditional rulers. The colonial force, moreover, was remarkably small in size and normally armed only with rifles that were left unloaded until a crisis actually arose. Rather than being a continuing visible presence in every remote hamlet of the colony, troops were typically quartered at the district or regional headquarters.

Despite the paucity of men under arms, however, the colonial military was mobile and could be dispatched quickly to a troubled area. If the local force was insufficient to contain the crisis, reinforcements could quickly be brought in from neighboring territories or other parts of the empire. The infusion of troops directly from Great Britain—armed with the latest in jet fighter planes and other modern weaponry—for example, was ultimately the crucial factor in suppressing the Kenya revolt of 1952–56. And, of course, the Congo crisis of 1960 and the rescue operations carried out by British and French paratroopers during the spate of mutinies in 1964 provided adequate demonstration that the mere size of the local militia was not the only fact to be taken into account in analyzing the role that the sanction of force played in maintaining political authority.[13]

EROSION OF THE COLONIAL BARGAINING STRATEGY. A further factor limiting the ability of the new nationalist elites to maintain order and stability in the post-colonial state was the undermining or dismantling of the preceding colonial bargaining strategy that had been effective in securing the semblance of stability. This is not meant to suggest that the colonial administration was a neutral arbiter, standing aloof from the competing claimants for the limited human and material resources of the colonial territory. Indeed, the officers of the colonial state were anything but neutral whenever the vital interests of the European metropole, the empire as a whole, or the local settlers, merchants, missionaries and other resident Europeans were directly challenged. There were nevertheless many occasions in which the administrators had to arbitrate conflict within the European community itself. This occurred, for example, when the needs of European mine owners, planters, and military recruiters for inexpensive manpower threatened the educational and proselytizing goals of the missionaries as well as the labor needs of the colonial administration itself in maintaining roads and other infrastructures. There was also an arbitrating role with respect to the growing conflicts between, on the one hand, those traditional authorities who continued to receive recognition by the colonial administrators and, on the other hand, the new groups of educated Africans who were needed at the lower or intermediate levels in staffing the colonial administration or assisting in the new European economic enterprises. Conflicts also arose between the aspirations of the burgeoning African merchant class and the better-financed Asian and Lebanese merchants who came in under the colonial umbrella. Admittedly—in its own interests—the colonial bureaucracy did provide negotiating machinery and carry out strategies of development that often limited interracial, interethnic, and interregional competition and conflict. The policy of Indirect Rule, for example, was one way in which the British administrators around the continent hoped to limit and contain political demands that could not be effectively regulated by the understaffed colonial bureaucracy. The "reserve" policy, which limited land settlement in an area to one ethnic group, was another.

Once the reins of power were transferred to African party leaders, however, it was apparent that many of the previous participants in colonial politics, linked with the economic and social transformation of colonial society, would either be forced out or compelled to assume a radically different role. European landowners in Kenya, for example, were compelled to emigrate or to reduce their holdings and largely withdraw from the political arena if they chose to remain in Kenya. Asian entrepreneurs in East Africa and Lebanese in the West in many instances were harassed about questions of citizenship, export of earnings, and other issues, and sometimes had their shops and other holdings confiscated. The traditional as well as the appointed chiefs, moreover, were dismissed in Tanzania and Guinea for having collaborated too closely with the European colonialists. Thus, the nationalists felt no need to arbitrate with respect to many of their former opponents.

Even those, however, who had been part of the broad coalition to unseat the colonial administration found themselves challenged by the party and governing elites at the center. Politics took primacy over other legitimate types of activities, and the party leaders increasingly turned against their fellow conspirators in the trade unions, the cooperative societies, the independent churches, student organizations, and ethnic political associations. Where the competing organizations were not actually banned or placed under severe restrictions, they were effectively subordinated to the dominant party or to the post-colonial state itself, and few new competitors were encouraged to appear on the scene. Consequently, in many new states the weakened condition of previous competitors to the political party leadership left only one other strong contestant in the field: the military. The continued presence, however, of a critical cadre of European officers in most post-colonial armies (Guinea in 1958 being an obvious exception) put the military into a different category. It was not necessarily viewed as an adversary, but as an institution which served at the pleasure of the new governing elite and could be brought into line by budget reductions and applying the lessons of the inherited civilian supremacy model. In Ghana, for example, Europeans still occupied key military posts in the early 1960s, and Kwame Nkrumah's oft-quoted admonition to the military cadets to refrain from political activity illustrates the strength of this self-deception.

THE TRANSITIONAL MILITARY ESTABLISHMENT. Although the party elites did increasingly rely on the post-colonial military, their tendency during the anti-imperial struggle was to view the colonial military as an "alien" institution which could be effectively controlled by the party leadership once independence was achieved. Although this proved to be a crucial mistake, the basis of their reasoning is understandable. The virtual monopolization of colonial officer ranks by Europeans, and even of key noncommissioned positions in the French and Portuguese colonial armies, provided very few career outlets in the military for Western-educated Africans who had been exposed to a cash economy and other aspects of a modern society. Even Indians, Goans, and other third parties were frequently given preference over qualified Africans with respect to noncommissioned officer posts. Also, the colonial army generally had played a negative role in terms of African liberation, supporting the colonial presence against guerrilla bands in Kenya and against trade unionists, student strikers, and other "progressive" forces around the continent. More significantly, the rank and file and the few Africans who did qualify for noncommissioned rank overwhelmingly tended to be recruited from the areas of the country which had been least exposed to modernizing influences. Lord Lugard in Nigeria, for example, made it an explicit policy of government to draw heavily upon the less developed north for recruits in preference to the better educated and economically transformed Igbos and Yorubas in the south.[14] The conscious stereotyping of ethnic groups with respect to the military tasks that they were assumed to be most capable of performing had perpetuated ethnic segregation in the army. By contrast, the party leaders were attempting to transcend ethnic differences and embrace national or Pan-African concepts. The tasks of the military, furthermore, were viewed as being largely ceremonial when they were not overtly repressive and as such not requiring an exceptional amount of education to be performed. Since the resort to the corvée had provided colonial administrators with a ready pool of free or cheap civilian labor, the colonial military was seldom called upon along the model of the U.S. Corps of Engineers for road construction, bridge building, or other projects associated with development. Finally, the conscious posting of soldiers to districts outside their ethnic homelands in order to avoid conflicts of loyalties with respect to the colonial administration had other consequences, not the least of which was that the low prestige of the soldiers was further aggravated by the absence of family, ethnic, and other restraints upon abuses of authority by the troops.

The party elites failed to see that the colonial military was in fact an outlet for modernization for those who were overlooked in the European strategy for economic development or in missionary planning for location of schools and clinics. However low the salaries might have been or how primitive the facilities, the military experience involved the recruit in a cash economy, and there was undoubtedly a lot of transmittal of money between the soldiers and their home areas. Since the European officers were concerned about having a healthy force, the recruit was exposed to at least the rudiments of modern sanitation and health. While the European colonial officers were not interested in African college graduates, they did impart to the raw recruits from less developed regions a certain level of skill with respect to literacy; to typing and other forms of technical training; and to driving and the repair of motor vehicles. The army, moreover, exposed the enlisted man to the European or African language which in many cases became the accepted lingua franca of a given territory. Furthermore, while the experience was not always transferable to other structures of modern society, the knowledge of bureaucracy, the chain of command, and other imperatives for the successful functioning of the military could be put to use by the discharged veteran in civilian situations.[15]

In addition to the continuing transforming influences of the colonial military, developments during the final stages of colonial rule brought about dramatic changes. Perhaps in anticipation of nationalist resistance activity which did not actually materialize, the British, French, and other colonialists had begun to introduce heavier armament, more modernized transport, updated communications facilities, and military aviation into the colonial armies. Other changes as well were made in the character of the colonial army. Since the pool of non-African immigrants had slowed considerably after World War II, for example, increasingly Africans were provided with the higher level of technical education needed for military modernization. This meant not only higher wages but also a respectable career alternative. A few even qualified for officer training as independence approached. Since the colonialists were interested in retaining the friendship and commitment of this new cadre of African officers, they were frequently sent to Europe for training and given, upon their return, perquisites that rivaled those available to educated Africans in the civil service, the clergy, the schools, and other civilian structures.

PARTY LEADERSHIP RELIANCE ON THE MILITARY. Having initially viewed the military as an unnecessary or at worst an alien institution, and then having perceived the post-colonial army as being automatically imbued with the ideal of subservience to civilian authority, the dominant party leaders in many countries went on to commit one further egregious error. The party leadership increasingly tended to rely heavily in maintaining its own shaky rule upon those two sanctions for authority—force and ritual—which are closely identified with the military. Inevitably this intensified the political role of the military at the expense of civilian authority.

Even Nkrumah, who had lectured most eloquently about the civilian supremacy model, increasingly relied on military ritual as a prop for his regime.

Mass rallies, the parading of tanks and other military equipment in Accra's Black Star Square (reminiscent of Red Square on May Day), the wearing of uniforms and ribbons, and the granting of chivalric honors gave a military flavor to what should have been civilian enterprises. The organization of the youth and workers into disciplined "brigades," the calls for heroism and sacrifice, and the constant references to "the nation under siege" evoked military ritual and imagery in the maintenance of the new state against its enemies, both domestic and foreign.

In addition to military-like ritual, the civilian party leaders increasingly called upon military force in dealing with a broad spectrum of political opponents. With respect to ethnic secessionists—such as the Ruwenzori movement in Uganda during the first Obote government—the resort to military action may have been understandable.[16] It was less acceptable when the leaders of the First Republic in Nigeria moved against the Yoruba leaders who were challenging the nature of the federal political compact, but who did not seek the dissolution of the Nigerian state. A political solution was similarly required in the dispute between Obote and the leaders of the Kingdom of Buganda, even though the history of Baganda exclusivism is a long one. Equally questionable was the use of the army in many states to put down student demonstrations on university campuses or labor unions striking for improvements in the conditions of employment.

Using the the military to cope with political situations that called for negotiation or arbitration had several major drawbacks. In the first place, it revealed the very weakness of the civilian leadership and the political party in their professed roles as unifiers of the nation-state, calling into question the regime's legitimacy. The military quickly came to the realization that its intervention was indispensable to the survival in power of the civilian governing elites. Both the military leadership and the troops, moreover, came to resent being thrust into basically political situations in which they had to bear the brunt of the hostility of the suppressed dissidents, hostility that should instead have been directed against the flawed political leadership.

There were other dangers as well. In cases where the military force failed to achieve its intended results, the army often turned on the civilian authorities to justify its own inadequacies in dealing with guerrilla warfare. This occurred, of course, in Algeria in 1958 when French paratroopers imposed de Gaulle upon the indecisive politicians of the French Fourth Republic. And it was the primary justification for the military overthrow of the monarchy in Ethiopia it 1974, when it was obvious that the Eritrean secession movement could not be easily contained. Thus, in abandoning the course of political bargaining and opting to dissolve the poorly structured federal relationship between Ethiopia and Eritrean, the Emperor and his advisors by default made the military the one indispensable element in keeping the post–World War II state intact and thereby sowed the seeds of their own destruction.[17]

SIGNALING CIVILIAN VULNERABILITY. Having once appreciated its mistake in augmenting the military's role with respect to basically political situations, the civilian party leaders further aggravated the relationship by signaling their fear of the political monster they had brought forth. Cutting military expenses might, in a previous period, have been regarded as a genuine commitment to reallocate resources to health, education, and other programs neglected by the colonialists. After independence, however, it became a challenge to the corporate interests of the military, which had now come to enjoy a partnership role in the political arena. Although many of the early hour justifications of African coups constitute pious rhetoric about defending the constitution or democracy, a significant portion of the post hoc rationale crassly relates to salaries, uniforms, housing, and other narrow corporate interests of the military. While the military might not move speedily with respect to the loftier ideals, they demonstrate no hesitation in addressing their own basic needs.

Secondly, the civilian leadership in many cases took overt steps to limit the effectiveness of flamboyant military leaders who enjoyed a popular base, and to manipulate promotions within the military itself. An early case was noted by Robert Price in his book on the Ghanaian military. Price concluded that the military's resentment of Nkrumah's removal of the very popular General Ankrah from his position as commander of the army was one of the major precipitating causes of the 1966 coup. It was the politicians—in the thinking of the Ghanaian military leaders—who had violated the civilian-military compact by striking at the professional integrity of the army.[18] Samuel Decalo provides many other examples of civilians moving against military personalities, including the conflict that was coming to a head between Milton Obote and Idi Amin in 1971, just as Obote took off for Singapore.[19]

The patent manifestation of fear of the military on the part of the civilian leaders is often signaled by the creation of independent military or paramilitary units with the stated political mission of protecting the head of the regime. Creation by Nkrumah of a President's Own Guard Regiment—recruited, trained, and equipped independently of the regular army—was a second professional irritant contributing to the 1966 coup in Ghana. Military leaders not unexpectedly raised the question: Against whom is the president being protected if the regular military is excluded from what it regards as one of its primary missions?

Even more challenging to both the integrity and the patriotism of the regular army has been the use of foreign troops to protect the leadership of the regime. Although it was undoubtedly warranted for the British to respond to requests from the heads of government of the three East African states in 1964, the intervention of British paratroops had very different results in Kenya and Tanzania than in Uganda. In the former states the incident led to the more effective subordination of the military to the state or the dominant party once the mutineers had been dismissed or punished. In Uganda,

the aftermath of the mutiny was the establishment of an uneasy truce between the civilian and military leadership, the former going to extraordinary
lengths to placate the latter with salary hikes and other perquisites.[20] These
efforts at budgetary bribery following the British paratroop intervention,
however, only served to reinforce the contempt of the military toward the
Obote government and were a factor in the subsequent Amin coup.

Finally, we might cite a case when reliance upon an external rescue force,
while not a direct factor in a coup, helped prepare the way for the widespread
acceptance of a military coup once it had occurred. Reference here is made
to the 1979 Rice Riots in Liberia, a year before the assassination of President
Tolbert. During the demonstrations Tolbert called upon Guinean troops and
planes to deal with the rioters after the Liberian military had largely refrained
from action. It was the politically subservient police that had fired on the
unarmed demonstrators. The Guinean troops were soon withdrawn, but
general resentment about the use of alien troops in Africa's oldest republic
was a feature of the year of ferment leading to the military coup of April
1980.[21] The Liberian case was different from similar neighborly rescues; a
Guinean rescue unit remained in Sierra Leone after the coup attempt there
in 1981, and a Senegalese force continues to provide protection to David
Jawara of The Gambia following the 1981 police coup in that country. Thus
the continuity of civilian rule was maintained despite the resentment of the
military regarding alien intrusions.

The Nature of Military Regimes

MODELS OF CIVIL-MILITARY RELATIONSHIPS. In analyzing the extent of politicization of the military in the new African states, we must appreciate that
the terms "military government" and "military intervention" cover a great
variety of political relationships between the military and civilian authorities.
Like the mythical walls between church and state in a liberal democracy or
between government and the economy in capitalist-oriented societies, the
political division between the domain of civil and military authorities even
in a society committed to the civilian supremacy model is not hard and fast.
The military, after all, is central to the political objective of maintaining the
independence of the state community. Like other actors in society it makes
political claims against the financial and other resources of the state in carrying out its primary mission. Conversely, regimes that are characterized as
"military governments" in fact must normally either co-opt a wide range of
civilian technicians or retrain soldiers to take on civilian skills in coping with
the day to day concerns of society.

Similar caution must be used to avoid treating the military of a particular
country as a monolith. In addition to the differences between the organization
and roles of military as opposed to paramilitary units, there are service

rivalries—an air force competes with an army for prestige and funding—as well as generational, regional, and ethnic imbalances that create tensions within the overall military group. In some cases, such as the January 1966 coup in Nigeria, the senior officers were effective in bringing most of their fellow officers as well as the troops along with them in taking control of the government in the wake of a coup. Other interventions have found one segment of the military (such as the air force in the abortive 1982 coup in Kenya) acting unilaterally against a civilian government or even against their own senior officers in a military regime (such as the 1979 intervention of Flight Lieutenant Rawlings against the Acheampong government in Ghana). Occasionally, one segment of the military undertakes a preemptive coup against a civilian regime to forestall action by another segment of the military. This was apparently the case in the December 1983 action of General Buhari that terminated the tenure of the Shagari government in Nigeria.

Rather than a bipolar model, which pits civilians against the military, the political relationship between civilian and military authorities is more appropriately analyzed in terms of a series of models along a continuum. Although the degree of intervention of the military into the political affairs of a state can be plotted along a line, there is no suggestion that a given military group proceeds logically from one point on the continuum to the next. Instead, the continuum is posited for the purposes of cross-national comparative analysis and to assess changes in degree of intervention of specific military groups.

At one end of the continuum is the *civilian supremacy* model of civil-military relations, the model subscribed to by political leaders both in Western-style democracies and in most Marxian socialist societies. Ironically, in addition to its being the norm in party-dominated African states such as Tanzania, Senegal, and Malawi, it is publicly stated to be the ideal even by most military leaders in Africa who have succeeded in toppling well-established civilian regimes. Essentially the civilian supremacy model requires that civilians rather than the military control decision-making with respect to the issue of war and peace, the determination of the size and general shape of the military establishment, the basic methods of recruiting both officers and enlisted personnel, the allocation of major privileges and rewards within the service, and, most importantly, the allocation of government revenues for the funding of all military and paramilitary activities. It is a model that depends for its proper functioning upon the existence of strong independent political counterforces in the economy, the schools, churches, professions, and other areas of the private sector.

Subsequent models are arrayed along the continuum in terms of the duration and scope of military intervention into the political arena. The minimal breach from the civilian supremacy relationship can be labeled the *watchdog* model. This suggests an intervention which is both limited in time and calculated to achieve a specific objective, such as assurance that the winning party in a contested election will actually be installed in office, exemplified by the April 1968 noncommissioned officers' coup in Sierra Leone. This action, the last of a series of coups which began a year earlier, put into power the All People's Congress of Siaka Stevens, which had successfully challenged the ruling Sierra Leone People's Party in the 1967 election but had been denied the fruits of its victory by a preemptive military coup.[22]

The second level of military involvement in politics—the *balance wheel* model—indicates a more extended intervention, with the military assuming full authority with respect to all instruments of violence but leaving the running of government in the hands of bureaucrats, judges, educators, and others who form part of a civil-military coalition. This model is represented by the July 1966 Gowan coup against Ironsi in Nigeria, which continued in effect until the actual commencement of the Biafran civil war.

The next two models on the continuum represent an even further in-depth and more pervasive involvement of the military in the running of the state. This is based on the assumption that the co-opted civilians are creatures of their own past and hence need to be either displaced or more closely supervised in order to achieve the objectives of the military intervention. The *direct rule* model is the more conservative of the two, assuming that the solutions which must be applied are more technical or technological and do not require a basic shift in ideology or a restructuring of the society. This position is exemplified by the Nigerian military experience from the outset of the civil war to the handover of authority in 1979. The more drastic version of in-depth intervention is the *social transformation* model (Ethiopia, Benin, Congo-Brazzaville), which assumes that there must be a complete break with past values and institutions and a restructuring of society if it is to achieve its multiple goals of nation-building, overcoming poverty, and popular democracy.

The last model on the continuum, the *atavistic* model, represents a situation in which military personnel penetrate every aspect of society, and military values and the so-called virtues of heroism, sacrifice, martyrdom through conflict, and blind obedience to authority become dominant norms in society. The obvious examples of this are Uganda under Amin and Equatorial Guinea under Macias Nguema. The atavistic model represents a calculated effort at creating disorder to root out all vestiges of civilized behavior. Amin was ultimately driven from power by the combined forces of Tanzanian regulars and Ugandan dissident refugees, but not before the decades- and even centuries-old political relationships among the peoples of Uganda were irreversibly destroyed. President Milton Obote returned in 1980 to preside over a radically different society and political system than the one from which he was forcibly excluded in 1971. The high cost which Uganda had to pay in terms of loss of hundreds of thousands of lives and refugees is too great a burden for any society.[23]

THE MANDATE OF THE MILITARY. It has been one of the hard lessons of

African politics that the military leaders who abandon the civilian supremacy model in favor of a greater degree of political intervention quickly discover that they have overestimated the depth of what they perceived as a popular mandate to govern, and immediately take on the mantle of guardian of the masses. The slogan of the Liberian People's Redemption Council—"In the cause of the people, the struggle continues"—illustrates this presumption of an ongoing popular mandate. In most instances it was not the popularity of the particular military group per se that contributed to the acceptance of the coup, but rather the lack of popularity of the civilian or military leadership that had preceded them in office. To the extent, moreover, that the destruction of the preceding regime was broadly accepted, it has been perceived by the participants as a mandate which the military was obliged to share with other significant dissident groups in society. Thus the very groups that had applauded the military intervention and provided it with popular acceptance are among the first to criticize any effort on the part of the military to give itself an unlimited mandate in terms of both time and scope of responsibilities. The lofty aims which the military initially proclaim soon give way to the pursuit of narrow corporate interests. Once the military, moreover, has proceeded beyond a narrow watchdog model, it sacrifices the neutral arbiter role which made it attractive to civilian dissidents in the first place, and it is perceived by its former co-conspirators as one of the more firmly entrenched competitors in the pursuit of scarce resources and privilege in society.

The syndrome of popular disenchantment is well illustrated in the cases of Ethiopia, Ghana, and Liberia. The military Dergue in Ethiopia appeared to forget very quickly that it was the broad-based hostility of students, labor leaders, and peasants toward the regime of Haile Selassie—combined with discontent over the progress of the Eritrean War—that had brought the imperial system to its knees. Hence, when the Dergue attempted to carry out a radical transformation of society, instead of the more limited goals embraced by the students and the labor leaders, the latter manifested their loss of confidence.[24] By that time, of course, the military was firmly in charge. Similarly, it was the Ghanaian market women who cheered most enthusiastically the second coming of Flight Lieutenant Jerry Rawlings during the New Year's Eve 1981 coup because of Rawlings's pledge to eliminate official corruption. Months later, however, the same people found themselves engaged in violent confrontation with Rawlings's troops who were attempting to deal with the black market corruption that had become a way of life among the market vendors. Finally, a parallel exists in the advent of Master Sergeant Samuel Doe to power in Liberia in April 1980. The students, opposition political leaders, editors, clergymen, and others who had participated in the year of ferment leading to President William Tolbert's demise quickly found themselves chafing under the moratorium placed on political activity by the People's Redemption Council during more than five years of military rule.

Ironically, it is the military itself, through the perpetuation of its tenure, that contributes most to undermining its own mandate. The commitment to the civilian supremacy model of civil-military relationships in Africa is not exclusive to civilian politicians. Indeed, it has become almost a sine qua non in the ritual of intervention that the coup leaders themselves in the early hours or days following their takeover of power publicly proclaim their commitment to an early return to civilian rule as soon as the factors which precipitated intervention have been eliminated. One recent example of this came in the Sudan where the leader of the April 1985 coup, General Abdel R. H. Swareddahab, pledged to restore civilian rule within six months of the ouster of President (and former General) Jaafar al-Nimeiry. It was a promise Swareddahab could not uphold. The frequency with which subsequent military leaders in Nigeria, Ghana, and elsewhere have undermined the efforts of their military predecessors to restore civilian rule does not negate the general proclaimed preference for civilian rule.

LIMITS ON MILITARY GOVERNANCE. The limits on the ability of the intervening military to control the machinery of state have been in many respects similar to the dilemma faced by the party leadership at independence, namely the need to rely upon others to provide the skills for economic planning, maintenance of the judicial system, and the other tasks of government. Just as the party leaders at independence initially had to rely upon expatriates, the military leaders following a coup have had to rely upon civilian bureaucrats, judges, teachers, and others in coping with the broad economic, social, and political questions that needed resolution; the specialized training and relatively insular experience of the military poorly prepare them for the tasks of governing. This is particularly true where a *social transformation* model is envisioned, but it applies as well to the more limited instances of the *watchdog* or *balance wheel* models. The departure of some experienced expatriate administrators at the time of independence deprived the civilian nationalists of certain "institutional memories" required for the continued functioning of key ministries; similarly, the assassination or departure of leading politicians impedes the ability of the military to effect a smooth consolidation of power. The modus operandi of the military, moreover, differs substantially from the rules and procedures which apply to civilian government. The military style of command through hierarchies is not readily adaptable to civilian politics. The latter requires constant negotiations among vested interests; tradeoffs in vertical, horizontal, and oblique directions; and occasional self-recognition and acceptance of failure as a healthy aspect of political behavior.

Taking on civilian tasks poses considerable risks for the military. Even if this involvement merely requires military supervision of civilian performances, it inevitably diverts the top military leadership from its primary mission of running the military establishment to the more complex task of running the state. A number of things thus occur that create internal tensions within the military. First of all, the easier access on the part of the top military to the new privileges associated with state power (as well as the extra-legal acquisitions of property) creates a gulf between senior and junior grade officers as well as between officers and the rank and file. Second, military leaders associated with governance of the state are called upon from time to time to make decisions which may be in the interest of the larger civilian community but do not necessarily satisfy the more narrow interests of the military. Thirdly, not all ethnic, religious, and other segments of society can be proportionally represented within the top military cadre. Hence, the appearance (if not the reality) of linkages of an ascriptive nature between the top brass and key ethnic leaders in the civilian sector creates ethnic tensions within the ranks of the military. In response to one or more of these developments, the collective nature of leadership, which may have characterized the initial coup group, ultimately gives way to one-man rule or governance by a narrowly based junta concerned about tightly controlling both the society and the military establishment as well. Thus distance is put between the top leadership and its own primary constituency. Any one of the preceding factors may be a specific cause of the succession of coups that occur within a single period of military governance.

Evaluating Military versus Civilian Performance

THE LEGITIMACY ISSUE. We have nothing approaching a truly scientific social science laboratory in which we can test the relative performance of civilian and military regimes.[25] The variables that must be taken into account are extensive even though most African states share a generalized situation of poverty, a recent history of colonial occupation, and a roughly similar set of problems in nation-building. Even when comparing military and civilian rule within a single state, where the range of variables is thereby reduced, it is difficult to know when to start counting developments or situations that must be credited to or charged against a civilian, as opposed to a military, regime. As previously noted, moreover, the range of models of civil-military relationships does inject a wide measure of uncertainty regarding crude analyses based upon more than fifty rather divergent cases of successful military intervention. Mindful of these problems, some broad generalizations can nonetheless be posited.

The first observation has to do with the frequent claims of military leaders that, despite the paucity of the numbers actually involved in a specific coup, military intervention has popular support. Thus, it is argued that military effort at governing has had a greater base of legitimacy than that of the civilians they displaced. What kind of test is being used to validate this claim? Dancing and demonstrations by jubilant market women at the announcement of a successful coup are not a reliable index. The very women, for example, who danced in front of Usher prison in Accra in January 1966 as Nkrumah's political prisoners were being released by the new military government had been photographed several days earlier giving President Nkrumah a triumphal farewell as he went off to China for a state visit. The 1974 student demonstrations, labor strikes, and other kinds of anomic behavior that greeted the Ethiopian coup could not be read by the military Dergue that toppled the Emperor as an abiding test of its legitimacy. Indeed, within weeks the military had to turn against its fellow revolutionaries.

In considering the claims to legitimacy by various military governing groups, there are few objective tests by which to evaluate the likelihood of their being more appropriate defenders of the society and its "constitution" than the civilians they have displaced. The military is not elected, nor does it have its mandate confirmed in a post-coup election. By contrast, at least some of the party regimes do in fact periodically have their mandate to govern tested. In addition to those states which have long permitted or have recently introduced a system of multi-party competition (e.g., Botswana and Senegal), several single-party states have permitted competition to take place at the legislative level in a modified primary election system.

Aside from referenda on new civilian constitutions (usually on a take-it-or-leave-it basis), there are few instances in which a military regime has permitted a popular referendum on policies to be pursued by the military regime, let alone one on its remaining in power. The closest thing to the latter was the referendum which the Ghanaian military provided in 1978 regarding its continuation in office as part of a unionist coalition of civilians and military leaders. Despite the many charges of rigging, the military only managed to record a 56 percent favorable vote.[26]

In many instances the critical test of legitimacy of an African military regime is externally applied. Parallel to the OAU principle that upholds the sanctity of the inherited colonial boundaries of African states, a similar posture of "live-and-let-live" applies with respect to the acceptance of any governing regime. African leaders generally accord recognition to other African governing groups whether civilian or military, exemplary or outrageous, well-trained or deficient in the art of governing, and whether supported by an elective majority or imposed by a handful of self-indulgent dissidents. It was a rare act in international politics of Africa for the Nigerian civilian leadership in 1980 to attempt to orchestrate a quarantine of the regime of Master Sergeant Doe following the assassination of President William Tolbert. The boycott partially succeeded only because Tolbert had been the Presiding Chairman of the OAU at the time of his death. Indeed, Idi Amin not only secured official international recognition of his regime, but was actually elected Chairman of the OAU during the apex of his domestic atrocities. No one attempted to topple his government until he had actually invaded Tanzania. Citing another case, it was France, rather than other African states, that dethroned Emperor Bokasso in Central Africa. Once entrenched in power, military regimes, like the civilians they displaced, do not have to earn a sort of Wilsonian right of international acceptance.

MAINTENANCE OF STABILITY. A further aspect of performance evaluation relates to the claim that the military can better maintain order and stability in the new African states than can the civilians they displaced. Despite the superior direct control which military regimes exercise over the instruments of violence, there is no overwhelming evidence that they have done a more creditable job of providing the order and stability required for economic development or for the political consolidation required in forging a nation from among highly heterogeneous societies.

More frequently, indeed, it is the military itself which is the major source of instability. This would include not only the *atavistic* models of military intervention provided by Idi Amin and others; it applies as well to those situations in which the very uncertainty and insecurity on the part of the coup leaders regarding the success of their intervention had led them to engage in significant destruction of property as well as the highly publicized and almost ritualistic killing of those identified with the previous order. Although the numbers were relatively limited, nevertheless the execution of previous military politicians by Jerry Rawlings in the Ghanaian coup of 1979 and the 1980 executions of thirteen Americo-Liberian civilian leaders following the Samuel Doe coup did provide the impression of a breakdown of public order. Even more broadly, the imposition of curfews, and restrictions on movement and political activities provide an increasing number of occasions where the military may—under the guise of maintaining order—exploit and extort the general public. By way of contrast, civilian regimes tend to place a higher priority upon educative, economic, group, and ritualistic sanctions. Military leaders tend to rely heavily upon the sanction with which they are most familiar—that of force. They secure the appearance of popular acceptance of their rule by securing a form of compliance based upon fear of physical reprisal.

ACCOMMODATING INTER-ETHNIC CONFLICT. Despite the military's being one of the few continuing institutions associated with the entire colonial state, and despite its claim to represent the defense of the whole nation against threats both domestic and external, the record of the military on accommodating interethnic conflict has been somewhat checkered. On balance, the military does not appear to have been more effective than civilian regimes in terms of reducing ethnic, religious, and regional conflicts or in balancing out the diverse claims against the state's limited economic resources. The military, moreover, cannot boast of a superior record in terms of maintaining the integrity of the original political boundaries. This has been part of a generally accepted compact which civilian and military regimes alike have upheld under the Charter of the Organization of African Unity. Indeed, among the few instances in which efforts were made at secession (e.g., Biafra), or in which international boundaries were initially violated (e.g., the Somali incursions into the Ogaden and Uganda's attacks on villages in northwest Tanzania), a military governing group dominated the political scene.

On further analysis, moreover, the argument of the military—based upon continuity from the colonial period that is the prime *national* institution— is flawed. It ignores the fact that ethnicity was very carefully taken into account as an instrument of control by the European administrators in the recruitment and assignment of Africans to the colonial army. It overlooks as well the fact that the colonial army supported the European bureaucracy rather than upholding the concept of an African national community.

Developments under civilian rule following independence further limited the ability of the post-colonial military to rise above its own ethnic problems. This was especially true where the departure of Europeans and the subsequent Africanization of the officer class brought advantages largely to those ethnic groups which had been more intensely exposed to mission education and other forces for modernization under colonial rule. These were often the same groups that dominated the political parties during the nationalist struggle. Career opportunities which had been viewed with disdain during the colonial period suddenly became—taking Uganda as a case in point— attractive to both the Baganda and the Lang'o educated elite. This turn of events was viewed with alarm by Idi Amin's group, the Kakwa (Nubi), whose home area in the north had under British rule been generally neglected in terms of modernization but who had been systematically recruited as non-commissioned officers.[27] The Ganda (Baganda) and Lang'o officers from the south were also suspect to the northern ethnic groups who were in general disproportionately recruited at the troops level. This situation was central to the comprehension of the 1971 Amin coup. Similar examples of parallel interethnic tensions within the post-independence military can be cited from around the continent.

The intervention of the military into post-independence politics further exacerbated the preexisting ethnic imbalances. In the 1958 coup in the Sudan, for example, the Northern Muslim Arabs expanded their influence under General Aboud to the detriment of the Nilotic Christians and traditionalists within the military, setting the stage for the decade-long civil war. In Nigeria, the Igbo officers who were prominent in the January 1966 coup (and who had as a group escaped assassination attempts), moved too precipitously in promoting their co-ethnics to the vacated positions within the military. This aroused the suspicions of the Hausa-Fulani and representatives of other ethnic groups in the military, who subsequently effectuated the July 1966 coup against Ironsi and his fellow Igbos. Still a third case is that of Liberia, which, following the 1980 coup, found a disproportionate number of the recently promoted officer cadre coming from the Krahn and other southeastern ethnic groups. These were the ethnic groups that had been only recently exposed to modern education and health care, but they were dominant within the group of eighteen noncommissioned officers who carried out the coup.

Even the two categories of cases which suggest that military forces are better able to achieve national integration than civilian political leaders are not unqualified successes in this regard. The first category consists of instances in which the military wing of a nationalist political movement makes a conscious effort to transcend ethnic differences within its ranks during the course of a revolutionary struggle against an autocratic regime. Rather than awaiting military victory, specific planning takes place during the military phase of the nationalist struggle regarding the nature of the civilian political system which will—*inter alia*—reduce ethnic considerations in decision-making. Thus, an effort is made to emulate the Yenan experience of the Chinese Communist Party following the Long March. FRELIMO in Mozambique and SWAPO in Namibia are the African examples that come quickly to mind.

On the other hand, involvement in military action to achieve nation-building goals may actually harden ethnic lines. The fact, for example, that the Mau Mau emergency was largely restricted to the Kikuyu and the related Embu and Meru groups subsequently provided the Kikuyu with an extraordinary claim to political preference over its ethnic competitors on the basis of its heroic efforts in challenging settler domination. In other cases where the ethnic base of resistance was broader, the absence of a unified military command and strategy on the part of those political groups fighting for liberation and control of the post-colonial state may actually exacerbate ethnic divisions within the new state. The ZANU/ZAPU split, reflected in the refusal of both parties to coordinate the tactics and strategies of the separate ZANLA and ZIPRA military wings, has perpetuated ethnic cleavage in post-independence Zimbabwe. And the MPLA government and the challenging UNITA forces in Angola represent two conflicting versions of broad ethnic coalitions forged under conditions of uncoordinated military action against a single colonial army.

The second category of cases—those instances in which the military appears to have done a more effective job in ameliorating ethnic conflict than was done by a preceding civilian regime—is virtually limited to two surviving examples. Until the early 1980s the Sudan could have constituted a third case. Unfortunately, the same General Jaafar al-Nimeiry who toppled a government in 1969—in order to provide a formula for ending the long-raging civil war—by the 1980's had undermined that national compact by administratively dividing the Christian Nilotic southern region and by imposing the Muslim Shar'ia law upon the entire country. Of the two extant cases of successful integration under military auspices, the lesser of the two is that of Burundi under the second military government, which Crawford Young suggests has made considerable strides in ameliorating the long-standing conflict between the Tusi and the Hutu caste groups that previously had resulted in the deaths or exile of tens of thousands of Barundi. This case should receive greater research attention in the future. The better documented case is that of Nigeria. The political system devised by the Nigerian military during the Biafran War and brought fully into existence in 1979 frontally addressed the question of ethnicity. The success of Nigerian military efforts at ethnic accommodation, of course, was seriously flawed by the New Year's Eve coup in 1983. The coup dismantled the ingenious electoral system introduced by the military which limited participation to political parties with greater than regional appeal and which required a broad national mandate for one to be elected president. Other aspects of the military experiment in reducing ethnic tensions, however, remain in place despite the 1983 coup. The nineteen-state federal system, which broke up most of the larger ethnic groupings, continues to function with respect to management of public programs and the administration of justice at the state level. The national bureaucracy, moreover, was broadly recruited from among regions and ethnic groups during the last years of military rule, and this process has also continued, despite the coup. Of equal significance has been the continuity of military efforts to equalize economic distribution throughout the republic. The formula for sharing the oil revenues, for example, and the establishment of respectable universities in each of the nineteen states continue as monuments to the military's success in accommodating interethnic rivalry in Africa's most populous country.

Having acknowledged the example of the Nigerian military, however, it must be noted that several civilian regimes elsewhere in Africa have been equally effective in dealing with the problems of ethnic and religious heterogeneity. The Revolutionary Party (Chama Cha Mapinduzi, the former TANU) in Tanzania, for example, has been a vital instrument in sublimating the differences among Tanzania's more than 120 ethnic groups. As noted in Chapter 3, Nyerere's use of Swahili, the introduction of a radical development ideology, and the conscious efforts at regional equalization of economic benefits have all been factors in Tanzania's success in nation-building. Although their strategies and tactics differ substantially from those of Tanzania, other civilian regimes in Senegal, Cameroon, Kenya, and the Ivory Coast have also been able to achieve a kind of static tension among competing ethnic groups, with conflict being ameliorated as a byproduct of a reasonable amount of success in economic development.

POPULAR CONTROL OVER GOVERNMENT. Closely related to the question of ethnic accommodation is the question of establishing popular government. There is little evidence to support the proposition that the African military has been more effective than civilian regimes in providing an environment receptive to the survival of consociational democracy. On the contrary, the rejection by the Ghanaian military in 1982 and by the Nigerian military in 1983 of the experiments in democracy launched by their military predecessors only adds to the litany of failure on the part of military experiments in the furtherance of democracy around the continent. Conversely, there has been a steady widening of the base of permitted competition within several of the political party states. This has come either through challenges being permitted by opposition parties that do in fact compete and have their ballots counted or through encouraging effective challenges at the legislative level within the confines of the single party itself. Through voluntary resignations of heads of state, moreover, major changes in political directions have already been achieved in Senegal and Cameroon, with other changes contemplated in Tanzania, Sierra Leone, and other countries which have experienced voluntary retirement of heads of state.

The denial of the democratic process, moreover, during periods of military intervention is not limited to the banning of political parties and elections. The restrictions are much broader, invariably involving a complete moratorium on all forms of political activity and legitimate discussion (as defined by the military); the imposition of curfews; the banning of independent newspapers and the arrest of journalists and editors; and the outlawing or restricting of the activities of trade unions, cooperatives, churches, and other pluralistic institutions. This provides ample evidence of a general intolerance by the military of any form of political competition, let alone dissent. Confrontation of ideas, however, is the essence of pluralistic democracy. I am not in any way suggesting that limits on civil liberties do not occur under civilian party regimes in Africa. It is rather the consistency of their application under military rule that undermines the military's professed commitment to democratic procedures. The modus operandi of the military, after all, dictates against the constant bargaining, open-ended discussion, and absence of closure that are requisites of a functioning democratic system.

ACHIEVEMENT OF ECONOMIC DEVELOPMENT. A substantial portion of the literature on the African military and economic development has been based upon certain theoretical assumptions about the modernizing disposition and capacity of the military. It is assumed that, unlike many other structures in African society, the new military is fully committed to modern technology as a necessary element in achieving effective defense and combat readiness.[28] Since indigenous or purchased technology is directly related to industrialization, it is further assumed that the military will place a high priority upon industrialization of African economies to ensure continued military preparedness. In contrast with churches, parties, and other institutions, the military as an institution is characterized by rational decision-making; management by objectives; achievement orientation in the selecting and assigning of personnel to specific tasks; and commitment to the idea of higher education— particularly in the technical fields and the need to maintain a modern system of communications.

To the extent that the foregoing is true (and it is certainly questionable with respect to many African armies), all it essentially confirms is that the military has a vested corporate stake either in (1) maintaining an industrialized economy which will produce the weaponry, communications systems, transport, and other material needed by the military itself; or (2) maintaining an economy that, through exports, can earn sufficient credits or secure enough funds through loans to be assured of a foreign source of needed military equipment. The Ethiopian Dergue is an excellent example of this tendency—despite its rhetoric about the transformation of the Ethiopian economy in the interest of the masses. The attributes noted above say nothing about the ability of the military to transfer its skills and attitudes to the governance of a national society or to blend the various corporate demands (including its own) into a workable package for the maintenance of a healthy national economy and society. There is nothing in the training of military officers per se, however, that makes them better qualified to comprehend the workings of complex industrial organizations, to cope with the problems of international finance, or to engage in the bargaining that must take place among the various participants in the market—whether that market is controlled or based on laissez faire principles.

No objective indices of growth provide indisputable proof that a given society which has experienced both extended periods of military rule and extended periods under a civilian regime fares better under the former than it does under the latter. In any event, it would be difficult in most circumstances to delineate where one economic initiative ends or begins, whether the weather has been a factor, and what other considerations have to be taken into account. There have been very few single case studies of the performance of a military regime in an African country. (One exception would be Donald Rothchild's appraisal of the Ghanaian experience during the second military intervention.[29] Rothchild notes the difficulties of controlling the variables which must be taken into account. Nevertheless, he confirms a rather negative judgment of the military's economic performance.) For the continent as a whole, however, certain gross data do suggest that civilian regimes fare better than military regimes. For example, only seven of the forty-five states in sub-Saharan Africa are self-sufficient in food production. Of these seven states, six have experienced unbroken periods of civilian rule since independence.[30] Congo-Brazzaville is the only exception, and it has a relatively small population. The remaining thirty-eight states that have encountered problems in food production break roughly even between military and civilian-dominated regimes. Despite the efforts of Nigerian, Ghanaian, and other military regimes to mount energetic programs to "Feed the Nation," they have failed miserably in meeting production goals. Also of interest is the revelation that Uganda, having endured the disastrous economic chaos of the Amin military period, did manage to achieve dramatic increases in agricultural production during the first two years of Obote's Second Republic.

Other gross data which suggest better performance of civilian versus military regimes are contained in the 1983 IBRD figures for growth of production for thirty-four African states, listed in rank order.[31] Of those states which have experienced unbroken civilian rule since independence or have experienced more years of civilian than military rule during the past decade, ten are in the upper half of the scale, and only four are in the lower half, whereas only seven of the states that have endured more years of military than civilian rule during the past decade (or since independence) are in the upper half of the scale, with twelve in the lower half.

With regard to the waste of scarce resources on nonproductive activities, the record on corruption during periods of military rule is not demonstrably better than the record in those same countries under civilian rule. The second coming of Jerry Rawlings was directed against alleged corruption by civilians; the first Rawlings coup was directed against his predecessor military colleagues! Both civilian and military regimes in Africa experience periods of puritanical posturing about corruption followed by periods of rampant rapaciousness. In the absence of hard data, the anecdotal material on civilian corruption tends to be no more outrageous than the material on military misdeeds (such as the cement scandal under the Nigerian military). Aside from illegal exactions, the escalating costs of military weaponry, barracks, uniforms, and the associated perquisites have become increasingly significant factors in explaining national budget deficits, adverse balance of payments problems, and the possibility of default on repayment of loans. Once in power, military regimes have gone far beyond correcting the low economic status of the military vis-à-vis other sectors of society. At the time of transfer of power to civilian hands, the military invariably has lacked the courage to bring the size of the military establishment down to the scale which would be reasonably required for defense. The Nigerian military in 1979 was a significant case in point.

Furthermore, on the question of development, the military as a corporate structure has not been visibly associated with development projects or programs. The most significant African use of the military in U.S. Corps of Engineers–type projects has occurred under civilian, not military-dominated, regimes. Sekou Touré in Guinea—following the dramatic achievement of independence in 1958 and faced with having to absorb the Guinean troops who were summarily dismissed from the French army without their pensions—decided to put the returned veterans and the military to work on projects of value to the nation. Similarly, Nyerere, following the 1964 mutiny, subordinated the military to the national political party and involved the military in the economic transformation of Tanzanian society. In states where the military has enjoyed political authority, it has generally refused to involve troops in activities which are described as civilian, such as collecting the garbage in Lagos during a sanitation workers' strike. The only exceptions to this rule have occurred when the issue was a highly sensitive political one (the Nigerian troops did help conduct a census during the extended military period) or when a situation was regarded as a crisis matter, such as the use of Ghanaian troops to move cocoa to market when vital export earnings from this mainstay of the Ghanaian economy had been threatened by lack of transport and fuel.

Transition to Civilian Rule

Despite the popular sense of resignation, if not popular approval, which appears to greet many military interventions in Africa, in the long run the commitment to the general principle of civilian rule seems to be a deeply held one on the part of Africa's modernized sector. What is applauded is not military rule but the demise of particular civilian regimes associated with corruption or failure of economic growth. The military itself, moreover, recognizes the underlying preference for the civilian supremacy model by making an early pledge to restore civilian rule once the situation which led to the coup has been eliminated.

How then can the transfer of authority take place in a peaceful manner and with some assurance of permanence? Admittedly, we enter this discussion with more trepidation than we manifested before the 1983 Nigerian coup, particularly since the full post mortem has not yet been conducted on the overthrow of the Shagari government. Nevertheless, the procedures followed in the Nigerian transition seem worth restating, since the same course will probably be pursued by the new military there and be followed as well in other states.

First of all, the transfer must be a genuine effort at restoring or refashioning civilian political institutions. The "civilianization of the military" along the lines of Atatürk or Nasser and Sadat has not produced viable civilian supremacy models in the few places where this has been attempted in Africa. The titles have changed, but the military-created parties in Zaire, Liberia and elsewhere do not function as genuine political parties. The emphasis in such regimes is upon the sanction of force rather than upon economic, educative, and other approaches to expansion of the base of popular participation in decision-making.

A second requisite for successful transfer of authority is that the situations or issues that invited military intervention in the first place should be substantially resolved prior to the military withdrawal. The military is often able to impose a rational and mutually beneficial solution to a problem that has defied civilian negotiation and bargaining. The civilian negotiating leaders are often bound by the rigid and entrenched interests of their respective constituencies and thus are unable to make those necessary concessions which might be regarded as a betrayal of vital interests. Thus, in Nigeria the military was able to provide a rational formula for the distribution of the revenues from oil in the Eastern Region and to cope with the problems of interethnic conflict by establishing a more workable federal system. Civilian politicians prior to the 1966 coup had been stalemated on these two fundamental questions.

Third, if the transfer is to succeed, the military must work closely with the prospective politicians who will be expected to make the new political, economic, and social system function effectively after the transfer of authority. Civilians must be intimately involved not only in the broad issues but also in the mechanics of how the new system will function. The legitimacy of the process requires, furthermore, that a realistic timetable be established for the return to civilian rule, with a series of incremental target dates determined and fairly faithfully adhered to.

Fourth, success of the civilian restoration requires that the military engage in the complicated self-denying act of consciously sharing power with other elements in the society. This requires that the military not only reduce its mission to one adequate for the defense of the nation, but also avoid even the appearance of entrenched clauses or informal understandings which would give legitimacy to a future military intervention. Paralleling a sharp reduction of its own political role, the military must be committed to a process which effectively permits respected civilian politicians—without regard to their previous roles—to participate in politics. And the base of institutionalized pluralism within the society must be expanded and strengthened with trade unions, cooperative societies, universities, churches, independent presses, and other forms of social and economic structures permitted to serve as strong effective counterpoints to the strength of both the military and the political parties.

One final caveat regarding the return to civilian rule relates to the extent of external funding and support for the military in particular African countries. During the early post-independence era the continuing external linkages with Britain and France, for example, proved during the rash of mutinies in East and West Africa to be a factor in averting a military takeover or guaranteeing a speedy return to civilian rule following military intervention. An even more recent case was the intervention of the French military in the overthrow of the former Colonel Bokasso, who had restyled himself Emperor of the Central African Empire. The long-term effect of these external linkages, however, has been to place the military at the center of the political struggle over the allocation of scarce resources. The increasingly high cost of modern weaponry and military technology as well as the perpetuation and expansion of the package of material benefits which the new military enjoys cannot be met from domestic production alone. They require loans, gifts, and other outlays from foreign sources. Economic aid from the Soviet Union to Africa has long been heavily oriented to military forms,[32] and the American assistance programs are increasingly skewed in that direction. Having become accustomed to imported weaponry, the military is reluctant to turn over the reins of power to civilian regimes that have edu-

cational, health, and other priorities with respect to the use of scarce resources. This problem is particularly acute where the military governing
group is engaged in one or more instances of rebellion and can only survive
because of massive infusions of outside military assistance—whether from
the East, the West, or the Libyans. There comes a point, however, as is
certainly true of Ethiopia today, when the question arises as to whether the
beleaguered military governing class has invited in a new colonial governing
class. No matter what the intentions with respect to reestablishing civilian
rule, the options are severely limited.

IX

U.S. POLICY TOWARD SUB–SAHARAN AFRICA
Continuities and Variations

Alexis de Tocqueville, writing in 1835 at the conclusion of Volume One of his insightful *Democracy in America*, speculated:

> There are now two great nations in the world which, starting from different points, seem to be advancing toward the same goal: the Russians and the Anglo-Americans.
>
> Both have grown in obscurity, and while the world's attention was occupied elsewhere, they have suddenly taken their place among the leading nations, making the world take note of their birth and of their greatness almost at the same instant.
>
> All other peoples seem to have nearly reached their national limits and to need nothing but to preserve them; but these two are growing. All others have halted or advanced only through great exertions; they alone march easily and quickly forward along the path whose end no eye can yet see.[1]

While that prophecy was proceeding to its fulfillment, there was one region of the globe that remained relatively untouched by the influence of either of these two major powers. That region, of course, is sub-Saharan Africa. Yet today if one were to believe the African coverage in the American or the Soviet press—or indeed the press in Africa itself—one might mistakenly conclude that the United States or the Soviets, or both, were behind every major crisis emerging within a region of crises.

Although the focus of this chapter will be upon American policies and practices with respect to sub-Saharan Africa, it is striking to consider the many parallels in attitudes and actions on the part of both major powers. Not least among these parallels is the fact that the late 1950s and early 1960s constituted a watershed for both countries in their relationships with the peoples of Africa. Whether it was by their choice or due to calculated exclusion by West European colonialists, the attention of the two major powers was largely directed elsewhere prior to the heralded "1960 Decade of African Independence."

When Americans did have contacts with Africa in the several centuries preceding that decade, the involvement was often intermittent, frequently negative in character, and usually marginal to the greater economic, cultural, and political interests that Americans manifested with respect to Europe, Latin America, and even Asia.[2] The most significant African-American connection, of course, was the heritage of the European-inspired slave trade, which found a good portion of the more than 11.5 million African captives deposited on the North American shores. The relationship between free whites and enslaved Blacks not only produced America's most tragic war, but it created a social, economic, and political crisis in race relations that is only now in the final stages of being resolved. The external implications, moreover, of slavery and the slave trade have also been significant both historically and in contemporary terms. Shortly after achieving its independence, for example, the fledgling republic devoted a considerable amount of its energies to the suppression of the transatlantic traffic in human cargo. It was the slave trade and the anomalies of slavery itself, furthermore, that gave the United States one of its few enduring direct links with Africa, namely the 1822 creation of Liberia as a refuge for freed persons of color. One of the lingering consequences of racial discord in the U.S. is that many Africans still tend to view this country's actions and intentions through the prism of racial discrimination—a situation from which they themselves were only recently liberated. This attitude will change as American Blacks in increasing numbers achieve elective and appointive office. Black officials of the stature of Ralph Bunche, Andrew Young, and Donald McHenry have already done much to alter it. The newly politicized American Blacks, moreover, have become an organized force seeking a more consistent and constructive U.S. policy toward Africa, particularly through the Black Caucus in the U.S. House of Representatives.

Although history cannot absolve the United States of the general taint of colonial expansionism, its record with respect to Africa is progressive. Even Liberia was not created as a political extension of America. It was the creature of private American philanthropic efforts, and indeed the survival of the settlements during much of the nineteenth century depended more on British, than on American, governmental efforts.[3] As the great partition of Africa took place in that century America resisted the siren call of Kipling and others that it in particular should "take up the white man's burden." The Berlin Conference of 1884 was the only one of the conclaves involved in the partition of Africa which found an American delegation in attendance, and that treaty was never submitted to the Senate for ratification—so intense was the anti-colonial sentiment. Similarly, despite the urging of the Allied powers in both World Wars, the United States categorically refused to undertake Mandate or Trusteeship responsibility for the conquered German and Italian dependencies in Africa.

The marginality of America's diplomatic concern is revealed in the fact that the U.S. missions in Liberia, Ethiopia, and South Africa only had legation status until well after the Second World War, and U.S. consular services were limited in number and scope. The same evidence of marginality is provided by two weighty studies produced by the Brookings Institution in the 1950s, surveying the gamut of American foreign policy in the first postwar decade.[4] The first of these studies dismissed sub-Saharan Africa in several sentences and a solitary footnote. The second devoted a single paragraph to Africa, stating that with the region "still firmly under European control, the U.S. has few direct responsibilities there, nor is the area one of rapidly developing crises." While that was a faulty analysis of Africa, it was an on-the-mark assessment of official U.S. lack of concern. Not until the end of the Eisenhower presidency was the Department of State administratively reorganized to deal with Africa as a region in itself apart from Western Europe or the Near East.

In strategic terms as well, the military significance of Dakar and Monrovia in the transatlantic supply lift of World War II was but a temporary interlude that did not alter the basic position that Africa was the direct military concern of America's NATO allies. The only direct contacts were the military training and supply agreements with Liberia and Ethiopia and the exchange of military attachés with South Africa. Trade and investment links were similarly limited in contrast with America's pre–1960 stakes in other world regions. Africa accounted for less than 2 percent of U.S. foreign trade. American investment (3 percent of the U.S. total overseas) was focused on the rubber and iron ore industries of Liberia and the mineral resources of Southern and Central Africa. In addition to gold, which is mystically linked to the health of the global monetary system, the significance of cobalt, chromium, manganese, and other steel alloys was already manifested prior to the 1950s, and interest did increase in the succeeding decades. While not exclusively linking Africa and the United States, the imports of tin, copper, and other metals from the area between Zaire and the Cape did supplement either U.S. domestic production or its other overseas sources of these minerals.

Official and private business relationships, of course, did not exhaust the forms of private contacts with Africa prior to the 1950s. Christian missionaries operated in many sectors of the sub-continent. Although frequently resented by Muslims and by adherents of traditional religions—and harassed or viewed with suspicion by colonial officials—American missionaries contributed substantially to educational and health services in selected regions. Private American foundations, such as the Phelps-Stokes Fund in education and the Rockefeller Foundation in medical research, were also positive forces for change. While American scholarly interest in Africa was minimal prior to the 1950s, the predominantly Black colleges, Northwestern University, and others did sow the seeds for the future.

The Era of African Independence

The sudden achievement of independence by Ghana in 1957 and Guinea in 1958 followed in rapid succession by more than a score of African states in the succeeding years brought dramatic changes in both official and private American contacts with Africa. Casual diplomacy was the first to be changed. With the exception of Guinea and Angola (discussed below), the independence of each new African state led to the quick establishment of a U.S. embassy and the potential inclusion of that country in American AID, Peace Corps, and other programs. The scope of the federal government's concern went far beyond the State Department. The Departments of Commerce, Defense, Labor, and the Treasury as well as the Export-Import Bank became actively concerned with currency stability, military crisis management, global labor linkages, and facilitating American access to trade and investment activities formerly monopolized by Europeans. During the 1960s the number of universities having major African area and language centers grew to over thirty, and the number of colleges offering two or more African courses grew to more than two-hundred.

What kind of analysis can be made of the American approach and attitudes toward Africa during this first twenty-five years of African independence? First of all, unlike the case with the Soviet Union, the U.S. national government does not monopolize American contacts, attitudes, and opinions with respect to Africa. State governments and cities may have direct contacts for trade, cultural, and other purposes. More significantly, private businessmen, Black Power groups, scholars, and missionaries have both independent general attitudes and special policy interests which often put them at odds with the national administration. Indeed, even within the federal government, sharp debates on substance and style occur when the same political party controls the White House, the Senate, and the House of Representatives; even more so when control is divided. Without, however, diminishing the role of Congress or the private sector, in the final analysis, it is the executive branch that bears the primary responsibility and controls the significant instruments of foreign policy. Hence our analysis will focus on the continuities as well as the subtle or bold contrasts in presidential policies during the first quarter-century of African Independence.

THE ABSOLUTE AND RELATIVE PRIORITY OF AFRICA IN AMERICAN FOREIGN POLICY FORMULATION. While it is true that there have been both quantitative and qualitative changes in American contacts, programs, and attitudes vis-á-vis Africa since 1960, its interests in other world regions have also increased. Indeed, America's old ties with Western Europe and its new links with the USSR and Eastern Europe began to absorb the attention of foreign policy thinkers in a much more intensive way almost two decades earlier, as it threw off its mantle of isolationism and fully accepted the role of a major power. Unfortunately, the awakening of America toward Africa occurred *pari passu* with U.S. concerns about the strategic, economic, and diplomatic significance of the Middle East, Latin America, and Asia. The populations and resources involved and the potential for crises demanding attention place these areas higher in the pecking order than Africa.

When, moreover, an African crisis or situation does command the immediate and concentrated attention of the Secretary of State or even the President, the tendency is not to view that situation in local or regional terms. Long before the "globalist" analysis of Henry Kissinger, the tendency was to view an African crisis in terms of how it affects American vital interests elsewhere. Hence, the delayed recognition of Guinean independence in 1958 and the muted U.S. posture in United Nations debates on African colonialism had to be weighed against what were assumed to be the higher stakes of maintaining NATO solidarity in the confrontation with the Soviet Union. Despite U.S. hostility toward apartheid, most administrations have moderated their condemnation of South Africa out of concern for continued Western access to its mineral wealth and out of strategic consideration of its geographical location. Diplomatic recognition of the MPLA government in Angola, for example, has been delayed because of the larger domestic and Western hemispheric concern regarding Cuba's global role—epitomized by the 25,000 Cuban troops in Angola. Finally, checking Colonel Muammar Qaddafi's support of terrorists and his interventions in Chad and the Western Sahara seemed to have greater priority than the equally valid American objective of preserving the OAU as a force for stability in Africa—hence the successful efforts to deny him the OAU chairmanship in 1982, despite the threat that American efforts posed to the survival of the OAU itself.

The globalist strategy not only diminishes the importance of African events to Africans themselves, but it also contributes to a superpower "zero-sum" mindset with respect to the major players.[5] Both superpowers have showed evidence of this train of thought. In the U.S. context, the zero-sum game has led to acrimonious policy debates about the U.S. having "lost" something that it never possessed in the first place and whose fate was, in any event, beyond the ability of Americans to control (such as in Ethiopia or Angola). This attitude of omniscience, which the zero-sum mentality encourages, causes one to overlook the fact that there are many other players in the so-called game. The Africans, of course, are the most significant of these, and they have often skillfully manipulated East/West rivalry to their economic, strategic, and other advantage. The players also include the former colonialists, the Chinese, the Japanese, the Israelis, and others that may be crucial in assessing the alleged gains and losses. But the attitude of "gains and losses" misses the point that few things are permanent at this stage of African development. Previous so-called losses to the Soviet bloc have included Egypt, the Sudan, Morocco, Guinea, Ghana, Somalia, and even Mozambique!—each of which now demonstrates an ability to pursue its own course of action. The globalist zero-sum approach has limited American

ability to construct a positive and consistent policy toward Africa. The glob-
alists, nevertheless, have been in the driver's seat for most of the past twenty-
five years—the Kennedy and Carter eras being only modified exceptions to
this.

THE INDIRECT NATURE OF AMERICAN INVOLVEMENT. A paradox in American
official attitudes of omniscience, however, is the persistence of the notion
that "Africa is still Europe's affair." Direct contacts between American and
African diplomats have multiplied in Africa, in Washington, at the United
Nations, and in other forums. Yet, in the face of a crisis, the knee-jerk
reaction of Washington is to defer to European initiatives. This was the case
in the early phases of the 1960s crisis in the Congo (Zaire) and was paralleled
by the automatic acceptance of the British and French paratroop rescues of
beleaguered civilian governments in East and West Africa in 1964. More
recently the Carter administration assumed that the British ultimately had
to play the central role in the resolution of the Zimbabwe-Rhodesia conflict,
since they legally retained the colonial overseer role. The latest manifestation
of this deference was Ronald Reagan's blunt admonition to President Mitterrand during the August 1983 crisis in Chad. To the chagrin of the French
President, he was informed by Reagan that Chad was, after all, "France's
historic responsibility." Mitterrand reluctantly obliged.

Although American businessmen, academics, missionaries, and even diplomats themselves might be irritated by the thinly veiled paternalism of
France and other American allies in Africa, it is clear that official Washington
regards this on balance as a bonus. The economic and military assistance
provided by the West Europeans directly, as well as collectively through
the EEC, diminishes the need for more lavish American aid being spread
more thinly around the African continent. The continuity of links through
the Commonwealth and the French Community (as well as the recently
renewed links between Portugal and both Angola and Mozambique) keeps
the Africans psychologically oriented to the West and reduces the need for
greater American diplomatic effort except where the issue or the country
has achieved special significance with respect to vital American interests.
The U.S. circle of friendly involvement is not limited to the former colonialists. Canada and West Germany, for example, have cooperated with the
other Western Contact Group members in dealing with Southern Africa.
Individually, as well, the Japanese, Israeli, South Korean, and Taiwan governments had been encouraged to pursue economic, educational, and other
objectives in Africa.[6]

The long-run trend has been to avoid the direct engagement of American
military personnel in the resolution of African crises, even though training
missions have been maintained in Liberia and—formerly—Ethiopia and provide support now in Morocco and Sudan. The direct U.S. involvement in
the extended Congo crises of the early 1960s, as well as the not-so-covert
actions of the CIA operatives in Angola in the mid-1970s, had damaging

repercussions.[7] Aside from the Viet Nam reaction syndrome in the United States itself, direct American involvement inevitably tarnished the U.S. image among the African elite. Whether justified or not, as the leading member of the Western capitalist group, America has come to be identified with the more negative aspects of the colonial experience. Furthermore, the direct involvement of U.S. military personnel either invites a counter-response from the USSR or provides legitimacy to the prior intrusion of Soviet supported forces. Hence, the Cold War comes to Africa in spite of African "non-alignment."

The "police action" in the Congo (Zaire) in the 1960s was not intended to be an American affair. Hoping to follow the precedent of the U.S. operation in Korea, African forces from Ghana, Liberia, Senegal, and Ethiopia were expected to bear the brunt of keeping the peace in Zaire. This collaborative effort quickly dissipated as the domestic policy contest between Prime Minister Patrice Lumumba and President Joseph Kasavubu took on the character of a great power ideological struggle between the United States and the USSR. African states quickly lined up into the "blocs" named after the cities where the struggle was defined (Casablanca, Brazzaville, and Monrovia). Significant though the Congo learning experience was, it took the Angola involvement to drive home the message. The Shaba crises during the Carter period and the Chadian chaos during the Reagan era have seen America providing logistical support, AWACs, and other forms of military assistance. Yet the direct military engagement has been left to the French, and increasingly to the Senegalese, Moroccan, and other African military forces. Any efforts to systematize and underwrite Africa's management of its own military crises, however, has been stoutly resisted and resented. Julius Nyerere spoke for many Africans when he characterized such a Western-inspired move as an effort to maintain existing corrupt regimes in power.[8]

In dealing with other matters as well, the U.S. has strongly supported collaborative African self-reliance. The Western Contact Group—as a case in point—has worked in tandem with the Frontline States in confronting Southern African issues. African-inspired efforts at regional economic cooperation, such as the ill-fated East African Community and ECOWAS, have been preferred channels for U.S. aid over assistance to a single country. The Reagan administration, for example, has been one of the more generous contributors to the success of the Southern African Development Coordinating Conference (SADCC) despite the implicit conflict with other Reagan policies with respect to South Africa.[9] SADCC has been viewed as a self-help effort in the spirit of the Marshall plan, since the nine states cooperate in a wide range of economic areas. Significantly, the list of donor countries to SADCC does not include Eastern bloc states. This undoubtedly was a major factor in American enthusiasm and support.

There are limitations, of course, in letting Africans, West Europeans, and others deal more directly with interests in Africa that are of concern to the

United States. One consequence is that the American administration finds itself informationally and psychologically unprepared to act decisively when a truly major crisis emerges. The U.S. risks proposing solutions that are unacceptable to those who have dealt with the region over a more considerable period of time. American actions or recommendations for crisis management thus appear either amateurish or provocative to Africans, West Europeans, and the Soviets alike.

EXPECTATIONS OF RECIPROCITY. Respect for African independence and support for cooperative self-reliance have been partially offset by American expectations of reciprocity. It is often viewed as a matter of moral principle that the quid pro quo for American economic assistance is diplomatic support from Africans on issues vital to the U.S. and the West. Hence, after the generous support which the Reagan administration has provided Zimbabwe, both directly and through SADCC, the Reagan officials were bitterly disappointed by Zimbabwe's abstention on the U.N. vote on the Korean Airlines Flight 007 tragedy, and by Zimbabwe's later sponsorship of the anti-U.S. resolution regarding Grenada. No account was taken of what Zimbabwe insisted were conflicts in information regarding the first or the role that Africans expected Zimbabwe to play as its Security Council representative on the second. In retaliation the American aid package to Zimbabwe was cut in half. There was also a long delay in providing Zimbabwe with food assistance to cope with the refugees who had fled across the border from Mozambique to escape the drought and the effects of the 1984 cyclones. Earlier, the Carter administration—after having secured a substantial Third World vote in condemnation of Soviet actions in Afghanistan—expressed its severe disappointment over the failure of many African states to follow the U.S. lead in boycotting the 1980 Moscow Olympics. Carter officials failed to appreciate African questioning regarding why the United States had not earlier supported them on the apartheid-related boycott of the 1976 Montreal Olympics. Finally, many African 234leaders—in responding to U.S. requests for support in curbing Iranian, Libyan, Palestinian, and other terrorist acts— wonder why the U.S. abstains or even vetoes resolutions condemning the destabilizing raids of South Africa into Angola, Lesotho, and Mozambique or why the U.S. has given tacit support to the links between South Africa and UNITA, the MNR, and other terrorists.

IDEOLOGICAL PURSUITS. Aside from the generalized goals of peace and stability, which would be conducive both to the enjoyment of human rights and to economic development, the approach of the United States to Africa has been at a fairly muted and uncomplicated level of ideology. On occasion a moral issue—such as the current Reagan anti-abortion posture—does intrude, but not for long. Politically the rhetoric of the Wilsonian and earlier eras regarding "national self-determination of all peoples" persisted in the American contribution to the debates in the Trusteeship Council and the General Assembly and were positive in terms of pressing the colonial powers to advance the timetables for African independence. That rhetoric was subsequently modified to include the phrase "responsible" self-government when it appeared that independence within the southern "white redoubt" could not be accomplished without an armed struggle. A return to the earlier Wilsonian position was signaled by Kissinger's Lusaka speech in April 1976, and by the Carter efforts in pressing for majority rule in Southern Africa.

Once African independence has been achieved, successive U.S. administrations have given strong political support to the goals of nation-building and economic development within the OAU-sanctioned inherited colonial boundaries. Indeed, the U.S. rejection of Katangan separation from Zaire in 1960 provided evidence of that position before the OAU was born. Similarly, the U.S. did not come to the aid of Somalia until after its troops had been driven out of the Ogaden province they had invaded. The only appearance of wavering on the issue of acceptance of pre-colonial boundaries came during the Nigerian civil war, when Congressional critics as well as churchmen, business leaders, and others questioned why "self-government" was not as legitimate a goal for the Igbos of Biafra as it was for the rest of Nigeria. Presidents Johnson and Nixon, however, remained firm in providing official acceptance of the concept of a united Nigeria.

Equally strong has been the expressed U.S. preference for multi-party democracy, with a broad base of pluralism regarding churches, trade unions, cooperatives, traditional associations, an independent press, and other non–government controlled social and economic groupings. Despite the preference, both Republican and Democratic administrations have been prepared to work with all but the most abusive manifestations of military atavism or one-party dictatorships, such as Idi Amin or Macias Nguema. The persistence of Wilsonian morality in international politics, however, has made it difficult for presidents to justify to Congress the continued economic and military aid to regimes which are not only corrupt but also lack demonstrated popular support.

In terms of the more economic aspects of ideology, Ronald Reagan is not alone among American presidents who have felt obliged to emphasize U.S. concern with strengthening the private sector in Africa.[10] In particular, this administration has been persistent in urging African governments to pay "realistic" prices to small farmers. There has, however, been a realization at both the official and the private levels in the U.S. that African national economies are a mix of the inherited state capitalism from the colonial era; the survival of traditional forms of both communalism and private enterprise; and the more recently introduced efforts at cooperativism and state welfarism. The African espousal of programs of socialist development is recognized by informed Americans to be often a requirement for political survival in some African states.[11] Ironically, the failure of "African socialism" to be equated with the Marxist-Leninist version of scientific socialism is—with obviously differing motives and conclusions—accepted by American and So-

viet politicians and theoreticians alike. In any event, as the case of Angola
has long demonstrated, advocacy of socialism has not been a sufficient de-
terrent to American capitalist investment in Africa. Indeed, American companies have been encouraged by the U.S. government to do business with
countries that span the political spectrum.

CONSTRAINTS ON AMERICAN ECONOMIC ASSISTANCE. Although the U.S. lacked
direct responsibilities for governing in Africa, the Fourth Point of Harry
Truman's 1949 Inaugural Message signaled a U.S. intent to provide technical
assistance and other forms of aid to Third World countries. As each new
African state appeared on the scene, it immediately (with the exceptions of
Guinea and Angola) became a candidate for U.S. aid. The Americans, as
well, have participated in the "North-South" dialogue regarding the more
equitable global sharing of the benefits of industrialization.

From the African perspective the American positions on "North-South"
sharing and on the extent of aid to Africa have been inadequate. By most
reckonings the roughly $9 billion which the U.S. has been contributing
annually—either directly or through the World Bank and other multilateral
efforts—constitutes roughly ten percent of all sources of foreign aid to Africa.
In common with the Soviet Union, there is no "natural" domestic constituency in the U.S.—including even the Congressional Black caucus—which
puts a higher priority on African aid as opposed to internal claims on scarce
resources. American officials insist that the more generous contributions of
our West European allies are attributable to two factors: the benefits they
derive diplomatically and economically from their continued links with Africa; and the abandoned global responsibilities elsewhere which the Americans have had to assume.

Unfortunately, the persistently desperate nature of African economic prospects makes it difficult for any administration to sustain enthusiastic Congressional support for African aid. Admittedly, many of the factors that make
two-thirds of the African nations candidates for the "Fourth World" category
are not of their own making. This would include, obviously, the colonial
legacy of underdevelopment, particularly with respect to modern economic
and bureaucratic skills but also with respect to the colonial emphasis upon
cash crop and mineral exports to the neglect of viable domestic economies.
Droughts, cyclones, and other natural disasters have also taken their toll on
development aspirations. Administration and Congressional critics, however, have difficulties in "selling" aid programs to the American public because part of the record of failure must be attributed to African leaders
themselves. Official corruption is a luxury that even well-endowed countries
can ill afford, yet it has become a way of life in many African states. The
world's largest pool of refugees, moreover, is only in part a consequence of
natural disaster. Scapegoatism regarding "alien" Africans, conflict among the
new countries, and internal policies bordering on genocide in some African
states have also aggravated the refugee situation. American support for Af-

rican food relief is tempered by a growing awareness of the local neglect of domestic food production. Coupled with the lack of political will to stem the flow of rural to urban migration and the failure to address the problems of family planning, neglect of agriculture has already produced a crisis in Africa more serious than that faced by any other world region. American aid is also difficult to defend given the lack of African political will in dealing with those traditional values and institutions—such as the attitudes toward cattle— which impose a drain on development. And finally, the conscious under- mining of workable economic institutions and the reckless experimentation with human lives by many African leaders in the name of an untested ideology must also be included in the reckoning.

Limited though the U.S. aid program may appear to be, Secretary Shultz recently asserted that it is still in the magnitude of ten times that provided by the Soviet Union. U.S. aid, moreover, tends by the ratio of five to one to favor economic over military assistance. This is almost the reverse of the Soviet ratio.[12] While American aid is disproportionately concentrated on relatively few African countries, it also involves relatively few American personnel—either military or civilian. A persistent characteristic of U.S. aid, moreover, is the speed with which the U.S. has responded to natural crises and the attention given to the problems of child development (nutrition and education). U.S. emphasis has also been placed upon the modest Peace Corps effort and other programs which maximize face-to-face relationships between Africans and Americans. Unfortunately, the inability to marshall long-term Congressional support means that emphasis is placed upon small economic projects with immediate and highly visible results, no matter how short- lived those benefits might be. Given the limited total allocation for Africa, moreover, the tendency has been to concentrate U.S. efforts either on coun- tries having historic linkages with the U.S., such as Liberia, or on the trouble spots. The consequences of this approach have been analyzed earlier. Thus, Liberia, Sudan, Morocco, Zaire, Kenya, and Ethiopia (pre–1974) or Somalia (post–1974) have received a disproportionate share of U.S. aid. In this re- spect, U.S. decision-making is not radically different from that of Soviet officials. And Republican presidents manifest the same tendencies as Demo- cratic ones. The distinctions between the Reagan and Carter periods on the use of aid are more subtle than substantial. Despite the bellicosity of the Reagan rhetoric, economic aid still predominates over military expenditures in sub-Saharan Africa. Despite the expectations of reciprocity from states like Zimbabwe, the U.S. has simultaneously applied both the "carrot" and the "stick" in terms of aid during the period of disenchantment.

THE SOUTHERN AFRICAN "TAR-BABY." The one area where the contrasts between the Reagan administration and its immediate predecessor are most pronounced is Southern Africa.[13] Even here, however, the continuities over the past several administrations are striking. First of all, events in Southern Africa have claimed a disproportionate share of the time, talents, and energies of whoever has been the Assistant Secretary of State for African Affairs. This does not mean that there has been a total neglect of such countries as Liberia, mineral-rich Zaire, Ethiopia or Somalia on the Horn, or Black Africa's most prosperous and populous state, Nigeria. The last-named—after all—is the second most important source of U.S. imported oil. But the fact is that U.S. policies with respect to Southern Africa have become a virtual litmus test to African leaders in measuring the sincerity of U.S. policies toward the continent as a whole. Secondly, the Ford, Carter, and Reagan administrations have repudiated the early Nixonian attitude of "benign neglect" or the "tar-baby" option in favor of a more activist stance with respect to Southern African liberation, even though the stances vary. Thirdly, each administration in the past decade has provided explicit condemnations of apartheid and has attempted to engage all the parties in the region—including South Africans—in a dialogue which would achieve a peaceful transition to some form of majority rule in Zimbabwe, Namibia, and South Africa itself. Fourthly, each administration has both explicitly and implicitly acknowledged the strategic significance of Southern Africa's cobalt, chromium, diamonds, uranium, and other mineral wealth to the health of the Western industrialized economies. Finally, the Ford, Carter, and Reagan administrations have shared the view that the presence of some 25,000 Cuban troops in Angola is a barrier to the normalization of Angola–American relations and to the stability of Southern Africa. Yet, all three regimes have maintained the substance of official contact with Angola without the formality of diplomatic recognition.[14]

Despite the continuities, the substance and the style of the Carter stance toward Southern Africa did represent a decided break with the past. It was not, moreover, simply an implementation of Secretary of State Henry Kissinger's April 1976 speech in Lusaka, as some have argued.[15] That speech had all the earmarks of a deathbed confession of past errors, and certainly the political will to apply the new approach was not in evidence. President Carter, on the other hand, engaged in more than rhetoric when he named to the U.N. ambassadorship a friend and Black civil rights activist who would have immediate access to the Oval Office. Andrew Young and his equally able successor, Donald McHenry, constituted visible recognition of the fact that there was a linkage between human rights in America and human rights elsewhere in the world—particularly Africa. In contrast with the benign neglect of the past, the Carter team vigorously pursued the goals of Southern African liberation. Acting in concert with both the other members of the Western Contact Group and the Frontline States, McHenry and other Americans played a key role in getting action on three fronts. First of all, they got the South Africans to cease supporting the Ian Smith regime, thereby making the Lancaster House conference possible. Second, after two decades of stonewalling, the South Africans were finally persuaded to sit down at the negotiating table and discuss the implementation of U.N. Resolution 435 on the independence of Namibia. And finally, Carter's Vice-President, Walter Mondale, was almost confrontational in making explicit to Prime Minister John Vorster that apartheid was not merely an internal South African problem but that it constituted a genuine threat to international peace. It was made clear that the real threat to regional stability was the challenge that South Africa posed to its Black African neighbors.

While the Carter administration saw only one of its three Southern African objectives accomplished during its watch, it created throughout the continent a receptivity to—if not an actual demand for—U.S. involvement. This had all but disappeared in the interim since the euphoria of the Kennedy era. The Carter initiatives created a climate which made it possible for Reagan operatives to immediately provide economic support both to Zimbabwe and SADCC. It also permitted Assistant Secretary of State Chester A. Crocker to continue dialogue with the MPLA government in Angola. Of equal significance, however, to the Reagan strategy of Constructive Engagement was the fact that the Carter posture provided Vorster's successor as Prime Minister (now President) P. W. Botha with the negative image of what could recur in 1985 if the Republic did not make significant strides toward Namibian independence and the restructuring of apartheid during the tenure of the less hostile and conservative Reagan.

The strategy of Constructive Engagement has had multiple objectives. For the U.S. and its allies, the restoration of political stability in the Southern African region was regarded as satisfying the economic and strategic needs of continued access to the mineral wealth of the area. It would also reassure the naval theorists who regarded South Africa as a vital link in the "sea lanes" strategy of safeguarding the flow of oil from the Persian Gulf. For South Africa the quid pro quo for Namibian independence and reform in race relations within South Africa was reduction in internal violent opposition toward so-called reforms and the elimination of the sanctuary support being provided by neighboring Black states to African National Congress (ANC) and other dissidents. For the Black states in the region, a rapprochement with South Africa was regarded by the Reagan officials as a policy of "realism." That is, security agreements with South Africa would constitute recognition of the military strength of the Republic but would also signal the elimination of South African support to UNITA in Angola, the MNR in Mozambique, and other "rebel" groups. In more positive terms, the superior industrial capacity in South Africa could be put to work in overcoming the shortages in development capital and technical skills needed in the Southern African region. This, incidentally, coincided with South Africa's own dream of a "constellation of states," economically linking countries within South Africa's "natural market."[16]

Since it was the South Africans who held most of the military and economic chips in the area, the Reagan administration has felt that they were the ones that needed the greatest convincing regarding the sincerity of the U.S. negotiating effort. Hence, a number of U.S. actions were explicitly or implicitly justified on these grounds. This would include, for example, the abstentions or vetoes cast in the U.N. Security Council on resolutions condemning South African incursions into neighboring states. The assumption that the U.S. government had to appear to be sympathetic to white South African problems lay behind the repealing of the Clark Amendment of 1974, which specifically barred covert CIA action in Angola. The more favorable diplomatic posture, or tilt, toward South Africa, exemplified by U.N. Ambassador Jeane Kirkpatrick's actions in meeting with South African military personnel early in her tenure, accounts for the increasing dialogue between the military attachés of each country. The tilt accounts, moreover, both for the U.S. government's favorable attitude toward an International Monetary Fund loan to South Africa and the Reagan administration's lack of support for efforts to restrict American private investment in the Republic.[17] Although the issues of white supremacy, mineral security, and South Africa in general are complex in terms of U.S. domestic politics, the tilt partially explains why the U.S. gave South Africa additional maneuvering time in Namibia by insisting upon a linkage between Namibian independence and the removal of Cuban troops from Angola.[18] Further, in cultivating the notion of "sympathetic understanding," President Reagan himself made public statements about the strategic importance of South Africa to the West, reminding Americans that the two countries had been allies in both World Wars (without noting that the Nationalist Party of Botha had actually opposed entering World War II against Germany).

Although the leaders of many African states regard American policies toward South Africa under the Reagan administration as a betrayal of both African liberation and America's own principles of human rights, the Reagan administration takes a different view. The Constructive Engagement approach, Chester Crocker and others argue, has been responsible for bringing regional peace to the Southern African area. American officials played an important role in the negotiations leading up to the Nkomati Accord between South Africa and Mozambique and to the Lusaka Agreement with Angola which was to de-escalate conflict along the Namibian-Angolan border. Constructive Engagement, however, has not noticeably advanced the struggle of SWAPO for Namibian independence, and indeed the U.S. introduction of the linkage between South African and Cuban troop withdrawal from Angola has once again sidetracked the cause of Namibian independence.

It is open to question, moreover, whether Constructive Engagement has been a serious factor in bringing about the recent changes in the structure of apartheid, including the granting of 99-year leaseholds to urban Blacks, the abolition of the Mixed Marriages Act, and the suspension of some minor apartheid laws and the forcible evacuation of African residents from designated white areas. In any event these changes have not convinced the Black majority that the process of dismantling apartheid has really begun in earnest.

The level of violence in 1984–86—particularly in areas that had not witnessed serious violence in the past—indicates a dramatic shift in Black attitudes with respect to the need for basic changes in race relations in South Africa. In this respect the American government has lagged considerably behind American church leaders, educators, labor unions, students, state and local officials, and—most significantly—American businessmen doing business in South Africa, in recognizing the need for the dismantling of apartheid. The policies and attitudes of the American government with respect to South Africa are vital to the maintenance of good relations with the rest of the African continent, for policies and practices with respect to apartheid have become the standard for judging American actions with respect to Black Africa as a whole.

NOTES

Chapter I: Introduction

1. Harold Lasswell, *Politics: Who Gets What, When, How?* (New York: Whittlesey House, 1936).
2. Meyer Fortes and E. E. Evans-Pritchard, eds., *African Political Systems* (London: Oxford University Press, 1940).
3. Paula Brown, "Patterns of Authority in West Africa," *Africa*, Vol. 21 (Oct. 1951), pp. 261–78; John Middleton and David Tait, eds., *Tribes Without Rulers* (London: Routledge and Kegan Paul, 1958); and Lucy Mair, *Primitive Government: A Study of Traditional Political Systems in Eastern Africa* (Bloomington: Indiana University Press, 1977), reprint of 1962 edition.

Chapter II: The Impact of Colonial Rule

1. C. Grove Haines, *Africa Today* (Baltimore: Johns Hopkins University Press, 1955), p. 3.
2. Philip D. Curtin, *The Atlantic Slave Trade: A Census* (Madison: University of Wisconsin Press, 1969). Despite challenges to Curtin's estimates, subsequent research by Paul E. Lovejoy seems to confirm the earlier research by Curtin. Cf. Lovejoy, "The Volume of the Atlantic Slave Trade: A Synthesis," *Journal of African History*, Vol. 23 (1982), pp. 473–502; and *Transformations in Slavery: A History of Slavery in Africa* (Cambridge: Cambridge University Press, 1983).
3. E. M. Winslow, *The Pattern of Imperialism: A Study in the Theories of Power* (New York: Columbia University Press, 1948).
4. V. I. Lenin, *Imperialism: The Highest Stage of Capitalism* (New York: International Publications, 1939).
5. Joseph Schumpeter, *Imperialism and Social Classes* (New York: August Kelly, 1951).
6. East Africa Royal Commission, *1953–1955 Report*, Cmd. 9475 (London: Her Majesty's Stationery Office, 1955).
7. The works of a number of scholars confirm my own observations on the nature of European colonial policies and practices. See, for example, Michael Crowder, "Independence as a Goal in French West African Politics: 1944–60," in William H. Lewis, ed., *French-Speaking Africa* (New York: Walker & Co., 1965), pp. 15–41. Also useful are the articles by William Roger Louis, Ronald Robinson, Tony Smith, John Hargreaves, Yves Person and others in Prosser Gifford and William Roger Louis, eds., *The Transfer of Power in Africa: Decolonization, 1940–1960* (New Haven: Yale University Press, 1982).
8. Félix Houphouet-Boigny "Black Africa and the French Union," *Foreign Affairs* (July 1957), pp. 593–99.
9. Crowder, "Independence as a Goal in French West African Politics: 1944–60."
10. Quoted in William B. Cohen, *Rulers of Empire: The French Colonial Service in Africa* (Stanford: Hoover Institution Press, 1971), p. 189.

11. Ibid., pp. 57ff.

12. Cf. Lewis H. Gann and Peter Duignan, *White Settlers in Tropical Africa* (Baltimore: Penguin, 1962).

13. Cf. Baron William M. H. Hailey, *Native Administration in the British African Territories*, Parts I–IV (London: HMSO, 1951).

14. Cf. Lord Frederick D. Lugard, *Dual Mandate in British Tropical Africa* (Edinburgh: 1922); and Sir Donald Cameron, *Principles of Native Administration and Their Application* (Dar es Salaam: Government Printer, 1930), and *My Tanganyika Experience and Some Nigeria* (London: Allen & Unwin, 1939).

15. Cf. Crawford Young, *Politics in the Congo* (Princeton: Princeton University Press, 1965), and Rene Lemarchand, *Political Awakening in the Congo: The Politics of Fragmentation* (Berkeley: University of California Press, 1964).

16. Cf. James Duffy, *Portugal in Africa* (Cambridge, Mass.: Harvard University Press, 1962); Charles R. Boxer, *Four Centuries of Portuguese Expansion, 1415–1825* (Johannesburg: Witwatersrand University Press, 1961).

17. John Marcum, *The Angola Revolution*, Vol. 1, *The Anatomy of An Explosion (1950–1962)* (Cambridge, Mass.: Massachusetts Institute of Technology Press, 1969), p. 4.

18. Cf. J. Gus Liebenow, "Responses to Planned Political Change in a Tanganyika Tribal Group," *American Political Science Review*, Vol. 50 (June 1956), pp. 442–61.

19. J. Spencer Trimingham, *Islam in West Africa* (London: Clarendon Press, 1959), pp. 229–30; and Robert O. Collins, "The Sudan: Link to the North," in Stanley Diamond and Fred G. Burke, eds., *The Transformation of East Africa: Studies in Political Anthropology* (New York: Basic Books, 1966), pp. 377–85

20. Hausa, Swahili, and others had been written in Arabic script, but even that gave way to the Latin script under colonial rule.

Chapter III: The Challenge of Nation-Building

1. Hans Kohn, *Nationalism: Its Meaning and History* (New York: Van Nostrand, 1955), pp. 9–10.

2. M. Crawford Young, "Comparative Claims to Political Sovereignty: Biafra, Katanga and Eritrea," in Donald Rothchild and Victor A. Olorunsola, eds., *State Versus Ethnic Claims: African Policy Dilemmas* (Boulder, Colo.: Westview Press, 1983), pp. 199–232.

3. Cf. Edmond J. Keller, "Ethiopia: Revolution, Class, and the National Question," *African Affairs*, Vol. 80 (October 1981), pp. 519–49.

4. Jacques J. Maquet, "Le Problème de la Domination Tutsi," *Zaire, Revue Congolaise*, Vol. 6 (1952), pp. 1011–16. Also Maquet, *The Premise of Inequality in Ruanda* (London: Oxford University Press, 1961).

5. Cf. Philip D. Curtin, *The Atlantic Slave Trade: A Census* (Madison: University of Wisconsin, 1969); and Paul E. Lovejoy, *Transformations in Slavery: A History of Slavery in Africa* (Cambridge: Cambridge University Press, 1983).

6. Cf. Edward A. Alpers, *Ivory and Slaves in East Africa* (London: Heinemann Educational Books, 1975).

7. Cf. also Robert O. Collins, *Europeans in Africa* (New York: Alfred A. Knopf, 1971).

8. Source: Elizabeth Hopkins, "Racial Minorities in British East Africa," in Stanley Diamond and Fred G. Burke, eds., *The Transformation of East Africa: Studies in Political Anthropology* (New York: Basic Books, 1966), pp. 83–153.

9. Cf. Wilfred H. Whitely, *To Plan Is to Choose* (Bloomington: Indiana University African Studies Program, 1973).

10. Jack Berry, "Language Systems and Literature," in John Paden and Edward Soja, *The African Experience* (Evanston, Ill.: Northwestern University Press, 1970), pp. 80–98.

11. Joseph Greenberg, "Linguistics," in Robert Lystad, ed., *The African World: A Survey of Social Research* (New York: Praeger, 1965), pp. 416–41; and David Dalby, "African Languages," *Africa South of the Sahara 1986*, 15th Edition (London: Europa Publications, 1985), pp. 136–39.

12. Robert O. Collins, "The Sudan: Link to the North," in Diamond and Burke, eds., *Transformation of East Africa*, pp. 377–85.

13. Whiteley, *To Plan Is to Choose*.

14. Ali Mazrui, "Language Policy After Amin," *Africa Report* (September October, 1979), pp. 20–22.

15. Cf. Pierre Alexandre, "Multilingualism," in Thomas A. Sebeok, ed., *Current Trends in Linguistics*, Vol. 7 (Linguistics in Sub-Saharan Africa) (The Hague: Mouton, 1971), pp. 654–64.

16. *The Swazi Observer* (Swaziland), 2 March 1984, p. 4.

17. In the Cameroon Republic, the competition is not between a European and an African language, but between French and English. This stems from the fact that the modern state was formed from the union of the former French Trust territory and a portion of the British Trust Territory of Cameroon. Cf. Ndiva Kofele-Kale, ed., *An African Experiment in Nation Building: The Bilingual Cameroon Republic Since Reunification* (Boulder, Colo.: Westview Press, 1980).

18. Barbara Harrell-Bond, "Local Languages and Literacy in West Africa," *AUFS Reports*, West Africa series, Vol. 17, No. 2 (1979).

19. Whiteley, "Language Policies of Independent African States," in Thomas A. Sebeok, ed., *Current Trends in Linguistics*, pp. 548–58.

20. Mubanga E. Kashoki, "Achieving Nationhood Through Language: The Challenge of Namibia," *Third World Quarterly, Vol. 4 (April 1982)*, p. 283.

21. Cf. John Spencer, "Colonial Language Policies," in Sebeok, ed., *Current Trends in Linguistics*, pp. 537–47.

22. Andre Lestage, *Literacy and Illiteracy*, UNESCO Educational Studies Document No. 42 (Paris: UNESCO, 1982); and UNESCO, Division of Statistics on Education, *Estimates and Projections of Illiteracy*, September 1978 (UNESCO, 1978); and UNESCO, Statistical Yearbook, 1982.

23. This ignores literacy in Arabic and even traditional languages. Harrell-Bond, "Local Languages and Literacy in West Africa," p. 5.

24. The figures for other areas are: South Asia, 16.9; Middle East and North America, 18.1; and Latin America, 62.3. IBRD *World Tables*, 3rd ed., Vol. I, Economic Data, 1983.

25. Cf. Liebenow, "The Sukuma," in Audrey I. Richards, ed., *East African Chiefs* (London: Faber & Faber, 1960), pp. 229–59.

26. Cf. David Apter, "Political Religion in the New Nations," in Clifford Geertz, ed., *Old Societies and New States: The Quest for Modernity in Asia and Africa* (Glencoe: Free Press, 1963), pp. 57–104.

27. Ibid., p. 77.

28. This is apparent in the excellent film *Benin Kingship Rituals*, referred to above.

29. Cf. Liebenow, *Liberia: The Evolution of Privilege* (Ithaca, N.Y.: Cornell University Press, 1969), pp. 96–99.

30. Kathleen Lockard, "Religion and Politics in Independent Uganda: Movement Toward Secularization," in James R. Scarritt, ed., *Analyzing Political Change in Africa* (Boulder, Colo.: Westview Press, 1980), pp. 40–73.

31. J. Spencer Trimingham, *A History of Islam in West Africa* (London: Oxford University Press, 1962), pp. 224–31.

32. Ruth Schacter Morgenthau, *Political Parties in French-Speaking West Africa* (London: Oxford University Press, 1964), pp. 231ff.

33. Richard V. Weekes, ed., *Muslim Peoples: A World Ethnographic Survey* (Westport, Conn.: Greenwood Press, 1978).

34. Cf. the three-part article by Donal B. Cruise O'Brien, "Revolutionary Islam in Senegal?" in *West Africa*, 5 July 1982, p. 1741; 12 July 1982, pp. 1815–1816; and 19 July 1982, pp. 1872–1873.

35. Roland Oliver, *The Missionary Factor in East Africa* (London: Longmans, Green & Co., 1952), pp. 138–49.

36. For further readings on Pan-Africanism, cf. Immanuel Wallerstein, *Africa: The Politics of Unity* (New York: Random House, 1967); Ali Mazrui, *Towards a Pax Africana: A Study of Ideology and Ambition* (Chicago: University of Chicago Press, 1967); and Colin Legum, *Pan-Africanism: A Short Political Guide* (New York: Praeger, 1965).

37. Wallerstein, *Africa: The Politics of Independence* (New York: Vintage Books, 1961), p. 103.

38. Cf. Liebenow, "The Quest for East African Unity: 'One Step Forward, Two Steps Backward'," in Mark W. DeLancey, ed., *Aspects of International Relations in Africa* (Bloomington: Indiana University African Studies Program, 1979), pp. 126–58.

39. Cf. Nelson Kasfir, "Soldiers as Policymakers in Nigeria," *AUFS Reports*, Africa, Vol. 17, No. 3 (1977).

40. Cf. Liebenow, *Liberia: The Evolution of Privilege*, and "Liberia: 'Dr. Doe and the Demise of Democracy,' " parts 1 and 2, *UFSI Reports*, 1984/17, 1984/18.

41. Warren Weinstein and Robert Schrire, *Political Conflict and Ethnic Strategies: A Case Study of the Burundi* (Syracuse, N.Y.: Maxwell School, Syracuse University, 1976), pp. 10–15.

42. Victor Dubois, "To Die in Burundi," Parts I and II, *AUFS Reports*, Africa, Vol. 16, Nos. 3 and 4 (1972).

43. Margaret Peil, "Host Reactions: Aliens in Ghana," in William A. Shack and Elliot P. Skinner, eds., *Strangers in African Societies* (Berkeley: University of California Press, 1979), pp. 123–40; and Niara Sudarkasa, "From Stranger to Alien: The Socio-Political History of the Nigerian Yoruba in Ghana, 1900–1970," ibid., pp. 141–68.

Chapter IV: South Africa: Apartheid and the Clash of Nationalisms

1. J. Gus Liebenow, "SADCC: Challenging the 'South African Connection'," *UFSI Reports*, 1982/No. 13, Africa.

2. Source: Leonard Thompson and Andrew Prior, *South African Politics* (New Haven: Yale University Press, 1982), p. 35. Note: official South African figures recently have assigned Africans to the Homelands, which has increased the proportions of Europeans, Coloureds, and Asians in the rest of South Africa.

3. For an insightful commentary on the nature of the ANC and other groups, cf. Thomas G. Karis, "Revolution in the Making: Black Politics in South Africa," *Foreign Affairs*, Vol. 62 (Winter 1983/84), pp. 378–406.

4. Karis, ibid., pp. 387–88.

5. Cf. Cornelius W. DeKiewiet, *A History of South Africa: Social and Economic* (London: Oxford University Press, 1941), pp. 19–21.

6. Heribert Adam, *Modernizing Racial Domination: The Dynamics of South African Politics* (Berkeley: University of California Press, 1971), pp. 23ff.

7. DeKiewiet, *History of South Africa*, pp. 30ff.

8. For an interesting comparison between the traits of pioneers on the North American frontier and those of the Afrikaners, cf. Howard Lamar and Leonard Thompson, eds., *The Frontier in History: North America and Southern Africa Compared* (New Haven: Yale University Press, 1981).

9. Thompson and Prior, *South African Politics*, pp. 30–33.

10. Ibid., pp. 107–109 and passim.

11. Leo Kuper, *Passive Resistance in South Africa* (New Haven: Yale University Press, 1957), p. 32.

12. Ibid.

13. Leo Marquard, *The Peoples and Policies of South Africa* (London: Oxford University Press, 1962), pp. 65–74.

14. William J. Foltz, "South Africa: What Kind of Change?" CSIS *Africa Notes*, No. 5 (Nov. 25, 1982), p. 2.

15. Kuper, *Passive Resistance in South Africa*, pp. 53–54.

16. Marquard, *Peoples and Policies of South Africa*, p. 173.

17. Kuper, *Passive Resistance in South Africa*, pp. 47–71.

18. Kogila A. Moodley, "Structural Inequality and Minority Anxiety: Responses of Middle Groups in South Africa," in Robert M. Price and Carl G. Rosberg, eds., *The Apartheid Regime: Political Power and Racial Domination* (Berkeley: University of California, Institute of International Studies, 1980), pp. 217–35.

19. Philip Bonner, "Black Trade Unions in South Africa Since World War II," in ibid., pp. 174–93.

20. Cf. Newell Stultz, "Some Implications of African 'Homelands' in South Africa," in ibid., pp. 194–216.

21. Lawrence Schlemmer, "The Stirring Giant: Observations on the Inkatha and Other Black Political Movements in South Africa," in ibid., p. 111–26.

22. Gwendolen M. Carter, *Which Way Is South Africa Going?* (Bloomington: Indiana University Press, 1980), pp. 28–48.

23. Ibid., p. 42.

24. Herman Giliomee, "The National Party and the Afrikaner Broederbond," in Price and Rosberg, eds., *The Apartheid Regime*, pp. 14–44.

25. Stultz, "Interpreting Constitutional Change in South Africa, " *Journal of Modern African Studies* Vol. 22 (Sept. 1984), pp. 353–80.

26. Liebenow, "Southern African Hegemony," Part I, *UFSI Reports*, 1984/No. 24, Africa, p. 8.

27. Adam, *Modernizing Racial Domination*, pp. 145–59.

28. Carter, *Which Way Is South Africa Going?*, pp. 87–92.

29. *Africa South of the Sahara, 1984–85*, 14th ed. (London: Europa Publications, Ltd., 1984), pp. 105–16.

30. Ibid.

31. Ibid., p. 115.

32. Deon Geldenhuys, "South Africa's Regional Policy," in Michael Clough, ed., *Changing Realities in Southern Africa: Implications for American Policy* (Berkeley: University of California Institute of International Studies, 1982), pp. 123–60.

33. Cf. Schlemmer, "The Stirring Giant."

34. Cf. Liebenow, "Southern African Hegemony," Parts I and II, Nos. 24 and 25.

35. Cf. Michael Clough, "From Southwest Africa to Namibia," in Clough, ed., *Changing Realities in Southern Africa*, pp. 61–91.

36. Cf. Liebenow, "South African Hegemony."

37. Cf. Liebenow, "SADCC."

38. Thomas Karis, "United States Policy toward South Africa," in Gwendolen M. Carter and Patrick O'Meara, eds., *Southern Africa: The Continuing Crisis*, 2nd ed. (Bloomington: Indiana University Press, 1982), pp. 313–63 passim.

39. Cf. Patrick O'Meara, "Zimbabwe: The Politics of Independence," in ibid., pp. 18–56.

Chapter V: The Crisis of Enduring Poverty

1. The World Bank, *Toward Sustained Development in Sub-Saharan Africa: A Joint Program of Action* (Washington, D.C.: The World Bank, 1984), p. v.

2. Ibid., pp. 57ff.

3. Speech in Tokyo, 13 January 1982. World Bank *News Release*.

4. South Africa, Zimbabwe, Malawi, Kenya, Ivory Coast, Cameroon, Swaziland, and Benin.

5. World Bank, *Toward Sustained Development*, tables 1–32.

6. Robert H. Bates, *Markets and States in Tropical Africa: The Political Basis of Agricultural Policies* (Berkeley: University of California Press, 1981).

7. "Ideology and Agriculture," *Harpers Magazine*, February 1985.

8. *Africa South of the Sahara, 1984–85*, 14th ed. (London: Europa Publications Ltd., 1984), pp. 107ff.

9. Ibid.

10. Ibid.

11. Cf. J. Gus Liebenow, "SADCC: Challenging the South African Connection," *UFSI Reports*, 1982/No. 13, Africa.

12. Cf. Robert Anton Mertz and Pamela MacDonald Mertz, *Arab Aid to Sub-Saharan Africa* (Boulder, Colo.: Westview Press, 1983).

13. Cf. Carl Widstrand, ed., *Water and Society: Conflicts in Development*, Part I, The Social and Ecological Effects of Water Development in Developing Countries (Oxford: Pergamon Press, 1978), passim.

14. John M. Hunter, Luis Rey, and David Scott, "Man-Made Lakes and Man-Made Diseases: Towards a Policy Resolution," *Social Science Medicine*, Vol. 16 (1982), pp. 1127–45.

15. Liebenow, "Bilharzia Control in Swaziland: The Dilemma of Political Development," *AUFS Reports*, 1980/No. 2, Africa, pp. 1ff, and John M. Hunter, "Past Explosion and Future Threat: Exacerbation of Red Water Disease (Schistosomiasis heamatobium) in the Upper Region of Ghana," *GeoJournal*, Vol. 4, 1981, pp. 305–13.

16. Hunter, "Progress and Concerns in the World Health Organization: Onchocerciasis Control Program in West Africa," *Social Science Medicine*, Vol. 15 (1981), pp. 261–75.

17. FAO *Monthly Report*, February 1985. The most acute cases of famine were Chad, Ethiopia, Mali, Mozambique, Niger, and Sudan. The others included Angola, Botswana, Burkina Faso, Burundi, Cape Verde, Kenya, Lesotho, Mauritania, Morocco, Rwanda, Senegal, Somalia, Tanzania, Zambia, and Zimbabwe.

18. World Bank, *Toward Sustained Development*, p. 68.

19. Bill Freund, *The Making of Contemporary Africa: The Development of African Society since 1800* (Bloomington: Indiana University Press, 1984), pp. 19–27.

20. Ibid., pp. 25–30.

21. Cf. John Iliffe, *The Emergence of African Capitalism* (Minneapolis: University of Minnesota Press, 1984).

22. Liebenow, *Colonial Rule and Political Development in Tanzania: The Case of*

the Makonde (Evanston, Ill.: Northwestern University Press, 1971), pp. 126ff.

23. Carl Eicher, "Facing Up to Africa's Food Crisis," *Foreign Affairs*, Vol. 61 (Fall 1982), pp. 151–74.

24. Cf. David and Marina Ottaway, *Afrocommunism* (New York: Africana Publishing House, 1981); and John W. Harbeson "Socialist Politics in Revolutionary Ethiopia," in Carl G. Rosberg and Thomas M. Callaghy, eds., *Socialism in Sub-Saharan Africa* (Berkeley: University of California Press, 1979), pp. 345–72.

25. Bates, *Markets and States in Tropical Africa*.

26. World Bank, *Accelerated Development in Sub-Saharan Africa: An Agenda for Action*, 1981, p. 55.

27. Bates citing the works of Donal Cruise O'Brien and others, in *Markets and States in Tropical Africa*, pp. 110–11.

28. For the most comprehensive study of the role of ideology in African politics, cf. M. Crawford Young, *Ideology and Development in Africa* (New Haven: Yale University Press, 1982).

29. Cf. Liebenow, "Malawi's Search for Food Self Sufficiency," *UFSI Reports*, Parts I and II, 1982/Nos. 30 and 31, Africa.

30. World Bank, *Toward Sustained Development*, pp. 70–75.

31. Cf. Rosberg and Callaghy, eds., *Socialism in Sub-Saharan Africa*, passim.

32. Kenneth Jowitt, "Scientific Socialist Regimes in Africa: Political Differentiation, Avoidance, and Unawareness," in ibid., pp. 133–73, passim.

33. Dean McHenry, Jr., "The Struggle for Rural Socialism in Tanzania," in ibid., pp. 37–60.

34. Cf. Liebenow, "Zimbabwe: A Political Balance Sheet," *AUFS Reports*, Parts I and II, 1981/Nos. 14 and 15, Africa.

35. Julius Nyerere, "Ujamaa: The Basis of African Socialism," in *Freedom and Unity* (London: Oxford University Press, 1966), pp. 62–71.

36. Milovan Djilas, *The New Classes* (New York: Praeger, 1966).

37. Sara S. Berry, "The Study of Inequality in African Societies," *SSRC Items*, Vol. 30, No. 1 (March 1976), pp. 10–11.

38. Eicher, "Facing Up to Africa's Food Crisis," p. 161.

39. For a discussion of the range of problems and options, cf. Timothy Shaw and Malcolm J. Grieve, "Dependence or Development: International Inequalities in Africa," in Mai Palmberg, ed., *Problems of Socialist Orientation in Africa* (Uppsala: Scandinavian Institute of African Studies, 1978), pp. 54–82.

40. Cf. John W. Harbeson, "Tanzanian Socialism in Transition: Agricultural Crisis and Policy Reform," *UFSI Reports*, 1983/No. 30, Africa.

41. U.N. General Assembly, Resolution 39/29, "Critical Economic Situation in Africa," 39th Session, Doc. A/RES/39/29, 7 December 1984.

42. Nyerere, *TANU's Policy on Socialism and Self-Reliance* (Dar es Salaam: TANU, 1967).

43. Walter Rodney, *How Europe Underdeveloped Africa* (London: Bogle L'ouverture, 1972).

44. Guy Arnold, *Aid in Africa* (London: K. Page, 1979).

45. Tony Hill, "Africa and the European Community: The Third Lomé Convention," *Africa South of the Sahara 1986*, pp. 60–69.

46. Robert W. Clower, George Dalton, Mitchell Harwitz, and A. A. Walters, *Growth Without Development: An Economic Survey of Liberia* (Evanston, Ill.: Northwestern University Press, 1966), pp. 23–61.

47. Ali Mazrui, "Continent of Coups," in "West Africa: A Special Report," *International Herald-Tribune*, 4–5 August 1984, p. 7.

48. For a provocative analysis of the impact of foreign assistance, cf. Karl Borgin and Kathleen Corbett, *The Destruction of a Continent: Africa and International Aid* (New York: Harcourt Brace Jovanovich, 1982).

49. The World Bank, *Toward Sustained Development*, p. 1.

Chapter VI: The Dilemma of Political Community in the Urban Context

1. *U.N. Demographic Yearbook, 1982: Special Topic: Marriage and Divorce Statistics*, 34th Edition (U.N., 1983), Table 1. Annual rates of increase, 1975–1982, included: Somalia (7.2), Djibouti (6.4), Kenya (3.4), Nigeria (3.3), Botswana (3.3), Sudan (3.1), Zambia (3.1), and Burundi (2.4). Ibid., Table 3.

2. U.N. Department of International Economic and Social Affairs, *Demographic Indicators of Countries: Estimates and Projections* (U.N., 1982), p. 39.

3. IBRD, *World Tables*, Vol. II: *Social Data*, 3rd ed. (1980–81), pp. 2ff.

4. Useful bibliographies on African urbanization include Hyacinth I. Ajaegbu, *African Urbanization: A Bibliography* (London: International African Institute, 1972); and Anthony M. O'Connor, *Urbanization in Tropical Africa: An Annotated Bibliography* (Boston: G. K. Hall, 1981).

5. Figures in this section are based upon *U.N. Demographic Yearbook*, ibid., Table 6; IBRD, *World Tables*, ibid.; and the U.N. Department of International Economic and Social Affairs, *Demographic Indicators of Countries* (U.N.: 1982), p. 399.

6. *U.N. Demographic Yearbook, 1982*, Table 8.

7. Cf. William Bascom, "Urbanism as a Traditional African Pattern," *Sociological Review*, Vol. 7 (1959), pp. 29–43; Daniel McCall, "The Dynamics of Urbanization in Africa," *Annals of American Academy of Political and Social Sciences*, No. 298 (1955), pp. 151–60.

8. Gideon Sjoberg, *The Pre-Industrial City: Past and Present* (Glencoe Ill.: Free Press, 1965).

9. Peter C. Lloyd, "The Yoruba Town Today," *Sociological Review*, Vol. 9 (1959), pp. 45–63.

10. Peter C. Lloyd, A. L. Mabogunje, and B. Awe, eds., *The City of Ibadan* (London: Cambridge University Press, 1967), p. 3.

11. Ibid., p. 39.

12. For a broader Third World study of this situation, cf. Joan Nelson, "Sojourners versus New Urbanites: Causes and Consequences of Temporary Versus Permanent Cityward Migration in Developing Countries," *Economic Development and Cultural Change* (July 1976), pp. 721–57. Also cf. IBRD, "Urbanization Patterns and Policies," *World Development Report*, August 1979, Ch. 6, pp. 72–85, 112.

13. Audrey I. Richards, ed., *Economic Development and Tribal Change: A Study of Immigrant Labour in Buganda* (Cambridge: W. Heffer and Sons, 1956), pp. 64–75, 149–51.

14. Phillip H. Gulliver, "Incentives in Labour Migration," *Human Organization*, Vol. 19 (1960), p. 161. Cf. also his *Labour Migration in a Rural Economy* (Kampala: EIASR, 1957).

15. Cited in J. Gus Liebenow, "Malawi's Search for Food Self Sufficiency," *UFSI Reports*, 1982/No. 3, Africa, Part I, pp. 8, 15.

16. Liebenow, *Colonial Rule and Political Development in Tanzania: The Case of the Makonde* (Evanston, Ill.: Northwestern University Press, 1971), pp. 17, 18, 157–60.

17. Kenneth Little, *West African Urbanization* (Cambridge: Cambridge University Press, 1971), pp. 7–23.

18. Cf. Margaret Peil, "Interethnic Contacts in Nigerian Cities," *Africa*, Vol. 45 (1975), p. 120–21.

19. Howard E. Wolpe, *Urban Politics of Nigeria: A Study of Port Harcourt* (Berkeley: University of California Press, 1974).

20. Abner Cohen, *Custom and Politics in Urban Africa: A Study of Hausa Migrants in Yoruba Towns* (Berkeley: University of California Press, 1969), pp. 183–214.

21. Margaret Peil, "Host Reactions: Aliens in Ghana," in William A. Shack and Elliot P. Skinner, eds., *Strangers in African Societies* (Berkeley: University of California Press, 1979), pp. 123–40; and Niara Sudarkasa, "From Stranger to Alien: The Socio-Political History of the Nigerian Yoruba in Ghana, 1900–1970," ibid., pp. 141–68.

22. Cf. Merran Fraenkel, *Tribe and Class in Monrovia* (London: Oxford University Press, 1964).

23. UNESCO, *Social Implications of Industrialization and Urbanization in Africa South of the Sahara* (Paris: UNESCO, 1956), p. 165.

24. Little, "Some Urban Patterns of Marriage and Domesticity in West Africa," *Sociological Review*, Vol. 7 (1959), pp. 65–82.

25. Cf. Robert H. Bates, *Markets and States in Tropical Africa* (Berkeley: University of California Press, 1981).

26. Peil, *Cities and Suburbs: Urban Life in West Africa* (New York: Africana, 1981), p. 8.

27. Michael Crowder, *Senegal: A Study of French Assimilation Policy* (London: Oxford University Press, 1961), p. 78.

28. Cf. Aristide Zolberg, *One-Party Government in the Ivory Coast* (Princeton: Princeton University Press, 1964), pp. 29–58 passim, and Crowder, *Senegal*, p. 66.

29. *United Nations Demographic Yearbook, 1982, Special Topics*, 34th Issue, Table 8.

30. J. van Velsen, "Labour Migration as a Positive Factor in the Continuity of Tonga Tribal Society," in Aidan Southall, ed., *Social Change in Modern Africa* (London: Oxford University Press, 1961), pp. 230–41.

31. Cf. Elliott J. Berg, "The Economics of the Migrant Labor System," in Hilda Kuper, ed., *Urbanization and the Migration of West Africa* (Berkeley and Los Angeles: University of California Press, 1965), pp. 160–84.

32. Joan Aldous, "Urbanization, The Extended Family and Kinship Ties in West Africa," *Social Forces* Vol. 41 (1962), pp. 6–12.

33. Aidan Southall notes other examples in *Social Change in Modern Africa* (London: Oxford University Press, 1961), p. 39.

34. Sandra Barnes, "Voluntary Associations in Metropolis: The Case of Lagos, Nigeria," *African Studies Review*, Vol. 18 (Sept. 1975), p. 83; and Barnes, "Voluntary Associations in Membership in Five West African Cities," *Urban Anthropology*, Vol. 6 (Spring 1977), pp. 83–106.

35. Kofi A. Busia, *Report on a Social Survey of Sekondi-Takoradi* (London: Crown Agents for the Colonies, 1950) and D. K. Fiawoo, "Urbanisation and Religion in Eastern Ghana," *Sociological Review*, Vol. 7 (July, 1959), pp. 83–97.

36. Little, *West African Urbanization*.

37. Peil, "Interethnic Contacts in Nigerian Cities."

38. Bates, *Markets and States in Tropical Africa*, pp. 38–39.

39. Cf. David Parkin, *Neighbours and Nationals in an African City Ward* (Berkeley: University of California Press, 1969), pp. 31–51, 180–92. The Baganda attempted to extend their original jurisdiction over Mengo into Kampala, with its immigrant population.

40. Leonard Plotnicov, *Strangers to the City: Urban Man in Jos, Nigeria* (Pittsburgh: University of Pittsburgh Press, 1967), p. 291.

41. In 1984 Mozambique attempted a similar policy of rustication. The government carried out the plan in two phases. During the first phase, a two-week voluntary relocation of urban unemployed had the government providing free transportation back to their towns and villages. In the second compulsory phase "appropriate instruments of coercion" would be used against those unemployed who had remained.

42. Cf. Liebenow, "Malawi: Clean Water for the Rural Poor," *AUFS Reports*, 1981/No. 40, Africa.

Chapter VII: Political Parties: The Quest for Popular Government

1. Sidney Hook, *The Hero in History: A Study in Limitation and Possibility* (Boston: Beacon Press, 1943), pp. 151–83.

2. The modern concept is based upon Max Weber, *Theory of Social and Economic Organizations*, translated and edited by H. H. Gerth and C. Wright Mills, *From Max Weber: Essays in Sociology* (New York: Oxford University Press, 1958), pp. 245–52 and passim. For one of the earliest applications to the African scene—Kwame Nkrumah of Ghana—cf. David Apter, *The Gold Coast in Transition* (Princeton: Princeton University Press, 1955), pp. 174, 296–97, 303, 323ff. See also William H. Friedland, "For a Sociological Concept of Charisma," *Social Forces*, Vol. 43 (October 1964), pp. 18–26.

3. Cf. the excellent discussion of the Poro in Liberia in Warren L. d'Azevedo, "A Tribal Reaction to Nationalism," Parts I–IV, *Liberian Studies Journal*, Vol. 1 (Spring 1969), pp. 99–116; Vol. 2 (1969), p. 43; Vol. 2 (1970), pp. 99–116; and Vol. 3 (1970–71), pp. 1–20. For the impact of the Poro in Sierra Leonean politics cf. D.J.R. Scott, "The Sierra Leone Election, May 1957," in J. M. Mackenzie and Kenneth Robinson, eds., *Five Elections in Africa: A Group of Electoral Studies* (London: Oxford University Press, 1960), p. 230; and Martin D. Kilson, *Political Change in a West African State: A Study of* the *Modernization Process in Sierra* Leone (Cambridge: Harvard University Press, 1966), pp. 256–58.

4. For one of the earliest comprehensive efforts to analyze African political parties, cf. Thomas Hodgkin, *African Political Parties: An Introductory Guide* (London: Penguin Books, 1961).

5. Maurice Duverger, *Political Parties: Their Organization and Activity in the Modern State* (London: Methuen and Co., 1954), and Anthony King, "Political Parties in Western Democracies: Some Skeptical Reflections," *Polity*, Vol. 2 (Winter 1969), pp. 111–41.

6. Cf. Introduction and Conclusions of James S. Coleman and Carl G. Rosberg, eds., *Political Parties and National Integration in Tropical Africa* (Berkeley: University of California, 1964), pp. 1–12, 655–91.

7. Cf. Peter C. Lloyd, "Traditional Rulers," in ibid., pp. 382–412; and Eliot J. Berg and Jeffrey Butler, "Trade Unions," in ibid., pp. 340–81.

8. Baron William H. Hailey, *An African Survey*, Rev. 1956 (London: Oxford University Press, 1957); and George H. T. Kimble, *Tropical Africa*, 2 vols. (New York: Twentieth Century Fund, 1960).

9. Liebenow, *Liberia: The Evolution of Privilege* (Ithaca, N.Y.: Cornell University Press, 1969), pp. 112–30; for a good history of the role of the African National Congress, cf. Thomas G. Karis, "Revolution in the Making: Black Politics in South Africa," *Foreign Affairs*, Vol. 62 (Winter 1983–84), pp. 378–406.

10. James S. Coleman, *Nigeria: Background to Nationalism* (Berkeley: University of California Press, 1958), pp. 264–65.

11. Hodgkin, *Nationalism in Colonial Africa* (New York: New York University Press, 1957), pp. 145–53.

12. Ernest Milcent, "Senegal," in Gwendolen Carter, ed., *African One-Party States* (Ithaca, N.Y.: Cornell University Press, 1962), p. 92.

13. Nelson Kasfir, "Cultural Sub-Nationalism in Uganda," in Victor A. Olorunsola, ed., *The Politics of Cultural Sub-Nationalism in Africa* (New York: Doubleday, 1972), pp. 47–148, passim.

14. Lloyd, "Traditional Rulers," pp. 382–412.

15. Harold D. Lasswell, Daniel Lerner, and C. Easton Rothwell, *The Comparative Study of Elites: An Introduction and Bibliography* (Stanford: Stanford University Press, 1952). See also Harold D. Lasswell and Daniel Lerner, eds., *World Revolutionary Elites* (Cambridge, Mass: MIT Press and UNESCO, 1965).

16. Ronald Segal, *African Profiles* (London: Penguin Books, 1962), p. 262.

17. Sophia Ripley Ames, *Nkrumah of Ghana* (Chicago: Rand McNally, 1961), pp. 71ff; and Thomas Howell and Jeffrey P. Rajasooria, eds., *Ghana and Nkrumah* (New York: Facts on File, 1972), pp. 13–14.

18. Lionel Cliffe, unpublished, "Nationalism and Reaction to Enforced Agricultural Change in Tanganyika during the Colonial Period," East African Institute of Social Research, Conference Papers, Makerere University, Kampala, Uganda, Dec. 1964.

19. Scholarly treatment of Kenya's struggle for independence is contained, inter alia, in Cherry J. Gertzel, *The Politics of Independent Kenya, 1963–68* (Evanston: Northwestern University Press, 1970); Guy Arnold, *Kenyatta and the Politics of Kenya* (London: J. M. Dent and Sons, 1974); and Jeremy Murray-Brown, *Kenyatta* (London: George Allen and Unwin, 1972).

20. Henry Bienen, *Tanzania: Party Transformation and Economic Development* (Princeton: Princeton University Press, 1967), pp. 163ff.

21. Cf. Ruth Schacter Morgenthau, *Political Parties in French-Speaking Africa* (London: Clarendon Press, 1964), pp. 226ff and L. Gray Cowan, "Guinea," in Carter, *African One-Party States*, pp. 201ff.

22. Lansine Kaba, "Guinean Politics: A Critical Historical Overview," *Journal of Modern African Studies, Vol. 15 (March 1977)*, pp. 25–46.

23. Cf. Hodgkin, *Nationalism in Colonial Africa*, pp. 29–59.

24. Cf. Lloyd, "Traditional Rulers."

25. Cf. G. Wesley Johnson, Jr., *The Emergence of Black Politics in Senegal: The Struggle for Power in the Four Communes, 1900–1920* (Stanford: Stanford University Press, 1971).

26. Schacter Morgenthau, *Political Parties in French-Speaking Africa.*

27. Cf. Kenneth Robinson, "Senegal: The Election to the Territorial Assembly, March, 1957," in Robinson and Mackenzie, eds., *Five Elections in Africa*, pp. 281–390.

28. Cf. Rene Lemarchand, *Political Awakening in the Congo: The Politics of Fragmentation* (Berkeley: University of California Press, 1964).

29. Ibid., p. 176.

30. Cf. Carl G. Rosberg and John Nottingham, *The Myth of 'Mau Mau': Nationalism in Kenya* (Nairobi: East African Publishing House, 1966).

31. Jon Kraus, "Political Change, Conflict, and Development in Ghana," in Philip Foster and Aristide R. Zolberg, eds., *Ghana and the Ivory Coast: Perspectives on Modernization* (Chicago: University of Chicago Press, 1971), pp. 73–102.

32. Liebenow, "Zimbabwe: A Political Balance Sheet" Parts I and II, *AUFS Reports*, 1981/Nos. 14 and 15, Africa.

33. Ruth Collier, "Political Change and Authoritarian Rule," in Phyllis Martin and Patrick O'Meara, *Africa* (Bloomington: Indiana University Press, 1977), pp. 295–310.

34. Susanne D. Mueller, "Government and Opposition in Kenya, 1966–69," *Journal of Modern African Studies*, Vol. 22 (1984), pp. 349–427, passim.

35. Apter, *The Gold Coast in Transition*, pp. 199–203.

36. Cranford Pratt, *The Critical Phase in Tanzania, 1945–1968: Nyerere and the Emergence of a Socialist Strategy* (Cambridge: Cambridge University Press, 1976), pp. 24ff.

37. Coleman and Rosberg, *Political Parties and National Integration*, p. 657.

38. Cf. Seymour Lipset, *The First New Nation: The United States in Historical and Comparative Perspective* (New York: Norton & Co., 1979), pp. 13–90.

39. Julius Nyerere, *Freedom and Socialism: Uhuru and Ujamaa* (Dar es Salaam: Oxford University Press, 1968), passim.

40. K. Oberg, "The Kingdom of Ankole in Uganda," in Meyer Fortes and E. E. Evans-Pritchard, eds., *African Political Systems* (London: Oxford University Press, 1940), pp. 121–64.

41. Edmond J. Keller, "The Ethiopian Revolution: Is It Socialist?" manuscript draft, March 1982.

42. Cf. Goran Hyden and Colin Leys, "Elections and Politics in Single Party Systems: The Case of Kenya and Tanzania," *British Journal of Political Science*, Vol. 2 (October 1972), pp. 416ff. Also Collier, "Political Change and Authoritarian Rule."

43 Cf. Lionel Cliffe, *One Party Democracy: The 1965 Tanzania General Elections* (Nairobi: East African Publishing House, 1967).

44. Collier, *Regimes in Tropical Africa: Changing Forms of Supremacy, 1945–1975* (Berkeley: University of California Press, 1982), Chs. 2, 3.

45. Cf. Sheldon Gellar, *Senegal: An African Nation Between Islam and the West* (Boulder, Colo.: Westview Press, 1984).

46. Cf. Lancine Sylla, "Succession of the Charismatic Leader: The Gordian Knot of African Politics," *Daedalus* (Spring 1982), pp. 11–28; and L. Gray Cowan, "Guinea," in Carter, ed., *African One-Party States*, pp. 149ff.

47. *Washington Times*, 30 March 1984, p. 1.

48. Cf. Collier, *Regimes in Tropical Africa*, pp. 95–117.

Chapter VIII: Military Intervention: Aberration or Way of Life?

1. Gwendolen Carter, ed., *African One-Party States* (Ithaca, N.Y.: Cornell University Press, 1962); James S. Coleman and Carl G. Rosberg, eds., *Political Parties and National Integration in Tropical Africa* (Berkeley: University of California Press, 1964); Carter, ed., *Five African States: Responses to Diversity* (Ithaca, N.Y.: Cornell University Press, 1963); William H. Lewis, ed., *French-Speaking Africa: The Search for Identity* (New York: Walker, 1965); Carter, ed., *National Unity and Regionalism in Eight African States* (Ithaca, N.Y.: Cornell University Press, 1966).

2. Michael Lofchie, "The Uganda Coup—Class Action by the Military," *Journal of Modern African Studies*, Vol. 10 (1972), pp. 19–35.

3. Robert M. Price, "A Theoretical Approach to Military Rule in New States: Reference Group Theory and the Ghanaian Case," *World Politics*, Vol. 23 (April 1971), pp. 399–430; "Military Officers and Political Leadership," *Comparative Politics*, Vol. 3 (April 1971), pp. 361–79.

4. Samuel Decalo, *Coups and Army Rule in Africa* (New Haven, Conn.: Yale University Press, 1976).

5. Cf. Claude E. Welch, Jr., *Soldier and State in Africa* (Evanston, Ill.: Northwestern University Press, 1970); "The African Military and Political Development" in Henry Bienen, ed., *The Military and Modernization* (Chicago: Aldine, Atherton, 1971); (with Arthur K. Smith) *Military Role and Rule: Perspectives on Civil-Military Relations* (North Scituate, Mass.: Duxbury Press, 1974).

6. Morris Janowitz, *Military Institutions and Coercion in the Developing Nations*, rev. ed. (Chicago: University of Chicago Press, 1977).

7. Samuel P. Huntington, *Political Order in Changing Societies* (New Haven, Conn.: Yale University Press, 1968).

8. Richard Sklar, *Nigerian Political Parties: Power in an Emergent African Nation* (Princeton, N.J.: Princeton University Press, 1963), pp. 28off.

9. Donald R. Morris, *The Washing of the Spears: A History of the Rise of the Zulu Nation Under Shaka and Its Fall in the Zulu War of 1879* (New York: Simon and Schuster, 1965).

10. Michael Crowder, ed., *West African Resistance: The Military Response to Colonial Occupation* (London: Hutchinson, 1978).

11. Lewis J. Greenstein, "Africans in a European War: The First World War in East Africa, with Special Reference to the Nandi of Kenya," Ph.D. thesis in History, Indiana University, Bloomington, 1975.

12. Carl G. Rosberg and John Nottingham, *The Myth of "Mau Mau": Nationalism in Kenya* (Stanford, Calif.: Hoover Institution, 1966).

13. Henry Bienen, "Public Order and the Military in Africa: Mutinies in Kenya, Uganda, and Tanganyika," in Henry Bienen, ed., *The Military Intervenes: Case Studies in Political Development* (New York: Russell Sage Foundation, 1968), pp. 35–69; M. Crawford Young, *Politics in the Congo: Decolonization and Independence* (Princeton, N.J.: Princeton University Press, 1965); and Ernest Lefever, *United Nations Peacekeeping in the Congo. 1960–64* (Washington, D.C.: Brookings Institution, 1966).

14. Lord Frederick D. Lugard, *The Dual Mandate· in British Tropical Africa* (Edinburgh: 1922), p. 577. Cf. also John Barrett, "The Rank and File of the Colonial Army in Nigeria, 1914–18," *Journal of Modern African Studies*, Vol. 15 (March 1977), pp. 105–108.

15. Several interesting studies of army veterans in Africa suggest that they did not play a modernizing role in society once they had returned to mufti. Cf. Eugene P. A. Schleh, "The Post-War Careers of Ex-Servicemen in Ghana and Uganda," *Journal of Modern African Studies*, Vol. 6 (1968), pp. 203–20; G. O. Olusanya, "The Role of Ex-Servicemen in Nigerian Politics," *Journal of Modern African Studies*, Vol. 6 (1968), pp. 221–32; and Rita Headrick, "African Soldiers in World War II," *Armed Forces and Society*, Vol. 4 (May 1978), pp. 501–26.

16. Nelson Kasfir, *The Shrinking Political Arena: Participation and Ethnicity in African Politics, with a Case Study of Uganda* (Berkeley: University of California Press, 1976).

17. Marina and David Ottaway, *Ethiopia: Empire in Revolution* (New York: Africana Publ. Co., 1978).

18. Robert Price, "Theoretical Approach to Military Rule."

19. Decalo, "The Politics of the Personalist Coup," in *Coups and Army Rule in Africa*, pp. 173–230.

20. Lofchie, "The Uganda Coup."

21. J. Gus Liebenow, "Liberia: The Dissolution of Privilege," Part 3, *AUFS Reports*, 1980/41, Africa, pp. 39–41.

22. Cf. Thomas S. Cox, *Civil-Military Relations in Sierra Leone: A Case Study of African Soldiers in Politics* (Cambridge, Mass.: Harvard University Press, 1976).

23 Tony Avirgan, *War in Uganda: The Legacy of Idi Amin* (Westport, Conn.: L. Hill, 1982).

24. Edmond J. Keller, "The Ethiopian Revolution at the Crossroads," *Current History*, Vol. 83 (March 1984), pp. 117ff.

25. Several interesting efforts in this direction are found in Robert W. Jackman, "Politicians in Uniform: Military Governments and Social Change in the Third World," *American Political Science Review*, Vol. 70 (December 1976), pp. 1078–97; Eric A. Nordlinger, "Soldiers in Mufti: The Impact of Military Rule upon Economic

and Social Change in the Non-Western States," *American Political Science Review*, Vol. 64 (December 1970), pp. 1131–48; and R. D. McKinlay and A. S. Cohan, "A Comparative Analysis of the Political and Economic Performance of Military and Civilian Regimes: A Cross-National Aggregate Study," *Comparative Politics*, Vol. 8 (October 1975), pp. 1–30.

26. Cf. Donald Rothchild, "Military Regime Performance: An Appraisal of the Ghana Experience, 1972–78," *Comparative Politics*, Vol. 12 (July 1980), pp. 459–79.

27. Aidan Southall, "General Amin and the Coup: Great Man or Historical Inevitability?" *Journal of Modern African Studies, Vol. 13* (1975), p. 89; and Ali Mazrui, *Soldiers and Kinsmen in Uganda: The Making of a Military Ethnocracy* (Beverly Hills, Calif.: Sage Publications, c. 1975).

28. Cf. Bienen, "Armed Forces and National Modernization: The Continuing Debate," *Symposium Papers* (Seoul, Korea: Korea Military Academy, September 1981).

29. The six civilian-dominated states are the Republic of South Africa, Zimbabwe, Malawi, Kenya, the Ivory Coast, and Cameroon. The military regime state is Congo-Brazzaville.

30. The *IBRD World Development Report*, 1983.

31. Cf. Frank M. Chiteji, "Superpower Diplomacy: Arming Africa," *Current History*, Vol. 83 (March 1984), pp. 125ff.

32. Robert D. Grey, "The Soviet Presence in Africa: An Analysis of Goals," *Journal of Modern African Studies*, Vol. 22 (1984), pp. 511–27.

Chapter IX: U.S. Policy toward Sub-Saharan Africa

1. Vol. I (1935), in J. P. Mayer and Max Lerner, eds. (New York: Harper and Row, 1966), pp. 378–79.

2. J. Gus Liebenow, "United States Policy in Africa South of the Sahara," in Stephen D. Kertesz, ed., *American Diplomacy in a New Era* (Notre Dame, Ind.: University of Notre Dame Press, 1961), pp. 236–69, for extended treatment of pre–1960 policy.

3. Cf. Liebenow, *Liberia: The Evolution of Privilege* (Ithaca, N.Y.: Cornell University Press, 1969).

4. William Reitzel, Morton A. Kaplan, and Constance G. Coblenz, *United States Foreign Policy, 1944–1955* (Washington, D.C.: 1956); Brookings Institution, *Major Problems of United States Foreign Policy, 1954* (Washington, D.C.: 1954), p. 289.

5. For an interesting perspective from a former State Department official, cf. Anthony Lake, "Africa: Do the Doable," *Foreign Policy Report* No. 54 (Spring 1984), pp. 102–21.

6. See Liebenow, "American Policy in Africa: The Reagan Years," *Current History*, Vol. 82 (March, 1983), pp. 97ff.

7. John Stockwell, *In Search of Enemies: A CIA Story* (New York: W. W. Norton, 1978).

8. Address by Julius Nyerere, 8 June 1978, quoted in AEI *Foreign Policy and Defense Review*, Vol. 1 (1979), p. 22.

9. Cf. Liebenow, "SADCC: Challenging the 'South African Connection'," *UFSI Reports*, 1982/No. 13, Africa.

10. Chester A. Crocker "The African Private Sector and U.S. Policy," U.S. Department of State, Bureau of Public Affairs, *Current Policy*, No. 348 (19 Nov. 1981), p. 1.

11. Chester A. Crocker, Mario Greznes, and Robert Henderson, "A U.S. Policy for the 80s," *Africa Report*, Vol. 26 (Jan.–Feb. 1981), p. 8.

12. Secretary of State Shultz, "The U.S. and Africa in the 1980s," U.S. Department of State, Bureau of Public Affairs, *Current Policy* No. 549 (15 Feb. 1984), p. 3.

13. See Liebenow, "American Policy in Africa: The Reagan Years."

14. Richard Deutsch, "The Cubans in Africa," *Africa Report* (Sept.–Oct. 1980), pp. 44–49.

15. E.g., Bayard Rustin and Carl Gershman, "Africa, Soviet Imperialism, and the Retreat of American Power," extracted from *Commentary* in AEI *Foreign Policy and Defense Review*, op. cit., pp. 8–10.

16. Crocker, Greznes, and Henderson, "A U.S. Policy for the '80s," p. 8.

17. David Anderson, "America in Africa, 1981," *Foreign Affairs*, Vol. 60 (1982), p. 664.

18. One of the earliest statements is contained in Crocker, "Namibia/Angola Linkages," *Africa Report*, Vol. 26 (Nov.–Dec. 1981), p. 10.

INDEX

African National Congress (ANC): origins of, 105–106, 208; sanctuaries, 120, 131; tactics of, 126

Agriculture: colonial regulation of, 25, 26, 163, 164; territorial specialization, 147–48; production decline, 154–55; ritual in traditional, 156; African attitudes toward, 163–67; cash and export orientation, 164; post-independence policies, 164–65; impact of price on production, 166–67

"Alien" Africans: vulnerability of, 187; expulsion from Ghana, 97; expulsion from Nigeria, 98. See Zongo quarters

Amhara. See Ethiopia

Amin, Idi: atavistic model of military rule, 252, 257; background of, 258. See also Uganda

Angola: ethnicity in UNITA and MPLA, 60, 259; role of Cuban troops, 131, 132, 135; UNITA forces, 132, 133; relations with U.S.A., 135, 271. See also Mestiços, Portuguese Colonial rule

Apartheid: defined, 102; rationale for, 109–11; legal structures of, 111–14, changes in, 280–81. See also South Africa

Arab bloc: impact on development, 148, 149

Ashanti: traditional military, 243

arop Moi, Daniel: role in Kenya nationalism, 93

Asians: in colonial economies, 27, 60, 67, 228; population in East Africa, 68; role in cities, 185; harassment in post-independence era, 68–69, 245; in colonial armies, 246

Associations, urban voluntary: as receiving institutions, 196–97; religious, 197; savings groups, 197; diversity of, 197–98

Awolowo, Chief Obafemi: on pacificism, 242. See also Nigeria

Baganda (Ganda): pre-colonial population of, 6; formation of state society, 7; imperial expansion of, 20–21, 219n; used by British in administration, 56; role of Kabaka in Uganda politics, 81; in post-independence army, 258; and Kabaka Yekka Party, 210, 223; conflict with Obote, 248

Banda, H. Kamuzu: self-reliance, 168, 177; urban attitudes, 202; background of, 215. See also Malawi

Belgian colonial rule: independence policy, 21, 35; mineral exploitation, 34; Leopold and Congo Free State, 34; role of Roman Catholic Church, 35, 85; Union Minière du Haut Katanga, 34, 35, 85, 162; African politics, 35, 36, 219; language policy, 35; education policy, 162, 216; urbanization, 185, 193–94. See also Burundi, Rwanda, Zaire

Benin (Dahomey): role of military, 252

Benin (Kingdom of, Nigeria): kingship rituals, 78

Berlin Conference (1884–85): division of Africa, 14, 21; U.S. role in, 268

Biafran secession, 52, 54, 91, 92, 259

Biko, Steve: death of, 106

Bilharzia. See Schistosomiasis

Bismarck, Otto von, 20

Bokasso, Emperor, 256, 265

Bophuthatswana: boundaries of, 115, 116; mineral resources in, 26, 116; political status of, 116; leadership of Lucas Mangope, 116; casinos and financing, 117

Botha, P.W.: 1983–84 constitutional change, 106–107, 111; opposition to, 119; "hidden" agenda, 120

Botswana: nationhood concept, 47, 50; religious role of Seretse Khama, 80; water resources in, 152; population distribution, 152; multi-party system, 224; role of military in, 242

British colonial rule: classification of dependencies, 24; "paramountcy of African interests," 24; settler territories, 30; creation of political institutions, 30, 31, 32, 216, 217–18; policy on independence, 31; African participation in politics, 31, 217, 218; administrative practice and behavior, 34, 163–64; attitude toward religion, 41

British Togoland: joined to Ghana, 39

Buganda. See Baganda

Burundi: concept of nation, 50; caste system, traditional, 61–62; Tusi/Hutu conflict, 61–62, 96–97, 259–60

Buthelezi, Chief Gatsha: attitudes on Homeland status, 116; idea of "multistan," 125; Inkatha Party and Zulu nationalism, 125. See also KwaZulu

Cameroon: Independence of, 34; resignation of Ahmadou Ahidjo, 232; Paul Biya, 232

Index   301

Lenin, V.I.: imperialist theories of, 18–19
Lesotho: concept of nation, 47; division of Sotho, 50; role of military in, 242
Liberia: imperialist expansion of, 20; ethnicity, 56; racial factor in, 61; language policy, 74; religion and politics, 80; Americo-Liberian domination, 94–95; True Whig Party, 208; 1980 Doe coup, 239, 250, 256–57; death of Tolbert, 250, 256; rice riots of 1979, 250; mandate of PRC, 253; ostracism of Doe regime, 256; ethnicity in the army, 258; "civilianization" of military, 264; U.S. role in founding, 268; strategic link to U.S., 269, 272; U.S. aid, 272; Poro, 292n
Literacy: rates for Africa 75, 76; Koranic schools, 159. See also Christian missionaries
Loans: Tanzanian indebtedness, 168; extent of African debts, 180. See also IMF
Lugard, Lord Frederick: policy on religion, 27, 41, 82; and Indirect Rule, 31; ethnicity and army recruitment, 246

Malawi: food production, 3, 168; water development, 3, 152–53; link with Rhodesias, 39; language policy, 72; and religion, 86; agricultural education, 166; membership in SADCC, 132; anti-urban bias, 202; strength of Malawi Congress Party, 206, 220, 224; civilian supremacy model, 251. See also Banda, H. Kamuzu
Mali (ancient), 38, 47
Mali (modern): 1960 union with Senegal, 39
Mandela, Nelson: detention of, 106
Manding: traders, 39; and nationalism, 82
Mansa Musa, 38
Marabout, 83. See also Tariqa
Masai: and modernization, 12; division of, 50
Marxism: imperialism, 18–19. See also Socialism
Mau Mau: origins of, 30, 243–44; ban on politics during emergency, 216; no links with KANU, 221; role of Kikuyu in, 259. See also Kenya; Kenyatta, Jomo
Mauritania: abolition of slavery, 4, 63; and Western Sahara, 54; population policy in, 141. See also Western Sahara
Mauritius: multi-party elections, 229
Menelik II. See Ethiopia
Mestiços: under Portuguese rule, 36–37; in MPLA, 60
Migration, urban: sex/age imbalance of, 187; push/pull factors, 187–88; causal theories regarding, 188, 195; as source of inter-ethnic conflict, 188–89, 198–99. See also Urbanites, Urbanization
Military/civil relations, models of: civilian supremacy, 250–51; watchdog, 251–52, 254; balance wheel, 252, 254; direct rule, 252, 254; social transformation, 252, 254; atavistic, 252

Military, colonial: use of force, 242; race and rank, 245, 246; ethnic factor in recruitment, 246; role of veterans, 295n; and modernization, 246, 247; nationalists' views of, 246, 247; career opportunities for Africans, 246, 247
Military, post-independence: civilian use of, 247–49; basis of legitimacy, 255–57; referenda and elections, 256; maintainence of public order, 257; role in ethnic conflict, 257–60; Africanization of officer corps, 258; assault on pluralism, 261; and modernization, 261–64; restoration of civilian rule, 264–66. See also Military intervention
Military intervention (coups): and political succession, 237; unforeseen in early 1960s; personality factor in, 238, 239, 249; multiple causes of, 238; organizational explaination of, 239; various sources of leadership, 239; party weakness as factor in, 240–42; as response to pacifism, 242
Minerals: discovery of diamonds, gold in South Africa, 108; strategic significance of southern Africa, 122, 123, 134; bauxite in Ghana, 141; basic ingredients of industrialization, 143–47; as energy sources, 143–47; steel alloys, 143–47; southern African production of, 145–46
Modernization: defined, 11, 12; in relation to industrialization, 142
Monomatapa: state building, 47
Mozambique: dependence on South Africa, 36, 126, 132; renewed relations with Portugal, 37, 65; FRELIMO, strength of, 224; anti-urban policy, 292n
Morocco: and Western Sahara, 54; religion and politics, 80; links with U.S., 272; role in Zaire crises, 273
MPLA. See Angola
Mugabe, Robert: relations with European minority, 37, 60; on South African oil embargo, 133. See also Zimbabwe, ZANU

Namibia: white population of, 104; South African Mandate, 129–31; liberation war, 130; U.S. policy toward, 278–79; Cuban troop "linkage," 280
Nandi; resistance to British rule, 243
Nation-building strategies: Pan-nationalist, 87–89; over-arching integrative, 89–91; pluralist accommodation, 91–93; static tension, 93; dominant ethnic, 94–95; selective isolation or exclusion, 95–96; selective expulsion, 96–98; irredentist, 98–100
Nation-state: origin of concept, 45–46
National Congress of British West Africa, 208
NCNC: origins of, 210; strength of, 240
Nationalizing elite: and communication, 48; political role of, 47; symbol creation, 49; establish moral code, 47

J. Gus Liebenow is Professor of Political Science at Indiana University, Bloomington. He is the author of numerous articles and several books, including *Liberia: The Evolution of Privilege.* and *Colonial Rule and Political Development in Tanzania: The Case of the Makonde.* He is the founding Director of the African Studies Program at Indiana University and Past President of the African Studies Association.